PRAISE FOR *People*

"An extraordinary true crime book that sheds light on one of the most horrific killings of the last decade. Difficult to put down . . . impossible to forget." —Minette Walters, author of *The Chameleon's Shadow* and *Disordered Minds*

"*People Who Eat Darkness* is an extraordinary, compulsive, and brilliant book. The account of the crime, the investigation and the trial—particularly in its knowledge and understanding of the Japan in which this tragedy took place—is both insightful and gripping; the attempt to understand Obara is fascinating but never ghoulish; and finally, and most of all, the compassion for Lucie Blackman and her family is very, very moving." —David Peace, author of the Red Riding quartet and the Tokyo trilogy

"A riveting and clear-eyed account of a family struggling to deal with unimaginable trauma. Richard Lloyd Parry combines extraordinary investigative skills with a natural storytelling ability to create an utterly compelling read. *People Who Eat Darkness* comes with the cast-iron guarantee that you will read to the very end." —Mo Hayder, author of *Gone* and *The Devil of Nanking*

"A masterpiece of writing this surely is, but it is more than that—it is a committed, compassionate, courageous act of journalism that changes the way we think. Everyone who has ever loved someone and held that life dear should read this stunning book, and shiver." —Chris Cleave, author of *Little Bee* and *Incendiary*

ALSO BY RICHARD LLOYD PARRY

In the Time of Madness: Indonesia on the Edge of Chaos

PEOPLE WHO EAT DARKNESS

PEOPLE WHO EAT DARKNESS THE TRUE STORY OF A YOUNG WOMAN WHO VANISHED FROM THE STREETS OF TOKYO—AND THE EVIL THAT SWALLOWED HER UP

RICHARD LLOYD PARRY

FARRAR, STRAUS AND GIROUX ■ NEW YORK

FOR MUM AND DAD

Farrar, Straus and Giroux
18 West 18th Street, New York 10011

Copyright © 2011, 2012 by Richard Lloyd Parry
All rights reserved
Printed in the United States of America
Originally published in 2011, in slightly different form, by Jonathan Cape, Great
    Britain, as People Who Eat Darkness: The Fate of Lucie Blackman
Published in the United States by Farrar, Straus and Giroux
First American edition, 2012

All materials from the notebooks, schoolbooks, and journals of Lucie Blackman are
reproduced by kind permission of the Estate of Lucie Blackman.

Library of Congress Cataloging-in-Publication Data
Parry, Richard Lloyd.
    People who eat darkness : the true story of a young woman who vanished from
    the streets of Tokyo—and the evil that swallowed her up / Richard Lloyd
    Parry. — 1st American ed.
        p. cm.
    Includes bibliographical references.
    ISBN 978-0-374-23059-3 (alk. paper)
    1. Blackman, Lucie Jane, 1978–2000.   2. Obara, Joji—Trials, litigation,
etc. 3. Murder—Investigation—Japan—Tokyo.   4. Young women—Crimes
against—Japan—Tokyo.   I. Title.

    HV6535.J33 T664 2012
    364.152'3092—dc23

                                                              2011047019

Designed by Abby Kagan

www.fsgbooks.com

10   9   8   7   6

Among the old men who secretly came to this "house of the sleeping beauties," there must be some who not only looked wistfully back to the vanished past but sought to forget the evil they had done through their lives . . . among them must be some who had made their successes by wrongdoing and kept their gains by repeated wrongdoing. They would not be men at peace with themselves. They would be among the defeated, rather—victims of terror. In their hearts as they lay against the flesh of naked young girls put to sleep would be more than fear of approaching death and regret for their lost youth. There might also be remorse, and the turmoil so common in the families of the successful. They would have no Buddha before whom to kneel. The naked girl would know nothing, would not open her eyes, if one of the old men were to hold her tight in his arms, shed cold tears, even sob and wail. The old man need feel no shame, no damage to his pride. The regrets and sadness could flow quite freely. And might not the "sleeping beauty" herself be a Buddha of sorts? And she was flesh and blood. Her young skin and scent might be forgiveness for the sad old men.

—YASUNARI KAWABATA, *House of the Sleeping Beauties*

CONTENTS

PEOPLE WHO EAT DARKNESS

MISSING

行方不明の英国人女性をさがしています。

ルーシー・ブラックマン
Lucie BLACKMAN

年　齢：21歳
身　長：175cm
体　格：中位
髪　の　色：金髪
瞳　の　色：青

7月1日(土)に、
東京で見かけられて以来、
行方が分かっていません。

A　g　e ： 21 years
Height ： 175cm Medium Build
Hair Color ： Blonde
Eye Color ： Blue

She was last seen in Tokyo
on Saturday July 1st. Since
then she has been missing.

もし本人を見かけた方、または
何か情報をお持ちの方は
警視庁麻布警察署
tel. 03-3479-0110
または最寄りの警察宛ご連絡を
お願いいたします。

If anyone has seen her, or has any
information relating to her, contact
Azabu Police Station
tel. 03-3479-0110
or your nearest police station.

ルーシー・ブラックマン（英国人女性）

Lucie BLACKMAN (British Female)

PROLOGUE: LIFE BEFORE DEATH

Lucie wakes up late, as usual. A line of daylight flares at the edge of the shrouded window and pierces the dim interior. A low, cramped, colorless space. There are posters and postcards on the walls, and blouses and dresses on overburdened hangers. On the floor, two human shapes on two futon mattresses: one head of blond hair, one of brown. They sleep in T-shirts, or naked beneath a single sheet, for even at night it is too hot and clammy for anything but the thinnest layer against the skin. Outside, crows are cawing and scuffling on the telegraph wires that tangle between the buildings. It was four in the morning when they went to sleep, and the plastic alarm clock shows that it is almost noon. The brown head remains huddled on its pillow as Lucie puts on her dressing gown and goes to the bathroom.

She refers to her home in Tokyo as the "shithouse"—the bathroom is one of the reasons why. Half a dozen people share it, plus their overnight guests, and the room is vile with their parings and detritus. Exhausted tubes of toothpaste curl on the edges of the sink, sodden lumps of soap drool on the floor of the shower, and the plughole wears a slimy cap of clotted hair, skin, and toenail clippings. Lucie's own vanity products, which are numerous and expensive, are brought into and removed from the bathroom on every visit, along with her combs, brushes, and makeup. Her toilet is lengthy and fastidious, a practiced drill of shampooing, rinsing, conditioning, soaping, toweling, patting, smoothing, cleansing, moisturizing, absorbing, tweez-ering, brushing, flossing, and blow-drying. Lucie epitomizes the distinction between simply taking a shower in the morning and *grooming*. If you were running late, you wouldn't want to find yourself behind her in the queue for the bathroom.

What does Lucie see when she looks into the mirror? A full, fair face, surrounded by naturally blond hair falling be-low the shoulder. A solid chin; strong, even, white teeth; cheeks that lift and dimple when she smiles. A rounded nose; sharp, closely plucked brows and small dark blue eyes that angle away from the horizontal. Lucie deplores her "slanty eyes" and spends long mirror hours wishing them away. They are subtly and unexpectedly exotic on a woman otherwise so fair com-plexioned, so blue eyed and long limbed.

Lucie is tall—five nine—with a good bust and hips. She pays anxious attention to the surges of her fluctuating weight. In May, after the effort of traveling to Japan, moving into the shithouse, and finding work, she was slimmer than this, but after a few weeks of late nights in the club, she has "drunk it back on again." On her worst days, she is filled with contempt for her own appearance. She feels bloated and saggy; she is tor-tured by self-consciousness about the birthmark on her thigh and the dark mole between her brows. A dispassionate observer might describe her with old-fashioned and faintly equivocal words such as "buxom" and "comely." The brown-haired girl on the other mattress, Lucie's best friend, Louise Phillips, is far more of a conventional beauty: slim, small, pert featured. But for most of the time, to other people at least, Lucie communi-cates a confidence and an ease. Her way of laughing, of moving her hands as she speaks, of shaking her hair, her habit of un-selfconsciously touching the person she is talking to—all of this lends her a charm that appeals to women as well as to men.

Lucie emerges from the bathroom. What does she do next? I know that she doesn't write in her diary, which has been neglected for almost two weeks. She doesn't call Scott, her boyfriend, who serves on the American aircraft carrier in the port city of Yokosuka. Later, among her personal possessions, her family will find an unsent postcard, addressed to her great friend from home, Samantha Burman. Perhaps she writes that card now.

> *Darling Sammy, just a little note from Tokyo to say how good it was to talk to you the other evening. I'm so glad you've found a lovely friend/guy/mate (whatever he is). I know it's easier for me over here as my everyday life has changed and Sundays are so different at the moment, but I wanted to let you know that life is incomplete without you and although I'm not sure when, we will be together soon, be it wherever I am, or me back home. I do love you and miss you terribly and always will. All my love, Lulu*

At half past one the telephone rings downstairs. One of the other flatmates answers and calls from below: it is for Lucie. Unlike Louise, who has her own cell phone, given to her by one of her customers, Lucie has had to rely on the shithouse's shared pay telephone. It is a clunky pink plastic box in the kitchen, fed by ¥10 coins; conversations on it can be overheard by anyone else who is downstairs. But Lucie will not have to put up with this unsatisfactory situation for much longer. In just a few hours, she will have a mobile of her own.

Louise is up by now and sits in the common living room during her friend's brief conversation. It was him, Lucie tells her after hanging up the pink receiver: the meeting has been postponed by an hour until three o'clock; he will call again and she will meet him at the railway station. Then they will have a late lunch, but she will be back in good time for the agreed eight o'clock rendezvous—a night of dancing with Louise and one of the other girls from the club. Lucie takes off her dressing gown and chooses her outfit for the day: her black dress, the silver necklace with the heart-shaped crystal pendant, and the Armani watch. Her sunglasses are in her black handbag. Three o'clock comes and goes. At three twenty the pink phone rings again for Lucie; he is on his way and will be at the station in ten minutes.

The crows flap and complain as Lucie steps outside. As she does, she experiences the small daily shock of reentry that every foreigner in Tokyo knows. A sudden, pulse-quickening awareness of the obvious: Here I am, *in Japan*. Every morning it takes her by surprise—the sudden consciousness of profound difference. Is it something unfamiliar about the angle of the light, or the way that sounds register in the summer air? Or is it the demeanor of the people on the street and in the cars and the trains—unobtrusive but purposeful; neat, courteous, and self-contained but intent, as if following secret orders?

Even after years and decades have passed, you never get over the excitement, the unique daily thrill, of living as a foreigner in Japan.

The shithouse—or Sasaki House, to give it its formal name—is a grimy plaster-covered building at the dead end of an alleyway. Lucie turns left out of it and walks past more exhausted-looking apartment buildings, a children's playground with wooden climbing frames, and an old-fashioned restaurant serving rice omelets and curry. Then comes a jewel in the midst of the drabness—a classical Noh theater, in smooth modernistic concrete, surrounded by sculpted hedges and a gravel garden.

Lucie turns right, and the neighborhood undergoes a sudden transformation. The atmosphere up to here has been shabby and suburban; now, less than five minutes from home, Lucie is walking along a main road in a big city. Railways and an expressway run above it on elevated piles. Five hundred yards further on is Sendagaya Station, where bus routes intersect with subway and commuter lines. It is a busy place on a Saturday afternoon, noisy with traffic and with people in short sleeves and summer dresses bustling in and out of the station and the Olympic Gymnasium on its far side. He's waiting there for Lucie, in front of the police station; his car is nearby.

Shortly before Lucie, Louise leaves the house on her own mission: to exchange a pair of shoes in Shibuya, the great shopping district of southwest Tokyo. She takes the train to Shibuya Station, where nine different lines deposit two and a half million passengers every day, and where Louise quickly becomes lost. She wanders confusedly among the Saturday crowds, along streets of shops and restaurants which, despite their dizzying diversity, somehow manage to be indistinguishable from one another. After much time wasting, she finds the shop she is looking for, then walks wearily back to the station.

Just after five o'clock, her mobile rings. The screen displays the words USER UNSENT. But the voice is that of Lucie, who should be heading home soon to prepare for the night ahead. Instead she is calling from inside a moving car. She's on the way to the "seaside," she says, where she will have lunch with him (although it is getting very late to talk of lunch). But there is no need to change their plans for the evening, she tells Louise; she will be home in good time, and she will call again in an hour or two to say exactly when. She sounds happy and cheerful, but self-conscious in the manner of someone whose conversation can be overheard. She is calling from his mobile, she tells Louise, so she cannot chat long.

Later, Louise would say that she was surprised by this development and that it was out of character for Lucie to get into a man's car and drive out of Tokyo with him. But it was very like her to make this call. Lucie and Louise have known one another since they were girls, and this is the kind of friendship they have. They phone one another just for the sake of it, to reaffirm closeness and trust, even when there is little to say.

It's an oppressively hot and humid summer afternoon. Louise visits her and Lucie's favorite shop, the department store Laforet, and buys shiny stickers and glitter to decorate their faces for their night of dancing. The sun sinks in the sky; the evening begins, spreading a cloak over the dim residential shabbiness and illuminating in neon the restaurants, bars, and clubs, all the places of promise and delight.

Two hours pass.

At six minutes past seven, when Louise is back at home, her cell phone rings again. It's Lucie, full of high spirits and excitement. He is *very* nice, she says. As promised, he has given her a new mobile phone—and a bottle of Dom Perignon champagne, which she and Louise can drink together later. It's not clear exactly where she is, and Louise doesn't think to ask. But she will be back within an hour.

At seventeen minutes past seven, Lucie calls the mobile phone of her boyfriend, Scott Fraser, but connects only to voice mail. She records a short but happy message, promising a meeting tomorrow.

There Lucie vanishes.

It's the beginning of a Saturday evening in Tokyo, but there will be no girls' night out and no date with Scott. In fact, there will be nothing else at all. Stored in the digital data bank of the telephone company, where it will be automatically erased in a few days' time, the mobile phone message is Lucie's last living trace.

■ ■ ■

When Lucie failed to return as promised, Louise's alarm was immediate and overwhelming. Later, people would point to this as a reason for suspicion: Why *would* Louise have got into such a panic, so soon? Her flatmates, who were sitting in the living room smoking marijuana, couldn't understand her agitation. Little more than an hour after Lucie's expected return, Louise was already telephoning her mother, Maureen Phillips, in Britain. "Something has happened to Lucie," she told her. Then she went to Casablanca, the hostess club in the entertainment district of Roppongi where the two of them worked.

"I remember that first day very clearly, the first of July," said a man who was there at the time. "It was a Saturday night, and it was Lucie and Louise's day off that week. Neither of them was supposed to work. But quite early on, Louise came in and said, 'Lucie's missing. She went to meet a customer. She's not come back.' Well, it's not so surprising. It's still only eight, nine o'clock. I said, 'It's normal, nothing really strange, Louise. Why are you so worried?' She said, 'Lucie's the kind of person who will come back, or if something happens she'll call me.' And it was true for them. What one was doing, the other one always knew about. They had a really strong relationship. Louise knew that something was wrong, right away."

Louise kept calling the club all night, asking if anyone had news of Lucie, but there was no news. She walked around Roppongi, visiting every one of the bars and clubs where she and Lucie used to go: Propaganda, Deep Blue, the Tokyo Sports Cafe, Geronimo's. She talked to the men who handed out flyers on Roppongi Crossing, asking if any of them had seen Lucie. Then she took a taxi to Shibuya and went to Fura, the club where the two of them had been planning to go that night. She knew that she wouldn't find her friend there—why would Lucie have gone on ahead alone, without coming home first, or at least calling her? But she couldn't think of anything else to do.

It rained for much of the night—warm, perspiration-inducing Tokyo summer rain. It was light by the time Louise returned to Sasaki House early on Sunday morning, having been into every bar that she could think of. Lucie was not at home, and there was no message from her.

Louise telephoned Caz, a Japanese man who worked at Casablanca as a waiter, and debated what to do. Caz called a few of the bigger hospitals, but none of them had heard of Lucie. Wasn't it at least possible, he suggested, that Lucie had decided to spend the night with her "nice" customer and simply failed to let Louise know? Louise said that it was unthinkable, and no one was closer to Lucie than Louise.

The obvious next step was to contact the police. But this prospect brought its own load of anxiety. Lucie and Louise had entered Japan as tourists, on ninety-day visas that explicitly forbade them from working. All the girls in the clubs, in fact most of the foreigners working in Roppongi, were in the same situation. They, and the clubs that employed them, were breaking the law.

On Monday morning, Caz took Louise to Azabu Police Station in Roppongi and filed a missing-person report. They explained that Lucie was a tourist on holiday in Tokyo who had gone out for the day with a Japanese man she'd met. They made no mention of hostessing or Casablanca or its customers.

The police showed little interest.

At three o'clock in the afternoon, Louise went to the British embassy in Tokyo. She spoke to the vice-consul, a Scot named Iain Ferguson, and told him the full story. Ferguson was the first of many people to express bafflement at the circumstances in which Lucie had gone out on that afternoon. "I asked what was known of the client and was taken aback to hear nothing," he wrote in a memo the next day. "According to Louise, girls within the club routinely, and with the club's consent, hand out their business cards and clients as a result often make private appointments with the girls. I stated I found that hard to believe, that the club would allow the girls to meet with clients without their knowledge. Louise however remained firm. Certainly Lucie had said nothing of her client, his name, anything of his car or even where they had gone other than the beach . . ."

Ferguson pressed Louise on Lucie's character. Was she capricious, unpredictable, unreliable? Was she naïve or easily influenced? "All of Louise's responses drew a consistent picture," he wrote, "of a confident, worldly-wise, intelligent individual who had the experience and judgment not to have foolishly put herself in danger." Why, then, had she got into a car with a complete stranger? "Louise could . . . not explain, restating that such behavior was out of character for Lucie."

No one has more experience than a consular officer of the folly of the British abroad. And no one understands better that, most of the time, when a young person "disappears" there is a predictably mundane explanation: a tiff between friends or lovers; drugs, or drunkenness, or sex. But Lucie had telephoned twice during the afternoon to update Louise on her whereabouts. Having called to say that she would be back within an hour, it was hard to imagine that she would not have done so again, even if her plans had changed. Iain Ferguson called Azabu Police Station and told them that the embassy was deeply concerned about Lucie and that they regarded it not as a simple missing-person case but as a probable abduction.

Louise left the embassy. In the two nights since Lucie's disappearance, she had hardly slept. She was in a torment of uncertainty and tension. It was unbearable to be alone, or to spend any time in the room she shared with Lucie. She went to the apartment of a friend, where other people who knew Lucie were also gathering.

Just before half past five, her mobile rang again, and she snatched it up.

"Hello?" Louise said.

—Am I speaking to Louise Phillips? said a voice.

"Yes, this is Louise. Who's this?"

—My name is Akira Takagi. Anyway, I'm ringing on behalf of Lucie Blackman.

"Lucie! My God, where is she? I've been so worried. Is she there?"

—I am with her. She is here. She is fine.

"Oh, God, thank God. Let me speak to Lucie. I need to speak to her."

It was a man's voice. He spoke English confidently but with a distinct Japanese accent. He was at all times calm and controlled and matter-of-fact, almost friendly, even when Louise became agitated and upset.

—She must not be disturbed now, the voice said. —Anyway, she is in our dormitory. She is studying and practicing a new way of life. She has so much to learn this week. She can't be disturbed.

To her friends, Louise was frantically mouthing, "It's him," and signaling for paper and a pen.

"Who is this?" she said. "Are you the one she went out with on Saturday?"

—I met Lucie on Sunday. She met my guru on Saturday, my group's leader.

"Your guru?"

—Yes, my guru. Anyway, they met on a train.

"But she . . . when I spoke to her, she was in a car."

—The traffic was bad, so bad, and she didn't want to be late to meet you. So she decided to take the train. Just before she got on the train she met my guru and she made a life-changing decision. Anyway, she decided to join his cult that night.

"A cult?"

—Yes.

"What d'you mean, a cult? What . . . Where is Lucie? Where is this cult?"

—It is in Chiba.

"What? Say that again. Can you spell it?"

—In Chiba. I spell it: C-H-I-B-A.

"Chiba. Chiba. And . . . what is it called?"

—It's the Newly Risen Religion.

"The what? What is . . ."

—The Newly Risen Religion.

The man calmly spelled this phrase out too, letter by letter.

Louise's thoughts were churning. "I have to speak to Lucie," she said. "Let me speak to her."

—She's not feeling too well, said the voice. —Anyway, she doesn't want to talk to anyone now. Maybe she will talk to you at the end of the week.

"Please," said Louise. "Please, please, let me talk to her."

The line went dead.

"Hello? Hello?" said Louise, but there was nobody there. She looked at the small silver telephone in her hands.

A few heartbeats later, it rang again.

With trembling fingers, she pressed the pick-up button.

—I'm so sorry, said the same voice. —The signal must have broken. Anyway, Lucie can't talk to you now. She's not feeling well. Maybe she will talk to you at the end of the week. But she has started a new life, and she won't be coming back. I know that she has a lot of debts, six or seven thousand pounds. But she is paying them off in a better way. Anyway, she just wants to let you and S'kotto know she's okay. She is planning a better life.

He said, quite distinctly, "S'kotto," the characteristic Japanese rendering of the unfamiliar English name Scott.

—She has written a letter to Casablanca to say that she will not be coming back to work.

There was a pause. Louise began to sob.

—Anyway, what is your address?

Louise said, "My address . . ."

—The address of your apartment, in Sendagaya.

"Why . . . why d'you need to know my address?"

—I want to send you some of Lucie's belongings.

Louise's dread, which up until now had been on behalf of her friend, suddenly became personal. "He wants to know where I live," she was thinking. "He's going to come after *me*." She said, "Well, Lucie knows it. She knows her address."

—She is not feeling too well now and she cannot remember.

"Oh, I can't remember either."

—Well . . . can you remember where your house is near?

"No, no, I can't remember."

—What about the street? Can you remember the street?

"No, I . . ."

—Anyway, I need to send her belongings back.

"I can't remember . . ."

—If it's a problem, don't worry.

"I haven't got it on me now . . ."

—That's okay. Don't worry.

Louise was overcome by panic and emotion. Weeping, she handed the phone to a friend, an Australian man who had lived in Tokyo for years.

"Hello," he said in Japanese. "Where is Lucie?"

After a few moments, he handed the phone back. "He'll only speak English," he said. "He only wants to speak to you."

But Louise had collected her thoughts. She realized that it was important to draw the conversation out, to try to find out where Lucie was.

"Hello," she said. "This is Louise again. So, can I join your cult?"

The voice seemed to hesitate. Then it said, —What religion are you?

Louise said, "Well, I'm a Catholic, but Lucie's a Catholic too. I don't mind changing. I want to change my life too."

—Anyway, it's up to Lucie. It's up to what she thinks. I will think about it.

"Please let me speak to Lucie," said Louise desperately.

—I'll speak to my guru and ask him.

"Please let me speak to her," Louise cried. "I'm begging you, please, let me speak to her."

—Anyway, I have to go now, the voice said. —I'm sorry. I just had to let you know that you won't see her again. Good-bye.

The cell phone line went dead for the second time.

■ ■ ■

Lucie disappeared on Saturday, July 1, 2000, at the midpoint of the first year of the twenty-first century. It took a week for the news to reach the world at large. The first report appeared the following Sunday, July 9, when a British newspaper carried a short article about a missing tourist named "Lucy Blackman." There were more detailed stories the next day in the British and Japanese papers. They named Louise Phillips, as well as Lucie's sister, Sophie Blackman, who was said to have flown to Tokyo to look for her, and her father, Tim, who was on his way there. Reference was made to a threatening phone call and the vague suggestion that she had been kidnapped by a cult. Two of the stories spoke of "fears" that she had been "forced into prostitution." Lucie was identified as a former British Airways stewardess, but the following day's news identified her as a "bar girl" or "nightclub hostess" in "Tokyo's red-light district." Now Japanese television had seized on the story and camera crews were prowling through Roppongi, looking for blond foreigners. The combination of the missing girl's youth, nationality, hair color, and the implications of the job she had been doing had tipped the story over the threshold that separates mere incident from news; it was now impossible to ignore. Within twenty-four hours, twenty British reporters and photographers and five separate television crews had flown to Tokyo, to join the dozen correspondents and freelancers permanently based there.

That day, thirty thousand posters were printed and distributed across the country, mostly in Tokyo and in Chiba, the prefecture immediately to the east of the capital.

"MISSING," ran the bilingual text along the top and, at the bottom, "Lucie BLACKMAN (British Female)."

Age: 21 years
Height: 175cm Medium Build
Hair Color: Blonde
Eye Color: Blue
She was last seen in Tokyo on Saturday July 1st. Since then she has been missing.
If anyone has seen her, or has any information relating to her, contact Azabu Police Station or your nearest police station.

The poster was dominated by the photograph of a girl in a short black dress sitting on a sofa. She had blond hair and white teeth exposed in a nervous smile. The camera looked down on her from above, making her face appear broad and childlike. With her large head, long hair, and firm chin, the girl in the poster looked like no one more than Alice in Wonderland.

■ ■ ■

Lucie Blackman was already dead. She died before I ever knew that such a person existed. In fact, it was only because she was dead—or missing, which was as much as anyone knew at the time—that I took an interest in her at all. I was the correspondent for a British newspaper, living in Tokyo. Lucie Blackman was a young British woman who had disappeared there—which is to say that, in the terms in which I first thought of her, she was a *story*.

At first the story was a puzzle, which developed over time into a profound mystery. Lucie emerged as a tragic victim, and finally as a cause, the subject of vigorous, bitter contestation in a Japanese court. The story attracted much attention in Japan and Britain, but it was fickle and inconsistent. For months at a time there would be no interest in Lucie's case, then some fresh development would bring a sudden demand for news and explanation. In its outlines the story was familiar enough—girl missing, body found, man charged—but, on inspection, it became so complicated and confusing, so fraught with bizarre turns and irrational developments that conventional reporting of it was almost inevitably unsatisfactory, provoking more unanswered questions than it could ever quell.

This quality of evasiveness, the sense in which it outstripped familiar categories of news, made the story fascinating. It was like an itch that no four columns of newspaper copy or three-minute television item could ever scratch. The story infected my dreams; even after months had passed, I found it impossible to forget Lucie Blackman. I followed the story from the beginning and through its successive stages, trying to craft something consistent and intelligible out of its kinks and knots and roughness. It took me ten years.

I had lived in Tokyo for most of my adult life and traveled across Asia and beyond. As a reporter of natural disasters and wars, I had seen something of grief and darkness. But Lucie's story brought me into contact with aspects of human experience that I had never glimpsed before. It was like the key to a trapdoor in a familiar room, a trapdoor concealing secrets—frightening, violent, monstrous existences to which I had been oblivious. This new knowledge made me feel obscurely embarrassed and naïve. It was as if I, the experienced reporter, had been missing something extraordinary in a city that it was my professional pride to know intimately.

It was only when she was slipping from public consciousness that I began to consider Lucie as a person rather than a story. I had met her family over the course of their visits to Japan. As a reporter of the case, I had been treated first with cautious mistrust and eventually with cautious friendship. Now I traveled back to Britain and visited the Blackman family on their home ground. I tracked down friends and acquaintances from the different stages of Lucie's life. One led to another; those who were at first reluctant to speak were eventually persuaded. To Lucie's parents, sister, and brother, I returned repeatedly over a period of years. The accumulated recordings of these interviews add up to several days.

I thought that grasping the essentials of a life that ended at twenty-one would be a simple task. At first glance, there was nothing obvious to distinguish Lucie Blackman from millions of others like her: a young, middle-class woman from the southeast of England, of moderate affluence and education. Lucie's life had been "ordinary," "normal"; by far the most remarkable thing about it was the way it ended. But the closer I looked, the more intriguing she became.

It should have been obvious, for we all know it from our own lives, but after twenty-one years, Lucie's personality and character were already too various, too complicated for any one person, even those closest to her, wholly to understand. Everyone who knew her knew someone subtly different. A few years on from childhood, her life was already a complexity of allegiances, emotions, and aspirations, often contradictory. Lucie was loyal, honest, and capable of deceit. She was confident, dependable, and vulnerable. She was straightforward and mysterious, open and secretive. I felt the helplessness of a biographer in sifting and reconciling this material, in doing justice to an entire life. I became fascinated by the process of learning about someone whom I had never known, and could never have known, someone of whom I would have been oblivious had she not died.

Within a few weeks of her disappearance, many, many people had heard the name Lucie Blackman and knew her face—or at least the version of it that appeared in the newspapers and on television, the Alice face of the girl in the missing-person poster. To them she was a victim, almost the symbol of a certain kind of victimhood: the young woman who comes to a ghastly end in an exotic land. So I hoped that I could do some service to Lucie Blackman, or to her memory, by restoring her status as a normal person, a woman complex and lovable in her ordinariness, with a life before death.

PART ONE LUCIE

1. THE WORLD THE RIGHT WAY ROUND

Even later, when she found it difficult to see any good in her husband, Lucie's mother, Jane, always acknowledged that Tim Blackman had saved their daughter's life.

Lucie had been twenty-one months old at the time, cared for by her father and mother in the cottage they rented in a small village in Sussex. Since infancy, she had been stricken with fierce bouts of tonsillitis, which drove up her temperature and swelled her throat. Her parents sponged her with water to cool her down, but the fevers lingered, and when one had passed another would seize hold within a few weeks. One day, Tim had come home early from work to help Jane care for the needy child. That night, he was awakened by a cry from his wife, who had gone in to look at her.

By the time he entered the nursery, Jane was already running downstairs.

"Lucie was motionless at the bottom of the cot, and she was clammy," Tim said. "I picked her out and put her on the floor, and she was turning gray in front of me, just the most sickly, blacky-gray color. Quite clearly the lifeblood wasn't being pumped round her body. I didn't know what to do. I was cuddling her on the floor, and Jane had run down to phone an ambulance. Lucie was completely quiet, wasn't breathing. I tried to force open her mouth. It was tightly shut, but I forced it open with two hands and held it open with the thumb of one hand and put my fingers in and pulled her tongue forward. I didn't know whether I was doing any good or not, but I did it, and then I put her head to one side, and then I breathed into her and then pushed the air out, breathed into her and pushed it out, and she started to breathe on her own again. I was sick with anxiety and worry, and then I saw the pink coming back to her skin, and by that time the ambulance had arrived, and the ambulance blokes were rushing up the tiny, weeny stairs, these great big blokes with all this huge, noisy kit on, big beefy chaps who were as big as the cottage. And they got their stretcher out and strapped her on and carried her downstairs and put her in the back of the ambulance. And after that she was fine."

Lucie had experienced a febrile convulsion, a muscle spasm caused by fever and dehydration that had caused her to swallow her own tongue, blocking off her breathing. A few moments longer, and she would have died. "I knew at that moment that I could not only have one child," Tim said. "I knew. I'd thought about it before, when Lucie was born. But at that moment, I knew that if anything had happened to her, and we didn't have any other children, it would be an absolutely terrible disaster."

■ ■ ■

Lucie had been born on September 1, 1978. Her name was from the Latin word for "light," and even in adulthood, her mother said, she craved brightness and illumination, and was uncomfortable in the dark, switching on all the bulbs in the house and going to sleep with a lamp turned on in her room.

Jane's labor had to be induced, and it lasted sixteen hours. Lucie's head was positioned against her mother's back, a "posterior presentation" that caused her great pain during the delivery.

But the eight-pound baby was healthy, and her parents experienced deep, but complicated, happiness at the birth of their first child. "I was delighted, absolutely delighted," said Jane. "But I think when you become a mother, you . . . I just wanted my mother to be there, because I was so proud I'd had a baby. But she wasn't there, so it was sad as well."

Jane remembered little but sadness from her own childhood. Her adult life, too, had been marked by clusters of crushing, overwhelming loss, which had bred in her a dry, dark humor, alternately self-deprecating and indignantly defensive. She was in her late forties when I first met her, a thin, attractive woman with short dark blond hair and sharp, vigilant features. Her outfits were tidy and demure. Long, delicate lashes ringed her eyes, but the girlishness that they might have suggested was dispelled by a fierce sense of rightness and a scathing intolerance of fools and snobs. Pride and self-pity were at war within Jane. She was like a fox, a stubborn, elegant fox in a navy blue skirt and jacket.

Her father had been a manager at the Elstree film studios, and she and her younger brother and sister had grown up in the outer London suburbs, a strict and rather drab middle-class life of homework and good table manners and the annual summer holiday in a gusty English seaside resort. When Jane was twelve, the family moved to south London. Before her first morning at her new school, Jane went in to kiss her mother goodbye and found her asleep after a night of headaches and insomnia. "I felt that something awful was going to happen," Jane said. "And I said to my father, 'She's not going to die, is she?' and he said, 'Oh no, don't be silly, of course not.' And then I came home from school that day, and she'd died. She'd had a brain tumor. And from then on my father was distraught. He was broken, a broken man, and I just had to be brave. That was the end of my childhood."

Jane's mother was forty years old at the time of her death. "My grandmother looked after us during the week, and at weekends it was Daddy," she said. "I remember him just crying all the time." Fifteen months after his wife's death, he married a woman in her mid-twenties. Jane was appalled. "But he had three children, and he just couldn't function. It was terrible. The truth is that I can't remember much of my childhood. When you've had a shock, and been through a time as painful as that, your brain makes you forget."

Jane left school at fifteen. She took a secretarial course and found a job at a big advertising agency. When she was nineteen, she traveled to Mallorca with a girlfriend and stayed there for six months, cleaning cars for a living. It was before the age of mass British tourism to Spain, and the Balearic Islands were still a select and exotic destination. The famous Manchester United footballer George Best was a visitor. "I didn't meet him, but I remember seeing him in these bars, surrounded by beauties," said Jane. "But I was very sensible, I was very careful. I've got the word 'sensible' running through my body like a stick of rock. Everyone else might have been swinging but I wasn't. I was just very boring."

In Mallorca, Jane's virtue was tested by a young man, a nodding acquaintance, who appeared at her front door one day and attempted to kiss her. "I was absolutely mortified, because I hardly knew him, and it was the middle of the afternoon. He was Swedish, I think. I hadn't given him any provocation, and it made me very wary after that. I liked the sun and the sea, I liked being in the outdoors, but I can't say it was a wild time, because I'm sensible. I never slept with anyone until I slept with my husband."

She was twenty-two when she met Tim, and living with her father and stepmother in Chislehurst in the London borough of Bromley. He was the older brother of a friend, and Jane had already heard all about him. "People said to me, 'That Tim's a right one,'" she remembered. "'A right one for the women.'"

Tim had just returned from the south of France, where he had been staying with a French girlfriend. "But he started flirting with me anyway, and I gave him one of my icy stares," said Jane. "I think I was the first person in his life who hadn't fallen for him just like that, so I was a challenge. But I had no confidence, if I'm honest. I had lots of very beautiful girlfriends who had men flocking round them, but at discos I was always the custodian of the handbags. Tim couldn't understand why I hadn't fallen for him hook, line, and sinker, and I couldn't understand why anyone would fancy me, and I think that's why I ended up marrying him." The wedding was eighteen months later, on Tim's twenty-third birthday, July 17, 1976.

Tim managed a shoe shop in the nearby town of Orpington, a relic of the dwindling chain of businesses that his father had once owned across the southeast. But the shop failed, and Tim found himself claiming the dole for six months. He ended up supporting his young family with odd jobs for friends and as a freelance painter and decorator. "We were living hand to mouth," he said. "They were very tricky, very tricky times in the early 1980s, and we didn't know where the next fifty pounds was coming from. But we were in this lovely place with our baby, this Laura Ashley–style cottage, and it was a very beautiful life. I loved that time when Lucie was little."

In May 1980, less than two years after the first baby, Jane gave birth to Sophie, and, three years after that, to Rupert. Tim found a business partner and moved from decorating into property development; in 1982 the family moved a few miles north to the genteel commuter town of Sevenoaks, in Kent. Here, their period of hardship at an end, Jane was able to create for her own family the childhood she had always wanted for herself, an idyll of flowers and pretty dresses and the laughter of little children.

The house where they lived, which Jane christened Daisy Cottage, overlooked a private prep school—Granville School, or *the* Granville School, as it insisted on being known. It was the fulfillment of all her fantasies, a place of such self-conscious tweeness that everyone who went there remembers it with a smile. The girls, as young as three years old, wore a uniform of blue-checked dresses and gray woolly bobble hats; at the spring festival, they put rings of flowers called chaplets in their hair. The school curriculum included the study of curtsying and maypole dancing. "Our bedroom looked directly over the playground," remembered Jane. "It was so perfect—at play-time, Lucie would come and wave to me and I could wave back." It was a school out of the past, out of the pages of an illustrated children's book. "Like living in la-la land," said Jane, "not like the real world at all."

From the beginning, Lucie was a grown-up, conscientious girl with a childish earnestness that made adults smile. When Jane gave her peas to shell, she would examine each one individually, rejecting any that displayed the smallest sign of imperfection. She loved dolls and would sit alongside her mother breast-feeding a plastic baby as Jane breast-fed Sophie. "She was so meticulous and tidy and neat," said Jane. "Like me from an early age." Sophie, by contrast, was "stroppy" and prone to tantrums, which her older sister gently and skillfully defused. The two sisters shared a big old-fashioned bed, and one Easter Sunday they spent the entire day living underneath it, taking their meals there, reading their picture books, and tending to their toys.

Lucie's school exercise books suggest how successfully Jane created for her children a world of innocence and delight.

Name: Lucy Blackman
Subject: News

Monday 20th May

To-day Daddy is going
to collect me from
school and we are
going to go home and
I am going to get
my Laura Ashley dress
and it is bluey
gray and it has
little flowers and then
I am going to in to Tescos
home and wear and
I am going to get Gemma
a preasnt but I don't
know what to get her
for her birthday treat
and she is having
four friends that is
me and Celia and
Charlotte and another
frend in her school
and I will be the
only one from Granville

friends friends friends friends

And from another exercise book:

Name: Lucy Blackman
Subject: Experiments

Light

I used a large mirror.
I looked at myself.
I saw my reflection.

I closed one eye.
I saw myself with one eye closed.

I touched my nose.
I saw myself with my right hand on my nose.

I clapped my hands.
I saw my hands clap.

ИIЯЯOЯ
MIRROR

I used a large mirror.
I put the mirror at the side.
I saw the world the right way round.

"Because my childhood was sad I always wanted to have a wonderful, happy family life," said Jane. "I'd put their slippers down the front of the stove so they'd be warm when they came home from school. When Rupert used to play rugby, I'd take a hot-water bottle and a flask of hot tea when I met him from school. My biggest fear was losing them. Even when they were little. I had these leather reins with a little picture of a bunny rabbit on them, these reins that I used to make Rupert wear. I'd have him on reins, and to the girls I'd say, 'You hold hands,' and in the supermarket if I lost sight of one of them I would feel . . . It was the worst thing for me, loss, because of what had happened to me. That was always my biggest fear—

losing. Because I'd lost my mother, I just couldn't bear the thought of ever losing the children. So I was a very protective—an overprotective—mother."

Lucie won a scholarship to Walthamstow Hall, a stalwart redbrick nineteenth-century institution founded for the daughters of Christian missionaries. She was a hard worker and might have been expected to flourish at "Wally Hall," which took pride in the number of girls it sent to university. And yet Lucie never quite fitted in there. "Walthamstow Hall was quite a posh school," said Jane. "A lot of girls on their birthday were given car keys. That was their birthday present, and that wasn't the league we were in at all." However, the darkest shadow over Lucie's teenage years was not money but illness.

At the age of twelve, she contracted mycoplasma pneumonia, a rare form of the illness, which laid her low for weeks. "She was very, very ill and no one knew what was the matter with her," said Jane. "She'd be propped up in bed on so many pillows, and I had to give her this treatment to get rid of the mucus, to pummel her back. There was a rattle when she breathed, you could hear it in her lungs." Afterwards Lucie was afflicted with a malaise that caused her legs to ache so much that she could barely walk, and put paid to two years of schoolwork. For weeks at a time she had no energy at all; the effort of descending a flight of stairs left her spent with exhaustion, and a series of doctors could give no assurances about when, or even if, her good health would return.

Jane Blackman had a strong belief in the hidden powers of the mind, and in her own gifts of prediction and intuition. She worked as a reflexologist—a masseuse and a therapist of the feet—and frequently, she said, she had found herself accurately foreseeing imminent events—the death of an elderly relative, the pregnancy of a patient before the woman was aware of it herself. "I just have feelings about things when I'm working," she said. "A voice will come into my head to tell me something and afterwards I'm right. It goes back to my sense of justice: I feel people's pain. People say I'm very empathetic, but I think if you've been through a lot yourself it gives you that ability."

It was during Lucie's long illness, her mother believed, that her daughter's own gift for supernatural perception first displayed itself.

Separately, both her parents began to notice a faint but distinctive smell in the master bedroom where Lucie was being nursed—the smell of cigars. No one in the family smoked them; Tim even called on the neighbors to confirm that the smoke was not coming through their shared wall. A few days later, Jane mentioned the strange smell to Lucie. It was a time when she was extremely weak, drifting between sleep and wakefulness, but it was still a surprise when she replied, "It's the man who sits on the end of my bed."

"What man?" asked Jane.

"In the night, there's this old man who comes and sits on the end of my bed sometimes, and he smokes cigars."

"Poof!" said Tim, telling the story later. "We all thought, 'Lucie's gone completely off her rocker.'"

Much later, after her strength had returned, Lucie visited the home of Jane's father and stepmother. She came across a photograph on a sideboard of an old man and asked who it was. Jane's own grandmother, Lucie's great-grandmother, was there that day, and the man was her husband, Hollis Etheridge, who had died years before.

"That's the man," said Lucie, "the one who came and sat at the end of my bed."

Throughout his life, he had been a smoker of cigars.

The disappearance of Lucie Blackman, the long months of uncertainty, and the discovery of her terrible fate added to the ill feeling between her parents. But it existed long before her death. The shrill, contending versions of the truth were the sound track to the last five years of Lucie's life.

In Jane's version, the breakdown of their marriage occurred at a precise moment in November 1995 in their latest home— a big six-bedroom Edwardian house in Sevenoaks, the place where Jane's dreams of domesticity had finally been fulfilled. "It was the house where I was going to have my Aga," she said, with a trace of self-mockery at the snugness of the image. "This was the place where it would all be. I would be round the kitchen, Aga cooking, and my children would be in there, and then grandchildren. It didn't quite work out like that."

It was Sunday afternoon, and the five members of the family were sitting together in the front room. A fire was burning in the grate. Jane had prepared what the children called "colored toast," striped with a tricolor of Marmite and apricot and strawberry jam. "We were watching *The Wonder Years*, which I used to love," Jane remembered. "We all used to love it. Tim had Rupert on his lap, and I'll never forget what he said. He said, 'I *love* being family,' as we all sat there together. I'll never forget it. 'I *love* being family.' That's what he said. And then the next day it was all over."

On Monday morning, Jane received a telephone call from a man, a stranger, who told her that Tim was sleeping with his wife. Confronted with the accusation that evening, Tim first denied, then admitted the affair. Jane demanded that he move out immediately. There was shouting and screaming. Overnight, black plastic bags were stuffed with clothes and belongings and tossed out windows. "I believed that Tim was a caring, family man," Jane said. "But after nineteen years of marriage, I realized that I'd lived with someone who didn't exist."

Tim acknowledged that he had been unfaithful to his wife. But rather than the sudden collapse of an apparently happy marriage, he spoke of a long, grinding slide into uncommunicativeness and antipathy. "When Jane was unhappy with something I had done, she would simply ignore me," he said. "There would be long weekends of stony-faced silence. It went on for weeks at a time, and then it lasted for months, months on end. I was the guilty party, according to the law and according to the whole standard procedure, and no one was particularly interested in whether there'd been a history to the breakdown. I'm sure that, in the children's eyes, I'd been the one who broke the family up. It's not quite as black and white as that, as anyone who's been in a similar situation would understand."

Jane and the three children spent an unhappy Christmas on their own in the big Edwardian house amid the unborn ghosts of future grandchildren. There was virtually no money from Tim, whose company had gone into liquidation. After the sale of their old home, Jane rented a small house, a grim brick cube in the less genteel quarters of Sevenoaks. It was a place with a history—its previous owner was Diana Goldsmith, a forty-four-year-old alcoholic who had inexplicably disappeared after dropping her children off at school. When Jane and the children moved in, the windows still carried traces of the dust that the detectives had used in their hunt for fingerprints. "The children and I used to say, 'I hope she's not under the bath,'" said Jane. "And it was only half a joke."

The following year, Diana Goldsmith's body was found buried in a garden in Bromley; her former lover was tried but acquitted of the murder. "Everyone hated that house," said Jane. "It was filthy dirty and had this horrible past. I'm not at all materialistic, but I like nice things which please the eye, and it offended my sense of beauty. Lucie hated that house."

It was her last home.

2. RULES

"A divorce makes you question everything," said Sophie Blackman, "because the only thing you know growing up is: this is Mum, this is Dad, this is your brother and sister, and this is how you fit in. When that changes, it really does throw open the question of who you are and why you exist. Rupert was thirteen, so he cried a lot but got on with it. I was fifteen and just at that point where everything is so awkward anyway, and I didn't know whether I was coming or going. Being seventeen, Lucie was that bit older. It wasn't that Lucie took Mum's side—there were no sides. But Lucie empathized with Mum, because it was Lucie who had always been like the mother to Rupert and me."

Sophie Blackman was the closest that I ever got to meeting Lucie Blackman in person. The two had been born less than two years apart and had lived together all their lives. Everyone who knew them commented on their striking resemblance, partly physical, but mostly the consequence of those unmistakable mannerisms and rhythms of speech that all siblings share.

Sophie was dry, caustic, and deeply loyal. Among the people Lucie left behind, there were those who needed and depended upon her more, but I don't think that anyone understood her as well as her sister.

Temperamentally, though, the two were very different.

Even as children, Lucie was girlish, conciliatory, and maternal, while Sophie was a stubborn, aggressive tomboy. As a teenager she was argumentative and tantrum prone, with a sarcastic and unsentimental wit. Like Jane, she was intolerant of idiots, but she was scathing too about her mother's preoccupation with the "mumbo jumbo" of superstition and the supernatural. She was naturally closest to Tim; with Jane, she argued violently. One of the consequences of the parents' separation was that this conflict between mother and daughter grew more bitter and intense.

Jane's dream of Edwardian coziness had died with her marriage, and in its absence a change came over the family. From being a strict and protective mother, Jane became strikingly liberal and permissive. Boyfriends and girlfriends were allowed, and even encouraged, to stay overnight; the teenage Rupert was mortified when his mother presented him with a packet of condoms. Friends remarked on the closeness between Lucie and Jane, more like that of two sisters than a mother and daughter. "It was the way they talked to each other, phone calls she'd make to her mum laughing and giggling," said Caroline Lawrence, who was at school with Lucie. "They used to wear each other's clothes. They even used to go out in the evenings together. I can understand that because my mum and I are very close, but I wouldn't go clubbing with her."

Conflicts were inevitable in a house of teenage children; very often, they were between Jane and Sophie. In these battles, it was Lucie who served as the peacemaker; to some people she seemed more even than a sister to Jane. "In that house she actually became like the mother figure," said Val Burman, a friend of Jane. "When Sophie used to scream and shout at Jane, it was always Lucie who would be the one to sort the problems out. She grew up quickly after Tim left. She became the mother, and Jane was the child."

––––––

Lucie didn't have the slim build or sharp features to qualify as straightforwardly beautiful, but the first thing that everyone remembered about her was the way she looked. Meticulous grooming was central to Lucie's idea of herself. Friends used to smile at the way she would do her hair and apply makeup for a walk to the shops or a morning jog. When she laughed, she would throw back her long hair and her shoulders would shake. With her height and her hair, Lucie stood out among her contemporaries; to Jane, she "lit up the room." "I was mesmerized by her the first time I saw her," said Val Burman. "I loved to hear her talking. She had a wonderful way with words. She could talk about anything, and you wanted to hear it. She could tell a story about a cube of sugar." The stream of words was punctuated by the darting movement of her fingers with their flashing, highly polished nails. "She was all hair and nails—it was as if she was talking with her hands," said Caroline Lawrence. "And people would notice her. That hair . . . I can remember being in the Dorset Arms in the town, waiting for her. There was a window, and she was crossing the road, and—I'm not joking—literally the whole pub just stopped and looked at her. Even the girls were looking at her. Just because she was this tall, blond bombshell strutting across the road."

Lucie loved new clothes and shopping for them. Like Jane, she loved the coziness of a home and took pleasure in her neatly ordered possessions. It was this fondness for luxury and comfort, as much as any other reason, that made life as a student unappealing to Lucie. She duly passed her exams and stayed on into the sixth form to take A levels, but, unlike most of the clever girls of Walthamstow Hall, she made no attempt to apply for university. She worked for a while in a pizza restaurant after her exams, later as a teaching assistant at a local private school. Then, through a family friend, she got a job at Banque de Société Générale, or "SocGen," a French investment bank in the City of London.

Lucie worked as an assistant to the dealers, inputting orders as they were called out from the trading floor. The traders were young, competitive, highly paid men; the atmosphere was fast-paced and aggressive. As a young, blond new arrival, Lucie was an immediate object of male attention. The men called her "Baps," in reference to her full bosom. She was only eighteen, but she thrived on the excitement and the atmosphere of flirtation. She loved the clothes and jewelry and the champagne after work in the City bars. "Everyone else was at university and we were working," said Caroline Lawrence, who had also left Walthamstow Hall to take a job in London. "We weren't earning a lot of money, but to us—seventeen, eighteen years old—we were rich. Lucie liked SocGen—the first taste of life outside Sevenoaks, in with all the City boys. We thought we were so grown up taking the train up there every day. I'd see her, in the rush hour, giving herself a French manicure, standing up. A French manicure is not like a normal manicure. You paint the nails a natural color, and then you have to paint the white tips. It's not easy at the best of times, and she could do it standing up. On a train."

The acquisition and disposal of money was the function of the City, and Lucie liked that too. She bought herself a car, a black Renault Clio, to make the predawn journey from Sevenoaks to London every morning in time for the opening of the financial markets. On weekends, she shopped in the Lakeside Shopping Centre in Thurrock; once, on a whim, Lucie and a friend visited Rigby & Peller, corsetieres to the queen, and purchased ten of their famous made-to-measure bras. But her salary, about $24,000, was a fraction of that of the men with whom she worked, and it was at SocGen that Lucie first went into debt. Credit cards, store cards, overdrafts, and hire purchases were a part of life for many workers in the City, but Lucie found it hard to get used to the idea. "I was infinitely more in debt than she was," said Caroline Ryan, who worked with her in the City. "But Lucie was a worrier. If she went a few pounds overdrawn, she wouldn't know what she was going to do."

Lucie worked for a year at SocGen but eventually grew restless there. The job in itself led nowhere, and a love affair with a younger trader at the firm ended badly, leaving her tearful and unhappy. Lucie liked the idea of traveling, but only if she could do it with a guaranteed degree of comfort and style. "That was Lucie's character," said Sophie. "She never had any interest in backpacking. You can't take a hair dryer and you don't wear makeup. Lucie liked to have manicured nails, and nice hair, she'd wear little-heeled shoes. She took care of her appearance, and that didn't fit with backpacking and grimy hostels. She didn't want that, but she did want to see different cultures, and people, and eat interesting food, and to do it in a way that was comfortable for her." The solution came after a year of working in the City, when Lucie successfully applied to work as an air stewardess for British Airways.

Here, on the face of it, was the perfect job for Lucie—pretty, personable, and with a decent command of conversational French. She began in May 1998 with a twenty-one-day training course in which she learned, among other lessons, how to deliver a baby, how to employ handcuffs, and how to deal with an onboard bomb (place it at the very back of the cabin, next to the exit, and wrap with wet cushions to absorb the blast). For the first eighteen months at the airline, she worked the short-haul routes to British and European cities; her first flight was the forty-minute hop to the island of Jersey. "I kept telling myself that planes are safer than crossing the road, that the journey to the airport is more dangerous than being on the plane," said Jane Blackman. "But when she made her first flight I felt sick to my stomach." Lucie was under instructions to telephone her mother after every flight; as long as she worked for British Airways, Jane would scan the departures and arrivals on Ceefax and relax only when she knew that her daughter's plane was safe and stationary on the ground.

■ ■ ■

Perhaps it was a consequence of her teenage illness, and those months of inactivity, but Lucie as a young woman was obsessed with method and technique, and with disciplining and ordering her life. She would write out lists of jobs to be done and tasks to be achieved, like incantations to keep inertia at bay. She collected books of self-help and self-improvement, and circulated them among her friends: guides to debt management, tummy flattening, and the boosting of self-esteem. A page from Lucie's diary records her preoccupations at the beginning of 1999 with fitness, beauty, health, and money.

NEW YEAR RESOLUTIONS!
  (1) GO TO THE GYM 3–4 TIMES PER WEEK.
  (2) TRY + DO 2 OTHER ACTIVITIES AS WELL.
  (3) STOP USING BOTH PHONES.
  (4) FROM MARCH START PUTTING MONEY
      AWAY.
  (5) STICK TO RULES.
  (6) SPEND MORE TIME WITH W+G//H+J.
  (7) SLEEP MORE.
  (8) LEARN ITALIAN.
  (9) SAVE ALL OF COMMISSIONS.
  (10) SCRUB AND TAN *EVERY OTHER* DAY.
  (11) LOTION ON DAYS IN BETWEEN.
  (12) DRINK MORE WATER.

Resolution 5 referred not to rules in general, but to *The Rules*, a popular American guide to dating and romance that Lucie strove to live by. *The Rules* set out a kind of emotional crash diet, a return to traditional, prefeminist modes of court-ship, in which sustained and energetic wooing was required of a man before he could expect any reward. In another diary, Lucie recorded her own summary of *The Rules*.

(1) Keep cool.
(2) Let him do all the work, the calling—everything.
(3) Keep your cards close to your chest—if he wants to know how you feel, he'll ask.
(4) Keep chat light.

YOU ARE NOT FALLING FOR HIM!!

Men were drawn to Lucie, and from her mid-teens she was rarely without a boyfriend. But, like the resolutions to save rather than spend and to talk less on the phone, the reticence and cool demanded by *The Rules* went against Lucie's nature. "When Lucie met someone, she'd give her all, and she had her heart broken a few times," said Sophie. "She wore her heart on her sleeve: 'this is what I am, this is what I'm like, take it or leave it.' And they'd take it for a while and then leave it." Lucie's friends became familiar with the pattern by which she met a new "chap," became rapidly besotted with him, only for one of them to lose interest. "She'd be madly in love," Sophie said, "and then about two months later she'd be repulsed at the mention of his name. She wanted very much to meet someone, settle down, have babies, and live in the countryside. And that meant she had to go through a lot of frogs."

There was Jim, who incurred the loathing of Lucie's female friends for the unforgivable act of dumping her on her eighteenth birthday. There was Robert, who lived above the local pizza restaurant and who deserted her for one of her best friends. There was Greg, who worked for SocGen; the split with him precipitated her departure for British Airways. And then there was the most glamorous and dangerous of them all: Marco—beautiful, wild, Italian, and doomed.

It was Sophie who first spotted Marco, when she was working as a barmaid at the Royal Oak Hotel in Sevenoaks. She identified him immediately as Lucie's type—tall, strapping, "gorgeous." "Marco really was handsome," Sophie said. "He had a history of working as a model. He was thirty—Lucie always had older boyfriends. On paper he was a real catch, and Lucie was pretty smitten with him. Then it turned out that everything on paper was complete bullshit."

At British Airways, Lucie had ten days off a month and she spent most of them with Marco. They went clubbing at the Ministry of Sound and Club 9 in London, and drinking in the Sevenoaks pubs the Vine, the Chimneys, and the Black Boy. Marco suffered from severe colds and spent long hours recovering from them in bed. During evenings out with Lucie, he frequently vanished for short stretches with one friend or another. "It just didn't click what was really going on," said Sophie. "It was so stupid and naïve of us."

Her friends found him vain and standoffish, but Lucie was becoming more and more serious about Marco. One weekend, he dropped her off at Heathrow and drove away in her car, with the promise that he would pick her up on her return the next day. But when she landed, Marco wasn't there. "He didn't pick her up, he didn't turn up at all, and Lucie was in a bit of a state," said Sophie. "She couldn't get hold of him. She didn't know where her car was, she didn't know where he was, she didn't know anything. Eventually, she rang a member of his family, his cousin or something. The cousin said, 'I was hoping this wouldn't happen again. This is what Marco does, you see. What exactly has he told you?' It turned out that he was a complete lying bastard."

Marco, it transpired, had never been a model. Moreover, he was a heavy user of cocaine. The disappearances in the pub, the susceptibility to "colds," and the long hours of recovery—suddenly, they made sense. In a rage, Sophie went to Marco's flat. He was in bed, stupefied after an extended binge of drugs and booze. The keys of Lucie's Renault Clio were on the table beside him. Sophie picked them up, gave Marco a valedictory punch, and stormed out to retrieve the car. Its door and back panel were scraped and dented by a collision.

Lucie was as caring and protective of her car as she was of her hair and fingernails: that was the end of her and Marco. Her unhappiness was intense but short-lived. Then, a few months later, came jolting news. Marco had committed suicide—or, according to another version of the story, had died of an accidental overdose of drugs. Whatever the truth, Lucie's handsome ex-boyfriend was dead.

3. LONG HAUL

It was becoming obvious that the life of an air stewardess wasn't for Lucie. By early 2000, it felt like a trap that she must urgently escape. To her colleagues, this was difficult to understand, for she had recently achieved the ambition of every British Airways cabin crew member: promotion from the short-haul jets that flew from Heathrow to the intercontinental flights out of Gatwick. The long-haul destinations were more exotic, more glamorous and, above all, better paid. As a junior flight attendant, Lucie's basic salary was paltry—an annual £8,336* before the deduction of tax. The same amount again came from the "allowances" that were added to her pay depending on the destinations, and the nature of the flights on which she worked. Flights that were very early, or long, overnight flights, and flights that required an unusually fast turnaround—all of these earned a bonus. There were allowances for breakfast, lunch, and dinner, based on the cost in local currency of a three-course meal in a five-star hotel. It was assumed as a matter of course that most employees would settle for a much cheaper meal and pocket the difference. So the least desirable flights were short hops within the United Kingdom; the most re-

*During the years covered in this book, one British pound was worth approximately $1.50.

warding were the expensive cities of Asia and the Americas: Miami, São Paulo, and the most lucrative of all, Tokyo.

Having moved to long haul, Lucie could expect to earn about £1,300 a month after tax. But however much she worried about money, she continued to edge deeper and deeper into debt. Lucie's scribbled accounts of expenditure and income for the end of 1998 listed a monthly payment of £764.87, more than half her income, on her Diners Club credit card account alone. Then there was the £200 monthly payment for her Renault Clio, a £47 payment for a bank loan, £89.96 for her Visa card, £10 for a Marks & Spencer credit card, as well as £70 in rent to Jane, a £32 gym membership, and a £140 mobile phone bill. By the time she had bought the makeup and shampoo and clothes that she needed for work, Lucie was spending a few hundred pounds more than she earned every month, and the interest on all her debts was making them harder to repay by the day.

She was tired and ill. The long overnight flights were bound to be draining, but they were not even fun. British Airways had fourteen thousand crew members; most of the time, Lucie stepped on to a flight with people she had never met before and would not see again. The occasional pleasure of working alongside a friend did not compensate for the monotony of repeatedly pouring tomato juice into plastic cups and offering the choice of chicken or beef. "One hotel room is much the same as another in any country," said Sophie. "She might be in Paris in the morning, Edinburgh in the afternoon, and she might be in Zimbabwe the following day. But she'd be stuck in the hotel, constantly jet-lagged and really not able to go out and enjoy the life and culture and food because she was knackered. Towards the end, she was quite unhappy—tired, miserable, she never saw the same people twice."

There was something almost sinister about the depth of

Lucie's exhaustion. "She'd sleep for fifteen hours on end," Sophie remembered. "She felt awful, began to be really unwell." It was beginning to resemble that alarming period eight years earlier, when she had been laid low for so many months by the postviral malaise. It was in this atmosphere of anxiety and exhaustion that Lucie began to talk about going to Japan.

The idea first came up late in 1999 or early in 2000; nobody remembered quite when or how. But it was clear that it had originated with Louise Phillips.

Louise was the closest of all Lucie's friends. The two had known one another since they were thirteen. Physically, they were a contrast: Louise was slim, small, dark haired, with a sheen of that fashionable prettiness that Lucie lacked. She, too, was a girl without a father; he had died suddenly of cancer when she was twelve. And the two friends' mannerisms, their mode of talking, their love of makeup and nail varnish marked them out as a pair; even their names were similar. Jane thought of them as "soul mates." Tim was more down-to-earth: "Louise could babble for England, just like Lucie," he said, "so they babbled all the time and found one another hysterically funny."

Their closeness was obvious in the trajectory of their careers; at each stage of her life, Lucie followed a path earlier marked out by her friend. Louise left school at sixteen and went to work for an investment bank in the City, as Lucie would two years later. Louise joined British Airways as a stewardess; Lucie followed. And it was on Louise's initiative that the two of them went to Tokyo to work off the debts that had become such a burden to Lucie.

Later events tainted perceptions of Louise, particularly among Lucie's friends and family. It was difficult to separate those feelings of suspicion and mistrust from the way Louise was regarded before Japan. But Samantha Burman, the daughter of Jane's friend Val, was wary of her. "She'd been Lucie's friend a lot longer than I, so I didn't say anything. But Lucie felt that Louise was the prettier one and Louise was the more confident one, that she was the uglier friend, trying to live in her shadow. I don't think Louise did anything to change Lucie's feeling about that."

The two of them had been working since they left school. They had often talked about taking a break to travel together, along the familiar backpackers' route through Thailand, Bali, and Australia. But Lucie had no taste for budget travel, and no money, in any case, for travel of any kind. It was Louise's older sister, Emma, who told them about Tokyo, where she had lived two years earlier. There, she promised them, they could live in an exciting and unusual city and also earn a great deal of money. What exactly Emma had been doing in Tokyo was vague to Lucie's other friends; it seemed to vary depending on who was being told the story.

Samantha Burman gathered that she had been working in "bars." Sophie recalled talk of "waitressing." Lucie's latest boyfriend, a young investment banker named Jamie Gascoigne, had the impression that Emma had performed with a "dance troupe." In a farewell letter circulated among her friends at British Airways, Lucie presented it as a plan from which she herself was rather detached. "My best friend Louise was going over there to stay with relatives and the opportunity came up for me to go too. I've no plans once I'm out there, maybe see the culture, learn the language or become a high class, well paid Geisha girl !!!!!! (Joke) Just a break for a few months, something different—they say a change is as good as a rest."

Louise, the girls explained, had an aunt living in Tokyo with whom they could stay rent-free, and this made the proposal seem safer, more comprehensible, and closer to home. It was only to her mother that Lucie explained what Emma Phillips had done in Tokyo and what she and Louise also intended to do. "She said she was thinking of going with Louise to Japan to work as a hostess to pay off her debts, and she made out that it was all going to be absolutely fine. She only knew what it involved from what Louise's sister had told her. She said you just pour people drinks and listen to them talk, and that they like to sing karaoke. Lucie loved singing, so to her that was money for old rope."

But Jane was not interested in the details. Her only concern was to prevent Lucie from going to Tokyo at any cost. "She kept reassuring me that she'd never do anything silly, she'd take extra care. But I just knew that something horrible would happen to her. I couldn't get it out of my head. I'd never even thought about Japan before, as a place. But as soon as she said it—Japan—this voice came into my head saying, 'Something terrible's going to happen.' Maybe it was more a thought, not necessarily a voice—a thought that came into my head. I was inconsolable. I didn't cry in front of her, but on my own I used to cry and cry."

Jamie Gascoigne was almost as dismayed as Jane. In the few months they had spent together, he had fallen deeply in love with Lucie, and the idea of being separated from her, even temporarily, was difficult to bear. Then one night, as they were in line at the cinema, Lucie told Jamie that she didn't want to be attached to him while she was in Japan. "I was totally gutted," he remembered. "I slid down the wall, didn't know what to say. We weren't rowing, we had no arguments. Over the space of the week before we split up, she just changed. It was as if someone was telling her what to do."

Others were puzzled by Lucie's behavior in the weeks before she flew to Japan, and the feeling grew stronger the closer the day approached. At home, Lucie embarked on a comprehensive spring cleaning, extreme even by her own high standards of neatness. "She went through everything, got rid of bin liners of stuff," said Jane. "Old letters, personal stuff. She got rid of lots of clothes. It was much more than just a clear-out, because her room was tidy anyway. It wasn't done as if she was going away for just a few months. She cleaned her room as if she was never coming back."

If Lucie saw less of old friends, she went out of her way to look up other people with whom she had formerly spent little time: cousins, godparents, peripheral aunts and uncles. "She did a lot of rounding up, which was a bit weird because it wasn't how Lucie had usually been," said Sophie. "She made a concerted effort to see lots of people before she went away. We wouldn't think anything of it if she'd come back. But because she never did, there was something odd about it."

Among the people whom Lucie particularly sought out was her father. After the separation from Jane in 1995, Tim Blackman had met and moved in with Josephine Burr, a divorced mother of four teenagers from Tim's birthplace, Ryde, on the Isle of Wight. He never lived with his family again, but he stayed in close touch with two of his children. During a period of particular acrimony with her mother, Sophie had gone to live with him in Ryde for a while, and Tim regularly drove over to Kent to take Rupert to rugby practice or for pub lunches. But of Lucie, he saw far less. The question of why and how this happened was part of the unceasing joust over the truth between Jane and Tim.

Jane was adamant that the decision was Lucie's. "Lucie was very disappointed in her father," she said. "But I never, ever, ever would have stopped him seeing the children—ever—because they're his children. Lucie chose not to see him, but I never, ever stopped her. You can't stop a grown child—if they're little, maybe you can. Lucie didn't see him for quite a few years, because she didn't want to see him, because she was angry with him. And I suppose because we were very close, she was very protective of me."

There is no doubt that Lucie reproached her father for her mother's pain—she said as much to several of her friends. But Tim also detected something subtler going on. "There was no benefit to the children in trying to explain away or justify my actions," he said. "That would never fall on receptive ears, except to say that I was very unhappy before it happened. I took the view that time would make a difference, and things would change, and that eventually they would come and see me. And with Lucie that was happening. She'd been down around Christmas a couple of times, and waterskiing in the summer. I'd see her a little bit in Sevenoaks; there wasn't a complete severing of ties. But it wasn't easy. For two, three years it was very difficult.

"This is where it gets very complicated. I know Jane very well, and I know how manipulative she can be. And she was a hundred percent vitriolic against me. There was simply *no way* she could have avoided manipulating the situation. Lucie would make an arrangement to come down to the island, to come and see me at the weekend. Then we'd get to Thursday that week—and, suddenly, it was too difficult to come. It's my belief that, most of the time, it was because there was a situation at home that she couldn't easily battle out. I was the easy sacrifice in her complicated status as eldest child supporting the devastated mother. She was stuck in a corner. And I could understand that, but it didn't make it hurt any the less."

Whatever pressures Lucie felt from her parents, the imminence of her departure eased them. Jane made a point of telling Lucie that she should see her father, and in mid-April, after she went in to British Airways for the last time to hand back her uniform, they met for dinner in a pub outside Sevenoaks. She sent him a text message a few nights earlier that

Tim kept on his phone long after Lucie had disappeared. Much later, when mementoes of Lucie had come to be very precious, he preserved it by copying it out exactly.

> 14.04.00 00:38 xxxxxxxxxxxxx good morning! my beautiful daddy. I love you so very much & can not wait to see your smiley face on tuesday. lots of love & snuggles . . . lula xx

Jane had always been a worrier, but her anxiety about Lucie's trip to Japan, and her campaign to foil it, verged on the absurd; it had about it something of a child's irrational fear for the well-being of a parent. The point of going to Japan for Lucie was to work off her debts, so Jane began collecting clippings from the newspaper about the grim state of the Japanese economy and casually leaving them on Lucie's bed. When these were ignored, she made an appointment on Lucie's behalf with a spirit medium, in the hope that wisdom from beyond the grave would prevail where her own entreaties had failed. (Lucie canceled the appointment.) Finally, hours before the flight to Tokyo, she considered the ultimate sanction—hiding Lucie's passport. Rupert Blackman remembered his mother standing on the stairs brandishing the passport and screaming down at his sister. "But I thought, 'If I do, she'll just get another one, and she'll be cross with me,'" said Jane. "And I didn't want her going to Japan cross with me."

Val Burman became irritated with Jane's flapping. "I don't understand why you're behaving the way you are," she told her friend. "Anyone would think you'd suffered a bereavement." And Jane replied, "It feels like that."

■ ■ ■

Lucie didn't completely stop being herself. In March, she added $1,500 to her debts by buying an immense iron bed from

Marks & Spencer. This gesture, so characteristic of Lucie, reassured her friends that she was at least planning to come back from Tokyo. "She called it her Princess Bed," said Sam Burman. "It was a big double bed with a metal frame, quite an old-fashioned style. It had a lovely thick mattress and beautiful linen that all matched. When Lucie came home, that was what she wanted: to be snuggled up in her own bed. She was always talking about it."

She was more reticent about another new feature of her life, one that illuminated some of her recent behavior: Alex, a young Australian, who was working as a barman in the Black Boy pub. Alex was eighteen years old, three years younger than Lucie; she met him less than a month before leaving for Japan. "He had curly brown hair, and he was a bit of a surfer type," Sophie remembered. "There was just something very vibrant about him. She really liked him, *really* liked him." Years after Lucie's death, Jamie Gascoigne had no idea that Lucie had left him for a new boyfriend, nor did their close mutual friend Sam Burman.

Among the mysteries of that period was Tuesday, May 2, Lucie's last night in Britain. Of her closest friends and immediate family, everyone had a different recollection of how she spent that day, and with whom. Tim Blackman was fairly sure that he was with Lucie that evening, having dinner in a restaurant in Sevenoaks with Sophie and Rupert. Sophie remembered clearly that Lucie had spent most of the evening with Alex. Jane's memory of the last few hours with her daughter was clouded by intense anxiety but didn't include Tim or Alex. The friends who remembered the most about Lucie's last night were Sam Burman and her mother, Val.

They were in no doubt that Lucie had been with them. "She was round at my mum's," Sam said. "And the thing that struck us the most was the fact that she hadn't made her list of things to do. She'd got a few bits together, but she wasn't all packed and organized like she usually was. And she was a bit sad about leaving, a bit reluctant. She kept pointing out the negatives but then talking herself back into it. It was as if she wasn't quite convinced, but she'd done it now and there was no going back. I think because she'd made a commitment to Louise, she didn't want to let her down."

Val remembers Lucie talking to her about Jane and about the atmosphere at home. "There was screaming in that house," Val said. "There was lots of screaming between Jane and Sophie and Sophie and Lucie. If she'd stuck with it, in a few years' time it would have righted itself and everything would have been a bit more bearable. But Lucie was the adult and Jane was the child at that time. Lucie told me it was a lot of pressure. They were arguing about her going away and I think that strengthened Lucie's resolve. Because maybe Lucie felt she didn't have a way out, and at that time going to Japan was a way out . . . She needed that break, even to the point of leaving Jane."

In Sophie's recollection of events, Alex came around to the house in the evening, and Sophie left him and Lucie together. "After I'd gone to bed," she said, "I began to think of the things I wanted to say to Lucie before she went away, and I thought I'd write them down. I began what was meant to be a farewell note, and it became something intense. I started to say how nice it was to have grown up having a big sister to protect me and look after me, and how she had helped me in hard parts of my life. It developed into an eighteen-page letter. I remember writing it, and I was really teary—not just a bit upset, I was properly sobbing. I always find it ghastly to say, 'It's almost as if I was writing to her for the last time.' But it was a painful experience. She was only going away for three months; she'd been away before. But there was something about this letter that was heartbreaking.

"There was something very final about it. On Lucie's trips with BA, we'd say goodbye but make plans. But when Lucie talked about Japan, I wasn't able to picture what it would be like when she got back. I found it difficult to create in my mind an image of her return."

The flight to Tokyo left at noon. It was Louise's mother, Maureen Phillips, who came for Lucie before dawn and drove the two friends to Heathrow. Lucie came into Sophie's room in the dark and kissed her goodbye. "She gave me a card, and I gave her my letter, and said, 'Don't open it until you're on the plane.' She lay down on my bed and snuggled up. We were both quite emotional. Then she had to go. I said, 'I love you,' and she left."

Lucie was twenty-one years old when she left home for good. How loved she was by her friends and her troubled family: sibling, or even mother, to her own mother, as well as to her brother and her sister. She had flown on many aeroplanes before, but this was the first time that she had traveled so far and so directly away from everyone with a claim upon her—and to a country through the looking glass, a place as distant and as obscure as anyone who knew her could imagine. Those who cared for her were anxious. In the last weeks, Lucie— whose heart had always seemed so open and clear—had ac- quired mysteries. No one, except Louise perhaps, knew the whole story of what the two of them expected in Japan and what they intended. Questions were asked, but the answers brought no clarity or satisfaction. The truth about Lucie Black- man was already becoming hazy.

PART TWO TOKYO

4. HIGH TOUCH TOWN

It takes fewer than twelve hours to fly from Heathrow to Narita Airport, but few single journeys bring such a dizzying sense of transition. Lucie and Louise lifted off to views of London rooftops, the fields of East Anglia, and the North Sea. By the time lunch had been served and the first film shown, they were above Siberia, where they remained for seven hours. Unimaginable volumes of empty space gaped on all sides; forty thousand feet below were expanses of tundra, churning mountain ranges blown with snow, dark rivers of vast width shining as the sun caught them. It was a journey that pitched the traveler forward through time as well as space. The two friends left at midday, flew through a long afternoon and evening, and landed at what their bodies registered as bedtime—blinking in the brightness of a Japanese morning.

"It's 9:13 here in Tokyo, making it 12:10 midnight behind in England," Lucie wrote in her diary minutes after arriving. "I am sitting on a suitcase at the railway underground feeling completely overwhelmed. I am very tired . . . also afraid, anxious & lost & v. hot! I only hope that I will look back at this with hindsight & laugh at my innocence—of how I was so unaware of what was in store for me."

For all their months flying as air stewardesses, neither Lucie nor Louise had ever been to a country so immediately and intriguingly alien. The barbed-wire guard towers of Narita

Airport looked out over paddies of green rice, and red, yellow, and black banners representing stylized carp fluttered from the tiled roofs of the houses. But these tokens of the Orient quickly gave way to the margins of Greater Tokyo, which overflowed the administrative boundaries of the city, sucking in satellite towns like a greedy amoeba. The railway rode high above a numb landscape of silvery-gray office buildings, low-rise apartments with metal fire escapes, and windowless love hotels with neon signs bearing names like Marie Celeste and Wonderland. Then came a sequence of bridges across broad, motionless rivers, and finally the view south to Tokyo Bay, with its islands of reclaimed land built over in glass and aluminum. In cloudy weather, the water was dark and oily and the buildings matte and dead. In sunlight, they shone silver: adamantine towers, immense goggling globes, the bristling power lines and bulbous storage tanks of power and petroleum plants, and the delicate curve of the Rainbow Bridge.

Thirty million people inhabited this megalopolis. Apart from the fleeting green of parks, shrines, temples, and the Imperial Palace, it was unbroken until the Okutama Mountains, forty miles to the west. Look out from Tokyo's highest skyscraper and, except on the very clearest of days, that was all you could see—Tokyo and then just more of Tokyo, gray, brown, and silver, spilling shapelessly in every direction.

And yet the impression created by this scale and density was the opposite of chaotic. Tokyo was clean and sharply defined to the eye, with none of the blaring squalor of many Asian cities. Sealed beneath a film of indifferent calm, there was a machine energy and ticktocking efficiency. For most first-time arrivals, it was an atmosphere unlike any they had encountered before; it produced a sensation not of straightforward exhilaration but of obscure excitement at mysterious possibilities. "It's so different already," Lucie wrote on the platform of Narita Airport Station, a few hundred yards into

Japan. "The most pristine train I have ever seen has just pulled away, aboard which stood a tiny man all in navy with the most immaculate white gloves. I've bought my first thing—a bottle of tap water top to toe in Japanese writing . . . I sit here and there is a warm breeze coming from somewhere & it is gently blowing on my face. I look up and pray it is the wind of change which is going to make all my dreams come true."

To arrive in Tokyo was to be transformed in a way that felt almost like a physical metamorphosis. For a start, there was the debilitation of jet lag: what felt in the bones like the middle of the night was actually day, and vice versa. Even more crippling was the sudden deprivation of language: at a stroke, the foreigner was rendered not only incapable of speech or comprehension but also illiterate. The relative smallness of the people, the lower height of doors and ceilings, the narrowness of chairs, even the smaller portions of food created the illusion of having grown measurably in size, like Alice down the rabbit hole. In twenty-first-century Tokyo, people rarely stared openly at foreigners, but always one was conscious of being the object of an unaccustomed attention from the rest of the human population—not outright gawping, neither unambiguous affection nor disapproval, but simply the discreet registering of difference. In Japan, you became a citizen of a new nation—that of the gaijin, the foreigner. It was a stimulating and frequently exhausting realm in which to live. "Life here means never taking life for granted, never not noticing," wrote the American expatriate writer Donald Richie. "It is with this live connection that the alert foreigner here lives. The electric current is turned on during all the waking hours: he or she is always occupied in noticing, evaluating, discovering and concluding . . . I like this life of never being able to take my life for granted."

But this was not to be the experience of Lucie and Louise. Without even knowing that they were making the choice, they turned away from the Japaneseness of Japan. Lucie had fifty-nine days to live, and she would spend them in a few hundred square yards of Tokyo engineered for the pleasure and profit of gaijin: Roppongi.

In daytime, at least, you could drive straight through Roppongi and scarcely notice the place. From inside a car, it was no more than a busier-than-usual junction on the eight-lane road between Shibuya and the moats of the Imperial Palace. The Shuto elevated expressway ran above Roppongi Avenue, forming a concrete canopy overhead and making a dingy crevasse of the main road. Commercials flashed from a giant screen mounted high on one corner of the crossing; the eye darted over a McDonald's, a pink coffee shop, a bank, a sushi bar. A pedestrian with time to take in the surroundings would notice the rows of eight- and ten-story buildings lining Outer Moat East Avenue, which cuts perpendicularly across Roppongi Avenue. Each one carried a narrow panel running vertically from roof to street level, bearing the names of the dozens of bars, clubs, and cafés within. The buildings were shabby concrete and beige tile; unlit tubes of neon sprouted from their façades, furred with dust and exhaust dirt. There were multiple pedestrian crossings and subway entrances, and engraved on the outer walls of the expressway, looking down over the crossing to north and south, Roppongi's mysterious motto, written in English: "High Touch Town."

During office hours, Roppongi gave itself over to people of the daylight—workers in the shops and restaurants, miniature schoolchildren in tiny uniforms, and the civil servants of the Japan Defense Agency in their walled compound north of the crossing. The changes began as afternoon became evening, and the suited population emptied the offices and filled the commuter trains. As the dark came in, individual neon lights began to twinkle on the sides of the buildings, and young foreign women began to converge on the fitness club behind Azabu Police Station. By the time they emerged two hours later, Roppongi was stirring from its vampire sleep. By mid-evening, the sound, smell, look, and touch of the area were transformed.

Early May, when Lucie and Louise arrived, was the point of transition from the cool to the hot months; over the weeks, the spring air became plump with heat and moisture. Nighttime was scarcely cooler than the day. In June, the rainy season began, a month of humidity so dense that it broke spontaneously on the skin. The summer brought out the fart smell of Tokyo's shallow sewers, an unexpected stench of the Third World, which blended with the smoke of pizzas, grilled chicken, fish, and perfume. (The one smell that one never encountered in Japan was that of human sweat.) The giant advertising screen glowed above the crossing, bathing it in changing images of cars, clothes, alcohol, food, and girls. The neon on the signs pulsed into life, masking the shabbiness of the concrete buildings. And the migraine hum of the expressway was blocked out by the chatter of the pavement, the human traffic that imparted to Roppongi all of its life and character.

Compressed into a radius of a few hundred yards from the crossing was all the untidy human and ethnic diversity absent from the rest of Japan. Roppongi was not especially trendy. For quality, variety, or good value, Tokyo had many more interesting entertainment districts—elegant Ginza, with its old-fashioned department stores and middle-aged gentility; the edgy street life of Shinjuku, with its gangsters and sex shows; and Shibuya, domain of the glazed, ultrafashionable young. Foreigners were to be seen all over Tokyo, of course, but only in Roppongi was their presence the entire point of the place. Most of the people on the streets were Japanese. But those who stood out were not, and the foreignness of the atmosphere was Roppongi's unique accent and identity.

There were foreigners who came here to be with other foreigners; there were Japanese who came here to be with foreigners; and then there were the foreigners, usually men, who came to be with the Japanese, mostly women, who wanted to be with foreign men. In Roppongi, you encountered people you would never meet anywhere else. This was the one place in Japan where that sense of exciting but oppressive separation, of gaijinness, lifted from the temples and shoulders.

Out of the mouth of the subway and across the swarming pedestrian crossing came faces from all over the world: Brazilian barmen, Iranian bricklayers, Russian models, German bankers, Irish students. Certain races monopolized certain trades: for some reason, for example, a foreigner who tried to sell you a framed photograph or picture (of a sunset, a smiling baby, a beautiful woman walking a poodle) would almost always be Israeli. Chinese and Korean women in long dresses lingered in front of "massage" parlors, seizing the sleeves of passing men and susurrating, "*Massāji, massāji, massāji* . . ." When the American aircraft carrier the USS *Kitty Hawk* was in dock at the port of Yokosuka, the drinking places were tight with the torsos of American sailors and marines. At these times, there was a high incidence of another phenomenon rare outside Roppongi: the bar fight.

Three groups above all stood out.

The first was the Africans. Black men in Japan fitted into a gaijin category of their own. Even in the center of Tokyo, they still drew stares, and nowhere else in the country was there such a concentration of them as on the four-hundred-yard stretch of Outer Moat East Avenue south of the crossing. Like other ethnic groups, they had a specialized function within the Roppongi machinery: the job of luring male passersby into the strip clubs, hostess bars, and lap-dancing parlors. A smaller clan of primped and spiky-haired Japanese boys catered to the native customer, but the rulers of the street were the Africans, men from Ghana, Nigeria, and Gambia. Many of them had been here for years, plenty spoke good Japanese. There was nothing overtly threatening about them; they smiled warmly as they accosted the male stroller, with one hand amiably placed on his shoulder and the other proffering a lurid flyer. Their patter followed him for several hundred yards, relayed from one tout to the next in a murmured baritone. "Good evening, sir!" it began. "Gentleman's club, best in Roppongi. Topless bar, sir, lovely ladies. Sexy girls, sir, topless, bottomless. Titty and ass, sir. Titty ass, asstittyass, tittyass-tittyasstitty. You com' up. Just look. Seven thousand yen, look. I give you three thousand yen half hour. Just com' and look see."

The police would have loved to arrest and deport these men, but almost all had Japanese wives. Sometimes these marriages were a legal fiction, renewed every year in return for a fixed sum in cash. But they gave the husbands the right to reside and work freely in Japan in whatever job they chose, and there was nothing that the police could do.

The second dominant tribe was the principal draw for much of the male nighttime population of Roppongi: the Roppongi girls, those Japanese women who liked foreign men. Periodically, the skimpiness of their dress and inhibitions made them the object of moral concern on the part of the Japanese media. Their appearance changed with the tides of Tokyo street fashion. In the early 1990s, a long-defunct dance club named Juliana's Tokyo had given birth to the style known as body-con—tight, revealing "body-conscious" outfits that were displayed to the full on the discotheque's famous raised dancing podiums. By Lucie and Louise's time, body-con had given way to the *ganguro*, a radically stylized look that combined deep orange artificially tanned skin, ash-gray dyed hair, white makeup, and white lipstick. Every Thursday, Friday, and

Saturday, tottering on platform boots of stiltlike height, pairs of these girls converged on Roppongi, resembling hallucinatory, Day-Glo golliwogs. They came on the commuter lines from the suburbs and commuter towns of the outlying prefectures. They spent the evening, and then the night, at clubs and bars with names like Motown, Gaspanic, and the Lexington Queen. At dawn every Friday, Saturday, and Sunday, a slightly smaller number of the unlucky ones made the melancholy journey back out of the city and home again on the first connecting train.

Then there was the third group among the street tribes of Roppongi: young Caucasian women, who worked as dancers, strippers, and hostesses. They began to appear on the streets in the middle of the evening, hair shining after their workouts at the fitness center. They wore jeans and T-shirts. Before entering their clubs and bars to dress and make themselves up, they would fuel up for the evening at McDonald's or KFC or the sushi restaurant on the crossing. They moved purposefully, without the diffidence of tourists, and for all the diversity of their origins—Australian, Kiwi, French, British, Ukrainian—they had something in common, apart from youth and prettiness. Something difficult to define: a set of the mouth or shoulders, suggesting defiance, irritation, even resentment. Unlike the friendly Japanese Roppongi girls, they were unapproachable. Lucie and Louise had come here to join their number.

Louise did, in fact, have a Japanese aunt, the wife of her mother's younger brother. But Masako lived in south London, not in Tokyo. The suggestion that she was to be the girls' host in Japan was a fib intended to ease the anxieties of Jane Blackman. Louise's sister, Emma, still had friends living in Tokyo and it was through one of them, a Scottish girl named Christabel, that the room had been booked in Sasaki House. The railway journey from the airport was complicated and trying, requiring repeated changes and steep flights of stairs. Their suitcases were dead weights in their hands, their high heels were painfully impractical, and they were sore and sweating when they hauled their belongings out of the stingingly expensive taxi that carried them on the final leg to their new home.

They had expected to arrive at a simple hostel, with crisply laundered bedding and an obliging manageress. Instead they found themselves in the category of Japanese accommodation known as the gaijin house—a guesthouse of single rooms, rented by Tokyo's transient foreign population of backpackers, English teachers, street vendors, and night workers. Dying potted plants and bicycles were propped against its outside walls. Huge black crows perched on the cat's cradle of utility wires overhead. "It was disgusting," Louise remembered. "We were just in shock. We looked in the lounge, and there were two people stoned on the sofa. We came up to the room and Christa was in there doing her hair. She was putting this thick, gloopy oil all over it—it looked like fat. And they were all smoking spliffs. The room stank. You could hardly see inside with the smoke."

The window of the tiny room was curtainless; Lucie and Louise had to drape it with sarongs to keep out the morning sun. Not that there was a great deal of light to exclude; the only view was that of the cement wall of the neighboring building. The futon mattresses were sheetless, the mirror was cracked, and the squat toilet in the bathroom was unspeakable. Transforming the "shithouse" into a livable space—with posters, postcards, candles, drapes—was the achievement of their first week in Tokyo. It was by far the pokiest place in which either of them had ever lived.

They slept for much of the next day, stunned by heat and jet lag. That evening, a Friday, they rode into Roppongi on borrowed bicycles with the half-formed ambition of finding jobs. Christa, who worked as a hostess herself, had given them the names of several clubs, but they were still finding their bearings when a good-looking young Japanese man approached and politely asked if he could be of assistance. Were Lucie and Louise looking for work? he asked. Were they interested in working as hostesses? If they came with him, he said, he could introduce them to people who might be able to help.

Warily, they followed the man up Outer Moat East Avenue and into one of the buildings with the neon-lit signboards. The first club had no vacancies, but at the second they were greeted warmly. The young guide was obviously well known to its manager, a gloomy man named Mr. Nishi. He looked them over, asked them a few rudimentary questions—age, nationality, where they were staying—and offered them jobs on the spot. Within days of arriving in Japan, Lucie and Louise were working as hostesses in a small Roppongi nightclub with the name of Casablanca.

5. GEISHA GIRL! (JOKE)

Unless you knew exactly what you were looking for, you could have passed by a thousand times and never cast a second glance at Club Casablanca. The building in which it nestled was brown and anonymous; from the street the only token of its existence was the long vertical signboard, where it was crowded out by the names of more exotic and intriguing establishments. There was Raki Raki, and the Gay Arts Stage, and Seventh Heaven, one of Tokyo's biggest strip clubs, whose lurid neon dominated the front of the building. Casablanca was on the sixth floor. The elevator opened to face a heavy-looking door plumply upholstered in padded leather and with a brassy plaque bearing the club's name.

Beyond it was a dimly lit room, perhaps twenty feet by sixty. To the left, rows of bottles glinted behind a low bar. To the right was an electric keyboard on a raised stand and the screen and speakers of a karaoke system. Around the walls were couches and armchairs in pale blue and twelve low tables. Framed prints or paintings were indistinctly visible on the walls.

An Asian man of indeterminate age and nationality guided the customer to one of the tables, on which stood a complicated glass siphon that dispensed water through a pump. A bucket of ice, metal tongs, and a chunky decanter of whiskey were brought—tools and ingredients for the blending of *mizuwari*, the whiskey-and-water mix that is the staple drink of the older salaryman. Despite the pompous details—the leather door, the black bow ties worn by the waiters and barman—it was a space wholly lacking in glamour. The whiskey in the decanter was cheap and sickly; the electric keyboard was crude and blurting; the water siphon, which tried so hard to be impressive, was merely baffling. The club strove for an effect of languid luxury, but the atmosphere was more cozy than sophisticated, with a droopy pretension suggesting the second-class lounge of one of the cheaper cruise liners, or a failing Las Vegas casino, or middle-class suburban England in the 1970s. You half expected the waiter to appear with a plate of pineapple chunks impaled on cocktail sticks with cubes of cheddar cheese.

But this was a Japanese establishment, and to a certain Japanese eye it had a crepuscular allure. The reasons for this were seated at the two tables closest to the bar: a group of foreign hostesses, most, but not all of them, Caucasian. "It was a rather dark place and I had a strange feeling about it," said Hajime Imura, a publisher who visited Casablanca a couple of times when Lucie worked there. "It had a kind of mysterious atmosphere, suspicious. There were girls of different colors of skin, perhaps Israeli or something. The room was dark, shades of black and blue. Dark chairs and tables. A Filipino singer, very loud. A middle-aged man who seemed to be the manager, a few waiters, maybe Filipino—Asian faces. About ten girls."

When the customer was comfortably settled with his mizu-wari, the manager would signal to the table of foreign girls. Two of them would detach themselves and walk over, and hostessing would commence.

What *was* a hostess exactly? To Western ears the word sounded laughably seedy and euphemistic, scarcely more respectable than "escort"—redolent of cheap perfume and dingy basements in Soho or Times Square. "We just freaked when we heard," said Sam Burman, who had a phone call from Lucie a few days after her arrival. "What did she mean, 'hostessing'? She seemed a bit nervous about telling me over the phone. I think she felt embarrassed because she'd told us one thing, and it hadn't worked out like that, and we were going to worry about her. The last thing she wanted any of us to do was to worry."

Sophie had the impression that the work involved "inane and dull conversations that she would have to smile at and laugh at. It wasn't like people sat there saying, 'Show us your tits' and 'How much d'you charge?' It's very different from that." Afterwards, when the question of what hostesses *really* did was a subject of discussion in British tabloid newspapers, Sophie came up with a way of explaining it to skeptical journalists. "The only difference between being a British Airways hostess and being at Casablanca," she said, "was the altitude."

Months later, Tim Blackman would receive a long and emotional letter from a kindly old gentleman named Ichiro Watanabe, a loyal customer at Casablanca, expressing his concern over Lucie's disappearance. "The club is far from the irresponsible reports by mass media aimed at vulgar gossips and based on groundless conjectures," he wrote in painstaking italic. "The ladie's [*sic*] job there is just only lighting customer's cigarette, making whisky and water for him, singing karaoke together and keeping company in talking. That's all, nothing else, just like she told her mother, 'a kind of waitressing.'" He added, "I've no mind to put in a good word for me. I dare want to say this fact *for her honor!*"

All of this, as far as it went, was true.

The club opened at nine. A little before then, in a narrow dressing room at the back, a dozen, and sometimes as many as fifteen, girls put on makeup and changed from jeans and T-shirts into dresses. They came from all over the world, although in the summer of 2000 there was a proportionately large British contingent. Apart from Lucie and Louise, there was Mandy from Lancashire and Helen from London, as well as Samantha from Australia, Hanna from Sweden, American Shannon, and Romanian Olivia. Three men worked in the club: Tetsuo Nishi, the manager, a pockmarked man in his fifties; Caz, the Japanese barman; and a Filipino singer whose name no one could remember. It was Caz and Nishi who decided which girls would sit with which customers, who rotated them strategically among the tables, and who gave them perfunctory instruction in the duties of a hostess. Much of this consisted of prohibitions: do not allow a customer to refill his own whiskey glass or light his own cigarette. But once seated, the only real task was to talk.

This wasn't as easy as it sounded. Few of the hostesses could say much more than "yes, thank you" and "excuse me" in Japanese, and although a customer would be unlikely to patronize Casablanca if he spoke no English, fluency and confidence varied widely. For some, a few hours with a foreign hostess was a kind of language lesson in itself. Certain men even took notes, and unselfconscious conversation, of the kind that one would naturally strike up with a stranger, was usually out of the question. And the customer, being a customer, could never be argued with, contradicted, or deserted. The novelist Mo Hayder worked as a hostess and compared it to "having to be nice to a work colleague in whom you're not too interested." "I'd ask where they worked, why they were in Tokyo. I'd flatter them and say, 'I like your tie.' The number of ties I've really loved!"

"You'd just talk rubbish to them," said Helen Dove, who worked in Casablanca at the same time as Lucie and Louise. "'How was *your* day today?' Or try to flatter their egos. 'You're such a good-looking man—sing to me.' They'd tell you how beautiful you were. You'd talk about England, about a business trip he had made to London. Within a few weeks I was starting to hate it. It was so boring, draining. The same conversations night after night, boring conversations with people you don't care about. Some girls were good, really friendly. I struggled with conversation. It was obviously completely fake. It didn't help that I couldn't sing, because there was a lot of karaoke and you had to be so enthusiastic about it, singing duets."

There was a good deal of traditional and straightforward lechery. "I suppose a lot of them talked about sex," said Helen. "I tried to avoid that subject as much as possible." But in four weeks of working at Casablanca, her only genuinely alarming encounter was with a man who had an obsession with Audrey Hepburn. "He went for brunettes with that look—pale skin and big eyes," she said. "There was one girl who left after two weeks because he was so creepy. He'd sit next to her and say things like, 'Now you are mine!' and 'I paid for you, now I own you!' and he'd grip her really tightly around the arm. She left, and then he started asking for me. I just stood up to him, wouldn't let him touch me."

More vexatious than the creeps were the bores. Every hostess routinely found herself engaging in conversations so incongruous or stultifying that if anyone else were present it would have been impossible not to laugh. Hajime Imura, the publisher, recalled entertaining Lucie with stories of his squid-fishing exploits. "I caught a great deal of squid on one occasion, and I told her about it," he told me. "I never heard back from her after that." Lucie was the object of an elaborate disquisition from one customer on the functioning of volcanoes. It culminated in the construction of a scale model of an active crater using the implements on the table: an ice bucket as the mountain, the water in the siphon as lava, and a cigarette as the source of smoke.

Old Mr. Watanabe had no problems finding conversation, as he revealed in his letter to Tim Blackman. The girls at Casablanca were unanimously fond of him because of his age, his extreme courtliness, and the regularity of his visits. They called him "Photo Man" because of his habit of taking countless photographs and then bringing sets of prints into the club on his next visit, carefully laid out in albums for presentation to the girls. He got his money's worth from Lucie. "We enjoyed interesting and informative conversations [for] about three hours," he recalled of one evening with her. "We talked about English history, literature, arts, authors, artists, the relation between Britain and Japan from old times, the similarity and difference of nature and mentality between both nations, and the sense of humor peculiar to English people that I like and respect most and so on." The effect of all this distilled earnestness on the average twenty-one-year-old hostess can only be imagined.

Casablanca might have been boring, and occasionally bizarre, but it was also strangely reassuring. Sealed within its dim blue cocoon, watched over by Caz and the unsmiling Nishi, the girls who worked there felt safe.

■ ■ ■

In Japan, where everything had its place, hostessing, hostesses, and hostess clubs did not exist in isolation. The jumble of nightlife establishments to be found in Roppongi—downmarket and upmarket, decent and disgraceful—was encompassed by a beautiful and suggestive term: *mizu shōbai*, literally, the "water trade." The phrase was mysterious. Did it refer to the drinking, which was an essential part of the nighttime experience? To the evanescence of its pleasures, flowing past like a stream? The image of water brought to mind sex, childbirth, and death by drowning. At one extreme, the mizu shōbai included the geisha, female entertainers of exceptional skill and refinement who were to be found only in the most old-fashioned quarters of Kyoto and Tokyo; at the other were hard-core S & M and torture clubs, where the most extreme degradation was exchanged for cash. In between extended a spectrum of sleaziness and elegance, cheapness and expense, openness and exclusivity.

Some Japanese would include within the mizu shōbai ordinary bars, pubs and karaoke parlors, but most definitions required the presence in some capacity of women attractive, at least notionally, to men. This might be no more than the mama-san of a tiny neighborhood "snack" (in Japanese, *sunakku*), a four-seat counter presided over by a middle-aged proprietress-barmaid whose active powers of seduction were on the wane. Some sunakku had younger waitress-hostesses who chatted and poured drinks under the mama-san's direction. The bigger of these shaded into the hostess bars and clubs, more likely to be found in larger cities, where female company, for conversation and karaoke, was provided at a price, along with drinks and snacks. "Gentlemen's clubs" were ones in which the female companions talked at the table but also stripped to nakedness during a public pole dance and in one-to-one "private" dances in a closed booth. The dancer writhed and gyrated astride the customer, who was allowed to touch and suckle her nipples and breasts, and who, in some places, could pay to go further. So, as the barmaid became a hostess, and the hostess overlapped with the stripper, so stripping evolved into prostitution.

No other race has expended the imagination and creativity that the Japanese have put into the packaging of paid sex, a response to the country's halfhearted and unenforceable anti-prostitution laws. The only thing that is strictly illegal is charging for conventional male-female intercourse. Fellatio and masturbation, in all their forms, are permitted. Proving that any given orgasm has been brought about legally and manually, rather than illicitly and vaginally, is, of course, impossible. In order to veil the obvious, sex businesses package their services under a bewildering range of names, so numerous and fast changing that it is a struggle for the nonspecialist to keep track.

In Roppongi there are "massage" parlors, where a perfunctory rubdown is the pretext for a manually administered happy ending. There are *fasshon herusu* ("fashion health") facilities offering a wider range of services, excluding conventional intercourse. This can be had at a *sōpurando* ("soap land"—the pretext here is an all-over wash by a woman who employs her body as a sponge). *Deri-heru* ("delivery health") is sexual pleasure delivered in a personal visit to your home or hotel. *Esute* (pronounced "ess-tay" and derived from the English "aesthetic salon") is sexual massage, subdivided into a diversity of genres. There is "Korean aesthetic salon" (massage and hand relief), and "Korean-style aesthetic salon" (the same as Korean aesthetic salon but with a naked masseuse). Further refinements, each subtly distinct from one another, include "Chinese aesthetic salons," "Taiwanese aesthetic salons," "Singaporean aesthetic salons," "sexy pubs," "lingerie pubs," "Peeping Tom pubs," "touch cabarets" and "Korean-style massage by Japanese housewife." In a "no-pants coffee shop," the waitresses are almost naked and will provide relief in return for a specified tip. In a "no-pants karaoke coffee shop," women without pants perform duets with the customers before, after, or during relief. In a "no-pants shabu-shabu," shabu-shabu hot pot is served rather than coffee.

The more expensive, exclusive, and respectable the mizu shōbai establishment, the more likely the women are to be Japanese. At the grubbier end, there are many more Thais, Filipinas, Chinese, and Koreans. "Western" women, meaning Europeans, Russians, North and South Americans, and Australasians, are generally found only in the middle band of the spectrum, from hostess to stripper, the zone in which talking and watching are the principal attractions, rather than touching. I speak of a spectrum, but it would be more accurate to think of shades not of bright and distinct color but of gray.

The practice of paying for female company has a long and noble history in Japan. The first references to geisha—highly trained female entertainers skilled in the arts of dancing, music, costume, makeup, and conversation—date back to the eighteenth century; a gulf of accomplishment and respectability separated them from the *oiran*, or courtesans, and the common prostitutes who frequented inns and teahouses. It was during the tizzy of faddish westernization in the 1920s that the first recognizable hostesses appeared—taxi dancers in the newly popular dance halls, and "café girls," whose company, and sometimes more, could be purchased along with coffee. During the same period, there was a short-lived and unsuccessful experiment with a kind of secular geisha, who wore flapper dresses instead of kimonos and played pianos and guitars rather than samisen. "Opinions still differ as to whether the nightclub entertainer and the bar girl of our day are as accomplished as was the geisha of old, but the geisha has gradually yielded to them," wrote the great American historian of Tokyo, Edward Seidensticker. "The story of the high life of this past century might be told as the retreat of one and the advance of the others."

The earliest foreign participants in the water trade were Korean and Chinese prostitutes, colonial subjects of the prewar Japanese empire. In 1945, Westerners appeared in large numbers, but as buyers rather than sellers, during the seven-year-long U.S. occupation. It was during this period, too, that Roppongi began to emerge as a place of recreation. Its name meant "six trees"; before the war, it had been a nondescript residential area dominated by a barracks of the Japanese Imperial Army. The U.S. military took over the barracks after the surrender, and around its entrance sprang up little bars catering to off-duty soldiers, with names such as Silk Hat, Green

Spot, and the Cherry. It was at this time that Roppongi's curious motto originated. Locals noticed that the American GIs would greet one another by slapping palms together above their heads. One could imagine the scene late at night, as a curious Japanese barman asked his customers about this, and the long, drunken attempt to explain the theory and practice of the high five. It was mistransliterated into Japanese as *hai tacchi*, or "high touch"—hence the slogan on the walls of the Roppongi expressway: "High Touch Town."

In 1956, Tokyo's first Italian restaurant opened in Roppongi, the beginning of a craze for exotica such as pizza and Chianti. Two years later, Tokyo Tower, an immense red, faux-Eiffel telecommunications mast, opened on Roppongi's southern edge. A private television station, TV Asahi, built its headquarters nearby, and in 1964 Roppongi acquired a subway station. This was the year of the Tokyo Olympics, symbolic of Japan's transformation from postwar destitution to wealth and international influence. By this time, the city had many hostess bars, but the women who worked in them were Japanese. In 1969, in another symbol of expanding affluence, Tokyo's first foreign hostess club opened in Roppongi under the name Casanova.

There were plenty of Japanese men who wanted to pay for time with hostesses—usually on company expenses, for the clubs were regarded as a respectable means of entertaining business contacts, closing contractual negotiations, and rewarding employees for loyalty and hard work. The opening of Casanova signaled the emergence of a new mizu shōbai demographic—salarymen with foreign clients and money, and the education and confidence to converse with foreign hostesses in English.

Casanova was dizzyingly expensive, but over the next thirty years it inspired many cheaper *kimpatsu*—"blondie"—clubs. An hour at Casanova cost ¥60,000, but Club Kai, which opened in 1992, and its successor, Club Cadeau, cost about ¥10,000 an hour.* The first clubs had employed female back-packers who happened to be passing through; soon club own-ers were placing advertisements in foreign newspapers and magazines and sending agents abroad to recruit and import suitable young women. But at any one time, the number of foreign hostess bars in Roppongi, excluding strip joints, was never very large. In Lucie's time, there was Casanova, Club Cadeau, Club Vincent, J Collection, One Eyed Jack's (the big-gest of them all, sister establishment to the "gentleman's club" Seventh Heaven), and Casablanca.

By 2000, Anne Allison was Robert O. Keohane Professor of Cultural Anthropology at Duke University in North Caro-lina. In 1981, as a doctoral student, she spent four months as the only foreigner in a Japanese hostess club in Roppongi. This fieldwork formed the basis of her doctoral thesis, later published as a full-length book: *Nightwork: Sexuality, Plea-sure, and Corporate Masculinity in a Tokyo Hostess Club*.

Much of it is a closely argued, densely theoretical treatise, heavy with phrases like "phallicized self-image" and discus-sions of Japanese concepts such as *jikokenjiyoku* ("the wish to expose oneself and have this self-exposure well received"). But it also contains moments of peculiar comedy as the unflappa-bly calm and analytical cultural anthropologist encountered the neurotically repressed patrons of the Floating World:

> I was sitting at a table of four, all men in their early forties. [They] spoke quietly and interestingly about relations be-tween the United States and Japan, universities, travel, and so on. At one point the Mama came up, asked them how

*When Lucie went missing in July 2000, one U.S. dollar was worth approxi-mately ¥106.

they were all doing, and told one of the men that he looked more handsome every time he came to the club. She smiled intimately, told them to enjoy themselves, and then went to the next table.

One of the men spoke about singing [karaoke] in a club like this, saying it wasn't a matter of enjoying it but of having to do it. "It's inevitable" (*shō ga nai*), he said. Someone asked me how tall I was, and they in turn told me how big their penises were. One said that his was 50 centimeters long. Another motioned with his arms to indicate that his was two feet long. Another said his was so big that he could jump rope with it, which made walking a big inconvenience.

Another hostess was called over, and I was assigned to a different table.

Professor Allison described, as another anthropologist might describe a coming-of-age ceremony in Micronesia, the dynamics of the arrival at the club of a new group of salarymen. First, the strained silence, as the workmates—bosses and underlings, young and middle-aged—sat down together for a night of prescribed "fun." Then the sense of release as the beer and mizuwari arrived, and the tendency of customers to behave drunkenly even before they had finished their first drink. Finally, the signal that the evening had begun in earnest—the inevitable sniggering reference to the breasts of one of the attending hostesses, sometimes accompanied by what the professor referred to as "the bop," a fleeting, chortling pat on the boob. "Breast talk becomes a signal that the time for play has just begun," Professor Allison wrote. "As often as I heard a comment about a breast made, it never failed to get the same reaction: surprise, glee, and release."

Yet for all this, she insisted that the club was not principally about carnality. "We were taught three things when we started. How to light our client's cigarettes, how to pour his drinks, and not to put our elbows on the table. We were also advised not to eat in front of him: it shows lack of subservience. Those rules aside, your job was to fulfill his fantasy. If he wanted you loud, you were loud. If he wanted you intelligent, you were intelligent. If he wanted you horny, you were horny. Sordid? Yes. Degrading? Yes. But one thing it wasn't was the White Slave Trade. The one thing the hostess bars are not about is sex."

The public telephone booths of Tokyo were full of printed flyers advertising prostitutes; what the hostess clubs offered was both more specialized and more costly. Unexpectedly, the more expensive and select a club, the less tolerant it was of touching and groping. "Other clubs in the mizu shōbai provide the service of masturbating a man to ejaculation," Professor Allison observes. "In the hostess clubs, by contrast, the masturbatory ejaculation is of the ego only."

Japanese sex, like Japanese society, is ordered and orderly. Japanese men like to know exactly what is expected of them and how they are meant to behave before entering any situation. And in the hostess clubs, they know that the only thing on offer is titillation . . . The Mama who owned and ran [my club] made one thing very clear: touching, now and then, with a client was OK; sex was a sackable offense. But most of the clients—Japanese clients anyway—did not expect sex. They expected flirtation and flattery, and that is what they got.

Within those parameters, you put up with whatever came your way. Some conversation was offensive, some was not, but the most important thing was not to be silent. One night you might discuss Tchaikovsky with a charming and courteous gentleman. The next night that same man might ask you how many times you climax each night, when you lost your virginity and compare your breasts with those of the two other hostesses at the table. Your job was to smile and pretend you found him entertaining. You made him believe that he was the most wonderful, most important man in the world, that you longed to jump into his bed. He made himself believe that this tall, beautiful Western woman was desperately in love with him, found him fascinating and was going to become his mistress that very night. They loved talking about sex and sometimes the conversations would become explicit or highly suggestive, but at the end of the evening, you went your separate ways. Neither side would be surprised or disappointed because neither side had expected anything else.

You tell him you wish he was your lover. He tells you he would like to take you home. You say that would be lovely, but my sister is in town and I have to show her the sights. It is the answer he was expecting; he might well have been frightened at any other.

The only people who did not understand and play by these rules were foreigners, Western men who were unable to grasp the Japanese obsession with ritual and role play. I remember a Frenchman being furious when his hostess wouldn't go back to his hotel. "Why on earth has she been coming on so strong all evening if she doesn't want to sleep with me?" he exploded.

The argument of *Nightwork* was that, rather than sex, hostess clubs were actually about work. By encouraging and subsidizing the salaryman to spend his evenings together with colleagues, clients, and hostesses (rather than at home with his wife and children), Japanese corporations enabled him to discharge stress and frustration in a way that served the corporations' ends—bonding with his workmates and building good relations with clients. The hostess club was both leisure *and* work; in colonizing the salaryman's after-office hours, as well as the working day, the company ensured that his first loyalty was not to his family but to his job. "They are tired when they arrive and the last thing they want to do is flog their wits to entertain either a client or a woman," Professor Allison wrote. "The hostess solves that problem. She entertains the client, flatters the man who is paying, and makes him look important and influential in front of others . . . If that same man went to a disco, he would probably fail to pick up a woman and go home feeling deflated and rejected. The hostess clubs remove the risk of failure."

How did Western women fit into all this? The truth, according to Allison, was that they were little more than a novelty: "Japanese men certainly fantasize about sleeping with Western women, but the reality of having one as a real wife or mistress frightens them. We might intrigue them, and there is certainly kudos in having a Western woman on your arm, but Western women are known to have opinions, to be neither obedient nor subservient." It was a fantasy that, by the consent of all concerned, was kept alive only for the evening and only within the club. And the club itself was closely monitored by a manager, waiters, or the presiding mama-san. "I cannot say that I enjoyed my time as a hostess," Anne Allison wrote. "It was hard work, and a lot of the time it was degrading. When you have to sit and smile politely while a man asks if you fart when you pee, and still smile when he says it for the tenth time, you get fed up. But I never felt threatened, I never felt compromised, and I never felt there was a situation I could not handle. And if I had felt in trouble, the Mama would have come to my aid. In Tokyo, even in its red-light district, I felt a lot safer than in New York."

■ ■ ■

If the job of being a hostess truly was confined to the inside of a hostess club, Lucie Blackman would be alive. But it was more complicated than that. Once she had entered the mizu shōbai, a woman was subject to pressures and temptations that shadowed her life in Japan, whether she was aware of them or not.

They were rooted in what was called *shisutemu*: "the system"—the tariff of charges and incentives imposed by each club on its customers and hostesses. At Casablanca, a customer paid ¥11,700 an hour, which included unlimited beer or mizuwari and the company of one or more girls. Out of this, a new hostess like Lucie was paid ¥2,000 an hour. For five hours' work a night, a hostess earned ¥10,000; at six nights a week, this came to ¥250,000 a month. But that was only the beginning of an arrangement of bonuses and compulsions that were the heart of "the system."

A girl who had impressed a man one night might be "requested" by him the next; for this, he paid a supplement and she received a ¥4,000 bonus, on the basis that she was bringing in business. If a customer ordered champagne or a "bottle keep"—a personal bottle of an expensive whiskey or brandy that was kept behind the bar for his private consumption—the hostesses in attendance shared a commission. Girls were encouraged to go on what were called *dōhan*—dinner dates with men who had taken a fancy to them and whom they brought back afterwards to the club. They enjoyed an evening out with an attractive young woman, she got time off work and a free dinner, and the club got more business.

Dōhan were not optional. At some clubs a dozen dōhan in a month brought a bonus of ¥100,000. At most clubs, including Casablanca, any girl who pulled in fewer than five dōhan a month, and fewer than fifteen "requests," faced the sack. Securing dōhan, for many hostesses, became an obsession and a source of deep anguish. It was not just a question of agreeing to dinner with men one disliked. As the month neared its end, an underperforming hostess would go on a dōhan with anyone who was willing. Male friends were recruited to make up the quota; sometimes a hostess in imminent danger of termination would pay the dōhan charge herself.

"In the changing room, by the toilet, there was a chart on the wall with everyone's name and the number of requests and dōhans you'd had that month," said Helen Dove. "You were really put to shame if there was a zero next to your name. I was so bad at it, I was always near the bottom of the list. I couldn't be bothered in the end. I completely lost enthusiasm. I'd rather talk to the other girls than pretend that I fancied these Japanese men. I'd had only one or two dōhans, a few requests. It got so bad, I ended up asking my landlord if he could do me a favor and pretend to be my dōhan."

She was sacked anyway, the week before Lucie went missing.

In the atmosphere of competition at Casablanca, rivalry was just as likely to flourish among the hostesses as friendship. But Lucie and Louise got on well with most people. "They were very close friends. They did everything together," Helen Dove remembered. "They were living together, they were cycling to work together, they'd socialize together. They got on very, very well. I found them . . . I don't know . . . naïve, quite young, a little bit foolish, a bit girly. They used to kiss each other when they met, even if they'd only been apart for a few hours. I thought that was sweet." Helen was struck, as many people were, by the attention Lucie paid to her hair and clothes and makeup. "I wouldn't say she was absolutely stunning, but she had a vivacious personality that made her attractive," she said. "She didn't strike me as being underconfident. Lovely hair, lovely personality, lovely and tall."

Customers liked her too. "She was different from Canadians or Americans with big laughs, women who are too bright and lively," said Mr. Imura, the squid-fishing publisher. "Her conversation was not over the top." Mr. Watanabe, the Photo

Man, was immediately impressed: "At first sight, I took in that she was from good family. She looked gentle, graceful, charming, and refined . . . I could really recognize her well breeding, good education, plentiful culture, and nice sensibility."

"It is obviously not the job of my dreams, but it's so easy," Lucie wrote in an e-mail to Sam Burman. "I am earning good money and it is so different from the UK. The men are so respectful. Obviously you get the odd one but so far I've met some really nice people." "The odd one" may refer to the unidentified customer who had offered her the equivalent of ¥1 million ($9,400) to sleep with him. In the version of this story that she recounted to her mother and sister, she laughed the offer off. As Louise remembered it, "She was furious and asked our manager to remove him."

The hostesses were instructed to collect business cards from the men they had entertained and to telephone and e-mail them to encourage their return to the club. A few of Lucie's e-mails have survived. In them, she strikes just the right note of chaste flirtation and noncommittal coquettishness.

From: lucieblackman@hotmail.com
To: Imura, Hajime
Date: Wednesday, June 21, 2000 3:01 AM

Dear Hajime,
I just wanted to write to you to say "Hello!" It is me Lucie here from Casablanca. I was the girl from London, with long blonde hair who you got on so well with . . .

    It was so good to meet you the other night at the club, I really enjoyed your company, and like we planned would love to meet up with you soon for dinner.

    . . . I am going to call you on Wednesday

between 1200 and 1600 so I can talk to you and make some plans to meet up. Maybe you are free sometime next week?

Well, I have to go now, but I will leave you with this message so you can find some time in your very busy schedule during Wednesday morning, then I will call you Wednesday afternoon, to finally talk to my new special friend.

I hope you have a lovely day, I know I will as I will be speaking to you soon.

Take care,

Lucie x

From: Imura, Hajime
To: lucieblackman@hotmail.com
Date: Wednesday, June 21, 2000 5:30 PM

Hello!
Thank you for your E-mail.

How are you, Lucie, a cute girl with long blonde hair, today? I always liked girls with blonde hair and also with short skirt. I hope everything is going well

Which cuisine do you like the best, French, Japanese, Chinese, etc.? Please choose one of them and go to a restaurant for dinner with me? How about next Tuesday? Do you have time to do? . . .

By the way, can you speak American English? I cannot speak Queen's English very well, because I eat rice and miso-soup every day. I suppose you could not quite catch what I said the other night. But I could understand what you said. So

```
please whisper at my ear whatever you like to
tell me.
    Enjoy yourself your life in Tokyo,
anyway . . .
    Hajime Imura
```

The secret of success in hostessing was to build up a stable of loyal customers for whom the girl, rather than the bar, was the attraction, and who regularly notched up requests, drink commissions, and dōhan.

Without at least a handful of regulars, it was difficult to survive. But Lucie got off to a good start in this respect. "I have a friend . . . who comes in every night in the last eight days," she wrote to Sam Burman. "It's excellent as he speaks really good English, isn't that bad looking and is part of the aristocracy therefore ultimately is loaded!! . . . He said if ever I needed to make up numbers [for requests] he'll come in any time." This was Kenji Suzuki, Lucie's most regular regular, her professional salvation and emotional burden.

Ken was in his forties and unmarried. He had large metal-rimmed spectacles, high cheekbones, and a wavy fringe of hair. His family may or may not have been descendants of the old, and long-abolished, Japanese feudal aristocracy, but he was undoubtedly well-off. With his elderly father, he ran an electronics company, but by 2000 the family business was struggling. In his many e-mails to Lucie, worry and loneliness gusted through the façade of brightness and cheer. He spoke of anxious meetings with clients, grueling business trips to Osaka. Some nights he would be in the office until eleven o'clock, with a six a.m. bullet-train journey the next morning. Booze and Lucie were his consolations. "I did not explain to you my troublesome situation and environment for my business," he wrote to her in his cheerfully inexact English. "You can imagine it is rubbish. I could drink around but I never became to SMILE until I met you, oh! what a poor guy, ho-hohohohohohoh."

He met Lucie halfway through her second week at Casablanca. Except during his out-of-town business trips, he wrote to her and visited the club almost every day. The crush he developed on Lucie—not even adolescent, but childish, almost infantile in its abjectness—would have been obvious from this attendance record alone. His e-mails spelled it out in cloying detail.

"Thank you for your patience last night," read his first message. "One thing that I can say to you now is that I will be sure to envy your future boyfriend in a Mad City, Tokyo."

The next day he was apologetic: "I was so drunk yesterday and always, so I want to chit-chat with you when I am sober and normal. It might be very boring for you, ha, ha, ha, ha, ha, ha, ha, ha."

Three days later: "I am interested in you because of being yourself. I know that you are the most CHARRRRRRRMING girl on this planet so far . . . See you soon! Kennnnnnnneeeeeeeeeeeeeeeeeeeeeeeeee."

Lucie had told him that one of the things she missed in Japan was black olives. On their first dōhan, they arrived at the restaurant, and a bowl of them had been placed on the table on Ken's instructions. He noticed that the glass of Lucie's watch was cracked; he had it repaired for her and gave her a Snoopy watch to wear in the meantime. "He is such a darling," she wrote to Sam. "On Friday night last week he took me for dinner again and picked me up in his little black Alfa Romeo sports car and took me to a beautiful restaurant in a hotel on the twelfth floor overlooking Tokyo. It was fab. He then came to the club with me which gets me a ¥4000 bonus."

"Tomorrow I have to wake up in the early morning for the important meeting," Ken wrote to Lucie on May 24. "However,

I will pop into CB to glance at your face even I cannot chit-chat tonight."

Less than two hours later: "I guess it is too early for you to say that you promise dinner will not only be tomorrow night. Having dinner with me may be too boring or too disgusting to stand. Just I warn you. Ha, ha, ha, ha, ha, ha, ha."

A week later:

To tell the truth, you have never left my mind even one second . . . Of course, I'm very much interested to get to know you more. However, I feel that I know you very well. Probably, you want to get to know me more more more ♪ How'd you like it? How'd you like it? Right? I strongly recommend that you should carefully do this nice man. He is sweet, smart and sexy, ha, ha, ha, ha, ha, ha, ha, ha, ha, ha , , , , ,

And on June 5:

Dear my sweet friend Lucie,
You saved my life. I have just come from the heavy and shit (Wooooops) meetings today. Although it is Monday, I am almost feeling today is Thursday. My tank for jokes (other people say a "brain") is dying. Today in some way it is very exciting but exhausted. In the early afternoon I climbed upto the top of Mt. Everest and in the late evening I was fallen into the bottom of the Mariana Trench in the Pacific Ocean, It is not just a normal up-down in a day. However, now I am floating on the surface because your sweet mail like a life jacket . . . please forgive my written English. I

am sure that you sometimes feel like
corresponding with Papua New Guineans or a 7
years old boy.

"[Ken] was wasted tonight so it was quite hard work," Lucie wrote in her diary. A few days later: "[Ken] . . . absolutely wasted—worst night so far in my opinion!!" But she displayed little self-consciousness about the relationship. A man more than twice her age, lonely, alcohol-dependent, and seemingly without other friends or attachments was besotted with her. At a time of crisis for his company, he was throwing away thousands of yen to spend every evening at her side. Far from discouraging him, she was behaving like an excited, delighted, appreciative sweetheart. And this, for someone in Lucie's position, was normal. More than normal, it was her professional duty. Hesitant, decent, infatuated, and loaded, Ken was the perfect customer. If she hadn't encouraged him, she would have lost her job.

Hostesses in Roppongi, the managers and waiters who ran the bars, even an anthropologist such as Anne Allison, all said the same thing: that hostessing was a game, governed by clear and binding rules, and that everyone—customers as well as girls—understood instinctively where the lines lay and when they were being crossed. But what if a man's judgment became blurred by loneliness or drink or love or lust? What if one side stopped recognizing the rules?

"I do not agree that I am a mad man, but many people say so," Kenji Suzuki wrote. "Alright. Even if I am mad, I were not mad with you last night at all and will not be mad with you in the near future either. Do not worry! Probably, you will soon be mad and angry with me sometimes . . . . . . Hahahahahahahhaha."

6. TOKYO IS THE EXTREME LAND

"During this time between arriving in Tokyo & buying this diary so much has occurred," Lucie wrote.

> 20 days is all it has been. We arrived in a shithouse, but slowly turned it into our home. We have survived mass starvation and drunk any weight that dropped off, right back on. We found jobs as hostesses at a club called Casablanca. We have drunk more alcohol in the last 20 days than I have ever consumed in my whole drinking lifetime . . .
>
> It has been an extremely hard & emotionally taxing 3 weeks. Tokyo is the extreme land. Only high as a kite or lower than you can imagine over here . . . never anything between the two.

Filling all of the next page, in giant, overlapping, individually shaded, graffiti-style letters, are the words TOKYO ROCKS.

Casablanca closed at two a.m., or after the last customers had left. The girls would help them on with their jackets, guide them unsteadily through the leather-clad door, and trill their thanks as the elevator rose to meet them.

"Goodbye, Yamada-san. Goodbye, Imoto-san. Please come again! Goodbye—see you soon!"

Then they would slip back inside, change out of their dresses, and escape into the humid darkness.

This was the moment, as the foreign hostesses were emerging from their clubs, that the Roppongi night turned on a pivot. There was a clear and inescapable choice. If you went home at this point, you would wake up tomorrow with something of the morning left—time to tidy up, go shopping, meet a friend for lunch. If you stayed out, you would be drinking until dawn. "There's no such thing as just one drink in Roppongi," the foreign investment bankers used to say, and Lucie knew the truth of this. "Last week was a bit mad," she wrote to Sam. "For some reason I got plastered every night from Wednesday onwards. You get so many drinks bought for you after work, and as work doesn't ever end before 2 really before you know it it's 7 a.m. daylight and you're falling round the streets of Tokyo. The bars here are very cool, you just can't help it."

There was Geronimo on Roppongi Crossing—cramped, raucous, and decorated with the severed ends of expensive silk ties, chopped off and presented as offerings by drunken bankers. There was Castillo, with its sign banning Iranians and its renowned DJ, Aki, who had an unmatched collection of records of the 1980s. Wall Street had a screen above the bar displaying stock prices; Gaspanic was the sweatiest and most carnal of them all, a grope pit of booze and dancing. The most popular place among the hostesses was the Tokyo Sports Cafe, which had the same management as the strip clubs Seventh Heaven and Private Eyes, and the One Eyed Jack's hostess bar next door. At this time of night, a group of hostesses rarely had to wait long for someone to buy their drinks. In the Sports Cafe, as in the clubs, they were paid a percentage on wine and champagne purchased by male friends. After being sacked by Casablanca, this was how Helen Dove made a living for a while—lingering in the Sports Cafe, making a ¥8,000-a-night commission on the drinks men bought for her.

Lucie enjoyed the nights—or early mornings—out after work. But no one loved them more than Louise.

One Saturday, Ken Suzuki took Lucie out to dinner. Afterward, she wrote e-mails in an Internet café and met Louise at midnight. At Geronimo there was a crowd of familiar faces. The girls drank shots of neat tequila. Louise was soon "slaughtered" and engaged in conversation with a man named Carl. "We then went to Wall Street," Lucie wrote, "where the night started to go really wrong."

Louise made a new friend. He was "a cute guy," Lucie recognized, but she sensed danger in him. He reminded her, she wrote, of her deceitfully self-destructive ex-boyfriend Marco. "Lou however by this point was too drunk for rational thinking." The three of them left Wall Street together and went on to a club called Deep Blue, "where Louise now decided she wanted something else to perk her up." Lucie went on: "We found some friends there and for me the night was getting good—then Lou started losing it."

The girlfriend of Louise's new friend arrived, but Louise was oblivious to her fizzing jealousy. "Lou was losing it more & more, kissing the guy in front of her blissfully unaware," Lucie wrote. Suddenly, the music had been switched off, the lights were up, and everyone in the club was watching a five-way brawl on the dance floor. "The girl went for Lou," Lucie wrote, "I went for the girl, the guy went for Lou, I went for the guy, the guy went for me, the bouncer went for the guy— *eventually* I went for the bags, I went back for Lou, we went to the lift, we got stalked by psycho man, & finally we got home."

"I never heard from Lucie that she was having a great time," Sophie said. "I'm sure that she was going out and getting drunk, partying hard—but I don't think she was happy. I don't say that because of her fate—I really don't think she was. I remember being worried that she wasn't happy.

"She was like me in that way. We'd . . . get involved in an act almost. If people around me are getting drunk, I'll get drunk, and if people around me are reading books in the library, I'll read books in the library. That's not to say that I always do what I don't want to do. But there's something quite genuine about that need to be accepted. Lucie did thrive on being well loved and popular, and she was. But, as she got older, she got involved in things that weren't really her.

"I think Lucie felt quite rejected out in Japan. I certainly got the impression quite early on that she wasn't having fun and that she was putting on an act—go out, join in, but never really feel content in your skin."

Lucie was still preoccupied by thoughts of home and the people she had left behind there. At Geronimo one night, the DJ played "Fields of Gold" by Sting, which reminded her of Alex, the young Australian barman in Sevenoaks. "I can't imagine what it'll be like finally to clap eyes on him," she wrote in her diary. "I get a 'flip' sensation in my stomach just thinking about it, sometimes it seems like tomorrow, other times it feels like a century away. All I think of is him . . . holding my hands, looking with his beautiful eyes boring into mine, catching his bottom lip with his teeth . . . Even at the bar, wasted, surrounded by the company of men, he's still in my every thought."

Money was a worry, as usual. At the end of May, three weeks after arriving in Tokyo, Lucie carried out one of her regular reviews of her finances. Her debts—including two bank loans, a bank overdraft, debts to her mother and father, a credit-card bill, and the balance on the "Princess Bed"—amounted to about $8,000. Minimal payments on all these, plus the rent on Sasaki House, the rental charge for her bicycle, and a modest ¥20,000 (about $188) a week for living expenses used up her entire hostessing income. It was obvious that it would take months to reduce her debts even slightly; her original plan of returning home in early August would have to be abandoned.

"There's nothing I can [do] except deal with it," she wrote, "but it's left me with a gutted feeling Alex & I won't work out and home now seems so much further away. I still feel such a huge sense of disorientation & being lost, yet every time I seem to settle on something—it changes."

But there was more bothering Lucie than money and an absent boyfriend. It came out in a passionate, lonely, and probably tipsy diary entry three weeks after arriving in Japan.

Date: 26/5—5:50AM

I don't know what's wrong but this place seems to be bringing out the absolute worst in me. I can not stop crying. I have such pain in my stomach—a real physical symptom of feeling absolutely crushed. I am so cried out, tears no longer come in one lot, they only come exhaust[ed]ly in waves.

I'm not coping well here. I can't pull myself out of this hole I've fallen into.

I've had to leave Lou in the Sports Cafe with Keenan— I couldn't stand it any longer. I feel so fucking horrible there—I hate it.

I feel so ugly & fat & invisible in there I constantly hate myself. I'm so average. Every single part of me from head to toe is completely average. I must have been kidding myself that I could make it out here. I hate the way I look, I hate my hair, I hate my face, I hate my nose, I hate my slanty eyes, I hate the mole on my face, I hate my teeth, I hate my chin, I hate my profile, I hate my neck, I hate my boobs, I hate my fat hips, I hate my fat stomach, I hate my flabby bum, I HATE my birthmark, I hate my bashed up legs, I feel so disgusting & ugly & average.

I am so fucking up to my neck in debt & so badly need to do well. This is not a bad thing to do with Lou & I'm really happy for her—but I'm a crap hostess. I've had 1 dohan only cos of Shannon, another stood me up—I mean how shit must you be for a dohan to stand you up? I only have [Ken] now—but how long will that last? Louise gets men falling over themselves to request her—I get fake no's & stood up.

Nishi gave her a tip & she's being so fab about it, but she's just falling so well into it—making heaps of friends & as usual no matter where I am—I feel alone.

It's not 7oaks, it's me.

I can't explain this feeling to anyone, this feeling of complete detest for myself & this feeling of being so average. I've tried so badly to understand why & to make Mum and Lou understand—but they think I'm being silly—but I really feel like this <u>so</u> much. It's a feeling of being so invisible, being no-one, feeling like I'm never a part of something & never quite fitting in.

. . . I know Lou has been all over the place for the last year, but she never has that feeling of no self worth.

The most beautiful men become spellbound. She always feels she deserves the best & becoming more radiant and confident all the time. I really am not joking & this sounds stupid but I am so exhausted with feeling this shit & feeling so lonely despite being with Lou every day & feeling so low & so up to my eyeballs with debt—I sometimes really can't be bothered to wait & find out what happens. I just want to disappear. I feel like I'm reeling & I don't know what to do.

I feel so outside.

I've nothing anywhere.

■ ■ ■

A man named Kai Miyazawa described to me the art of running a hostess club. Kai would have been a striking figure anywhere, and among middle-aged men in Japan he was outstanding.

He was in his mid-fifties, with a handsome, lined face and graying hair pulled up high above his forehead and tied in a ponytail. He wore a flower-embroidered shirt unbuttoned a third of the way down the chest and bright orange trousers bound with a striped white and orange belt. There was a silver chain around his neck, on his left wrist another chain and a chunky silver watch, and on his feet a pair of cowboy boots.

Kai was a living history of foreign hostess bars in Roppongi. In 1969, at the age of eighteen, he had visited the original kimpatsu club, Casanova, and been enraptured by the beauties who worked there. For the next twenty years, he spent most evenings in Roppongi, indulging his fascination. One day a friend remarked that if he loved foreign girls so much, he should set up a place of his own. Club Kai opened in 1992, to be succeeded a year later by Club Cadeau. It was hard work, and Kai struggled to make money. He was constantly having to move to cheaper premises, or landing in trouble with the local yakuza, the Japanese mafia. "Running a business—I don't know it well," he said. "What I do know is *girls*."

Kai was proud of Club Cadeau. As its manager, as well as owner, he watched over his hostesses with the concentration of a gambler over a hand of cards. He knew each of their strengths and weaknesses; he deployed them carefully and deliberately, at the moment of optimum moneymaking advantage. To the unobservant customer, quietly becoming sozzled over the course of an evening, the coming and going of different hostesses seemed a natural process, an ebb and flow as of the tides. But Kai controlled everything, like a ponytailed Zeus peering down upon the world from the bar of Mount Olympus.

He rarely took to the floor of the club himself; only with the very best customers would he sit for a brief exchange of pleasantries. Kai's job was to monitor the room, tuning in to the invisible frequencies and vibrations that surrounded each grouping of hostess and customer, gauging the aura around each man and how it fluctuated over the course of the evening. He had to be aware all the time at what point in the cycle of the "system" each customer had reached and how he might be detained a little while longer. "If a customer stays for just one hour, I make no money," said Kai. "He pays ten thousand yen. I pay the girls three thousand yen, so, after the rent and the drinks, I'm left with two thousand yen, something like that. If a customer stays for one hour, I don't care. After one hour— then I care."

On entering the club, the customer would be seated with one of the most attractive girls. This was his hostess honeymoon: the welcome was deferential, the girls were beautiful, the whiskey was warm in the belly, and the dimness of the lighting cast a veil of erotic promise over the tawdry surroundings. Girl and customer started to talk. Kai was watching. "First I give him a beautiful girl with a nice character," he said. "And then I'm checking to see how they get on, have they connected?" If not, then Kai would mutter in the ear of the waiter, who muttered in the ear of girl number one. She politely excused herself, to be replaced immediately by a second hostess. Perhaps this girl would hit it off with the customer. She had to detain him only until the end of the first hour and the beginning of the second. If she succeeded in this, then the first hand had gone to Kai.

"Past one hour, even one minute, I'll pick that girl up and move her to another table, and leave him with an ugly girl. If he wants to talk to the pretty one again, he can request her— ¥3,000. Or he might say, 'I want her again,' and you say, 'I'm sorry, she's not available—wait half an hour.'" By that time, the customer would be into his third hour, with a bill of ¥30,000 and rising.

"You watch them," Kai said, with the smile of an experienced huntsman recalling the stalking of an elk. "You know what they are thinking. So if he's going to the toilet and he checks his watch just before he goes in, then you know that he's planning to leave. So then you give him the best girl in the club. She is waiting for him when he comes out, the girl of his dreams." She would hand him a hot towel as he closed the toilet door behind him and lead him by the hand back to the table. He would decide to stay for one more round of whiskey and water—but his new girlfriend wanted to drink champagne (at ¥30,000 a bottle). Ticktock, ticktock: soon the fourth hour had begun. In three hours and one minute, the customer had spent close to ¥80,000. And now his champagne dream girl was whisked away.

"You have to look inside these men," Kai said. "You have to read their brains *inside*. I'm a genius at this."

Part of his skill was in finding the right girls. Kai sized them up like an expert horse trader. "The girls need to be under twenty-two," he said. "It's very important they look nice, like flowers. Inside the club, if only one of the girls is beautiful, all the others look beautiful too. Roppongi is small. If one girl is beautiful, the word spreads, everyone is talking about her, people are lining up. My club at that time had the most beautiful girls, the most fantastic girls. When girls came to Tokyo, they had a list of which club to work in—number one was One Eyed Jack's, because it's the biggest. Second was my club, Cadeau. Sometimes I was at the top." At the peak of business, in the early 1990s, the harvest of girls from the streets of Roppongi was not enough to meet demand. Kai and his British wife, herself a former hostess, placed advertisements abroad and went on scouting trips to Britain, Sweden, Czechoslovakia, France, and Germany to source fresh talent.

Kai, as he said, knew foreign girls. He loved foreign girls; he made his living from them. And he despised them. The way he expressed his contempt was casual, unimpassioned, offhand. After the enthusiasm with which he talked about running the club, it came as a shock. But it was born of a reciprocal contempt from the hostesses themselves, or Kai's perception of one—a condescension and indifference that was racist in character.

"Only ten percent of them are normal girls, girls with an identity who know why they are in Japan," he said. "Only ten percent of them like Japan, are interested in the country, the culture." Most of the girls he recruited in Tokyo, he said, were travelers who had found themselves in Thailand, following the backpacker trail, through the druggy tourist islands of the south with their full moon parties and unconstrained supplies of marijuana, Ecstasy, and cocaine. "So they run out of money. Then they hear that in Japan they can make money easily. So they come over, work for three months, and when they have made their money, they go back to Thailand. They don't like it here. They don't respect yellow people. They're just after the money.

"Ninety percent of them can't get jobs in their own country. Only ten percent have a reason to be in Japan. They have no idea—they're just party girls. They take drugs, chase boys. Everyone takes drugs—at the weekend they always take Ecstasy, they party like crazy. The drug culture here is crazy, crazy, crazy. Crazy. Only the East Europeans don't do it too much, because they send all their money back home to their families.

"Maybe twenty, thirty percent of them have sexual problems. What does that mean? That means their father fucked them, a lot. They used to tell me about it, because I'm easy to talk to. They say to me, 'Kai, my father is still my boyfriend.' Because of that, they're always angry. Maybe seventy, eighty percent of them are divorced back in their country. This kind of background, this troubled background.

"They have no friends. They cannot communicate with people. And then they go to Thailand and they can make friends at last because they meet other people like them. The communication is drugs. At weekends, that's what they share. Maybe ninety percent of them sleep with their customers, you know. Why not? It doesn't hurt, it feels good, you get money, you get rich—no problem!"

When Kai talked this way, he was expressing his sense of moral superiority, and this was hard to take seriously. I didn't believe that nine out of ten hostesses prostituted themselves. I didn't believe the other percentages he bandied around. They were just a pompous way of making the misogynistic generalization: *all hostesses are whores.* On the other hand, there was no doubt that the women he described—druggy, fucked up, and lost—were present in Roppongi in large numbers, as strippers and also in the hostess clubs. But Kai's disgust spoke of something else. No man was in a weaker position to pass judgment on hostesses. The fact that he did indicated his own hypocrisy but also suggested something of the general Japanese attitude.

After spending a little time in Roppongi, one's eyes became attuned to its spectrum, and it became possible to perceive the differences between a waitress and hostess, stripper and "massage" girl. But to most people, these distinctions were not obvious, and not especially interesting. "Some hostesses don't consider themselves part of the mizu shōbai because they are not having sexual intercourse," said Mizuho Fukushima, a female member of Japan's parliament who campaigned for the rights of foreign women in Japan. "But people outside consider what they are doing part of the sex industry."

Anne Allison writes, "There is something dirty about [the hostess], the sexuality she evokes, and the world of the mizu shōbai she represents. All of this sexual dirtiness, in turn, makes the woman who works in this world ineligible for respectable marriage, ineligible therefore to become a respectable mother with legitimate children . . . in a culture where motherhood is considered 'natural' for women, the mizu shōbai woman is constructed as a female who transgresses her nature. For this she is degraded; for this, however, she is also enjoyed."

■ ■ ■

Lucie's low lasted through the end of May and into June. By the second week of the month, her mood lifted a little, and she began to think again of the future. "Really been struggling with these awful emotions," she wrote. "But feel OK today. Suddenly realise I don't want to be here until Nov/Dec—I need fresh air, big spaces. I've felt this way ever since I arrived."

On Friday, the two girls left the club and dropped into Wall Street to meet Louise's new boyfriend, a Frenchman named Côme ("like at the end of Lancôme," she explained to Sam), who had promised to bring along a friend to meet Lucie. The bar was crowded; the men were late. "As they are not there we grab a drink and sit down," she wrote to Sam, "when MR. SEX GOD OF THE CENTURY STROLLS IN!" Louise, in quick time, "allured him" in their direction. "We start chatting and he is a babe," Lucie wrote. "His name is Scott and he is twenty, an American from Texas and an accent to melt you, blue eyes, 6 foot 2, huge shoulders, washboard stomach, blond straight brown hair, cute arse, he could get a modeling contract in a flash but actual job—wait for it—he is a US Navy Marine!!! Are you thinking uniform?? I did too!" Already, she was thinking tactically. "I decided just to enjoy the evening for what it was," she wrote, "and so long as I didn't pander after him as I'm sure many do, & didn't sleep with him—or do anything like that I was in a no lose situation. I kept very cool and confident & he was like a bee to a honey pot."

They moved on to Roppongi's oldest disco, Lexington Queen. Champagne was ordered; Lucie and Scott danced. "We got on like a house on fire. He is a fab dancer. And we were just owning the dance floor together and I loved it." They went to a third bar, named Hideout. By this time the sun was rising in the sky. Côme was helplessly drunk, and Louise decided to see him home. Scott had long before missed the train back to his aircraft carrier, so Lucie made a decision. Still mindful of *The Rules*, she gave him what she called the "Fuck Off Speech," and then she invited him home.

Lucie recorded the Fuck Off Speech on a special page of her diary headed "Quotes!! Tokyo Memories." It went: "Look, you're cute. I'm sure loads of girls would sleep with you, but if that's what you want from me—you've picked the wrong girl—so just fuck off now if so."

Back in Sasaki House, she kissed Scott but refused to allow him upstairs. "At first I think he was a bit disappointed, but at the end of the day—anyone can have a load of one night stands but really all of us want some one to love, & have someone to love us back. So I did what I knew would completely mesmerise him about me over any other girl here. I gave him beautiful soft kisses with enough tease in them to keep him hooked, long warm cuddles & tenderness . . . & it worked."

Lucie met Scott on Friday, June 9, 2000. The twenty-two days that followed were ones of happiness and excitement. They arranged to meet again early on Sunday evening. While Lucie was getting ready, Alex the barman called her from Seven-oaks. Only a few days before, this would have been the most exciting event of the week; today, he was a footnote. "As usual it was good to hear from him," she acknowledged in her diary, "but feel he is getting more distant every time . . . So, back to Scott."

Half an hour late, thanks to Alex, she arrived at the rendezvous, Almond, the pink coffee shop on Roppongi Crossing. "He was in jeans & a blue top. He didn't see me as his back was to me. I tapped him on the shoulder & he turned round—he is absolutely beautiful. His eyes were bluer than I remembered, his smile more warm, and his kiss more breathtaking."

They took the train to Harajuku, the weekend resort of the Tokyo young, and walked down Omotesando, the most romantic street in Japan and the closest thing in Asia to a Parisian boulevard—a wide, tree-lined avenue that gently sloped down towards the entrance of the Meiji Shrine. "We got on so well," Lucie wrote. "I feel very comfortable around him, & very comfortable with myself around him . . . We talked loads, but where we were being so chuffed & smiley we lost about 80% of our trail of conversations—it was a really cool feeling. I felt like I was drunk—a really giggly feeling. But all the time I kept very cool."

They had dinner in an Italian restaurant, then crossed one of the long pedestrian bridges that span the avenue at the height of the plane trees. In the heat and wet of June, the leaves were their greenest and most rich. "As we walked over, we began kissing," Lucie wrote. "It was dark, & the lights of Tokyo went as far as the eye could see, Omote-sando was buzzing with life & as we kissed I lost myself and felt as though my heart had leapt up into my throat . . . as I pulled away an enormous sense of contentment rushed over me."

At the back of her diary, Lucie drew a picture of this moment—kissing Scott on the bridge over the beautiful avenue of trees.

Lucie wrote: "Today I think is the first time as long as I remember that I—100%—can say I am content. I have never had so little, yet felt I have so much."

After meeting Scott, the days flew by. "Average day and average night," Lucie wrote on the Monday after their first date, "made fantastic as I was walking on air." The next morning she woke up early, hungover and exhausted, and had to go to Tokyo Disneyland, far on the eastern fringes of the city, with Louise and a customer of hers. "It was absolutely pissing with rain and we both felt like shit . . . When we arrived I felt fine and was really jumpy and excited." On Wednesday morning, there was a crisis when Lucie looked in the mirror and found her lip painfully studded with cold sores. She canceled her date that night with Scott. "I'd have felt shitty—not to mention extremely self-conscious—and unattractive." Instead she went on a dōhan with Ken at the Georgian Club, "the most beautiful restaurant I've ever seen—I felt like a Princess."

By the hostess's code (some clubs even required girls to sign a document promising as much), one never, ever spoke to a customer about an "outside" boyfriend or lover. But it is clear that Ken could sense the difference, a slackening of Lucie's interest in him. The sustaining illusion, for which he was paying extravagantly, became harder to maintain. Ken's defensive anxiety glimmered through his e-mails to her.

"You do not need to apologise anything to me at all," he wrote breezily in mid-June. "I understand that a hostess job absorbs a lot of energy from you more than you have imagined . . . Anyway, I thought that your boyfriend was also coming to Japan, ha, ha, ha, ha, ha, , , , , , , , , ," But a few days later, he was full of affection and need: "I am missing you so much. See you on Sunday, I hope!" Sunday came and went with no reply from Lucie. A tone of timid reproof could be heard in his next message.

```
I guess that I could not communicate with you
well. I thought that you would like to have
dinner with meeeeeeeeeeeeee. Anyway, I would
appreciate it if you would let me know when you
changed your mind.
```

Two and a half hours later came another message with the subject line "Sayonara!!":

```
I am sure that my small heart is to be broken as
usual. But, it is OK, my young lady! I just wish
that you will have present [sic] time in Tokyo.
Au revoir!
```

Lucie, of course, had spent the weekend falling ever more deeply for Scott.

The night before her next date with him, she was awake until 6:00 a.m., "my stomach flipping . . . keeping my body awake while my eyes are aching to sleep." They met in the middle of the afternoon, sat under a tree in Yoyogi Park, "and just talked & talked & talked." The sun was warm; people lay stretched out on the grass, or danced to a band that was playing in the open air. "It slowly grew darker so we decided to make a move," Lucie wrote. "Scott will never know that we then engaged in one of the most incredible conversations of probably our entire relationship which made me connect with him more than he will ever realise."

Musicians and street performers gathered on the weekend in the plaza between Harajuku Station and Yoyogi Park. Lucie and Scott passed a brilliant and spectacular juggler, and paused to watch him. This led to a conversation about talents and personal accomplishments, about people who have them, and those who don't. Lucie wrote: "He then said how one of his largest insecurities (& fears that this will always be) was that he felt SO AVERAGE. I felt my legs buckle & I nearly cried (without meaning to be too ridiculous)."

From Scott, Lucie had heard the articulation of her own thoughts. "I just couldn't believe it & still (as I write this 1 wk after) I can not describe the sensation I felt—all I could liken it to was a feeling of huge relief/connection that this person you are embarking on a relationship [with] felt this too & it makes me feel no longer so afraid or lost. If he ever saw this he'd probably think I'd lost the plot—but maybe one day I will reveal I feel the same so that his fears dissolve too."

They had dinner together at a steak restaurant. Scott, unsurprisingly, "missed" the last train home and stayed the night with Lucie. "It was a beautiful day," she wrote. "I am so glad I stuck it out that 1st night—it's amazing how these little decisions we make everyday change our life's path in an instant."

■ ■ ■

The summer of 2000 was a time of political tumult in Asia. On May 14, Prime Minister Keizo Obuchi had died in the hospital, six weeks after collapsing with a sudden stroke. On June 13, as Lucie and Louise visited Disneyland, the leaders of North and South Korea met to discuss peace for the first time since the Korean War. All over Japan, candidates were addressing crowds and loudspeaker vans were blaring party slogans in the campaign for a general election.

None of this public drama touched Lucie and her world.

On Tuesday, June 20, she met Scott again for breakfast and another day in the sun in Yoyogi Park. "I feel we fit, just like a key in a lock," she wrote. "My feelings grow with every fear I learn of, doubt I hear & passion I feel."

On Wednesday, she had a dōhan with an investment banker named Seiji. The following night, it was a salaryman named Shoji, who worked for JVC.

On Friday evening, she sat in Casablanca with a Mr. Kowa, who spoke excellent English with a faint lisp. Louise also sat with them for a while. He drank champagne and cognac.

Before he left, he promised to call to arrange a dōhan the following week.

Sunday was Japan's election day. Lucie spent the weekend with Scott, ignoring abject e-mails from Ken.

On Tuesday, she went to a workout class at the gym. On Wednesday, June 28, she had a dōhan with old Mr. Watanabe, Photo Man. They agreed to meet for dinner the following Tuesday.

On Thursday, she saw Scott again. By this stage she had fallen hopelessly behind in writing in her diary, but later he recalled the meeting. "She was deliriously happy," he said. "I had told her I loved her and she said she was glad I had said it first. She told me, 'I feel the same about you. I think the world of you.' Lucie said she felt so strongly about me that she had butterflies in her stomach and felt queasy. She told me her legs had gone weak when I said what I felt."

On Friday, June 30, she sent an e-mail to her mother, Jane, who had not heard from her for several days and had been anxiously asking for news. Its subject line was "I'm still alive!"

PART THREE THE SEARCH

FACIAL IMAGING TEAM
SO13 Criminal Intelligence Branch,
Room 1632, New Wing,
New Scotland Yard,
London SW1H 0BG

METROPOLITAN POLICE

Tel: 0171 230 0000
Fax: 0171 230 0000

FIT Ref: NW058/00

E-FIT
COMPOSITE IMAGE

WARNING:
This E-FIT Composite Image MUST NOT BE ALTERED, COLOURED, TINTED or CHANGED in ANY WAY without the prior consent and/or supervision of both the WITNESS and the COMPILER. To do so could be construed as TAMPERING WITH EVIDENCE.

7. SOMETHING TERRIBLE HAS HAPPENED

Lucie Blackman and Louise Phillips were born in the same year, attended the same school, loved the same music and clothes, and lived twelve miles from each other. One thing divided them, meaningless to the two friends themselves but reflected in the judgments and perceptions of others: the invisible fissure of English social class.

The Blackmans—privately educated, the children of businessmen, residents of the genteel town of Sevenoaks—spoke in the accents of the Home Counties. Louise's pronunciation identified her as the child of working-class southeast London. Her father was a successful builder who settled his family in a big house in the village of Keston, outside Bromley. His death at the age of fifty-one was a terrible blow to his wife and two young daughters' affluently secure, upwardly mobile life. Louise was able to attend Walthamstow Hall only thanks to a scholarship. This, along with her accent, immediately separated her from the other girls there. The snootier among them referred to her as the "guttersnipe."

A different personality would have been crushed by such snobbery, but Louise met it with defiance and scorn. She was fearless in the face of bullies; at school, she saw off Lucie's would-be tormentors as well as her own. As a teenager, she was wild and adventurous. Lucie's other schoolmates did their underage drinking in the Sevenoaks pubs, but Louise took her to thrillingly sophisticated bars and clubs in Camden and south London. The Blackmans treated Louise with affection, although she was sometimes conscious of their disapproval and of being seen as a bad influence over her friend. If the two teenagers stayed out too long or too late, it was Louise, Lucie often felt, who ended up getting the blame for transgressions in which Lucie had been a willing and active partner.

Louise was intimate with Lucie's insecurities and saw at close hand the effect of her parents' separation and divorce. She took an early dislike to Tim, partly because of his disapproval of her, and also for what she saw as his habit of undermining Lucie's confidence with casually critical remarks about his daughter's weight or appearance. She knew that Lucie rarely felt confident in her looks and that she looked on wistfully as Louise felled men with her prettiness. But Louise had deep vulnerabilities of her own.

The death of her father affected her badly. For years she struggled with a self-destructive hopelessness that expressed itself in anorexia nervosa. It was Lucie, more than anyone else, who saw her through this painful period. This was what other people missed in their friendship—the extent to which Louise depended on, and idolized, Lucie, with her talent for languages and drawing and cookery, her loyalty and her sense of humor.

Louise's original intention had been to go to Japan alone. She was delighted when Lucie agreed to come too and had even paid for half of her ticket. But Louise insisted that she had not pressured her friend. The move to Tokyo fitted the pattern that had been established at school, of Lucie following in Louise's footsteps. She wanted to go, and she had plenty to escape from.

"The debts really bothered her," Louise told me much later. "She'd wake up in the middle of the night worrying. She needed a quick solution. She couldn't see any other way of paying them off that wouldn't take years and years. I think that she felt guilty about getting away from her mum. It wasn't that she wanted to escape Jane. But she wanted to be carefree, she wanted to be able to act like a twenty-one-year-old. Jane didn't want her to go, but it wasn't really because she thought that something bad would happen to Lucie. I mean, Jane believed that herself, but most of all she just didn't want to be left behind."

The first few weeks in Tokyo were bewildering for both women, but harder for Lucie. Her failure to flourish as a hostess, and Louise's success, imparted an unfamiliar tension into their friendship, although neither of them spoke of it. But by June it was as if a corner had been turned. "The first month emotionally has been hard in different ways for both of us," Lucie wrote to Louise one day. "But since yesterday I feel the closest I have ever felt to you I think. You truly are my soul mate and you know in me things no one does, you see in me what [o]thers miss. You only have to walk into the room and you can sense my mood in an instant."

When they woke up late on the morning of Saturday, July 1, both girls were full of optimism. Lucie, finally, had begun to acquire a roster of regular customers. Louise had patched things up after a row with her French boyfriend, Côme. The night before in Casablanca, the two of them had sat with a pair of pleasant young salarymen named Yoshida and Tanaka, who had agreed to take them out on a double dōhan the following week.

They left the club at two thirty, took a taxi home together, and sat up until four in the morning drinking tea in the kitchen and eating buttered toast. "We were both so excited," Louise said. "We thought, 'We've done it.' We'd been there two months, we were being paid on Monday, and everything was going great. We both felt that we'd got through the rubbish bit and that it was going to be fine now."

It was Saturday afternoon when Lucie walked out for the last time. It was Monday morning when Louise went to the police and Monday afternoon when she had received the bizarre telephone call. But it was late on Monday evening, more than two days after Lucie's disappearance, before Louise could bring herself to tell anyone in the Blackman family what had happened. This was the middle of the afternoon in Britain; Jane was at home when the call came, about to go out to the post office with a parcel of sweets for Tokyo. Even after Lucie's safe arrival in Japan, she had remained inconsolably tense; this news, the confirmation of all her fears, pitched her into a torment of panic and dread. Sophie and Rupert were summoned home to the small house in Sevenoaks, Val and Samantha Burman immediately came over, and Jamie Gascoigne drove down from London as soon as he heard.

The information was impossible to digest. Not only that Lucie was missing but also the strange details of the phone call that Louise had tearfully recounted: a "newly risen religion," " training," "Akira Takagi" and "Chiba"—whatever or wherever they all were. "It was absolute pandemonium in the house," said Rupert Blackman, who was a sixteen-year-old schoolboy at the time. "Mum was like a headless chicken. What do you do when someone goes missing in Japan? No one knew what to do. I was there on the Internet, looking up 'newly risen religion.' I remember getting in touch with an old judo instructor of mine to ask for his advice, because of the connection with Japan. And then something comes over you, and suddenly it's as if you lift off the planet, and you're far above, looking down, and you've got to find this person, like the needle in the proverbial haystack. It's very strange. I could never express what that felt like. The feeling when you've lost something— that's bad enough. But when you've lost some*one*, it's awful. And to lose someone in a shopping center is one thing, but to lose someone in a different continent—you don't know where to start. You know no one there; it's a completely different culture. It was the worst place in the world for that to happen."

After she began to absorb the news, Jane telephoned Tim at his home in the Isle of Wight. He was sitting in his back garden, enjoying the late-afternoon sunshine. It was the first time that they had spoken since their divorce. There are two versions of the conversation that followed: hers and his.

JANE: Tim, Tim, it's Jane. Something terrible has happened—Lucie's disappeared.

TIM: Well, I don't know what you expect me to do about it.

JANE: Our daughter's disappeared in Japan. Can't you . . . Won't you go out and bring her home?

TIM: I'm sure that the Foreign Office and the police are on to it. There's nothing much we can do that they can't.

JANE: But, Tim . . .

TIM: Look, I'm in the middle of a barbecue. Bye.

JANE: Oh, Tim, please . . .

TIM: Fuck off.

He hangs up.

JANE: Lucie's gone missing! You've got to do something!

TIM: Whoa, hang on, slow down. Is that Jane? Slow down, Jane—what's happened?

JANE: Our little girl's gone missing in Japan! You must go and bring her back!

TIM: What do you mean, gone missing? What's happened exactly? Try to calm dow—

JANE: You bastard! I told you: she's gone missing, you shit. You're not going to go, are you?

TIM: Jane . . . I . . . I can't decide in eight seconds. It's a lot to take in. Tell me what's happened again. I'm just having a barbec—

JANE: You fucking bastard! Something terrible has happened to your own daughter! You just don't give a shit about anyone, do you?

She hangs up.

So it was Sophie who announced that she would fly to Tokyo the following day; Jamie Gascoigne would go with her. "We know that she's in Chiba, so I'll go there and find her," she told her mother. "If she's been kidnapped by a religious cult, then I'll offer myself in her place. I'll bring her home."

■ ■ ■

Sophie and Jamie were twenty and twenty-three years old, and neither had ever traveled so far from home before. For seven days, they were alone in Japan. Even while Jamie was Lucie's boyfriend, Sophie had never liked him much; it was her mother's idea that he accompany her. They spent a fruitless week shuttling between the British embassy, where they were shown anxious, but helpless, concern, and Azabu Police Station in Roppongi, where they were met with remote indifference.

Louise had already filed a report on Lucie's disappearance, a single piece of paper in a room of filing cabinets. But they did learn something about Chiba, which was not only a city of nine hundred thousand people but also the name of a prefecture of five million more, an area as large as Kent and Greater London combined. They also learned that "newly risen religion" was a direct translation of the Japanese term used to describe New Age cults, and that there were several thousand of them.

Jane, in Sevenoaks, was nearly incoherent with anxiety, but Sophie talked every few hours to her father, Tim. They discussed the dilemma faced in many such situations: whether to go public or not. Someone must know what had happened to Lucie. Someone must have seen her on the day she vanished. The only way to reach such witnesses was with a public appeal for information. On the other hand, if she had been taken by a kidnapper seeking a ransom, then a demand for payment, and the opportunity for negotiation, would eventually follow. If the abduction had been carried out for purposes other than money—rape, for example—then her captor might be facing his own dilemma over what to do with his living captive. Either way, a hue and cry in the media could panic the abductor into irreversible action. "There was a risk that if we went public, Lucie could wind up dead," said Sophie. "There was also the danger that if we kept it out of the news, then any chance to find her would be lost."

The police wanted nothing to do with journalists. The embassy said that the choice lay with the family but gave the impression of agreeing with the police. Sophie had arrived intending to march up to the front door of Lucie's abductor and compel him to hand her over by the force of her sisterly will. But immediately things had become complicated. There were so many pieces that had to be manipulated and lined up in sequence, like a Rubik's cube: police, embassy, media, even Sophie's bickering parents. Each one had to be dealt with in precisely the right way, even when their interests collided.

Sophie's sleep was disturbed by jet lag and anxiety. One night she dreamed that she was trapped inside a video game, which was also a Hollywood film. Sophie was an action hero, a James Bond or Bruce Willis, out to save the world before time ran out. But instead of defusing the bombs, saving the hostages, and killing the terrorists, she had to motivate the police, keep on good terms with the diplomats, engage the journalists, and mediate between her parents, before somebody out there, the unknown and faceless villain, murdered her sister.

"We had a choice," Sophie said. "Get all that we could from the police and stay away from journalists, or keep the case high profile, put pressure on the investigation, but learn nothing from the police at all. And we chose the media." In fact, the decision was taken out of the Blackmans' hands. In London, without consulting the family, Louise Phillips's sister, Emma, had gone to *The Daily Telegraph*. Within a few days the story was in all the British papers; the confusion of the reporters was evident.

> Fears were growing last night that former British Airways hostess Lucie Blackman is being held as a sex slave by an evil Japanese cult. (*The Sun*)

> Police fear that Lucie Blackman, 21, may now be forced into prostitution as "bait" for the weird group. (*Daily Mirror*)

> Police are investigating whether Lucie Blackman was abducted by one of the customers at the late night members' club Casablanca, where the 21-year-old was paid to talk to drinkers. (*The Independent*)

> Lucie Blackman's fate could lie in the hands of the Japanese "mafia." (*Sevenoaks Courier*)

For journalists in Tokyo, it was a troublesome story. The Japanese police bluntly refused to comment. The British embassy had little to say either, although it said it more politely. The club managers and foreign hostesses in Roppongi were defensive and wary; those who could be persuaded to speak articulated only puzzlement and concern. Sophie Blackman's response to media inquiries was one of truculent contempt. The mystery of the missing stewardess was intriguing but not compelling: all over the world and every day, people disappeared, often for uninteresting reasons. Lucie would quickly have been forgotten if it hadn't been for her father, Tim, who landed in Tokyo the following Tuesday, ten days after Lucie had gone missing, and immediately did one of the things that he would come to do best: he held a press conference.

In Britain, just as in Japan, powerful conventions govern the way that people under the load of unbearable stress are expected to behave in public. We like our anguished victims to be passive, confused, and broken; where those characteristics are absent, suspicion flourishes.

The way that the Blackmans presented themselves in Tokyo was the opposite of conventional.

A Japanese family, deprived of their daughter in sinister circumstances, would shuffle before the cameras with downcast eyes. Their words would be halting and few. They would express love for their child, anxiety for her safety, and appeal to the good nature of her abductors to give her back. There would be tears, and even apology, or something close to it, for "causing inconvenience" by their plight. The journalists' questions, too, would be conventional. What was your daughter's character? What is your message to the kidnapper? The unhappy family would shuffle off again, and little more would be heard from them. Responsibility for dealing with the press, for solving the mystery—responsibility for everything, in fact—would be entrusted without question to the police.

In Britain, there is a little more room for the expression of individual anger and resentment, but only within limits. An unspoken code governs people in the situation of the Blackmans, as strict in its way as old formalities of mourning. Before encountering Tim and Sophie in Tokyo, I had had no idea of its existence. It was their indifference to the conventions, from the very beginning, that made them so obvious.

Tim's first press conference was in the British embassy the morning after his arrival in Tokyo. The room was packed with people, cameras, and television lights; every seat was taken and there were reporters standing in the aisles. The embassy press secretary sat at a table on a podium alongside Tim and Sophie Blackman. She made a brief introduction, in those tones of exaggerated softness and poignancy which are reserved for public discussion of tragedies concerning the young. Then Tim spoke. He was a tall, solid man in his late forties, with direct blue eyes and a head of thick, reddish-blond hair. He was confident, articulate, almost brisk. "V. composed," I scrawled in my notes, "impressively so—no lump in throat, no obvious emotion. Big sideburns."

Yes, said Tim, in answer to the first question, he had met the police yesterday, immediately after his arrival. His impression was that they were following all available leads. Yes, Lucie had kept in touch with him by telephone while she was away and sounded happy. Asked about the telephone call from "Akira Takagi" and the suggestion that Lucie had joined a cult, he was confidently dismissive. "Lucie is a Roman Catholic," he said. "She did not take a great interest in religion generally, and the thought that she might suddenly become interested in a religious cult over a Saturday afternoon is very unlikely."

Lucie did have debts, he acknowledged, but nothing out of the ordinary—a "managed" overdraft and credit-card bill of a few thousand pounds. He and Sophie were in Tokyo, he explained, to assist the police and the media. "Lucie is a very noticeable young lady on a Japanese road or sitting in a Japanese car," he said. "A member of the public who may have seen her walking, or with someone driving through a gateway, may come forward and provide us with the vital clue we need."

His answers were prompt and efficient; as a provider of information he could not be faulted. But—from the point of view of the photographers and reporters and TV cameramen—that was not his role. Occasionally, in press conferences and in conversations over the telephone, Tim would pause before delivering an answer. The pause would extend and lengthen until it filled the room with tension. At these moments, one had an inkling of great, gaping emotion held in check. But a silent pause cannot be quoted, cannot be photographed. And then Tim would answer in his steady, emphatic, matter-of-fact, almost ironic voice. He was articulate but never gave the impression of being overprepared. He didn't refer to notes. From time to time, he would glance sideways at Sophie; sometimes, they would exchange a smile. He seemed at home on the podium, even relaxed. The next day, the less scrupulous papers would pepper their stories with phrases like "frantic dad Tim," "distraught sister Sophie," and "fighting back tears." They were lies. It was hard to imagine a calmer or more focused pair.

One British reporter raised his hand to ask about Lucie's current boyfriend. Tim said that he didn't know him but understood that he was a foreigner and had been interviewed by the police. The same question was put to Sophie, who had said little so far. The embassy press secretary had earlier advised that Sophie not attend the press conference, fearing that the media would attempt to provoke from her a distraught reaction. If so, the media were disappointed. "Of course she mentioned him, she's my sister," Sophie replied with a curling lip. "She said she'd met a chap over here, she had started dating, and that's all you need to know. The details of what she said are none of your business."

The photographers were crouching, lurking at the bottom of the podium, their lenses angled upwards. They were waiting for the shot that would make the following day's papers: a finger brushing away a tear, a face crumpled with anxiety and despond, even just the clenched hands of father and daughter. But there was nothing of the kind. As the press conference came to an end, I realized that there was something else about Tim that was disconcerting, something about his appearance. In most ways, it was conventional enough: he wore a blazer, dark trousers, and tasseled leather shoes . . . Then I spotted it.

As the lights and cameras were being dismantled, a Japanese reporter I knew approached with a frown on his face. "What was your impression of Mr. Blackman?" he asked. "And why was he not wearing any socks?"

"I'm a yachtsman," Tim told me years later. "So I rarely wear socks, unless I have to. And it is very hot in Tokyo at that time of year." As for the emotional dynamics of that press conference: "We decided early on that there'd be no simpering and crying. None of that."

Tim was born in Kent in 1953 and went to school in the Isle of Wight. His father, who also loved boats, was a stern man. Tim, the youngest of three children, was, by his own reckoning, "a complete pain." "I was the youngest, the little one, very irreverent, and my father at the time seemed very strict and growling," he said. "I never knew where to stop. I expect they would describe me today as a bit hyperactive." At school, Tim played the four-string banjo in a successful bluegrass band. It performed at music festivals and even pressed an LP, which "rocketed into obscurity." With no urge to go to university, he enjoyed himself for a few years, earning the reputation as a cocky flirt, which was the first that Jane knew of him.

By Tim's account, the marriage was troubled from close to the very beginning and became more and more miserable as the years passed. Its final years, and the first few years after its collapse, were ones of professional strain as well as personal unhappiness, with the slow failure of the family shoe shops and then the disastrous collapse of Tim's property company. But by 2000, he had resurrected the business, become the contented partner of Josephine Burr and stepfather to her four teenagers, and rebuilt his relationship with his own children, including, eventually, Lucie.

The idea that Lucie would go to Japan emerged gradually, over several conversations. Tim knew that she was unhappy at British Airways and that the long-haul schedule was making her ill again. He knew, too, that she had debts: Lucie asked him directly if he would pay them off. "I helped her manage them," he said. "I gave her bits and pieces, but I wasn't really in a position to write out a check for five thousand pounds, and I'm not sure that's something you want to get into the habit of doing. Of course, I live with the idea that if I'd paid her debts she wouldn't have gone to Tokyo. But I don't know that for a fact, and I'm not going to beat myself up about it, because there's no way out if you get into that trap. It's not going to make any difference to anything."

Before her departure, Lucie made no mention at all of hostessing. "I assume Lucie thought I would disapprove, and I would have done. Because it was unseemly. It was not what her intellect was for. I'm a man, and I know that, however safe this business was supposed to be, males leer at females. But it was a good while before she told me the full story. In retrospect, I was the typical gullible dad."

There were regular telephone conversations with Lucie after she had left and the odd postcard. At first she was homesick and fed up. Everything was expensive, and she struggled to make ends meet. Tim urged her to come home, but Lucie wouldn't abandon Louise. After a few weeks, she described to him the job she was doing. "She said it was a bit strange but quite good fun: Western girls pouring drinks, including three or four British girls, and then these funny Japanese people. She said they all talked like this: *hwah–hwi–hwah–hwi–hwor.* Then afterwards, the girls would have a few beers and cycle home. And she told me she'd met a lovely U.S. marine, this chap Scott. She'd prattle on happily, about this and that. By that time it was obvious she was beginning to enjoy it all a lot more."

Then came the telephone call from Jane. Whichever version of it one accepts, it is clear that Tim reacted to the news of Lucie's disappearance with greater calm and detachment than his ex-wife. "I've been asked so many times what I felt at that moment," he said. "And I don't know what I felt. It was all rather unreal. There was Jane on the phone, screaming, calling me every name under the sun. And there was I, sitting in the back garden, listening to the blue tits in the trees."

And then, within a matter of hours, before anything had become clear, Sophie was on her way to Tokyo to offer herself as a sacrifice for Lucie. Tim knew nothing about Japan. Like his son, Rupert, he telephoned anyone he knew who had some experience or knowledge of the country—business contacts, the friends of relatives. A Japanese acquaintance of his brother told Tim that a single British girl missing in Tokyo would not be likely to command the serious attention of the Japanese police. "I heard this kind of thing from more than one person," Tim said. "And that is when I did start to panic. Just the realization that you're completely in the hands of very, very distant foreign agencies, and absolutely dependent on them to resolve this life-and-death problem. And I was being told that it's not likely that they'd do it."

At around this time, the calls started coming from journalists. "Jane was giving the conventional response to phone calls at two in the morning—two words with lots of *f*'s," Tim said. "I was different. Journalists started ringing me up, so I told them what I knew. Suddenly I found the story starting to build. So I thought, 'If we're going to have an effect on things out there, people have got to know she's missing.'

"Then Sophie would ring from Tokyo and say, 'I'm totally stuck. The police are hardly talking to me.' It dawned on me, if we could whip up a huge amount of interest in the UK, it could make a difference. I announced that I'd be traveling out to Japan myself—that produced more interest." Tim was discovering the power that an individual, at the right moment, can exert over the media, the power of creating headlines. He made another important discovery too.

At the end of July, on the southern island of Okinawa, the Japanese government was to host the summit meeting of the leaders of the Group of Eight industrialized countries. Vladimir Putin, Jacques Chirac, and Bill Clinton would all be passing through Tokyo on their way to Okinawa; Tony Blair would be there too, preceded a week before by his foreign minister, Robin Cook.

"I knew about the G8," said Tim. "And I thought, 'If there's this summit out there, the whole world and his mother will be watching Japan, and this will help us. If we can get people back home interested, if we can get the *electorate* concerned about Lucie and what's happened to her, then any politician, including the prime minister, is going to be duty bound to ask questions—otherwise it looks like he's a crap bloke.'"

This was the challenge that Tim had set himself before he had even set foot in Japan: to turn Lucie and her disappearance into a cause célèbre, a problem that the most powerful men in both countries would have to confront.

"It was a race against time," said Tim. "On the one hand, it would be enormous PR; it would put Lucie on all the television screens around Japan. On the other, it would put the heat under the Tokyo police, because the prime minister of England was talking about it to the prime minister of Japan. I could see that a mile off."

Tim said, "It was as if I was a giant great earth digger, a JCB, and I had to get to a particular point—and that point was finding Lucie. And I was in a town, and if I chose I could go the proper way, all around the houses and alleys and lanes. But the place I wanted to be was over there, so I decided, 'I'm just going to drive there directly, in a straight line. Straight across, from point A to point B. And if things get in the way, then I'll just have to drive through them.'"

This determination, at times resembling a kind of excitement, would come to be held against Tim, but it was also what sustained him. Peering down at the landscape as the plane came in to land at Narita, he was stricken with confusion and anxiety. "I felt this overwhelming devastation at the prospect of finding Lucie down there. The drive into the city is just awe-inspiring, just out of this world. It's so vast and teeming and foreign. I just looked at it and I thought, 'Jesus Christ, what's going to happen? What *is* going to happen?'" But there was an urgent job at hand: to knock the British media into shape.

Tim checked into the Diamond Hotel, where Sophie was staying. A pack of reporters, photographers, and television crews had arrived on the same plane, and they all checked in there too. Among much of the British press, there was an uncertainty about where the story of Lucie's disappearance would lead. It hinged on one question: What exactly does a hostess *do*? If hostesses were essentially call girls, then it would be a vivid, but short-lived, story, about a young woman who willingly succumbed to a world of vice and suffered unfortunate, but predictable, consequences. There would be sympathy for the family, but it would be limited; no prime minister would meet with the father of a missing prostitute. Tim's challenge was to present Lucie as an innocent young woman—naïve perhaps, out of her depth, but in a situation in which enough ordinary British people could imagine their own daughters.

This was something that only Tim and Sophie could do, and—given the cynicism of the British media—they were miraculously successful.

There was much lurid reporting on the "red-light district"

of Roppongi. ("Peril of Jap Vice Trap," ran one headline in the *People*: "Middle class English roses who descend into twilight world of sin.") There was plenty of cheerfully racist generalization about the Japanese male and his fancied penchant for Western blondes. ("The men can be twisted sexually because of their restricted upbringing," a "Tokyo insider" explained to the *Daily Record*.) But Lucie and her family were treated with careful respect. She was styled as "the former British Airways stewardess" far more often than "bar girl Lucie." No one questioned the family's explanation about the nature of Lucie's debts, or drew attention to the fact that, having entered Japan on a tourist visa, she had been working illegally. And however titillating the stories of "posh British girls selling their bodies," it was made clear that this had not been Lucie's situation. "Lucie's job as a hostess was to provide company for male drinkers," the most scabrous of the red-top tabloids, *The Sun*, explained with gentlemanly punctiliousness. "There is no suggestion she was involved in anything more than that."

Instead of the sordid moral story of a young woman's undoing, the headlines told a much more compelling human tale, which ordinary newspaper readers could relate to personally, about a devoted and suffering family and a beloved child lost abroad.

I Will Never Leave Without My Lucie, I Just Pray That She's Safe. (*Express*)

I'm Not Leaving Without My Sis. (*The Sun*)

Family Pleas for "Cult" Woman. (*The Daily Telegraph*)

"Why Us?" Agony of Missing "Cult Slave" Lucie as Hunt Goes On. (*The Sun*)

"I said to Sophie, 'If we don't give them the story, they'll make it up,'" Tim told me. "What we wanted to do was gain the high ground, and we gained it by giving them this personal story about Sophie and I. And we gained so much sympathy that there wasn't a lot to be gained by trying to cut that down. We played the game: we provided detailed information, we were restrained, we were not abusive, then we went out for dinner with the hacks in the evenings."

To tabloid reporters used to resentment and hostility from their subjects, Tim's relaxed charm was disarming, almost off-putting. He would always take the call, respond to the e-mail, pose for the photograph. He was more than accommodating; at times, he seemed almost enthusiastic. To the more cynical among the reporters, his helpfulness raised suspicions— was there more to this family than met the eye? But they were outweighed by the ease, and indeed the pleasure, of working with Tim.

In all the time I knew him, there was just one occasion when he displayed straightforward pain and despair. It was during a press conference at the British embassy at the end of July, his sixth in three weeks. There had been no sign of Lucie; the police had no leads, no significant information of any kind to report. The traveling British press had flown back to London, and the turnout of local journalists was a fraction of that two weeks before.

Tim and Sophie looked tired and grave. There were no smiles or glances between them. Tim wore socks.

"We are all starting to feel very desperate and upset that Lucie is being kept somewhere in difficult conditions where she will be extremely upset herself," said Tim. "And I therefore, as her father, beg of them humbly to please just release her to us again." His voice faltered and he cast his eyes down, as if holding back tears. Sophie's eyes glistened.

Chanka-chanka-chanka-chanka! went the photographers'

flashes. The few cameramen in the room zoomed in on Tim's downcast face. It was the picture opportunity that had been withheld all this time.

Years later, I asked Tim about that moment. What was it that, after all those weeks, had broken his façade of cheerful calm?

"I probably shouldn't be telling you this," he said, after a pause. "But the tears—well, we planned that in advance."

■ ■ ■

Within a few days, Tim and Sophie had established a routine, gruelingly tied to the Japanese and British news cycles. London was eight hours behind Tokyo, so they would be up until the early hours calling friends and family and giving telephone interviews to the afternoon radio and television. A few hours' sleep, and then the phone would start ringing early in the Tokyo morning for the evening and late-night news. Over breakfast, they would brief the British journalists who were staying at the hotel—there would be requests for new photographs of Lucie and arrangements to be made for interviews later in the day. At the end of morning, they would call in at the embassy, a ten-minute walk from the hotel along the green moat and gray walls of the Imperial Palace. At lunchtime they might be whisked across the city to the studios of TV Asahi or Tokyo Broadcasting System for the "wide shows," the daytime magazine programs aimed at Japanese housewives. Afternoons were for the Tokyo Metropolitan Police.

Sophie had found the police sluggish and indifferent, but at Tim's first meeting with them, they went to some trouble to make a good impression. A convoy of black minibuses, flanked by motorcycle outriders and with darkened windows, collected the Blackmans from the embassy. A team of Japanese television reporters chased behind in a van of their own. "There was a lot of gesticulating out of windows, a lot of lurching around corners, a lot of heavy right foot, rather unnecessarily trying to rush through the Tokyo traffic," Tim remembered. "I didn't see the point, really." The destination was Azabu Police Station, 150 yards from Roppongi Crossing. Like everything to do with the Japanese police, the headquarters of the investigation was a strange combination of the cozy, the feckless, and the sinister.

The police station was a blank structure of nine gray concrete stories. In front, a young constable stood self-consciously on guard, a revolver on his belt and in his hands a weapon that resembled a domestic broom handle. Displayed on the front of the building was an image of Peepo, a grinning pixie who was the mascot of the Tokyo Metropolitan Police. Above was a bilingual banner whose English portion read, MAKE SURE AGAIN ALL THE DOORS & WINDOWS ARE LOCKED. Below were posters of wanted criminals, including gangsters, suspected murderers, and the grinning, life-sized cutouts of three fugitive members of the Aum Shinrikyo cult, which had released homemade nerve gas on the Japanese subway five years earlier.

"We were astonished by a few things," said Tim. "I expected we'd be in a much grander kind of police station. The interior of the building was like something out of the fifties. Completely bland, slightly grimy—just a worn-out, utilitarian nick." The most striking thing of all was the complete lack of any visible technology. The police had radios, but where one would have anticipated humming laptops, there were banks of old-fashioned filing cabinets and mounds of paper. "We expected the normal monitors and all that kind of stuff," Tim said. "We were taken into a sort of operations room, with loads and loads of little gray desks, with identical people walking round in their identical white shirts with identically rolled-up sleeves, and not a computer in sight."

The afternoons at the police station followed a pattern.

Tim and Sophie would be led into a tiny meeting room, with two chairs facing a sofa across a low table. A young woman would bring in cups of green tea, whose yellowy hue and luke-warm temperature reminded Tim of "bodily fluids"—"I never got used to the taste, but I always drank it." After a pause, there would be a commotion of bows and handshakes as the senior officers entered the room.

Japanese names are not easy to remember for the new-comer; Sophie's method of distinguishing between the senior officers was by their haircuts. There was Superintendent Mi-tsuzane, a smiling, reserved, bespectacled man with a pale parting, and Naoki Maruyama, a younger, spiky-haired man in the fast track of the National Police Agency, who spoke fluent English. On meeting Tim and Sophie for the first time, each would present a business card, proffered with both hands, and inscribed on opposite sides with English and Japanese. The card of Superintendent Mitsuzane bore the following thicket of information:

Akira Mitsuzane
Police Superintendent
Administrator of Special Investigation
First Criminal Investigation Division
Criminal Investigation Bureau
Tokyo Metropolitan Police Department
2-1-1 Kasumigaseki
Chiyoda-ku, Tokyo 100–8929

Superintendent Mitsuzane spoke little English, and the ne-cessity of interpretation prolonged these meetings. But they would have been drawn out anyway, as the detectives went over and over the same ground with amnesiac repetitiveness.

They wanted to know about Lucie's education, about her career before she came to Japan, and her reasons for coming out. The subject that seemed to obsess them, and to which they returned again and again, was that of her debts. They took copies of Tim and Sophie's passports; there were forms to fill in and formal statements to sign. What, they asked, was Lucie's character? Why exactly did Tim believe that a crime had been committed? Tim replied, "Lucie just isn't the kind of person to wander off on her own. She never has done, and there's no reason to think she would now. She went out to meet someone. She called her friend to say that she was about to come home, and she never came back. It's reasonable to conclude that she's being held against her will."

Superintendent Mitsuzane nodded and smiled distantly. But the explanation had evidently been accepted. As the presence of such a senior officer indicated, the case was being upgraded from a simple missing-person inquiry to a criminal investigation. "It was a complete transformation from the reception that Sophie had been getting the week before, when they'd been turfing her out of the police station," said Tim. He had no doubt that the press coverage of the case, the early-morning and late-night interviews, were the reason for this change of mood.

As they left the police station, Tim and Sophie would usually see Louise Phillips, going into an interview of her own. She seemed to be there all the time—and rather than being friendly and reassuring, their encounters with her were strained. Sophie remembered being disgusted by how well turned out Louise was—manicured and made up, even in a police station, with her best friend lost. Louise, it seemed to them, was uncomfortable with, even embarrassed by Tim and Sophie's presence. She said that the detectives had asked her not to talk to them.

Dark would be coming on by the time they stepped out again onto Roppongi Avenue. The hostesses would be emerging for the evening ahead, trickling out of the Tipness gym just behind the police station. Tim and Sophie would take a taxi back to the Diamond Hotel and sit in its restaurant drinking glasses of beer. Around this time, members of the British press pack would muster in the lobby and head out excitedly in twos and threes for another night of "research"—visiting girlie bars on expenses. On the television in the corner, Tim and Sophie watched themselves, dubbed into Japanese, in the interviews they had given that morning.

The bar of the hotel featured an automated piano that would play plonking show tunes throughout the early evening. Seated at the piano stool was the effigy of a giant white rabbit in waistcoat and bow tie, as large as a man. The rabbit's face was sad and resigned; his whiskers vibrated to the sound of the piano. But no one else in the bar seemed to regard him as unusual or comic, or to pay him any mind at all. Tim and Sophie sipped their beer and stared at the white rabbit. Nothing could have chimed better with their sense of absurdity and despair, as they contemplated the end of a day on the wrong side of the looking glass.

8. UNINTELLIGIBLE SPEECH

Tony Blair met Tim and Sophie in the Hotel New Otani, Tokyo, one afternoon in July 2000. It was a moment when he was at the height of his power and popular esteem, both at home and abroad. In a summit meeting that afternoon with the Japanese prime minister, Yoshiro Mori, Blair thanked the Tokyo police for their efforts and asked that "everything possible be done" to find Lucie. Mr. Mori had been briefed on the case. "The Tokyo Metropolitan Police are doing all they can to find Lucie-san," he said. "I want them to continue to do so."

Tim Blackman's instincts had been exactly right. For Blair, with his carefully burnished image as the sincere, empathetic family man, the case was impossible to ignore; the lines he delivered to the television cameras could have been scripted for him by Tim. "It is obviously an appallingly disturbing story and every parent's nightmare, to have their child working abroad and then disappear," he said, standing alongside father and sister. "It's a tragic case and obviously the family are at their wits' end, but they're staying here and they're going to fight to see that their daughter's whereabouts and what happened to her is discovered."

"The pressure needs to come from the top," Tim said. "If I stamp my feet, they'll think I'm a nuisance, but if it's coming from the Japanese prime minister, from their boss's boss's boss's boss, it'll have far more of an effect."

As if in response to these high-level discussions, the To-kyo police showed signs of vigorous activity. Forty detectives were said to be working on the case; thirty thousand missing-person posters had been printed and distributed across the country. When asked, the police would provide disarmingly precise figures for the number of calls received from the public—twenty-three one day, nineteen two days later. But they would say nothing about the quality of the information or their overall progress in the case. "Please be assured," Super-intendent Mitsuzane would tell Tim, with his remote, kindly smile, "we are doing everything that we can."

The Blackmans had made their choice, and they had pitched their camp with the media. With that, they cut off perma-nently any relationship of trust with the police.

One day Tim and Sophie went to the police station to pick up Lucie's possessions, which had been removed from Sasaki House. Everything had been meticulously sorted and inven-toried; everything had to be signed for. There were Lucie's makeup and manicure kit, her self-help books, all sealed in individual plastic bags and listed in the police ledger. There was the Tiffany necklace that Jamie had given her, the emo-tional goodbye letter from Sophie, and the postcard that she had been writing to Sam Burman. Lucie's diary was retained by the police, as a potential source of clues and evidence. So-phie took to wearing Lucie's clothes, because she had brought with her so few of her own. The two sisters resembled one an-other so closely anyway, in build and features; now Sophie was even dressed as Lucie, and this added to the atmosphere of ghostliness and poignancy.

Alone with the police clerk, Tim and Sophie wept as they sorted through Lucie's possessions.

The most painful sight of all was a toy that Lucie had had since she was a tiny girl. Its name was Pover, a childish at-tempt at the name "Rover." It was a battered dog with long soft ears, which Lucie used to suck and nuzzle. Even as a young woman, Lucie never left Pover behind. He had accompanied her on all her trips with British Airways, growing mangier and more bedraggled with the years. He had gone with Lucie to Tokyo—and now here he was. "And that was a really bad sign," said Tim. "That was a very, very bad moment. It brought home what we were facing. Because if she'd gone away anywhere by choice, this thing would have been stuck in her handbag. But it was here. It all said: 'I planned to come back. I didn't.'"

"Dealing with the press," Tim told me later, "it was a game. And I enjoyed it, if I'm honest: I did enjoy it. That doesn't mean that I was enjoying the situation I was in. But we felt that if we showed great strength then everyone else would respond, because they knew that we wouldn't give up. When I met Tony Blair, I didn't want to be patted on the head, and told, 'Oh poor you, how awful, never mind.' If I was strong, I'd make a bigger demand on his resolve. That's what you can do from a position of strength.

"What people didn't realize was that I was in an appalling mental state. Really, I had no grip on the bits and pieces of the case. It was as if I'd lost my memory. I couldn't understand what people were saying to me. I didn't understand what I was doing there. In retrospect, I can see that I was seriously affected by the shock of it. With a job to do, which was to keep Lucie's face in the media, I was able to be very lucid. Behind the scenes, I was absolutely cretinous."

Like her father, Sophie Blackman self-consciously made the decision to be "strong"; unlike him, her resolve often manifested itself as anger or disgust. Rather than sad or despairing, Sophie appeared constantly cross, with the police, and above all with journalists, to whom she displayed undisguised contempt. Politeness, humor, charm—none of them seemed to quell Sophie's truculence. She was so rude that it was difficult to feel sorry for her, and for Sophie, a proud and defensive young woman, this was probably the point. For she was at the beginning of the most crushing experience of her life, one that would mark her for years and come close to killing her as well as her sister.

In Japan, Sophie had a constant sensation of low-level nausea. The discombobulation of jet lag, the feeling of being at one remove from reality, never passed, and from the moment of landing she never had an uninterrupted night's sleep. "I'd sleep an hour and then the phone would ring," she said. "And it'd take a moment for me to realize where I was and what I was doing and what was at stake. And then the nausea. I remember that—just months and months of nausea. I'd wake up, in the crisp hotel sheets and with the cool of the air-conditioning and the darkness of the heavy curtains. And for a fraction of a second, I'd be thinking, 'This is nice—where am I?' For the briefest of moments I'd be content. And then I'd come to, and the phone would be ringing, and I'd be thinking, 'Is this the bad news? Is my sister dead?' I had that for most of a year—waves of nausea, anxiety, and fear. Knowing what happened to Lucie, to know her fate, was the most devastating, the saddest thing in my life, but it was a relief compared to the previous nine months."

At this moment, in the middle of July, came another consequence of the press coverage: volunteers began to step forward, strangers who wanted to help in the hunt for Lucie.

A week after Tim's arrival, his partner, Josephine Burr, flew out to be with him. That night they had dinner with Sophie in a Roppongi restaurant called Bellini's, in the middle of the street where the Ghanaian men lured passersby into the strip clubs. At a nearby table sat a foreign couple: a beautiful young woman and a tall, bulky, floppy-haired man in his late thirties, who recognized Tim and Sophie from the television. He introduced himself as Huw Shakeshaft, a British financial adviser with a small independent business in Tokyo. Huw had moved to Tokyo four years earlier, and since then he had rarely strayed a mile from Roppongi Crossing. His office was opposite the Defense Agency. His apartment was on the other side of the expressway. Roppongi's restaurants and bars were his dining room, the foreign bankers and stockbrokers who lingered there were his clients, and the hostesses in the clubs were his girlfriends. "Sir Huw of Roppongi" was what they called him; he prided himself on knowing everyone. He was a creature of the district, as naturally at home there as a monkey in a rain forest.

Huw had never met Lucie, but he knew all about what had happened and badly wanted to help. "If you want to find your daughter, forget about the people at the embassy, because they're useless," he told Tim. "You're going to need an office, and you're going to need dedicated phone lines. All that I can do for you."

Huw led Tim from the restaurant to a cash machine around the corner. There he withdrew ¥200,000, the equivalent of $1,900, and handed it over on the spot. Then he took him to a bar over the road, where a British friend of Huw's gave him ¥100,000 more.

Tim was overwhelmed. His property business had been on hold for a two weeks; he was paying more than $300 a night for the rooms at the Diamond Hotel, plus the costs of food, taxis, and telephone calls. "I was borrowing money from the bank. I was borrowing from my brother-in-law, so this was fantastic," said Tim. "Huw was hugely generous." As they parted, Huw gave Tim his card and told him to come to his office the following morning.

Its position was ideal, on the third floor of a building fifty yards up from Casablanca. There was a spare phone with an answering machine, which they immediately decided to use as a "hotline" for tips and information from the kind of people—such as hostesses working on tourist visas—who would not necessarily welcome contact with the police. Overnight, Huw had already put out e-mails to friends and colleagues appealing for help on the Blackmans' behalf. One investment banker was offering his services as a driver in the evenings and on weekends. Another expatriate, working for a detergent manufacturer, suggested putting Lucie's photograph on bottles of laundry fluid. Huw's small staff could help with interpretation, and his girlfriend, Tania, the multilingual Russian model and hostess with whom he had been dining the night before, would act as a guide.

They all went back to Bellini's that night and toasted the new arrangement. Huw told the restaurant manager that Tim and his family could dine there as often as they liked, and that all their bills were to be charged to his own account.

The office and the hotline gave Tim a new sense of purpose. Offers of help were coming from Britain too, and soon a team of helpers was converging on Roppongi. "We were getting these people calling all the time," said Tim. "Most of them were well-meaning, but some of them were chancers. We weren't in the best state of mind to distinguish between the two." One self-styled "private detective" came out from Britain for a week, interviewed a lot of hostesses, and presented a bill for $18,000. (It was paid, like many of the expenses, by Brian Malcolm, the wealthy businessman who was married to Tim's sister.) More useful was Adam Whittington, a young Australian barman and former soldier who had trained as a bodyguard and was a friend of Samantha Burman. Adam was small, sandy haired, and unobtrusive; he would end up spending weeks in Tokyo, conducting his own discreet enquiries. He often teamed up with two Japanese reporters, both fluent

English-speakers, who gave much of their own time to the hunt for Lucie: Toshi Maeda of the *Japan Times* and Kentaro Katayama of the private television company TBS.

Tim gave another press conference at the embassy and unveiled the Lucie Blackman Hotline. The British airline Virgin Atlantic paid for flyers and posters to be printed, carrying the telephone number. With a base established and a team assembled, there was leisure now to draw breath and to consider the most important question of all: What on earth had become of Lucie?

■ ■ ■

"At no point back then did I allow myself to think that Lucie might no longer be alive," Tim said. "I couldn't contemplate that. Everything would have just stopped." This possibility having been blocked out, there wasn't much that could positively be said. Lucie had gone out for a meeting with a man; in her conversations with Louise that day, she had sounded happy and relaxed. The phone call from Akira Takagi was obviously a hoax, a red herring lobbed by someone who wanted to throw the investigation off the scent. But it proved that someone knew where Lucie was and strengthened the assumption that she was being held against her will. But by whom? And where?

The obvious person to start with was Lucie's boyfriend, the American marine Scott Fraser. No one who met Scott found him to be anything but straightforward, and his alibi was unimpeachable: throughout the day of Lucie's disappearance, he had been on duty aboard the USS *Kitty Hawk*. Two other interviews were of the highest priority: with Lucie's best friend, Louise Phillips, and Kenji Suzuki, her most avid customer and number-one dōhan.

Sophie knew the password to Lucie's e-mail account. She quickly printed out its contents and handed them to the police. The correspondence with Ken stood out. It was plain that he had developed a crush on Lucie; obvious too was the suppressed jealousy and peevishness of his last few messages. But the police assured Tim that they had interviewed Ken and eliminated him as a suspect. Louise, on the other hand, was being questioned every day. Her constant presence at the police station, and her coolness towards the Blackmans, kindled the family's resentment and suspicion.

To the most crucial parts of the story, Louise was the only witness. There was no reason to believe that she was making anything up, but parts of her story were suspiciously vague. The details of the telephone call from Akira Takagi were strange beyond anyone's capacity for invention, and Louise's delay in reporting the disappearance and informing the family could be explained as the result of simple panic and confusion. But why didn't she know more about the man whom Lucie had gone out to meet that day?

Louise and Lucie had been best friends for a decade. They worked together, ate and drank together, and shared a living space the size of a large cupboard. And—among everyone who knew her—Lucie was notorious for her garrulousness. "She couldn't tell a story in under eighty thousand words—it was impossible for her," said Sophie. "It was painful, the amount of detail she would give you." Surely, with a dōhan the next day, and the promise of a mobile phone from a new and wealthy customer, Lucie would be bubbling with anticipation about the man she was going to meet. And yet Louise insisted that she had no idea who he was.

Tim and Sophie implored Louise to search her memory about the men whom Lucie had entertained before her disappearance. Ken Suzuki? No, Louise said, Ken was "a sweetheart" who could never do anything sinister. What about the old Photo Man, Watanabe? But that was even more unthinkable. Then there was the Mr. Kowa who had suggested a dōhan the week before Lucie disappeared. "Not Kowa," Louise said. "It wouldn't be Kowa."

Dozens of calls began to come in to the Lucie Hotline. Many were from journalists requesting interviews; the rest were a jumble. With the help of Huw Shakeshaft's staff, they were all assiduously translated and logged.

- Sighting of a girl at Kagoshima Airport who looked like Lucie. She was holding a small bag and got into a silver Mercedes.
- Mumbled, unintelligible speech with laughter.
- A Japanese man saw a few Western girls in a car. A girl who looked like Lucie showed him numbers on her hands, apparently asking him to call the number she indicated. When dialed, the number was nonexistent.
- Sighting of Lucie on 1 July at 12.30 p.m. on Mt. Fuji. She was wearing a one-piece white dress.
- No information, but caller was moved by family's devoted care for Lucie.
- Mumbled, unintelligible speech with laughter.
- Male, sounded young and embarrassed. Wants to go on a date with Sophie. Said Sophie was cool.

The calls came from every corner of the country. Each was returned and followed up, sometimes with great trouble. One tip gave the address of an apartment in the northern island of Hokkaido, where Lucie had been spotted. Adam and Tania flew five hundred miles to investigate but found the place empty and abandoned. Even when the information was detailed, it was of little help. Time and again, all over the Japanese archipelago, well-meaning and public-spirited people were noticing tall blond foreign women and wondering whether they might be the girl on the missing-person poster. But in the absence of any more precise information, what was to be done about that?

After a while, Tim and his helpers began to suspect that to many Japanese, light-haired foreigners all looked the same. One day, Sophie and Adam were on the main Roppongi road showing photographs of Lucie to passersby. Everyone was polite and sympathetic; some of the shopkeepers took posters to display in their windows. But one pair of Japanese girls reacted with electrified excitement. Yes, they said, they had seen the girl in the photograph—in fact, they had seen her just moments ago in a shop across the road. With racing hearts, Sophie and Adam ran across the street with one of the girls, who pointed through the shop window. A tall, fair European woman was standing in front of a refrigerator of soft drinks. "That's her, that's her!" shouted the girl. The woman turned around— and it was Josephine Burr, Tim's partner, twenty years older than Lucie, who had been quietly and obliviously shopping for her lunch.

■ ■ ■

Jane Blackman had never had any urge to go out to Japan. For one thing, she had sixteen-year-old Rupert to look after, and she hated the idea of cameras and press conferences and questions. When reporters called, she put the phone down or closed the door in their faces. "If you are a parent, if you have a very close relationship with your child, then maybe you have some idea of what I am going through," she said in her one public statement. "I have no desire to speak with the press about how I am feeling." Jane was not sleeping, and hardly eating, although she continued to see her reflexology patients. She would drink brandy at breakfast to get through the morning. She kept in touch with Sophie by telephone and e-mail, although after their last disastrous exchange she and Tim did not attempt to communicate directly. From Sevenoaks, there was little of practical use that Jane could contribute. But it was unbearable to be doing nothing.

Perhaps because of her own interest in the spiritual, Jane gave more credence than anyone else to the possibility that her daughter had indeed joined a "newly risen religion," and she spent fruitless hours learning about Japanese cults. Early on, a couple of her patients offered to put her in touch with mediums, and soon a series of psychics, healers, and channelers were calling of their own accord. "They'd say, 'If you'll pay for it, I'll travel out to Japan and find Lucie,'" Jane told me. "And I remember thinking, 'Well, if you're so psychic, why d'you need to travel there at all?'" But in the absence of anything else to do, Jane ended up spending a lot of time with people who claimed to have supernatural gifts.

There was a man named Keith, who had "worked closely" with the Metropolitan Police on "several" missing-person cases, and Betty, a medium, healer, poet, and "vitamin/mineral therapist." Jane drove as far as the Lake District to meet one lady spiritualist; later, she would receive tape recordings of her seances, full of moaning and crying and the honking of trumpets blown by invisible spirits. One psychic achieved his connection to the spirit world by holding a ring of Lucie's; another dowsed over a map of Japan. Jane wrote long e-mails to Sophie setting out the information that each of them provided. It was profuse, optimistic, bizarrely detailed, and uselessly vague.

> Lucie is being held in a run-down house by a sewage works.
> She is on a small island owned by the yakuza.
> She is in a Georgian building with servants and gaming tables.
> She was taken there in a rusty green van.

She was taken there in a floating gin palace.

He captor is a man with bad skin and a scar on his right cheek.

Her captor is a Japanese woman with a single plait.

Louise knows more than she is letting on. Don't trust her!

One of the Japanese police is bent. Don't trust him!

They are Japanese mafia.

They are an Arab organisation.

Lucie's hair has been cropped.

Lucie is being drugged.

Lucie is not being physically harmed.

She sailed from Yokohama.

I am getting the name Kiriashi.

Where is Okenhowa?

What is Tishumo, Toshimo or Tushima?

Look for the crossroads with the fountain and the temple nearby.

Check the phone bill.

Choose the second private detective.

The man, he keeps snakes.

On a bare shoulder, I see the tattoo of a rose.

Tim was not immune to the claims of such people. An elderly Australian dowser known as Mahogany Bob flew out from Queensland, his expenses paid by a British tabloid newspaper. He carried a pair of divining rods that were supposed to rotate and cross when the trail was warm. For several days, Tim, Sophie, Adam, and Tania drove around Tokyo with him, knocking on doors wherever the rods wobbled. They talked their way into private homes, offices, and even on board a cargo ship docked in Tokyo Bay, but with no result. Mahogany Bob grew increasingly tired, and after a few days, he announced that Lucie appeared to be dead, that there was nothing more he could do, and flew home.

Jane had the idea of flying a hypnotist out to Tokyo. The point would be to put Louise into a trance in an effort to find out what she really knew. But it came to nothing. "I feel as if I am completely losing my sense of reality with all this," she wrote in an e-mail to Sophie. "Please let me know what is going on as I feel so alone." But at the end of July there was still nothing to tell.

In Britain, tabloid newspaper attention was dominated by an even more wretched story: Sarah Payne, an eight-year-old Sussex girl, had disappeared on the same day as Lucie and was found raped and murdered two weeks later. In the Diamond Hotel, the journalists began to settle up their bills and check out, first the expensive television crews and then the newspaper reporters and photographers. The interest of the Japanese media was dwindling too. Tim and Sophie's weekly press conferences drew smaller and smaller audiences. Even their calculated display of emotion failed to excite much interest.

Tim asked the Tokyo Metropolitan Police to take part in a joint press conference; they declined. He wrote to Tony Blair, asking him to send "MI6 officers or Scotland Yard CID" to look for Lucie. "You know how sometimes you have a nightmare, dreaming of some terrible thing happening to you?" Tim said. "And you know the relief when you wake up, wipe the sweat off your face and think, 'I'm glad that was just a dream'? My situation is reversed."

In a few days, it would be an entire month since Lucie had disappeared. It was as if she had been swallowed up by a hole in the ground. And then August came, the hottest and most torpid month of the Japanese year, and everything began to happen all at once.

9. THE FLICKERING LIGHT

Tim and Sophie were sitting in the Azabu Police Station one afternoon when a junior officer bustled in and began to speak in urgent tones to Superintendent Mitsuzane. A folder of documents was presented and gravely examined. After a whispered discussion, the superintendent placed one of them on the table in front of the Blackmans. He kept the top part of it obscured; all they could see was the very bottom of the page.

It was Lucie's handwritten signature. And yet it was not by Lucie. The signature was an attempt at an imitation of Lucie's hand, close enough that it must have been copied from an original but not close enough to fool her father and sister.

It was late July, and the letter had just been delivered, having been postmarked in Chiba prefecture the day before. It was a word-processed, printed letter, written in English, purporting to be from Lucie and addressed to her family. "I have disappeared by my own free will and I do not wish to be found," it said. "Don't worry about me. I'm fine. I want you to return to England and I'll call you there." Tim and Sophie had no more than a glimpse of a few lines, but it was obvious that the language was stilted and unnatural, and no more Lucie's than the signature. The other giveaway was the date at the top of the first page. It was July 17, 2000, Tim's forty-seventh birthday. Lucie never forgot a family birthday, and yet it was unmentioned in the letter.

It was another hoax. But what did it mean? The police said that it contained "information that could only have been known to Lucie"—apparently detailed references to her various debts. So that meant that she was alive—didn't it? Or did it prove only that she had been alive, and in the hands of the writer, between her disappearance and the forging of this strange letter?

Tim and Sophie had sworn that they would not leave Japan without Lucie. But it had become impossible to stay. It was not only the time off work, the separation from friends and family, and the financial burden of living in the world's most expensive city. The mental pressure was unsupportable; Tim had the sensation that, unnoticed by those around him, he was silently going mad. So they agreed to work in relays of two weeks at a time; to maintain a family presence in Tokyo but to alternate, so that Sophie would leave as Tim arrived, and vice versa.

Tim flew back to Britain with Josephine Burr on August 4. It was three and a half weeks since he had gone out to Tokyo, and thirty-four days since Lucie had gone missing. From Heathrow Airport, they took the train to Portsmouth and then the ferry to their home in the town of Ryde, on the Isle of Wight. Tim and Jo lived in a big old vicarage on a hill above the sea, full of the rowdy energy of Jo's four teenage children. But the pleasure of being home was stifled by the horror of Lucie's disappearance.

The next day, a Saturday, Tim received a telephone call from a man who introduced himself as Mike Hills.

Tim had an indistinct memory of having spoken briefly to Mr. Hills several weeks earlier. At the time he had been just one more stranger offering help and hope, although more intriguing than most. His voice had immediately identified him as a Londoner, but he lived in the Netherlands. He had explained that he had "contacts" in Japan, some of them in the "underworld," who might be able to help Tim find Lucie. Numbed and bewildered by the parade of psychics, dowsers, private detectives, and other Lucie spotters, Tim had listened politely but given it little thought.

But now Mike Hills was on the phone again, with a more detailed, and extraordinary, story to tell. He worked, he said, in "import/export" and did a lot of business in Japan. Specifically, he sold guns, which were purchased by middlemen in Tokyo before being sold on to the yakuza. This trade, he matter-of-factly explained, occurred with the connivance of certain government officials in Tokyo, but recently a difficulty had arisen. Business was being hampered by the large and active inquiry into Lucie's disappearance. Questions were being asked, and investigative noses were being poked into activities that were usually ignored by the police. The squeeze was making the denizens of the Tokyo underworld unusually cautious.

A "consignment of small arms," for example, dispatched by Mike Hills, was stuck in a "bonded store" and could not be released because the customs officers were nervous about accepting the usual bribe. The Lucie mystery was making everyone edgy. Mike Hills's arms-dealer friends wanted her to be found and sent home as soon as possible so that they could get on with their business. And, according to Hills, they had the wherewithal to find her. It would cost money, he told Tim over the phone, but he believed that he could help to get Lucie back.

"It was very difficult to take in," Tim remembered. "I'd just got back from those awful weeks in Tokyo. I was jet-lagged, and exhausted, and very, very unhappy. And here's this Cockney bloke on the end of a phone in Holland somewhere with this staggering story. He said, 'Look, don't make a decision now. But let's get together in person and talk about it.'"

They arranged to meet the following Tuesday, in three days' time, across the English Channel in the Belgian port of Ostend.

The next day Mike Hills called again with stirring news. He had made inquiries with his "man on the inside"—a Mr. Nakani—who had ascertained that Lucie was indeed alive and well. She had been kidnapped and sold (by whom, it was not clear) as part of a trade in foreign women carried out by people connected to, but not a part of, the yakuza. Mr. Nakani, it seemed, knew people who knew Lucie's captors, and there was no doubt that, with their help, she could be bought back. The whole operation would cost $50,000, some of which would have to be paid in advance. Mike Hills would be transferring the first installment of $12,500 on Monday from his own private funds, so Tim was to bring this money with him to their meeting on Tuesday as reimbursement.

"She's still in Tokyo," said Mike. "They will get her back, Tim. Your daughter will come home very soon."

Mike Hills also sent a fax bearing a photograph of himself. It was indistinct, but it showed lined, ruined skin, a regretful smile full of crooked teeth—a grimy, likable, untrustworthy face.

For Tim, this was a great deal of information to absorb. But there was no question of ignoring it. "We did not have a clue where Lucie was," he said. "Then this guy comes forward and says he has information about where she might be. You would have to be pretty brave to say, 'Well, sorry, no.'"

Along with excitement and a strangled sense of relief, Tim felt frightened. He called Adam Whittington, the young Australian bodyguard, who had just returned to London himself, and asked him to come with him to Ostend. They took the fast catamaran from Dover. As instructed, Tim was carrying $12,500 in cash, which he had withdrawn from the bank the day before. "It was so way beyond my life experience," said Tim. "I just didn't know what to expect. This could have been some kind of elaborate trap. It could have been someone who wanted to bump me off because of what I was doing in Japan.

It could have been anything. It was like something on TV, except that on TV you know the thing will be resolved by the time the news starts at ten o'clock, because it always is. In reality, you don't know what the hell will happen next."

Mike Hills was waiting for them in the ferry terminal. "He had a dark suit on, thinning hair slicked right back," Adam remembered. "He was about fifty-five maybe, and he looked like he'd had a hard life. His teeth were disgusting, all black, like he'd been a chain-smoker or had a disease. Tim introduced me as a friend or a cousin, and he said that we could go to a café just round the corner."

On the way, they passed a marina, and Mike began to talk about Tim's great passion: yachting. "He had this shabby suit on, very down-at-heel, but he knew what he was talking about when it came to boats," Tim said. "He talked about how he'd been skippering on a Swan 42 one time, and how they'd replaced the deck. I asked him what they'd used and he talked about teak laid on ply, crosscut teak. All very detailed, technical and accurate—no bullshit there. I got the impression he was ex–merchant navy, and very bright-eyed and sharp behind this rather tatty exterior."

At one point Tim commented that Mike was not what he had expected and that he did not fit the image of a wealthy international arms dealer.

Mike smiled. "That's the last thing I want to look like," he said.

The café was dim and narrow, with heavy leather chairs; its owner greeted Mike warmly. Even before the coffee had been ordered, he was talking business. The situation in Japan, it became clear, had moved on since the last conversation—faster and further than Tim was prepared for.

Mike's men in Tokyo knew who had Lucie and where she was. They would pay $50,000 in exchange for her, and after she had been handed over, they would administer a beating to her captors "to prevent this sort of thing happening again." And all of this was going to happen in the next few days.

Mike said that Tim and Adam both needed to return quickly to Japan and to have a second payment of $25,000 ready there to be paid on Lucie's release. Secrecy was essential. Tim had too prominent a media profile, so the point of contact would have to be Adam, who should carry a dedicated mobile phone to be used only for communications with Mike and his intermediaries. Once Lucie was free and safely back home, the last payment of $12,500 would be made.

Mike was talking as if it had all been agreed, and Lucie was all but home, as if, in just a few days, with the processing of a couple of bank transfers, the pain and nausea of the past month would be dissolved. But Tim was still filled with doubt and confusion. Who was Mike Hills? What guarantees were there that any of this was true? From inside his shabby suit, Mike produced a copy of his passport, a water bill addressed to his home in the Dutch town of Breskens, and the name and telephone number of a friend, identified as Billy, who was said to have worked with him in import/export and who would vouch for him.

Surname:	Hills
Given names:	Michael Joseph
Date of birth:	26 June 43
Place of Birth:	London

Tim observed that these documents did not go very far in proving his bona fides.

"I understand your concern, but what other assurance can I give to you?" Mike asked. "I live in Holland, so the only people I can give you are here, or in South Africa, Spain . . . I feel like I'm applying for a bloody job."

Mike told Tim, "I'm sorry if this is not to your liking, but

I am not going to pay all of this money on my own. I feel you should pay if not all, then a part. I think you would do the same in my place, as I am willing to use what is around me to help you . . . The only guarantee I give is that if you agree to the terms, and if everyone does as they are asked, there is no reason why this thing cannot be over."

Before handing over the money, Tim hand wrote a contract setting out the terms of the agreement, to which both signed their names.

"What happens if things don't go right?" Tim asked.

"If my instructions are not carried out," Mike replied, "I will personally rip off someone's head."

Tim told me, "It was ridiculous. I was already picturing a dark street corner, and a car pulling up, and Lucie being pushed out towards us by the elbow, and a hand taking a case of money. It was as live as that. I could see the whole scenario. Lucie's face distraught, raddled by the drugs she'd been given . . ."

He reached into his own briefcase and handed over to Mike Hills the wad of 125 hundred-dollar bills.

Young Adam Whittington was the right person to take to a meeting like this: calm, quiet, shrewd, observant. He had been a soldier, a bodyguard, and a barman, and would end up as a police officer in central London; he was nobody's fool. On the catamaran back to Dover, Tim asked Adam whether he had made a wise decision. "Mike said all the right things," Adam told me later. "He knew exactly what Tim was going to ask; he never hesitated at all. All the time they were talking, I was just listening to him, trying to pick faults in the story: Is he bullshitting? Is he a con man? But there was no reason not to believe him. If I was Tim, and if it had been my daughter, I would have done exactly the same."

The following day, Tim and Adam boarded a flight back to Tokyo. It was less than a week since they had left; the white rabbit was still playing the piano at the Diamond Hotel. Tim went to the British embassy and told them the outline of the Mike Hills story: that an intermediary was in contact with Lucie's kidnappers and that she was expected to be released very soon. Far from being skeptical, the diplomats responded with concern. A room was readied in the embassy compound where Lucie could be taken care of, and a doctor was put on standby. Adam rented a mobile phone and Tim faxed the number to Mike Hills. "We will not give the number to anyone else," he wrote. "So when it goes off I will probably have a heart attack. We are very ready for this operation, Mike, so I hope you can pull it off. Could be your friend for life."

The only thing left to do then was to wait.

It was a struggle to fill the time. The usual diversions—interviews with journalists and press conferences—had been strictly forbidden by Mike Hills. Tim went into Huw Shakeshaft's office, where the volunteers were still at work, monitoring the calls on the Lucie Hotline. They were the usual mixture of the useless, the irrelevant, and the bizarre.

- Sighting of a girl resembling Lucie on 28 July at 18.00 at the Just Co store in Nagoya. She had a perm and was holding hands with a man who was about 177cm tall. They got into an old silver car on the fourth floor of a car park.
- A child with a message of encouragement.
- Unnamed caller expressed the opinion that Matakado island in Ehime prefecture is a suspicious place.
- Sighting of a girl resembling Lucie in a tent at Fujisawa beach. There were a lot of Mexicans in the area having a party.

The Japanese police were almost completely uncommunicative. A prime ministerial secretary replied on behalf of Tony

Blair, declining Tim's suggestion that MI6 agents be sent to Tokyo. But Mike Hills was reassuring, and Tim spoke to him every day. "That was one thing that was so persuasive about Mike," he said. "He was always available. He had one of those telephones which you could use anywhere in the world, those super-roaming quad-band intergalactic gizmos which, back then, were quite a thing. He was always phoning with updates. I never had any problem getting hold of him." Everything was in hand, Mike said; all that was necessary was patience. But it was hard to think about anything other than the small, conventional mobile phone that Adam carried in his pocket.

Tim and Adam passed the time in Roppongi, drinking in the Sports Cafe and dining at Bellini's. It was there one evening that the contact telephone suddenly began to ring. Tim and Adam looked at one another. Adam fumbled to answer it. "I picked it up and said hello," Adam remembered, "and there was a Japanese guy at the other end, starting to say something, and then, after a split second, the line disconnected. I said, 'Hello? Hello?' but he'd gone. Tim and I, our eyes lit up: this must be them, finally getting in contact. But the phone never rang again."

After a few days without any word from the kidnappers, Tim was becoming impatient. Mike apologized. The meeting to hand over the second installment of money had not taken place as scheduled, he explained; the intermediaries for the people holding Lucie had simply not turned up. But the lines of communication were still open, and Mike offered to get hold of a recent photograph of Lucie and a lock of her hair, to prove beyond question that the story was true.

Then, after Tim had been back in Tokyo a week, Mike called again with bad news: Lucie was no longer in Japan. The details were precise. Alarmed by the intense interest in the case, her captors had decided that the safest thing was to get rid of her. They had found three men willing to buy her. The sale had been transacted at a place called Tenkai. Soon after, Lucie had been smuggled onto a container ship called the *Leo J*. She was with four other young Western women, who were destined to be put on the market as sex slaves. But Mike was not ready to give up. His people had been tracking Lucie's progress—one of them had even managed to get onto the ship and would report on its progress and the well-being of its human cargo.

Tim put down the phone in a turmoil of irritation and confusion. Then he called a friend who contacted Lloyd's Register and inquired about the existence of a merchant vessel called the *Leo J*. To Tim's amazement, the ship really did exist.

MV *Leo J*
Gross Register Tonnage: 12,004 tons
Flag: Antigua & Barbuda
Manager/Owner: Mare Schiffahrtsgesellschaft MBH & Co.,
    Haren, Germany.

The *Leo J* had indeed left Osaka on August 10, then docked at the Japanese ports of Kobe, Moji, Tokuyama, and then Hong Kong. It was now on its way to Manila.

The following morning, there was a fax from Mike containing a page of black-and-white photographs. They were almost completely indistinct, but one appeared to picture the inside of a house, and another showed three smiling Asian men seated on a train with a briefcase. "This place is Tenkai," Mike had written below the first. Below the second: "Bag with money. They are on their way to Tenkai."

"My People are moveing there buts [*sic*] now it seems," the attached page read. "They have paid for some answers and now they are following them up."

On August 24, a British businessman, who insisted on remaining anonymous, contacted the *Japan Times* offering a reward of £100,000 for information leading to Lucie's safe return.

A few days later, Mike's source on the *Leo J* passed on more dismaying news: the five sex slaves, including Lucie, had been transferred to another vessel, the *Aramac*, which was now on its way to Australia. The rescue plan was hastily adapted—the new ship would be intercepted at the city of Darwin, and Mike would fly there himself to meet Adam. For this he would need another $10,000, to cover his own expenses and those of his "people."

Tim transferred the money to Mike's bank in the Netherlands.

Adam flew to Darwin and checked into the hotel where they had agreed to meet.

Mike never appeared.

At the port of Darwin, nobody could tell Adam anything about a ship called the *Aramac*. Tim tried calling the quad-band phone but could not get through. Eventually an e-mail arrived from Mike explaining that he was not in Australia but in Hong Kong.

He sounded tense and exasperated. The problem was the £100,000 reward, which had once again stirred up anxieties among Mike's people. "The Darwin end is now off thanks to the 100,000-pound offer, people [should] know the damage they can do making that kind of offer," he wrote scoldingly. "That has changed a lot of the other people's plans and things are not as they were before . . . Please before you say anything to people ask me first because we don't want things getting hot."

A few more days passed. Mike called from Hong Kong to say that he was going to meet his "man on the inside" to collect Lucie.

He called again to report that the man had been murdered in his car.

Adam said to Tim, "He's playing games. He's really bullshitting us now. He's making us go round the world; he's not producing anything. He's always asking for more money."

Rather impatiently, Mike agreed to send Tim proof that he really was in Hong Kong, as he insisted. Tim asked what had happened to the promised photograph of Lucie and the lock of her hair. They were waiting for Mike in Holland, Mike said, in a private PO box accessible only to him.

The conversations went back and forth. They went on for weeks. In Tokyo, meanwhile, the Japanese police were slowly tracking down leads. Tim and Sophie alternately came and went. Adam, and the few close friends who knew about Mike Hills, told Tim that he was being conned. At the end of August, he flew back to the Isle of Wight, having failed once again to bring Lucie home. At least once every day he spoke to Mike Hills, who talked of his struggles to reestablish contact with the sex slavers. But he never again sent any money to Mike.

One evening in the middle of September, a month and a half after their first and only encounter, Tim was driving home after a day of meetings. On a whim, he dialed Mike, not on the quad-band roaming telephone but at his home in Holland. A woman answered. Tim put on an impersonation of a Japanese speaking English.

"Haroo," he said. "Can I speak with Mistar Hirruz?"

"I'm awfully sorry," said Mrs. Hills. "He's just popped out."

"He no Hong Kong?"

"No, no, he's here in Holland. He's just gone down the shop. He'll be back in a mo."

Tim hung up. A few moments later, Mike called.

"I just had my wife on the phone from Holland," he said.

"She just got a strange call from someone. Sounded Japanese. You don't . . . D'you know who that was?"

"No idea, Mike, no idea," said Tim. "Where are you, by the way? Are you still in Hong Kong?"

"Tim," said Mike, in tones of exasperation, "I told you before, I'm telling you again: *I'm in Hong Kong.*"

Tim had bought a digital tape recorder in Narita Airport and after this exchange he began recording these conversations. But it became harder and harder to get through to Mike Hills. Eventually, he stopped calling altogether.

Mike was a con man, of course. His story was all lies.

In October 2000, Tim got a call from another stranger. His name was Brian Winder, and he was the father of a twenty-four-year-old investment banker named Paul. In March, Paul Winder had been trekking across the jungles of Colombia with a botanist friend. They were hunting for rare orchids, but one week they disappeared in the area close to the border with Panama known as the Darién Gap. Nothing more had been heard from them. It was assumed that they had been kidnapped by one of the various groups of bandits, revolutionaries, and drug smugglers that operate in the lawless area. His parents were beginning to resign themselves to Paul's death, when they got an intriguing call at their family home in Essex. The man at the other end of the line spoke plausibly of "underworld contacts" in Panama who knew the whereabouts of their son. Brian paid £5,000 to the man, who had bad teeth and a Cockney accent, but nothing had ever come of it, and no one had any idea where Paul Winder was.

Mike Hills hadn't even bothered to use a different name.

The Winders had been to the Essex police and now Tim went to see them too. He made a long statement setting out the whole story and handed over his tape recordings and the collected fax and e-mail correspondence from Hills. Charges were filed and an arrest warrant issued, but Mike's whereabouts were unclear. He seemed to have left Holland for Alicante in Spain. There was talk of extraditing him, but after a few months, Tim heard nothing more.

To the joy of his family, Paul Winder and his friend were released by their guerrilla captors after nine months of captivity and arrived back in Britain in time for Christmas 2000.

Tim had almost forgotten about the whole affair when he got a phone call from one of the Essex detectives two years later. A pair of traffic policemen in central London had been questioning an illegally parked motorist and asked to see his driver's licence. When they ran the details through the computer, they discovered that Michael Joseph Hills had an outstanding arrest warrant against his name.

Mike went on trial at Chelmsford Crown Court in April 2003, charged with two counts of obtaining property by deception. His address was given as a bed-and-breakfast in Waterloo. He pleaded guilty and said that he had needed to pay for treatment for his wife, who was dying of cancer. But the judge said that there was no evidence that this was how the money had been spent. Mike Hills's criminal record listed convictions for deception and theft dating back to the 1970s. He was sent to prison for three and a half years.

Before sentencing, Mike said, "At the end of the day, it was me that took the money, no one else. I'd like to be in a position to pay these people back. It would be nice."

Journalists called Tim about the verdict and quoted him saying the kind of things that people are expected to say in such circumstances: terrible, evil, despicable, abominable, preying on misfortune. All of this was true. "But even at the time," Tim told me later, "I was aware that without this candle flicker of hope I would have been in a terrible state. This single thing, this safety line that I was holding on to, was actually keeping me buoyant. All the time, there was a faint possibility that this man might bring Lucie back. It kept my head above water."

Tim understood that there was more to it than a simple story of an evil con man and an innocent victim. He had needed Mike Hills, and, in some sense, out of grief and need, he had created him. Mike was Tim's version of the psychics to whom Jane was so susceptible. One promised deliverance based on supernatural insights; the other offered cruder and more palpable tools—bags of cash, guns, beatings.

"When I realized it was all lies, that was my concern," Tim said, "that this lifeline had been wrenched out of my hands. I wasn't concerned about the money, or whether I'd been conned. I felt no hurt about having been targeted or being the victim of a crime. Those things weren't of any interest or importance to me at all. The only soreness I had was the soreness of my hand, where this safety line had been wrenched out of it."

This was what I admired in Tim, and what was also so off-putting about him: even in confusion and grief, he had the capacity to step back and scrutinize his own situation in all its psychological complexity. How many men in his situation—humiliated, as many people would see it, by a con man—would have the courage and clear-sightedness to say, "It was money well spent"?

"I didn't feel angry," Tim said. "I just felt as if I was falling into an abyss—no lifeline and no hope. Where were we going to find it now, the next bit of hope?"

10. S & M

Whatever the answer, it had to lie in Roppongi.

Another family in similar circumstances would have shunned the area, repelled by the place where their sister and daughter had come to harm. But the Blackmans spent many nights there—because it seemed to be the maze where Lucie had lost her way, and also because it had worked its fascination upon them.

August was the height of the Japanese summer. Even in the center of Tokyo, invisible cicadas whined and sneered in the trees. The air conditioners pumped out hot air, making the streets more oppressive than ever, and the neon of the lights diffused to a glow in the soft wet air. After dinner in Bellini's on Huw Shakeshaft's tab, Tim and Sophie and their helpers would disperse among the bars and clubs, looking for traces of Lucie.

Tim visited Club Cadeau and One Eyed Jack's, and one of the clubs where girls danced around a pole and stripped to their bikini bottoms. One night he dropped in at Casablanca, where Lucie had worked. "The whole thing was weird," he said. "This cramped little room, with these fairly mediocre Western girls and very animated Japanese guys pretending to be able to speak English. It was sleazy and grim. But I didn't relate Lucie to it, because I knew that she never related to it herself. If she'd been saying, 'It's really fantastic, I love it!' I'd've thought,

'What's the girl on?' But she never liked it, and in a strange way that was comforting."

The Blackmans met with an ambivalent reception from the practitioners of the water trade. Everyone recognized Tim and Sophie from the television, and there was a degree of sympathy and human concern. But Lucie's disappearance was bringing unwelcome illumination to businesses that were accustomed to operating in the dimness of semilegality. Practices that had gone unquestioned for decades, such as the hiring of foreign girls on tourist visas, were facing uncomfortable scrutiny. Plenty of the hostesses and barmen and mama-sans would not talk to the Blackmans, and there was little sign that Superintendent Mitsuzane and his detectives were pressing them very hard either. This made Tim furious. He became convinced that there was a "conspiracy of silence" uniting the police and the bar owners. "If Lucie had gone off for an arranged meeting with a customer, someone at that club knows who it is," he said. "They've got to cut across the imaginary boundary that exists between the authorities and the people who run the hostess industry." He had a suggestion, which wouldn't have won him any friends in Roppongi. "Gather up the people in the club—the manager, the owner, and the girls—stick them in prison for four to six weeks, and let them decide if they want to talk about it," he said. "And then do it again until something happens."

Some people were scandalized by Tim's nights out in Roppongi. Nobody would say it to his face, but among some of the Japanese journalists, and a few people at the British embassy, there were mutterings that Tim was "enjoying" himself a bit too much. Even those who were best disposed towards him were puzzled sometimes. "I like Tim, I really do, but sometimes the way he behaved was just . . . strange," said one Japanese man who spent long hours of his own time helping the Blackmans. "Like, we'd be out in some hostess club, supposed to be talking to the manager or the mama-san about Lucie, and about the girls who worked there and what they knew, and could they help us. And instead of asking serious questions about his daughter, Tim would be, like, checking out the girls. We'd have a drink and he'd whisper to me, 'Look at her!' or 'She's gorgeous.' And I didn't know what to say."

Sinister facts became evident during those nights out in Roppongi. One was the abundance of illegal drugs.

In Japan, the penalties for possession of even small quantities of soft drugs are harsh, and they are far less a feature of youth culture than in Europe and America. But in Roppongi there were Israeli and Iranian dealers who would sell cannabis, cocaine, and even heroin. "Everybody dabbled," Huw Shakeshaft said, and by "everybody" he meant everyone he knew: the traders and barmen and hostesses. "Barry" was the euphemism for powdered cocaine—after the throaty American singer Barry *White*. "Jeremy," more puzzlingly, meant the same thing, as Huw explained. "Jeremy is Jeremy Clarkson—because he presented a program called *Top Gear*. Top Gear: gear. Gear: drugs. Or people would say, 'Are you long?' as in, 'Do you have a "long" trading position in the markets?'" "Are you long?" meant "Have you got any cocaine?"

The most popular substance among hostesses was *shabu*, known in English as ice or crystal meth, a potent amphetamine that could be snorted, smoked, injected, or even inserted in lumps into the anus. The rush it imparted could transform a stilted conversation with a dreary customer into a thrilling and hilarious flirtation. Shabu was the only thing that got some hostesses through the night. Around Tim and Sophie, people in Roppongi tended to be careful, but one night Adam Whittington, with characteristic unobtrusiveness, was drinking in a bar with Louise and a group of her friends. One of the girls—not Louise—invited him into the toilets and offered him shabu to snort; Adam declined.

Did Lucie take drugs? Could the man she was meeting have been offering to give her something more than a mobile phone? Louise denied it, but Louise's recollections were so hazy. Lucie's family all agreed that she could not have been a serious user, but she had had one lethally druggy boyfriend and had worked in an environment—the City of London in the mid-1990s—where casual use of cocaine was epidemic. An early line in her diary jauntily referred to her and Louise's shopping expeditions in Tokyo and their "never ending quest for . . . music (anything but Craig David), postcards & drugs!" To her friends, she had always seemed more of a boozer than a snorter, stoner, or pill popper. But, at the very least, the opportunities had been there.

The second alarming thing was the number of stories about other Western hostesses who had disappeared or been attacked by customers. Many of them were no more than vague rumors, the usual late-night, third-hand anecdotes about the acquaintance of the sister of a friend. But there were a few well-attested cases of foreign girls who had come to grief in Roppongi.

Three years earlier, a twenty-seven-year-old Canadian hostess named Tiffany Fordham had stepped out of a bar after a night in Roppongi and never been seen again. The case remained officially open, but the police had effectively given up. As recently as the spring of 2000, three unnamed New Zealand girls were reported to have escaped by leaping from the window of a second-floor room where they had been held and raped repeatedly by a group of yakuza.

One night Huw Shakeshaft had introduced two friends of his, Isobel Parker, a young Australian, and Clara Mendez, a Canadian. This was during Tim's first visit to Japan; he was in the depths of shock and funk, and the information imparted by the two women passed through him like solid objects through a ghost.

Isobel and Clara were examples of a Roppongi phenomenon: former hostesses who had ended up marrying rich Western bankers whom they had met as customers. Both told similar stories, of dōhan with a wealthy Japanese customer who took them to an apartment by the sea, of drinking a drugged glass of wine, and of regaining consciousness hours later, naked in the man's bed. Isobel Parker had woken up to find the man filming her naked body with a video camera. In a surge of alarm and anger, she had snatched the tape from the machine. Instead of taking it to the police, she had succeeded in blackmailing the man. In return for the video, he had paid her several hundred thousand yen.

Years had passed, and neither girl could remember exactly where she had been taken. But they seemed to be describing the same place—a resort by the sea, with a large number of concrete buildings containing holiday apartments. There had been palm trees there, and the wind had rustled their leaves as it blew off the water.

■■■

One day in August, a Japanese man called the Lucie Hotline in a highly excited and agitated state. His name was Makoto Ono, and he said that he possessed crucial information that could be imparted only in person. Tim and Adam went to see him at an address in Yoyogi, close to the gaijin house where Lucie had lived. The taxi dropped them off in front of a nondescript residential building, and they took the elevator to an apartment on its upper floors. It was no ordinary apartment. One of its rooms had been fitted out with lights, cameras, and beds. Another contained banks of machines for dubbing videotape. Unsavory photographic magazines in Japanese and English lay on the tables, and there were posters of naked women on the walls.

It came to Tim and Adam that they were inside a small pornographic-film studio.

Makoto Ono was a short, stocky man in his early forties, dressed in T-shirt and trainers. There was nothing obviously seedy about him. He had formerly run a small computer business, he explained. Now he was a producer of adult videos. Adam and Tim attempted to remain as nonchalant about all this as Mr. Ono evidently was, but they could not stop their eyes darting towards the open door of the room with the beds and the cameras. But the rest of the studio was quiet. To their disappointment and relief, they understood that no filming was under way at the moment.

Mr. Ono explained that, as well as being a pornographer, he was a sadomasochist. He referred to it as his *shumi*—his hobby or pastime. Like many Japanese hobbyists, he pursued his sadomasochistic interests as a member of a group—an S & M "circle," whose members shared videos, magazines, and fantasies, and who sometimes held orgies together with girls rented for the occasion.

Until ten years ago, he had been a member of a circle run by a man named Ryuji Matsuda, a wealthy businessman from the neighboring port city of Yokohama. He had first met him at a session where like-minded hobbyists pooled resources to hire a few girls (often university students working for pocket money), trussed them up in leather and ropes, and photographed them in a room fitted out as a "dungeon." He had immediately been alarmed by Matsuda, who was what Japanese, borrowing the English word, referred to as a "maniac." His sexual appetites were extreme, and they repelled the more moderately sadistic Ono. All the members of the circle bragged about their exploits—or fantasies—but there was something chilling about the way Matsuda talked. "I have a daughter my-self," Ono said, turning to Tim. "It's a hobby for me, but there is still a line that should not be crossed."

Matsuda's favorite fantasy was to take sadistic sex to its ulti-mate conclusion. He would abduct a woman, he said, a big, blond foreign woman with large breasts, and film the scene as he tortured her to death in his private dungeon.

"As a man," he used to ask Ono, "don't you long to do one big thing, just once in your lifetime?"

"That was ten years ago," Ono said. "Such a childish plan. What kind of a person would do such a thing?"

Ono had fallen in with a new circle of more gentlemanly sadists and cut his ties with the Matsuda group. But he had stayed in touch with one of its remaining members, a man named Akio Takamoto. Like most members of the Matsuda group, he was outwardly a highly respectable figure, a fifty-two-year-old senior manager for Fuji Film, whose head office was a few hundred yards from Roppongi. In mid-July, the week after news of Lucie's disappearance, Takamoto had con-tacted Ono in a state of excitement and anxiety.

"He came to this office, very upset," Ono recalled. "He was jabbering away, saying, 'I must speak to Matsuda.' He kept saying, 'He did it. Finally, Matsuda did it.' Then he said, 'Per-haps there is a video, so we should go together to his place and steal it.'"

With a chill, Ono suddenly understood. His friend Taka-moto believed that the braggart Matsuda had finally enacted his fantasy and kidnapped Lucie Blackman.

Matsuda had recently acquired a new "dungeon," Taka-moto told him, a secret den where he could indulge his enthu-siasms. But rather than showing it off to his S & M chums, he had refused to take anyone there, which Takamoto found suspicious. And once, Takamoto remembered, while elaborat-ing on his kidnap plan, Matsuda had suggested a method of confusing the police—by making out that the missing victim had joined a religious cult.

Ono couldn't deny how likely it seemed. "There's something about Matsuda," he said. "He's the kind of person who would think nothing of killing. He treats women like dolls." After Takamoto had left, Ono went straight to Azabu Police Station and told them the whole story. The detectives listened with interest, took down the names and addresses of everyone he mentioned, and told Ono that they would need to speak to him again.

Takamoto returned to see Ono the following week, full of agitation; again, he expressed his conviction that Matsuda had killed Lucie. Then two weeks passed, and there was no further word from Takamoto, and no word from the police. One morning Ono got a phone call from another acquaintance. Takamoto's wife had been in touch with this man, reporting that her husband had failed to come home from work the night before. Did Ono have any idea where he might be?

Ono did in fact know something that few others did, including Takamoto's family: the respectable Fuji Film executive had a "dungeon" of his own, a small rented apartment a few train stops from his house.

Ono left his porn studio early that afternoon and went to the place.

It was a single room on the second floor of an old and decaying wooden building, the cheapest kind of apartment. Ono knocked, but there was no reply. He tried the door, which opened on to a tiny entryway. A pair of Takamoto's shoes lay side by side, so he must be at home. Ono slid open the paper door that divided the entryway from the apartment room. The first thing he noticed was a strong smell, of cars and latrines. The room was cluttered with piles of books, magazines, and videotapes, and Ono glimpsed the screen of a computer. Then he saw a pair of pale legs beside a cupboard.

It was Takamoto, obviously dead. He was hanging by a rope attached to a wall-mounted hook. He was not dangling but slumped against the wall, his feet trailing the floor; and he was naked from the waist down. The smell was petrol from an overturned can, which had soaked into the tatami mats on the floor, and excrement, apparently human, that was drooling out of Takamoto's mouth.

Ono stepped shakily outside and telephoned the police.

There was one other detail that he immediately registered in the few seconds he was in the room. On the walls, distinctive with their blue borders and white lettering in English and Japanese, were several missing-person posters bearing the smiling face of Lucie Blackman.

Within an hour or two, twenty police officers were on the scene, both uniformed and plainclothes. Ono talked to them at length over the next few days.

They told him that, based on his information, they had summoned Takamoto for questioning just three days earlier, on August 5. It was a Saturday, and the police had not wanted to embarrass him by asking him to be absent from work. Takamoto had told them his fears about Matsuda. The next day he had paid the paltry rent—¥20,000 a month—on his sex den. On Monday, he had said goodbye to his family and gone to work as normal. Sometime between that afternoon and the following day, he had died.

The magazines and videos in the apartment were pornographic; the computer, which was new, contained files of hardcore pornography downloaded from the Internet. Most of the images were of white women in postures of humiliation. The neighbors confirmed that the quiet bespectacled salaryman came by the apartment most days in the early evening, although they had no idea who he was or what he was up to. Rather tentatively, the police concluded that it was an accidental death caused by autoerotic asphyxia, the practice by which a masturbating man temporarily cuts off the supply of oxygen to his brain to intensify the sensation of orgasm. This dangerous game has caused many deaths over the years, although distraught families often prefer to announce publicly that the death was a suicide.

Ono didn't believe it.

Could Takamoto have killed himself out of fear of being exposed as a sadomasochist by the inquiries of the police? But if his aim had been to *avoid* censure and humiliation, why would he end his life in such a grotesque way? And the Lucie posters on the walls—why hadn't Takamoto mentioned them to his friend Ono, since they had talked about the case so much? Had they, in fact, been put up by someone else—after Takamoto's death, perhaps—to put the police off the trail? Could the petrol on the floor have been the beginning of an attempt to burn the place down, by an intruder who found himself suddenly interrupted?

According to Ono, the crucial clue lay in the vilest detail of all, the filth that filled Takamoto's mouth and smeared his face. According to the police, it belonged to the dead man himself. "Ono told us that if you've got someone else's smeared all over you, that's kinky," Adam Whittington recalled later. "But if it's your own, it's a sign of disrespect. It's an insult."

This was why Ono had summoned Tim and Adam: to convey his belief that Matsuda had kidnapped Lucie and had murdered Takamoto because he had guessed the truth.

■ ■ ■

"I certainly met some strange people during the course of this whole thing," Tim told me. "But that was probably the strangest of all. I mean, the whole idea that he was suggesting . . . it couldn't be worse, could it? Perhaps it could . . . At any rate, I was quite dysfunctional by that point, and perhaps that saved me. Because if I'd really taken in what this might have meant for my daughter, and her fate . . . Well, I couldn't take it in, and that was just as well."

But Adam had taken everything in, including the specific information that Mr. Ono had given them as they left: the addresses of the secret dens of both the late Mr. Takamoto and his alleged killer, Mr. Matsuda.

A few days later, Adam set out for Matsuda's dungeon with Yoshi Kuroda, a Japanese journalist who was helping the Blackmans. They parked in a residential area of Yokohama, a neighborhood of low apartment buildings, a dusty, old-fashioned kind of district, where old ladies walked small dogs in the evenings and where you never saw children. From the outside, the building looked less like a torture chamber than a storage shed. A wooden fence surrounded it. After climbing over, Adam could make a circuit of the building concealed from view, as Yoshi kept a nervous watch. There were drapes on the inside of the windows, but between two of them was a gap through which a fraction of the interior could be made out. Adam glimpsed a carpeted floor; videotapes were scattered across it.

A sharp tap with a stone was all that was needed to break the pane. Adam, small and fit, reached through to release the latch, climbed through the window, and let Yoshi in through the front door.

They found themselves inside a single rectangular room; a sheet had been hung rather crudely at one end to conceal a dingy sink. The drapes on the windows filtered out most of the light, but they could make out chairs, a television and video player, and mattresses on the floor. There were pornographic magazines and many, many videotapes. Their labels bore photographs of Japanese and Western women. Most of them were commercially produced, although there were a few that looked homemade. "Then there were sex toys everywhere, littering the place," Adam said. "Dildos, clamps—vile, sick things. Harnesses, straps, and things I'd never seen before. One of them had tubes for inserting inside a woman. It had some kind of clamps to hold the legs apart, and then this tube that must have gone between the legs." Instruments of humiliation and pain, designed for pleasure.

They shuffled through the labels on the videotapes, looking for something that might suggest a connection to Lucie. But there was nothing. The walls were bare: no missing-person posters here. Their hearts were racing, for they found themselves in an authentic dungeon, a place of sexual degradation, the kind of which everyone has heard but that no one ever expects to see for himself. It was unspeakable and bizarre. It was so extreme and unthinkable that it had come to seem inevitable, almost a matter of logic, that it contained the answer to the mystery. So to find it lifeless and empty was an intense disappointment. Her friends had looked everywhere for Lucie, and now they had followed her trail here, to the darkest chamber of the human heart, a world of manacles and excretion and death—and still she was not here. It would have been easier to discover a gang of sadomasochists in mid-orgy, or a coven of witches engaged in a human sacrifice: some palpable, visible evil, something that could be engaged with blows, anything but what confronted them at every corner: the stubborn absence of a girl.

The room was lifeless and unclean. A sheen of dust coated the glossy, textured vibrators and the outspread pages of the magazines. Adam scrutinized the floor, the mattresses, and the sink, looking for blond hair. After that, there was little more to do. Yoshi knocked on a few of the nearby doors, but none of the neighbors knew anything about the place or the man who rented it; none had seen or heard anything suspicious.

Later, Yoshi went alone to the apartment where Takamoto had died. It had been emptied of its contents and cleaned. He even called at the hanged man's former home, three stops down the commuter line that he had taken to work every day. When Takamoto's widow opened the door, Yoshi was appalled by how young and beautiful she was. After introducing himself as a reporter, he didn't know what to say. "I tried to talk to her, but she just cried," he said. "It was so tragic, so sad. He had this wife, and beautiful kids and a beautiful house, and he just died like that. There'd been other journalists there before, and she was desperate. She was begging me, 'Please leave, just leave.' I felt so bad, and I left."

Finally, Yoshi called at the home of Matsuda himself, in a more affluent suburb of Yokohama. He could have rung the bell here too, but instead he took up a discreet position across the road. Eventually Matsuda emerged, a stocky, vigorous-looking man in middle age, with a full round face and a head of bristly hair. Yoshi contemplated approaching him and introducing himself, but he refrained. Instead he took photographs through a long-lensed camera, as Matsuda came out of his front door and drove away.

But what to do with these pictures, or with any of this information? For a few weeks, Ono pestered Tim and Adam with calls and visits, repeating his conviction that Matsuda had to be involved in Lucie's disappearance. But Adam had begun to wonder about him and his motivation. He was persuasive, but who could tell what grudges and feuds might flourish between estranged sadists? "He was like a kid in his own action movie," Adam remembered. "He wanted to get involved in everything. He was getting off on it, to be honest. Towards the end he was quite annoying, trying to run the whole thing, telling us to do this and do that. I would have done something if there was any proper information. But all I had was this Japanese guy spinning on a merry-go-round.

"I went to the police station with Tim, and we told them what Ono had said. But they had all that anyway—the names, the address where Matsuda lived. What they did with it, your guess is as good as mine. When we talked to them about it, there was no reaction at all. They listened, they took some notes, and then they showed us the door."

11. THE MAN-SHAPED HOLE

The first day of September was Lucie's twenty-second birthday. It might have been a day of despair, but the Blackmans made it the occasion for a series of events to invigorate flagging media interest in the case. In Sevenoaks, Jane and Rupert Blackman released one thousand pink and yellow balloons above the town's famous cricket ground, the Vine. Sophie had wanted to do the same thing in Tokyo, but the police refused permission on the grounds that the floating balloons would distract the attention of motorists. Instead, Sophie handed out flyers at Roppongi Crossing; above her, Lucie's face and the number of the hotline were broadcast on the giant screen. The day before, Sophie had put on a black dress and been filmed as she walked from Sasaki House to Sendagaya Station, as her sister had done on that Saturday in July. The hope was that television stations would broadcast the sequence, and that new memories would be shaken loose from witnesses. But a reconstruction in itself was not enough. Without some fresh development to report, the story was dwindling and fading.

What more could Lucie's family do to help her? The only thing left was money. In the late summer and early autumn, a series of rewards was offered, each several times larger than the last. The announcements generated a brief flurry of sightings, which quickly subsided into silence. Like the doses of an

addictive drug, a bigger and bigger financial incentive produced over time a smaller and smaller effect.

Tim's family put up a reward of £9,500 for information
leading to Lucie. An Australian tourist contacted the BBC to
report a sighting of Lucie in Hong Kong, "shouting incoher-
ently and talking gibberish" as she withdrew money from a
cash machine. Tim spoke to the man, but the girl he described
was not tall enough to be Lucie.

The anonymous British businessman increased the reward
to £100,000. A call came to the Tokyo police from the Gulf
state of Qatar, where Lucie had been seen walking down a
street. The British embassy in Doha investigated; the tip came
to nothing.

Tim and Sophie continued to shuttle back and forth. Even
during the time spent back home in Britain, it was impossible
to concentrate on work or adjust to the routines of day-to-day
life. Tim's business was grinding to a halt; the hunt for Lucie
had personally cost him tens of thousands of pounds. It was a
measure of his desperation that in mid-October he made an
appeal to the "newly risen religion" that was holding Lucie—
a detail from the "Akira Takagi" phone call that had been
scoffed at as an absurd red herring for all these months. "Perhaps the possibility that Lucie was taken to some sort of cult
should be given a bit more thought," Tim told a small gathering of journalists at his ninth press conference. "I can understand that it may be difficult to return Lucie because of the
media attention. But it is possible to do so and I would be
pleased to receive some information as to how we could meet
in complete confidence. If indeed she was initiated into a cult,
I would understand that there may be a cost of money for the
expense of her training. If it's a question of money, I know
that the family would be able to find it."

At this stage, the question everyone else was asking—
What had happened to Lucie?—was of very little interest to

Tim. Who cared what had happened, as long as she could be returned home? "I've heard horror stories about girls who've gone missing," he said. "Drugged, taken away, photographed, abused, then returned. I would be overjoyed at this point if that would be Lucie's fate. We can make it all better once I get her home. But I've got to find her first."

The anonymous businessman increased the reward to £500,000.

One day, Tim was out in Roppongi with a sheaf of missing-person posters. He was taping them to telegraph poles along the main street. A policeman approached and sternly explained that this was not allowed. If Tim did not take them down immediately, the officer said, he would just have to do it himself later.

"No," said Tim.

"Please cooperate," said the policeman.

Tim shook his head and held out his hands with the wrists clenched together, submitting to arrest.

The policeman stamped off, his bluff called, and Tim moved on to the next telegraph pole. But it was already plastered with small paper flyers bearing photographs of seminaked women, advertisements for local "fashion health parlors," "soap lands," and "aesthetic salons." Tim plucked off a few of them for closer examination; in his other hand, he held the Lucie posters. He looked from the photograph of his missing daughter to the advertisements for the sex clubs and back again. Then he held the flyers up with a look of incomprehension. "But these are all right?" he said.

In public, Tim had adopted a policy of icy praise for the police and their "meticulous" investigations. But privately his resentment was increasing. The crux of the problem was the telephone call made to Louise by "Akira Takagi" two days after

Lucie's disappearance. Obviously, this had come from some-one who knew where Lucie was, if not the kidnapper himself. Trace the telephone number and its owner, and you would have a crucial witness. But to Tim's fury, the police insisted that this was impossible. One day, this would be put down to technical difficulties. But the next time, the detectives would explain that a court order was necessary to scrutinize private commercial telephone records. Yes, they assured Tim, an ap-plication had been made with the court, but it would take time. "Please be patient," said Superintendent Mitsuzane.

By September, patience had run out, not only among the Blackmans but also among diplomats at the British embassy. The lord chancellor, Derry Irvine, happened to be visiting Tokyo. He once again raised the case with the Japanese prime minister, and he asked the justice minister to assist in tracing the telephone records. One afternoon, Tim went to the police station with Alan Sutton, the stern, white-bearded consul general. As so often with the police, the conversation slid and slithered and proved impossible to bring to its point.

"Superintendent Mitsuzane," Sutton began, "you told me that telephone records are not preserved. Our information is that the data is, in fact, there. Why is the telephone company not complying with the court order?"

"Our problem is the law in Japan," Mitsuzane replied. "Another is the question of whether they actually keep the records. We have been continuing our checks. We have been doing everything that we need to do. We will be able to ob-tain a court warrant."

Tim said, "But you told me twice that an application had already been made with the court."

"Regrettably, we couldn't get the information because it was not kept," Mitsuzane replied.

Sutton quoted from a letter from the Japanese telephone

corporation NTT, saying exactly the opposite: although it was a complicated process, mobile calls could in fact be traced through the company's computers.

Mitsuzane smiled. "We have not received any information from NTT." At this, Alan Sutton lost his temper. "Perhaps you don't appreciate the high level to which the matter has gone. Lord Irvine, the lord chancellor of the United Kingdom, has received assurances from your minister of justice. The Tokyo Metropolitan Police are expected to do their job. I will be asked by my own government about your performance. How am I to respond? The police *must* obtain that information. A girl's life is at stake."

Tim said, "After ten weeks, I now want full information, not insults. If you don't trust me, then who do you trust?"

Superintendent Mitsuzane smiled. "The telephone company tells us it is not possible," he said. "We have to comply with the law."

■ ■ ■

For Lucie's friends and family back in Britain, deprived by their distance from Tokyo of the power to provide any help at all, the strain of her continuing absence was unrelenting. While his father and sister were addressing press conferences and grappling with detectives, sixteen-year-old Rupert Blackman found himself having to return to a new term at school. Everyone knew about his sister; over the summer, Rupert himself had acquired an unspoken celebrity. Erstwhile rivals and enemies treated him with gentleness and respect, although Rupert could take no satisfaction in this. "That period was awful," he said. "Whenever I went to bed I used to have a fag on the windowsill with the window open. I'd be looking up at the stars and thinking about Lucie. I didn't know where she was, but maybe she was looking up at that star too. Was she even in

Japan anymore? Was she out on a boat? Was she in a cult? That's the worst thing—not knowing. Not knowing what emotion to feel. You've got so many emotions inside you—you're ready to pick one of them. But you don't know which one is correct, whether you're meant to be mourning, or whether you're meant to be strong, or whether you're meant to be . . . anything." Any kind of news about the case made him squirm. "I hated it when I was round at a mate's house, and they'd flick on the telly and a documentary would come up about Lucie. It was like sitting down with your parents and watching something sexually graphic. It was the same kind of emotion, the feeling that this is not right at all."

Lucie's school friend Gayle Blackman (despite the coincidence of their uncommon name, there was no blood relation between them) became fixated on the conviction that she was still alive and kept a diary addressed to her friend to show to her when she eventually came back. "I had this image that we'd sit on that bloody expensive bed she'd bought just before she left and read it together, having a laugh," said Gayle. "Then I came to my senses. I thought, 'You're an idiot. You're never going to see her again. She's not coming back.'"

Jane Blackman had made a brief visit to Tokyo in August. The following month, she overcame her aversion to journalists and gave her first press conference. Compared to Tim's public style, Jane was wrenchingly straightforward and unselfconscious. "Tomorrow it will be three months since Lucie went missing," she said. "I'm here to appeal to the women of Japan—the mothers, the daughters, the sisters, the aunts, and the grandmothers—anyone who can give us or the police those vital clues which can help us to solve this dreadful mystery. We believe that someone out there knows what happened to Lucie and we desperately want that witness to come forward. A tall, blond, slim, good-looking girl can't simply vanish—someone must have seen her. Please, please, will a witness come forward? Her family wants her back. Her brother, sister, father, and I want her back. You, whoever you are, have had her long enough. To whoever is holding her, please, I beg you, from the bottom of my heart, please let her go now. If it is a man on his own, you've had her long enough. I can't believe the Japanese people can't help. We know you care. We know how family-oriented you are.

"As the mother of a daughter who is like a sister to me, it's the worst nightmare and it never goes away. I don't sleep. My life is just on hold. I don't function correctly. I feel as if my heart has been ripped out. It breaks my heart. My most loving daughter, so full of life that she lights up a room . . ." Jane trailed off. "As a family, we will never give up looking for Lucie and we will never take no for an answer."

But an awful prospect was presenting itself, almost worse than the idea that Lucie was dead: the possibility that no one would ever know what had happened to her, that she would forever remain one of the missing. "I think most of all is the fear that in ten, twenty years' time, even five years' time, I'm going to still be here, still looking," Sophie told a Japanese journalist in Tokyo. "I'm not willing to do that. I am not pre-pared to give up my life because someone has taken away Lucie. I'm not willing to do that. So it's going to be over. I hope it's going to be over soon. But she's not just disappeared."

Jane was accompanied by the latest addition to the unofficial Lucie Blackman investigation—retired chief superintendent David Seaborn Davies, a smiling Welshman known as Dai. As a young officer in the Metropolitan Police, Dai Davies had served for several years in the Vice Squad, but he had ended his career as head of the Royalty Protection Squad—Queen Elizabeth II's chief bodyguard. He had visited Japan three years earlier to compare notes with members of the Japanese Impe-rial Guard and been warmly entertained by them. The following year he retired from the Met to become an "international security consultant" with a partnership that went by the name the AgenC. Dai was an acquaintance of Jane Blackman's brother. He was confident that, with his decades of experience and his Japanese police contacts, he would be able to bring a bit of professional rigor to the uncoordinated efforts of the family and crack open Superintendent Mitsuzane's defensive shell. Brian Malcolm, Tim's wealthy brother-in-law, agreed to pay him £800 a day, plus expenses—a discount of £400 a day on the AgenC's usual rate.

Dai had a neat little mustache and wore gray suits and paisley ties. He was warm and chummy and persuasive, with a self-deprecating charm. But the challenges of operating in Tokyo were far beyond anything that he had anticipated. By the time he arrived in late summer 2000, most of his contacts in the Imperial Guard had retired or moved on. Those who remained were unable or unwilling to give him useful introductions. The bodyguards of Emperor Akihito, it became obvious, moved in a different world from the detectives of Roppongi. Dismayingly, he was informed that by operating in Japan as a private investigator without a license, he faced potential arrest. And having turned up anyway, under the guise of a concerned "friend of the family," he had no more success than Tim and Adam. The Tokyo Metropolitan Police treated him with polite disdain. The club owners and bar managers were suspicious and uncooperative. Virtually the only people who could be induced to talk to him were hostesses. Dai referred to this as a "wall of silence," which was one way of admitting that he was completely stuck. Without any knowledge of Japanese, and without the resources to hire interpreters, he had to rely on the goodwill of local journalists and volunteers, just like everyone else on the unofficial Lucie team. "No one would agree to see me," he told me six years later. "I used to wonder: Was I giving value for money? Was I just playing at being detective?

How far could I go with the resources I had? . . . When you work as a policeman and you have all these resources at your disposal, it's different—the information is found, the job gets done. But when you're working on your own, as often as not you have to pay . . . I suppose with hindsight it was somewhat pretentious of me to think that as a single individual I could make a huge difference anyway. With hindsight."

Dai Davies got on well with journalists. He would go on to play a similar role in other highly publicized cases involving missing British citizens; the "ex-Yard officer"—or even "super-sleuth"—was regularly quoted in the newspapers or interviewed on television, "blasting" the Portuguese police investigating the disappearance of the British toddler Madeleine McCann, for example, or pronouncing on the German investigation into the disappearance of another Kent girl, Louise Kerton. His "crucial role" in the Lucie investigation was often referred to by journalists, prompting ironic reflections on Tim's part.

"Dai Davies, the Great Dai Davies," he said. "It made me livid the other day when he was on TV saying, "Oh yes, I was out [in Tokyo], 'helping' the investigation." We paid him forty-eight grand to be there! For him to spend nights in pole-dancing clubs talking to managers."

But Dai did add at least one piece of information to the pile of fragments that the Blackmans had raked together.

In September, he tracked down a woman named Mandy Wallace, a former hostess, who had returned to her home in Blackpool after several weeks at Casablanca. She had worked there at the same time as Lucie, and she described a man who had come into the club one night in late June and sat with Lucie, a high-spending, brandy-drinking man who had left Mandy feeling vaguely uncomfortable. Dai's detective instincts seized on this information. He persuaded a friend from the Scotland Yard Facial Imaging Team to come with him to Blackpool. There he produced a photofit, based on Mandy's description, which was quickly sent to Tokyo and shown to anyone who might recognize it.

It was a grotesque and horrifying image: wide, fleshy, with a coarse nose, heavy, lascivious lips, and a sprout of dense, upthrusting hair. The neck of the man in the photofit was solid with muscle; wide spectacles partially concealed expressionless eyes. It was the face of someone merciless, implacable, and alien, beyond the reach of human empathy, beyond understanding. No artist could have created a more vivid emblem of the pain of the two-month search, and the hopelessness of the searchers.

■ ■ ■

By October, Mike Hills had exposed himself as a fraud, the trail of the S & M circles had led nowhere, and Tim and Sophie Blackman's private effort to find Lucie, based out of Huw Shakeshaft's office in Roppongi, was falling to pieces.

Partly, this was a consequence of exhaustion, despair, and the simple expense of maintaining a presence in Japan. But there was another reason—a growing hostility towards Tim among the volunteers looking for Lucie, veering at times into outright hatred.

The man who turned most violently against him was Huw Shakeshaft himself. Huw had quickly become resentful of Tim's presence in his office and accused him of being insensitive to its function as a place of business. He was irritated by the missing-person posters attached to its walls and about Tim's "rude and offhand" attitude towards his staff. He was furious that Tim had given interviews there in his absence and entertained journalists at Bellini's on his tab. But the source of his fury went deeper than this. At root, it was inspired by Tim's demeanor, based on passionate convictions about behavior appropriate for someone in his situation.

Tim's articulateness and composure kept the story of Lucie's disappearance alive long after it would naturally have faded away. But his refusal to take the role of conventional victim continued to make him an object of suspicion. Because he did not appear distraught, the reasoning seemed to go, he must not *be* distraught—and for a man with a missing daughter to be free of distress was immoral. "I was at this time becoming aware of the apparent lack of concern that Tim seemed to exhibit concerning this whole difficult situation, feeling that he showed none of the usual reactions that one sees or experiences when faced with extreme familial trauma," wrote Huw Shakeshaft, in a ten-page, four-thousand-word document detailing his dislike for Tim. "He just seemed more interested in how much money we could raise for him and when his next TV interview was."

Other people had complaints about money and Tim's alleged preoccupation with it. Adam Whittington's association with the Blackmans would end in a painful argument about how much he was owed. One participant in the hunt for Lucie, who asked not to be named, recalled overhearing Tim talking on the telephone to Jo Burr and their discussions of "ways they could make money out of the situation." "I believed [Tim] was someone in dire need of help," wrote Huw, who had given so freely and generously when the two of them had first met. "Unfortunately I now believe, as evidenced by Tim Blackman's subsequent behavior, that this was not the case and he was beginning to enjoy his celebrity."

Years later, I spent two evenings with Huw talking about the Lucie case. He spent much of the time railing against Tim. At one point I asked if he really thought that Tim had been "enjoying" his situation. "He seemed to be, when he was drunk at four or five in the morning," he said. "You can do the level of 'research' you need to and still get home by one, sober . . . All I know is that he saw Lucie two or three times in five years, or three years, or whatever it was since the divorce. He's a man who hadn't taken the time out to see his own daughter. My read on him as a person—he's very self-absorbed. If you look at how he handled the divorce and what he actually did to them, I think he's very capable of being extremely cold . . . I think you can safely say he was ego-led."

Accusations of egotism and intemperance sounded strange in the mouth of Huw, a man whose conversation was littered with the names of Hollywood actors with whom he was acquainted, who talked freely of the heart attacks he had suffered because of overindulgence during his years in Roppongi, and who had a failed marriage of his own and a young son from whom he lived apart. But he was not alone in his judgment on Tim. In the second half of 2000, it became common to hear this kind of talk in Tokyo—usually sotto voce and accompanied by frowns and regretful shakes of the head—at dinner parties in expat apartments, at Sunday brunches in five-star hotels, and at embassy cocktail receptions. Tim Blackman, father to a missing girl, was "enjoying himself."

The families of the missing are doubly burdened: first by the pain of their ordeal, and then by our expectations of them, expectations of a standard of behavior higher than we require of ourselves.

As humans, we seek naturally to help fellow creatures in distress. But most of us, whether we are conscious of it or not, expect something back—the flattery of helplessness and of need. Tim hid his pain and panic behind a screen of energetic concentration and activity, which deprived people of this comforting response. But Jane Blackman delivered it. Jane's pain was unconstrained and heartfelt. She needed help, appreciated it warmly, and her helpers were immediately able to feel themselves to be doers of good.

The mounting hostility towards Tim seemed to begin when

Jane started visiting Japan, and this was not a coincidence. Among the volunteers in Tokyo, Tim said little about his ex-wife, but to people she trusted, Jane talked freely about the failure of her marriage, or her view of it. Huw, Adam, and Dai all came away with an uncomplicated picture of a wronged wife and a philandering husband, who had neglected his family after walking out on them. Goodwill ebbed away from Tim and towards Jane. It was as if there was a limited quantity of it available to the Blackmans, and it had to be divided between them.

Perhaps sensing this shift, Tim gave an interview to a British Sunday tabloid, which did nothing to improve his standing among the people looking for Lucie. He talked of his pain at Lucie's disappearance and compared it to the experience of becoming estranged from her after the collapse of his marriage. "Jane is devastated and I can understand that," he told the *Sunday People.* "But I find it difficult to feel an ounce of sympathy for her. It's the same as when I couldn't see Lucie before. Obviously, this is worse, but Jane's going through now what she helped put me through previously. So I am emotionally cold towards Jane's suffering."

Since their brief and unhappy conversation over the telephone, Jane and Tim had not spoken; and they carefully timed their visits to Tokyo to avoid ever meeting. After Jane and Dai Davies left Japan at the beginning of October, Tim stayed at home in the Isle of Wight. Sophie had gone home too; Adam Whittington had left at the end of August. The answering machine attached to the Lucie Hotline was checked and logged by the staff of the British consulate.

- Caller saw a girl who looked like Lucie on 2 Oct at around 1 p.m. near an optician near Kinshicho. She was walking down the street with a man. He added

that there are lots of indecent clubs/bars where Asian and European girls are working.
- Caller said that he had information about a religious organization. Asked that a Japanese-speaking British person call him back.
- Background music only.

But for the first time since Lucie had disappeared three months earlier, none of her family was in Tokyo looking for her.

■ ■ ■

I lived in Tokyo throughout the Lucie Blackman time. I followed the case intently and wrote about it for my newspaper. I tried to answer the obvious questions put to me by my editors, questions that a British reader might ask, a person without particular knowledge of Japan. Some of them were settled quickly enough—about Lucie's life in Tokyo and the peculiar role of the foreign hostess. But to the biggest question of all— *What happened to her?*—there was no answer. And, lacking one, people began to pose other questions, such as, *Was she on drugs?* and *What did the best friend know?* and *What about the father?*

As a reporter, I moved across Japan's public surface. By day, I encountered bureaucrats, politicians, academics, professionals; in my own time, I relaxed with people like me, who loved Japan and thought that they understood it well enough, even if they would never call it home. Roppongi was a place for occasional rowdy nights out; male friends of a certain temperament would go to the titty bars for their stag nights. Now, as a reporter in search of Lucie Blackman, I found myself visiting them myself and paying a tariffed sum of money for conversations with attractive, and knowing, young women. At first the clubs were alert and hostile to journalists—more than once, there were scuffles between bouncers and suspiciously nosy "customers" with notebooks and cameras. But the water trade quickly found its level again. Even Casablanca, which had shut its doors within a few days of Lucie's disappearance, reopened at the end of August under a new name: Greengrass.

I spent long nights there, or in One Eyed Jack's, or in the Tokyo Sports Cafe, alone, or with a friend, pressing drinks on hostesses who knew less about Lucie Blackman than I did but who had all heard rumors: about cults, or rape gangs, or S & M circles. Roppongi, formerly so crude and neon bright, came to seem dark and damp and mysterious; creatures lurked beneath its stones. I would arrive home at 4:00 a.m., drunk and with clothes steeped in cigarette smoke, my pockets stuffed with napkins bearing scrawled notes. And in sleep, I dreamed one of the oldest male dreams of all: of being the knight who rides to the dark tower, slays the dragon, frees the missing damsel, and basks forever in the glory.

At Azabu Police Station, I submitted to repeated fobbings off. At the British embassy, I was patiently told the obvious. I formed alliances with Japanese reporters, who would pass on what little they had picked up from the police in return for my gleanings from the Blackman family. I even mounted a photograph of Lucie on a piece of cardboard and kept it in my bag to show to people as I went about life in Tokyo. Everyone recognized the girl in the picture, but nobody had seen her.

Even when there was nothing new to report, it was impossible to forget the case. People don't dissolve into particles. *Something* had happened. So much information had been assembled—about Lucie, about Roppongi, about hostesses, and about the events of that Saturday afternoon. But at the core, there was a hollow, a gaping space. People hated the void and wanted it to be filled. They wanted Tim to fill it, with pain and anger, all the obvious and easily comprehensible emotions, and when he refused to supply them, they resented him for it.

Nobody knew what fitted into the hole. And yet everyone knew. It was a hole in the shape of a person, the person who had taken Lucie and done harm to her. Everyone knew this, deep down, and they knew that the person had to be a man.

I hated the duty—which every reporter must face from time to time—of speaking to the bereaved and scared, to the victims of loss. I was always afraid of getting the tone, the register, wrong, of appearing too cold and brisk, or bogusly concerned and sympathetic. I had to steel myself to call the Blackmans—Jane with her grief, Sophie with her defensiveness and aggression, and Tim with his intolerable helpfulness and charm. But by October, they had all gone sadly home, and it started to become possible to pass days without thinking about Lucie. And then one evening a Japanese reporter friend phoned and said that the Tokyo police were about to make an arrest, and that this seemed at last to be the man who fitted into the man-shaped hole.

12. DIGNITY OF THE POLICE

Christabel Mackenzie had come to Tokyo to escape, although not from any of the conventional hardships of the runaway. Her father was a well-known Scottish lawyer, and her mother was an academic at Edinburgh University. Christa was clever and pretty and grew up in cultured affluence; a life of upper-middle-class respectability was hers for the taking. But wealthy Edinburgh was smug and airless; Christa wanted independence and excitement. She dropped out of school and worked as a receptionist, dropped back in to sixth-form college and took a couple of A levels, then moved to London and a job in a department store.

London never felt far enough from home. A woman she knew had lived in Japan and told Christa about the excitements and opportunities there. She had landed in Tokyo in January 1995, alone, at the age of nineteen. She would live there for most of the next seven years.

Christa had quickly discovered one of the defining features of life as a foreigner in Japan and the reason it attracts so many misfits of different kinds: personal alienation, that inescapable sense of being different from everyone else, is canceled out by the larger, universal alienation of being a gaijin. "I really loved Japan," Christa told me. "I still do, although it's a love/hate thing too. There are some things I find appalling and some things that I love. But there was a lot of freedom, because no matter what you do there, you're a freak, aren't you? People are going to stare at you anyway, so you can stop worrying about it and let your hair down. And you're making good money, so you can *really* let your hair down. You're so far away, you feel that anything you do is going to be insulated from your real life."

Christa was tall, blond, and wild. She briefly took a job as an English teacher, but the work bored her; within a few weeks she was a hostess in a small club called Fraîche. It was in Akasaka, the district adjoining, and upmarket of, Roppongi, a resort of Japanese salarymen rather than young gaijin. A handful of authentic geisha still worked in Akasaka in traditional teahouses patronized by Japanese politicians and the executives of the country's biggest companies. But such people rarely walked into Fraîche. Most of Christa's customers were lonely, charmless men, for whom a couple of hours spent talking in English to a pretty young foreign girl was an exotic, and otherwise unobtainable, pleasure.

"There was a small bar, a karaoke machine, six to eight girls," she said. "It was a tame place. Sometimes there were customers who were aggressive or mean or had bad breath, but only a few of them were really unpleasant. Most of them were fine—the biggest drag was the boredom. The dōhans were stress-free—just dinner somewhere in Akasaka, and then back to the club." The most successful hostesses adopted a persona of naïve innocence; customers often seemed reassured by the sensation of conversing with someone less intelligent than them. Christa could never bring herself to play dumb and developed other means of filling the time: silly drinking games (and she liked to drink), flirtatious conversational gambits, and drugs.

The mid-1990s represented the last wheezing gasp of Japan's bubble economy, but there was still a lot of loose money in Tokyo and startling rewards for hostesses with the right tactics: stories circulated about girls who had been given Rolexes, gold bars, even apartments by infatuated customers. Akasaka's greater respectability compared to Roppongi was reflected in the money paid to its hostesses. Having earned $180 a week in London, Christa was now being paid ¥3,000 (close to $30) an hour, and that was before bonuses for requests and dōhan.

One night a man whom she hadn't seen before came into the club. From the depth of the manager's bows and the obsequiousness of his welcome, she knew that he must be an established and high-spending customer. He introduced himself as Yuji Honda, and it was immediately obvious that he was a cut above the average patron of Club Fraîche.

He was a short man in his early forties, with a manner and bearing quite different from the typical salaryman. His face was unremarkable, but he wore an expensive-looking jacket with an open-necked silk shirt. He spoke good English, and unlike many of the customers, he was never obviously lecherous, or clownish, or pitiable. "He had this strained kind of arrogance and confidence about him that I always found amusing," Christa said. "Because he wasn't particularly good-looking or winning in his personality. But I did find him intriguing, not like most of the other customers. He was difficult to figure out. There were oddities about him.

"He had a bit of a swagger, sort of an arrogant way of walking. And there was something odd about the way he talked. It's difficult to describe—it was almost like a lisp, something funny about the shape of his mouth. It was almost like a baby's mouth. He used to slip his tongue in and out, like a lizard." And he sweated—even in the air-conditioned chill of the club, he would frequently produce a small hand towel and mop his face and neck and brow.

Christa and Yuji spent all of that first evening together; he promised her that he would come to see her again. It had all the makings of the perfect dōhan relationship.

For a month, they went out for dinner every week. Each evening he pulled up in a different car: a white Rolls-Royce convertible, and three kinds of Porsche. Christa made a point of not being impressed by money, but she recognized that this, by any hostess's definition, was the dream customer. Once, Yuji took her for a lavish Chinese banquet, complete with dishes of jellyfish and shark-fin soup; another time, they dined on fugu, the famous puffer fish, which can be poisonous unless it is correctly, and expensively, prepared. He didn't talk much about himself, but the display of money was evidently important to Yuji; someone in the club told Christa that his family was the fifth richest in Japan. "He was really into fugu—he said that he ate it every day," Christa remembered. "That was just one example of the way he showed off. I always find it funny when people think that because they've got money, they are a fabulous person." This was how Christa regarded Yuji—unusual, mildly ludicrous, and harmless.

One night in May 1995, he picked her up after work and suggested a drive to the seaside. It was three a.m., but Christa was never one to let conventional notions about bedtime get in the way of an adventure, and she was curious to see the holiday home Yuji had described. They drove there in the white Rolls-Royce. Christa was shivering in the powerful air-conditioning, but Yuji was sweating in his thin silk shirt. "It was really noticeable," she said. "I thought that he must be on coke or speed or something, although he wasn't. And he was a really bad driver. He always had his foot either hard down on the accelerator or on the brake, never anything in between." Christa was only vaguely aware of the direction in which they were driving, but after an hour or so, they arrived at a marina where yachts were moored. Next to it were apartment buildings containing holiday flats; tall palm trees shook ragged leaves in the wind off the sea. As Yuji had talked about this place, Christa imagined a beach house along Californian or Australian lines, a villa with its own garden and a private swimming pool. The reality was a disappointment: a large building containing dozens of identical cramped apartments. "As soon as I saw the place, I thought, 'What am I doing here?'" she said. "I thought, 'This guy doesn't really have as much money as he says.'"

The apartment was on the third floor, a small, slightly shabby bachelor pad with a single living room facing onto a thin strip of balcony, a narrow kitchen, and a still smaller partitioned-off area that appeared to be a bedroom. There was nothing glamorous or seductive about the place. The sofa was luridly upholstered in thick fabric bearing a pattern of creeping foliage and cabbage roses. Behind it was a sideboard laden with bottles of different shapes and colors. "His apartment was really naff," Christa said. "Kitsch, like maybe his mother decorated the place for him. All the furniture seemed kind of seventies—grandmotherly and floral, that kind of feeling."

They sat down to drink beer and eat the fugu, which Yuji had brought with him. Then he produced an electric guitar and plugged it into an amplifier. A recorded backing track started up and he began playing and singing along. The song was "Samba Pa Ti" by Carlos Santana, of whom Yuji was an enthusiastic devotee. He even had a photograph of himself with the singer in the United States. "I quite liked Santana, but playing along to him on a karaoke track—well, I thought that was pretty naff too," Christa said. "By now, it had started to get light outside, and I was thinking that this had all gone on long enough." She told Yuji that she wanted to go back to Tokyo, but he said he had one more thing to show her. He described it as a rare wine from the Philippines; it was among the clutter of bottles on the sideboard. He poured a measure of it into a small glass from a crystal decanter and handed it to Christa, who downed it in a single draught as she stood by the window.

For other women in the same situation, that was the last thing they knew: the acrid, chemical taste of the "wine" going down. But months of hard drinking had made Christa tolerant of the most powerful intoxicants. "I had no expectation at all of anything being wrong," she said. "And I think he'd cottoned on that I liked to drink a lot and that I was the sort of person who always took on a challenge. I drank it because that was the kind of thing I did then—I was into being tough. I can remember standing at the window as it came on, realizing what had happened and that this could be a very big problem. I had time to reflect on what was happening. I remember thinking, 'Oh, fuck.' It was like going under a general anesthetic. I was already too drugged to feel afraid."

She woke up in the darkness lying alone in a bed. She understood immediately what had happened and the kind of thing that must have taken place while she was unconscious. "I remember thinking, 'How do I feel?' and trying to work out what exactly had happened to me. But I didn't feel sore. And I had my clothes on. I thought that I must have been asleep a long time, because he'd bothered to dress me."

They had driven to the apartment in the early hours of Saturday morning. It was now Saturday evening—Christa had been unconscious for more than twelve hours. Yuji was there, behaving almost as though nothing had happened. It was as if he was waiting for her to say something, to hurl an accusation—but Christa was silent. "I just wanted to get home. I remember thinking, 'If he doesn't take me back, how will I get to Tokyo?' because I had no idea where I was. But he did drive me back." Christa felt hungover in the car, but she often did in those days. Otherwise she was calm.

She said, "It seems pretty strange to me now, the way I behaved. But the thing with hostessing is that it's like a game, for the girls and the guys. The girls are trying to get money, with no intention of giving anything back. And the guys are trying to get as far as they can, without giving any more than they would normally pay in the club. When I woke up that day I was angry, but I felt like it was partly my own doing to be in that situation. I think that's pretty typical from what I've heard—that women who've been raped feel partly responsible.

"I thought I'd understood the rules, but I hadn't. I was naïve in that way. So I felt he'd won the game. I was pissed off, but I didn't really reflect on it that much. I wasn't really conscious of the dangerousness of the situation. It wasn't until years later that I realized. Actually, I didn't want to think about it, because if I'd admitted how dangerous it was I would have had to change the way I lived my life."

Yuji dropped Christa off at home later that evening. The following week she went back to work at the club. He didn't come in again.

Christa stayed in Japan, living the life of the hostess. She moved to different clubs in new Japanese cities. She would work for a few months, accumulating cash, and then spend weeks traveling for pleasure, to India, Iceland, Canada.

In 1999 she was living in Sapporo, in the far north of Japan. There she met a foreign girl who had stories of a wealthy man who preyed on hostesses in Tokyo, taking them to a seaside apartment and drugging them. It could only be Yuji Honda. It was the first time that she had consciously thought about the incident in years.

A few months later, Christa was living in Japan's second city, Osaka, when she got a telephone call from an old friend, a former Tokyo hostess who had moved back to London. The girl's younger sister was coming out to Japan with a friend—would Christa meet up with them in Tokyo?

The caller was Emma Phillips. The pair bound for Tokyo were Louise Phillips and Lucie Blackman.

Christa booked the room in Sasaki House. It was she who was waiting for them when they arrived, smoking spliffs and having her hair dressed in the oil that so revolted Louise. The three women spent that evening together. Lucie and Louise found Christa intimidatingly self-assured, but she was charmed, and even touched, by them.

"They were so excited and vibrant—two young girls on their first big trip, their first break for independence. I remember thinking that Lucie was like me when I was nineteen, physically, I mean—tall and blond and so on. And Louise and Emma could be identical twins. So it was strange when they walked in the room, like looking five years back in time at me and Emma. And I remember thinking straightaway that Lucie was [Yuji's] type—if I was his type, then she would be too—and feeling a bit worried for them because they were so green. But they were happy and enthusiastic, and I wanted them to have a good time. I didn't want to put a downer on it, so I didn't say anything about him. But I did think of him, which was odd because he wasn't someone I normally thought about."

Two months later, she was back in Osaka when Emma called with the news that Lucie had gone missing. "She said that she'd gone out with a customer from work on a drive to the sea, and she hadn't come home. I was immediately sure, absolutely sure, that it was Yuji."

She phoned Louise, who was incoherent with distress. Christa said, "I thought that he'd let her go after she'd come round from the drug, like I did. I thought she'd come back." But after two days, there was still no sign of Lucie. Christa took the bullet train to Tokyo and went directly to Azabu Police Station.

■ ■ ■

Japan has the cuddliest police in the world. To many Japanese, the mere sight of *omawari-san* (literally, "Honourable Mr. Go

Around," the expression for the cop on the beat) provokes feelings of tender pride more conventionally aroused by children or small, appealing animals. To the foreigner, too, there is something touchingly nostalgic about their neat navy blue uniforms and clunky, old-fashioned bikes. It is hard to believe that the handguns they carry at their hips contain real bullets and impossible to imagine them ever being fired (prudently, they are attached to their uniforms by a cord, like a child's mittens). And then there is the symbol of the Tokyo Metropolitan Police, the country's proudest and most prestigious force: not a stern mastiff, or a watchful hawk, but a cheerful orange fairy named Peepo. The police are one of the things that impart to Tokyo its quaint, innocent, 1950s flavor: a tribe of earnest Boy Scouts, protecting the city from evildoers.

On the face of it, they are astonishingly and uniquely successful. Japan, like most nations, goes through spasms of anxiety about youthful delinquency and the erosion of traditional morals. But the essential fact remains: by every measure, Japan is the safest and least crime-ridden country on earth. Offenses like muggings, burglary, and drug dealing, which city dwellers in the rest of the world have learned to accept as part of everyday life, are between four and eight times lower than in the West.

Violent crime is rarer still, and for all of this the Japanese police proudly take credit. They believe that because Japan has the world's lowest crime rate, they must therefore be the world's greatest crime fighters. For years, this was the view of the Japanese population. One encounters little of the low-level cynicism that the inhabitants of other world cities instinctively feel towards the forces of law and order. But in 2000, at the time that Christa Mackenzie went to Azabu Police Station, this loyal consensus was unraveling.

After a series of scandals, the Japanese police were facing their most vociferous criticism in decades. Across the country, police officers had been exposed for sexual harassment, brib-ery, blackmail, drug taking, assault, and simple professional incompetence.* *The Yomiuri Shimbun*, one of the most conser-vative and pro-establishment of the country's newspapers, called the situation "a disgrace, the likes of which have not been witnessed in a long time." An editorial in the same newspaper said that "to straighten out this organisation, which has com-pletely lost discipline, the only solution is complete, drastic reform." An opinion poll showed that 60 percent of Japanese did not trust the police, compared to 26 percent in the previous

---

*Several of the most notorious scandals were about missing persons. The most appalling concerned the murder the previous December of a nineteen-year-old boy named Masakazu Sudo, whose body had been found in a forest in Tochigi prefecture, north of Tokyo. Sudo had been missing for more than a month, and his parents had a good idea why. Three other youths, whom they identified by name, had been holding the young man captive, marching him to cash machines and loan shops, and forcing him to take out and hand over large sums of money.

The Sudos went repeatedly to the police, but the police refused to in-vestigate, insinuating that Masakazu was a delinquent, and even a drug user, himself. Then one day, on the orders of his captors, he called his parents on a mobile telephone. They happened to be in the police station at the time, and they begged the sergeant on duty, who was still refusing to look into the case, to pose as a friend of their son and speak to the kidnappers. The officer took the phone—and immediately introduced himself as a policeman. Soon after, Masakazu Sudo was taken into the forest and strangled. One of the three killers, who were eventually tried and convicted of murder, turned out to be the son of another local officer.

Equally alarming, from the point of view of the Blackman family, was the case of a ten-year-old Japanese girl from Niigata who had gone missing in 1990. Ten years passed without a hint of what had happened to her, until in February 2000 she turned up at a local hospital. For almost a decade, she had been held captive in a single room in a house a few hundred yards from a police station. Her abductor was a convicted child molester. Four years earlier the police had received a tip that he was holding her, but they had not even bothered to knock on his door.

survey two years earlier. It was in this atmosphere of defensiveness and anxiety that the investigation into Lucie's disappearance began.

By their own account, the police had moved with unusual speed. "I want you to understand how quickly we liaised among ourselves," said Chief Superintendent Fusanori Matsumoto, the head of Azabu Police Station and the man who supervised the first days of the Lucie Blackman investigation. "We were motivated by our instincts as veterans. And then there was the fact that this girl was British, and the fact that she had been a cabin attendant for a famous company such as British Airways, a job that many girls aspire to."*

The converse of this, although the superintendent would never have spelled it out, was that if the missing woman had been, for example, a Chinese or a Bangladeshi whose previous career had been in a fish-canning factory or a massage parlor, his interest in the case would have been drastically reduced. "At first they didn't take it all that seriously," one person close to the investigation told me. "It was just another girl who had gone missing in Roppongi. In Tokyo, girls go missing quite often—Filipinas, Thais, Chinese. It's impossible to investigate them all." What marked this case out from others was not merely the nationality of the victim, or the identity of her former

---

*One of the cultural differences revealed by the Lucie case was the differing international attitudes to flight attendants. In Britain, the figure of the "trolley dolly" is regarded with as much mockery as admiration. But in Japan, air stewardesses are a high-altitude elite, the epitome of feminine glamour and sophistication. At the height of their ascendancy, in the bubble years of the late 1980s, they were from time to time chosen as brides by pop stars and sumo wrestlers. For many Japanese, it was incomprehensible, indeed highly suspicious, that a woman would choose to give up a job at British Airways to become a bar hostess in Roppongi.

employer, but the intense external pressure that quickly came to bear on the police.

First it was just Sophie Blackman visiting the police station, demanding answers. But soon she was accompanied by Alan Sutton, the formidable British consul general, whose staff were on the phone every day. Then Tim Blackman arrived, and soon—and unbelievably—he was talking to Tony Blair. The detectives, and many of the Japanese reporters, were astounded by this last development. The equivalent situation—a Japanese prime minister intervening in the search for a mislaid mizu shōbai girl—was unthinkable. ("That Mr. Blackman," Chief Superintendent Matsumoto asked me at one point in our interview, as if it were the only possible explanation, "was he a *friend* of Prime Minister Blair?")

And then Tony Blair was taking the problem to the Japanese prime minister, who had no choice but to express his own concern and determination—and all of this under the noses of dozens of reporters. "We had an understanding with the Japanese media, we knew how to handle them," said Chief Superintendent Matsumoto. "But we had no idea how to deal with the foreign media. It was very annoying."

Matsumoto telephoned Jane Blackman in Sevenoaks and heard from her what everyone who knew Lucie would repeat: it was inconceivable that she would have gone off on her own without explanation. On July 11, a special investigation headquarters was established in Azabu Police Station to look into the case, headed by one of the most experienced detectives in Tokyo, Toshiaki Udo. Superintendent Udo was second in command of Tokyo's First Criminal Investigation Division, and his men were the elite of the Tokyo Metropolitan Police. They handled the greatest and most sensational crimes in the country: murders, rapes, kidnappings, armed robberies. For fame and glamour, they were the equivalent of Scotland Yard's

Flying Squad, the fictionalized heroes of film, television, and novels. Superintendent Udo had worked on Japan's biggest postwar criminal investigation—into the apocalyptic religious cult Aum Shinrikyo, which released sarin nerve gas on the Tokyo subway during the morning rush hour in 1995. He was a rather tall, oval-faced man, with wide and intense eyes that gave him an expression of constant mild surprise. He had about him the air of a kindly deputy headmaster rather than a tough detective, and it was difficult to imagine him expressing extremes of any kind of emotion. But the search for Lucie literally shook him. "I worked on many big cases, on many famous cases," he told me. "But when the responsibility of solving the Lucie case was given to me, my body trembled physically with the tension. I sensed, by instinct, that it would turn out to be a serious crime. I could smell it. I knew that we couldn't ignore it."

His immediate subordinate was Akira Mitsuzane, who would deal face-to-face with the Blackman family. It had taken over a week for the police system to wake up, clear its throat, and decide that there was work for it to do—and by its own standards, that was good going.

■■■

What did the detectives do for the next few weeks? It is difficult to reconstruct the sequence of events fully, but nothing happened fast. By the time Udo's special investigation headquarters had been established, Matsumoto's officers had already confirmed the basic facts of Louise's story: the status of the two girls in Japan, their residence at Sasaki House and employment at Casablanca. This took three days. But from the moment that Louise reported Lucie's disappearance on July 3, it was more than six weeks before they made any concrete progress at all.

Early checks were run on religious cults in Chiba prefecture. ("There are so many, though," said one detective. "We
need more information.") But other exceedingly obvious leads
remained unpursued. Almost two weeks after Lucie's disappearance, the police had still not spoken to Lucie's boyfriend,
Scott Fraser, nor had they made any efforts to interview anyone called Akira Takagi, the name by which the mysterious
caller had identified himself. "It could be a fictitious name," a
spokesman said. "We do not want people of the same name to
be unnecessarily troubled."

The police did go to Casablanca, interviewed its hostesses,
and combed through the club's records. Some, but not all, customers left business cards; those who were entertaining on business were given receipts with the names of their companies, of
which the club kept a copy. But having harvested this information, it took an inexplicably long time to process. It was well
into August, for example, before anyone called on Hajime
Imura, the publisher who had entertained Lucie with his squid-
fishing exploits.

Instead, the police questioned Louise Phillips over and over
again. Her first full day at Azabu Police Station was July 4,
the Tuesday after Lucie's disappearance. For the next five weeks,
from Monday to Saturday, she was there every day.

The interrogations took place in a ten-foot-square room
containing a table at which Louise sat with two detectives and
a police interpreter. They began first thing in the morning and
often went on until night. From the beginning, she was struck
both by the warmth and tenderheartedness of the individual
officers, and their capacity for punishingly long working hours.

Every day, the police would bring lunch to Louise—several
times, the wife of one officer or other presented her with a
bento, a lunch box of small delicacies that she had personally
prepared. The police provided an apartment for Louise to stay
in and paid her a per diem allowance of ¥5,000. (Unabashed

by this generosity, she would save the money up and buy herself a camera.) Louise's confusion and anxiety frequently reduced her to helpless tears; more than once, she noticed that her female interpreter, and even the interrogating male officers, also had tears in their eyes.

But the content of the interviews did not inspire confidence. It was obvious that Louise was a key witness: Lucie's oldest friend and closest companion, and the last person known to have seen her. The length of her interrogation might have been justified if there had been new ground to cover. But for much of the time the detectives just asked the same few questions, over and over again. Their meticulousness was impressive, sometimes awe-inspiring. But their undifferentiated interest in absolutely everything suggested to Louise that they had little instinct for what might have happened, had not begun to narrow down their investigation, and apparently didn't know where to begin.

"They wanted to know everywhere we'd been, all that we'd done, everything about Lucie in such detail, from before we even came to Japan," Louise said. "They were amazing. They were all working so hard. They wanted to know about Lucie's birthmark, the birthmark she had at the top of her leg. And Lucie's health, when she was younger. They were asking about my boyfriend, and my other friends, and all the people we lived with, and all the customers in the club. They wanted to know if any of the customers had had tattoos. But it was just the same questions, over and over again, for days and days."

Rather hesitantly, they asked if she and Lucie were lesbians (she spluttered with laughter at the suggestion). They wanted to know in detail about Lucie's sex life: her relationship with Scott, the frequency of their nights together, the kind of contraception they had used. "They were asking me for about a week if Lucie had ever had chlamydia," said Louise. "Why, I never understood. Some of the questions were so random, and they went on and on for hours and hours and hours."

"I had a good impression of Louise," Superintendent Matsumoto told me. "Even so, we had to consider a range of possible scenarios. Could she have been part of a plot against her friend, for example? Suppose Lucie and Louise had fallen in love with the same man, and Louise wanted him for herself, and she had disposed of her friend? Or killed Lucie to steal money?" Some of the scenarios entertained by the investigators were bizarre. "We had information from people in the clubs that Lucie might be in North Korea, or that she might be a spy," Matsumoto said. "We didn't give it much consideration, because she had had so little money."

The question of whether drugs might have come into it was quickly settled. "Louise wasn't using drugs, judging from the color of her face," Matsumoto said. "And from her physical state when she was talking with us for long hours. There were no bubbles around her mouth, as you sometimes see in drug users. She wasn't thin, and she didn't get tired easily. There were none of those signs." In other words, because a person was not pallid and emaciated and foaming at the mouth, she could not be a user of illegal drugs. This was an elderly maiden aunt's view of narcotics and their effect. Coming from a proud detective, it was comically naïve, another sign of the innocence and unworldliness of the Japanese police, who faced so little serious crime that they sometimes had only the crudest idea of what it looked like.

The detectives who took over the investigation after Matsumoto were not so innocent. One day Louise arrived in the interrogation room to see Lucie's diary lying on the table accompanied by a Japanese translation.

"Good morning, Louise-san," the detective began and picked up the documents on the desk. "Louise, have you or Lucie ever taken drugs in Japan?"

"No, no, never," said Louise, shaking her head.

"Are you sure?" said the detective, leafing through the diary.

"Oh yes, I'm sure. Never."

For most of the time, the police did not give the impression of disbelieving Louise; their motive in questioning her at such length appeared to be genuine assiduousness rather than suspicion. But now the atmosphere had chilled.

The detective asked Louise, "Why did Lucie write in her diary, 'We have been on a never ending quest for music, postcards and drugs'?"

Louise's mind spun over and over. "I thought, 'If they think she's a drug taker, it'll look really bad.' So I said, 'Oh, she was looking for some paracetamol or Nurofen, something like that.'"

"You have not taken illegal drugs in Japan?" said the detective.

"No, no."

"You are quite sure?"

"Yes."

"Louise, you have the words 'I am a liar' written on your forehead."

"He was right," Louise told me. "I told them the whole story after that."

By the standards of many twenty-one-year-old British women, there wasn't so much to tell. "I mean, there were lots of drugs around, but we just weren't really that into them," said Louise. "Once, some of the people in our house were taking magic mushrooms, and neither of us liked the idea. Lucie said, 'I'd hate to be hallucinating, to be out of control like that.'" The two girls had never had supplies of their own marijuana, but they had taken drags of the spliffs that were passed around the living room of Sasaki House. And Louise said that they had taken tablets of Ecstasy when they were out clubbing in Roppongi—Louise twice (once on the occasion of the fight in Deep Blue) and Lucie once. They had been planning to buy more on the evening of July 1, the night out that had never happened.

In normal circumstances, such an admission would have landed a foreigner in Japan in terrible trouble: possession of a drug like Ecstasy, even in the smallest quantities and for personal use, was a grave crime. "But I knew I had to tell the truth, and I told them the whole story," Louise said. "I told them when, where, how much. And they were fine about it. It was more important to find Lucie. They worked so hard, they were working round the clock. I was there until late and they'd be there until a couple of hours after me. A couple of them had to take time off for exhaustion."

13. THE PALM TREES BY THE SEA

Roppongi—at least the Roppongi of foreign hostesses and their customers—was a village; in the space of two days, everyone in its parish knew of Lucie's disappearance. A week later, it was a headline across Britain and Japan. Two days after that, her face was on thirty thousand missing-person posters. All over Tokyo—and in London, Melbourne, Tel Aviv, and Kiev—Roppongi hostesses, active and retired, were going through the same experience as Christabel Mackenzie, of sudden, jolting reacquaintance with a memory repressed: Clara from Canada, Isobel and Charmaine from Australia, Ronia from Israel, Katie from America, Lana from Britain, and Tanya from Ukraine. Each recalled a different name: Yuji, Koji, Saito, Akira. But the experience was the same: a well-dressed, middle-aged English-speaker with an expensive car; a drive to a seaside apartment among palm trees; a single sip of a drink, then darkness, followed many hours later by dizzy, nauseated consciousness.

Some of the girls knew one another. A few had cautiously shared their stories. All of them, when they heard the story of Lucie, had the same reaction: it *had* to be him.

Almost all had chosen not to go to the police, for the same reasons—because they were anxious about their visa status, because they didn't know exactly what happened to them while unconscious, or because they knew very well and couldn't bring themselves to look the experience in the face. One exception was the young American woman, Katie Vickers. Her experience vindicated the decision of the others. Katie Vickers's story is an unanswerable reproach to the Tokyo Metropolitan Police.

In 1997, she had been working at Club Cadeau. For Katie, the smartly dressed middle-aged man came by the name of Koji. The drink he gave her was gin and tonic. Her first sip of it was the last thing she remembered.

Fifteen hours had passed by the time she awoke, lying on a sofa in her underwear. Koji explained that there had been a gas leak, and that he had a terrible headache too. He drove her halfway back to Tokyo, then put her in a cab, her handbag stuffed with cash and taxi vouchers.

Christa Mackenzie had come around feeling no more than badly hungover. But Katie was left reeling with nausea, which lasted for days. She staggered into Club Cadeau, her lips blue and her speech slurred. The club was owned and managed by Kai Miyazawa, the ponytailed businessman who would explain to me the secrets of the bar business. When he saw Katie, he sent her to a doctor and went with her the next day to Azabu Police Station.

The reaction of the officers on duty dismayed them. "We were not even taken into a private room or asked to take a seat, just simply left standing at the reception desk," Katie wrote later. "The officers showed no interest whatsoever to help us or take any further action. They would not make a formal report, just wrote down some notes on a piece of scrap paper . . . They said they could not investigate my incident because of a lack of evidence . . . I was able to give an accurate description of the man and clearly describe the location. I also gave them the mobile telephone number written by 'Koji' himself. This I feel was sufficient evidence to at least research who the man was, and if he had any prior criminal records. I was made to feel as if I were a nuisance and just wasting police time."

Kai even called a policeman he knew personally. "But in the end, they say, 'Kai, these foreign women, hostesses—they all take drugs. It's her personal problem—just forget about it.' I tell Katie, and she's very angry. For a week she keeps on about it, so I go and talk to them again. But again they say, 'Forget it, forget it.'"

Katie was still living in Tokyo three years later, when Lucie disappeared. As soon as she heard the news, she went back to Azabu Police Station. A female detective recorded a few more details this time but showed no particular interest or concern. Once again, Kai called his detective friend. "But he moved jobs—now he's in a different department," Kai told me. "He says, 'This is not my business.' But now I think one hundred percent that I am right: this must be the same guy."

In July, the police were considering three possible explanations for Lucie's disappearance: a religious cult, a crime involving the trade in illegal drugs, or something to do with the yakuza (hence the questions to Louise about men with tattoos, the badge of the Japanese gangster). They were obvious and sensible lines of inquiry, given the character of Roppongi and of crime in Japan generally. But the police were being told another story, about a criminal who had been operating for years under their noses. Was it this suggestion—of willful negligence on their own part—that explained why, at the beginning at least, they refused to hear it?

Christa Mackenzie had traveled from Osaka to Tokyo to tell the police about "Yuji." Katie Vickers related the story of "Koji." Huw Shakeshaft's friends Isobel Parker and Clara Mendez, who had shared their story with the shell-shocked Tim Blackman, went to them with different names but the same narrative. All four met with indifference. "It was a month before they took anything I said seriously," said Christa. "They were so slow to pick things up. It was partly inertia—they didn't seem interested for a while. They were saying, 'Well, yes, but she's probably joined a religious cult.' Just not listening to people who told them that Lucie wasn't that kind of person at all. But they genuinely thought it was a possibility. Or maybe they just wanted to believe it because they couldn't be bothered to follow through on the alternative."

The police had barely set up their investigation headquarters when the first of the fake letters arrived, signed in Lucie's name. It was the one dated July 17—Tim's birthday—and postmarked Chiba, and Louise recognized it immediately as a forgery. The signature was impressively accurate, but the spelling was poor. The extracts shown to Tim and Sophie had been carefully bowdlerized—in its entirety, it was violent, graphic and angry.

The detectives had forbidden Louise from taking notes, but when they were out of the room, she scribbled down a few phrases on a scrap of paper:

—Louise I love you like a sister but as a matter of fact you fuck up my plans by making me famous.
—he took me to the hotel and fucked me—fuck hostesses
—I want to be what I want to be
—Purpose of coming to Japan is for money yes that is a fact
—wanted to escape
—I begged him to call you
—Tell Scott that I love him, but I don't want to be with him any more
—not innocent had several happenings
—fucked customers with money
—Louise you think you know me but you don't

"It was all really hard language," Louise said. "It was awful." She was spending all day in the police station and going back alone to the police apartment. Her sleep was lurid with nightmares. For a few days, Christa stayed with her, but she was in the grip of her own guilt—for not going to the police earlier and because she had ignored the inner prompting to warn Lucie when she first met her. Instead of giving comfort, she and Louise compounded each other's despair.

"I couldn't stop imagining where Lucie might be," Louise said. "I thought she must be kept in a room, but what kind of room? Every night I thought, 'Is she hungry? Is she cold? Does she have enough to eat and drink? What if she's having her period?' Then I thought that she's been raped, tortured. I imagined there were six guys there, doing awful things to her. I imagined a row of prison cells, room after room. I never believed in my heart she was dead. I thought if she'd died, I'd feel it in my heart."

■ ■ ■

For Kai, the owner of Club Cadeau, the summer of 2000 was also a trying time. "The story about Lucie Blackman was on TV every day," he said. "Everyone's going crazy. All the journalists are in Roppongi, crazy, crazy, interviewing people, and no one is coming to my club." Then one day in August, a telephone call came from Azabu Police Station, the first contact since he and Katie had been fobbed off in the week of Lucie's disappearance. It was one of Superintendent Udo's detectives. "He says, 'I heard that back in July you talked to my colleague. Please come to Azabu Police Station.' I say, 'Fuck off. It's surrounded by journalists. I have a club, I'm trying to make a business, and I don't need this shit. This is bad for business. I just want it all to be over quickly. Come to my office and bring a car. We'll talk, and then we'll go for a drive.' Then I call Katie."

Having got nowhere with drugs, gangsters, or gurus, the investigators were being compelled to consider other possibilities. Two detectives, Usami and Asano, drove Kai and Katie out of Tokyo to look for the place where she had been taken and drugged by "Koji." She had only a vague idea of the direction—south and west of Tokyo, along the Miura Peninsula. Kai recollected the drive vividly; he claimed much of the credit for what followed. "For some reason I said to the police, 'Take a right down here,'" he told me. "Maybe some god was pulling me."

Soon they had reached Zushi Marina, two miles down the coast. When it was new, in the 1970s, this had been a famous and glamorous resort, a place where rich couples retired and where Tokyo celebrities bought holiday apartments with a view of Mount Fuji. The Nobel Prize–winning novelist Yasunari Kawabata had gassed himself to death here in 1972. Boats and water, tall apartment buildings with balconies, and—a rare sight this far north—hundreds of tall palm trees. Katie knew the place immediately. "It gave me chicken skin, the whole thing," Kai told me. "I have chicken skin now, talking about it. Because I was right after all. I knew from the beginning, just knew. And I was right. I knew I was one hundred percent right, and I was right. At that moment, I thought I was really great!"

Isobel Parker and Clara Mendez had told their story to Tim in his first days in Tokyo. Much like the police, in his own state of stifled dread and stupefaction, he had completely missed its significance. After that, the progress of the investigation, or the lack of it, was carefully concealed from him. "The father would come to see us and ask how the investigation was going," a retired senior detective told me. "But all we could say was, 'The investigation is proceeding well.' To be frank, we were not comfortable that he was giving all these big press conferences. He would say, 'Why don't you tell me more?' and we would reply, 'Because the press is there in the background. If we tell you what we are doing, you might tell the press, and that could jeopardize our investigation.'"

The police lied to Tim about their progress. At first, it was probably to conceal how little they knew. But later it was because they didn't want their suspect to learn how hotly they were breathing down his neck. This was partly what made the investigation so baffling.

By late summer the detectives were, in fact, tracking down telephone records. They wanted to identify the origin of the calls made to the pink pay phone in Sasaki House by the man Lucie was to have met that day, and to identify the owner of the numbers that "Koji" and "Yuji" had given to Katie and Christa. They had known about these numbers in early July (in Katie's case since 1997), but it seems only to have been in August that they seriously began to investigate them.

It was an immensely time-consuming and complicated exercise. For any given number, the telephone companies recorded only outgoing, not incoming, calls. It was impossible to start with the pink phone, for example, and trace backwards to the mystery caller. The telephone number given to Christa turned out to have been registered in the name of a Hajime Tanaka, a name as common in Japanese as Michael Smith or Paul Jones. The account had been opened with a public health insurance card that turned out to be fake. The address to which it was registered was real, but no one of that name lived there. The second cell phone, whose number Katie had, was charged with prepaid vouchers, requiring no contract and no billing, the kind of phone popular with people who had something to hide. Every time the detectives asked for telephone records, they had to obtain a warrant from a judge. It could take as long as a week to prepare the necessary documents, present them to the court, and wait for the result.

The detectives began with the pink phone. They knew approximately what time Lucie's customer had called her on the day she disappeared, and they blocked out a time period six minutes before and after that moment. Then they asked the telephone companies to search through all of their subscriber numbers to find out which of them had called the pink phone during that period. Such an exercise involved the scanning of millions of accounts; the companies took a lot of convincing even to attempt it.

"It had never been done before," a former senior detective told me. "It took several days and required many of their staff. This happened after Prime Minister Blair's visit and after he had asked the Japanese government for special cooperation. Having been asked in that manner, we had no choice but to do this to maintain the dignity of the Japanese police."

The search produced a single eleven-digit number. Further checks revealed that it was the number of another anonymous, prepaid cell phone. But the circumstances of its purchase were intriguing. It had been sold in an electronics shop in Tokyo in June 2000, one of a batch of seventy phones bought by a single customer. The name he had given was bogus, and the sale had been made just a few days before the introduction of a law requiring that buyers of such mobiles show proof of address and identity. But now the detectives had the numbers of the other phones from the same batch, all of them owned, they could assume, by the man who had telephoned Lucie and met up with her that day.

Only about ten of them had ever been activated. Now, with fresh warrants, they were able to identify the numbers that had been dialed from those ten numbers and then the numbers that had been called from those. They referred among themselves to "parent," "child," and "grandchild" numbers; the information was recorded in complicated charts resembling family trees. Eventually, in this thicket of digits, they uncovered the number of Louise's mobile phone: this was the call that Lucie had made to Louise on the Saturday evening to say that she would soon be coming home—Lucie's last call.

The telephone company was able to identify the relay

station that had transmitted the call. It was in the town of Zushi.

Katie Vickers had identified the Zushi Marina apartment complex as the place where she had been taken by "Koji." Now the detectives took the other girls there. Christa, Clara, and Isobel all recognized the marina as the place where they had been drugged and undressed. But none could remember with certainty the individual apartment, or even the building. The detectives procured a list of all the apartment owners and ran criminal-record checks on each one. Plenty of old offenses came up, but among the hundreds of names, there was only a single sex offender.

He was the owner of apartment 4314, and his file contained details of two offenses. In 1983, he had paid a small fine after driving into the back of another motorist. Then in October 1998—just two years ago—he had been arrested for peeping at a woman in a ladies' lavatory in the seaside town of Shirahama in western Japan, with a camera in his hand—the second time he had been caught in such an act. To start with, he had given the police a false name, the Japanese media reported later, and described himself as a "nonfiction writer." He pleaded guilty and was fined by the Summary Court without ever having to go to trial. The penalty was ¥9,000, less than the cost of an hour with a hostess at Casablanca or Club Cadeau.

The criminal file contained a mug shot of the man, taken at the time of his arrest, and the police were also able to call up the photograph on his driver's license. They identified cars registered in his name, several companies of which he was listed as president, and numerous properties owned by these companies across Japan.

The photographs of the man were placed in an album containing scores of other faces. Christa, Katie, Clara, and Isobel each identified him as their customer and assailant. "It was a really weird picture," Clara remembered. "His eyes were hardly open, like they'd picked him up out of the gutter. If you didn't know, you'd think he was drunk or something. But I think that he was just trying to make it difficult for them to photograph him by looking away."

They tracked one of the man's cars, a white Mercedes-Benz sports car, through the surveillance cameras that monitor Japan's highways. They confirmed that he had traveled from Tokyo to Zushi on the day of Lucie's disappearance and made several journeys in the days that followed, to and from the city, and up and down the Miura Peninsula.

Superintendent Udo ordered a watch to be kept on the man. Rather than risking detection with a fixed tail, he had him tracked by individual officers in different positions who radioed the suspect's movements to one another. In any one day, there might be ten different people following the suspect, on foot, on motorcycle, or in a car. Udo referred to this style of surveillance as the "pinpoint method." It was not completely reliable, and the detectives often lost their man. One day he went for a drive in the direction of Chiba, where he disappeared. And the next day, the foul, angry letter signed in Lucie's name arrived at Azabu Police Station bearing a Chiba postmark.

■ ■ ■

By the end of September, Superintendent Udo was confident that he had found his man. His movements on the day that Lucie disappeared and the stories of the other hostesses left no doubt. But proof was lacking. In Katie Vickers herself, the police were no more interested than when they had turned her away three years earlier; she and the other women were a means to an end. "What was important was to find out what happened to Lucie, how he had killed her, and where her body was," Udo said. "That was our goal—to find out what had happened to Lucie."

The detectives began to look into the background of their suspect and his movements over the past few weeks. His companies owned properties from the island of Hokkaido in the north to Kyushu in the south. Some of these were rented apartments, but several of them were personal residences, including three apartments in central Tokyo, and a huge two-story house with a swimming pool in the affluent suburb of Den-en Chofu. There was also a property in a village called Moroiso, on the west coast of the Miura Peninsula, sixteen miles south of Zushi. It was a coastline marked with rocky inlets and beaches, where the homes of fishermen stood beside blocks of holiday apartments. The suspect owned an apartment in a building called Blue Sea Aburatsubo.

The detectives called on their colleagues in the town of Misaki, the police station closest to Moroiso. The patrolmen there had an interesting story to tell.

On July 6, three officers had gone to Blue Sea Aburatsubo, after a complaint from its caretaker, Ms. Abe. A man had turned up suddenly that afternoon and entered apartment 401, which had been unused for several years. He didn't have a key for the place and, without consulting the caretaker, he had summoned a locksmith to open the door. He had left his sports car, a two-seater Mercedes, alongside the building. Ms. Abe's partner, Mr. Hirokawa, reported that it had been full of lumpy objects covered by white sheets; only the driver's seat had been clear. The suspicious man was now in his room, and unusual bangs could be heard. Inspector Naoki Harada and one of his officers climbed the stairs and knocked on the door. As they approached, they heard a loud bumping noise from within.

There was no reply at first. They rang the bell again, and spoke into the intercom, identifying themselves as policemen and asking to be allowed in. Eventually a man opened the door. He was short and middle-aged, with thinning hair. "He was half naked and wearing something like pajama trousers," Inspector Harada said later. "I was struck by the beads of sweat on his face and chest, and his trembling. He was panting, too. I had the impression that he was sweating from every pore, and he was very dirty. I thought he must have been doing some really vigorous work."

The man said something about changing his clothes and closed the door; there were more bangs from within. When the man appeared again, Inspector Harada stepped inside the entryway of the apartment. "I saw some kind of tool in the corridor, and pieces of concrete scattered around," he said. "There was a kind of linen bag in the back room, with something in it. It was something round and gray with a diameter of about twenty centimeters [eight inches]."

But the man strenuously refused to allow the police to inspect the house and insisted that he was doing nothing more than retiling his bathroom. "Showing you inside my room is like showing you my naked body," he said angrily. Inspector Harada replied, "I'm not interested in your naked body—just let me look inside and I'll leave." But lacking a warrant, or any evidence of a specific crime, the policemen had no right to force entry or carry out a search. After radioing back to their station, and confirming that the man was indeed the legal owner of the property, they retreated down the stairs.

The most bizarre part of the story came a little later when the man called them back up to the apartment. "He stood in front holding something wrapped in paper," Inspector Harada said. "He opened it, as if cradling a baby. I saw the head of a dog. He said, 'My beloved dog died. I thought you'd think it strange if you saw this body, so I didn't want to let you in.'"

One policeman remembered that the body of the creature was frozen and stiff. He said, "It was not something that had died that day or the day before."

"I thought he might be doing something serious like disposing of a body," Inspector Harada would say in court, years later. But the local police never followed up on the incident of the man with the dead dog and never made any connection with the reports just a few days later that a foreign girl had disappeared after being driven to the sea.

■ ■ ■

Between July and October, six letters were sent to the heads of Azabu Police Station and the First Investigation Section. Two were in the same imperfect English and signed with the same fake signature in the name of Lucie Blackman. One was in Japanese and eight pages long, purportedly from an unidentified "acquaintance" of Lucie, who had met her "at a certain place." It stated that Lucie suffered from schizophrenia and had multiple personalities, and that she had accumulated huge debts that she was paying off by working as a prostitute. "It was not kidnap—she used men," the writer hissed. Superintendent Udo had the fingerprints of the suspect from his arrest in the public lavatory, but no prints of any kind were to be found on the letters or their envelopes.

At the beginning of October, an especially fat envelope arrived at Azabu Police Station. It contained a wad of ¥10,000 notes—¥1,187,000 in total. The accompanying letter, once more signed by "Lucie," explained that this was to pay off her debts of £7,418 (about $11,000). It said that, because of her debts, Lucie had decided to disappear for a while and that eventually she would leave Japan. The enclosed money was to be disbursed to her creditors by Sophie—and, however many posters were distributed with her photograph, she was determined to escape to a place where nobody knew her.

For all their efforts at surveillance, the police never observed their suspect in the act of withdrawing the money from the bank or posting any of the letters. But they did become aware of a disturbing development: on October 1, he had purchased a boat.

It was a twenty-foot fiberglass Yamaha fishing boat. It had been bought for ¥3.5 million, about $33,000, from a dealership in Yokohama and was delivered to the Seabornia Marina, a few hundred yards across the bay from the apartment at Blue Sea Aburatsubo. A few days later, the suspect had gone into the maritime-supplies store at Seabornia and bought a compass and a length of anchor rope. He told the manager of the shop, Hideo Kawaguchi, that he wanted to anchor somewhere very deep and that he would need one thousand yards of rope. "There is a spot of one thousand yards, out in Sagami Bay," Mr. Kawaguchi remembered, "but it's very difficult to weigh anchor at that depth. I told him that you need a very heavy anchor, and you have to connect one long rope to another. He told me he was very experienced, but I doubted it, because an experienced sailor would never ask for a rope that long."

Most visitors at the shop wore shorts and sandals, but this customer came in a pin-striped suit, tie, and black leather shoes. "I had the feeling he was a bit strange," said Mr. Kawaguchi. "His manner was unusual, and he was sweating a lot."

Ten minutes after he had left the shop, the detectives arrived, wanting to know everything that had been said and cautioning the staff not to talk to anyone about their strange customer.

Superintendent Udo suddenly had a lot to think about. What possible reason could the suspect have for buying a boat? It was the end of the sailing season, and he seemed to have had no previous interest in the sea. The talk of anchor rope and Sagami Bay suggested an obvious explanation: he had something he wished to dispose of, and he planned to do so in the depths of the ocean.

Sailings out of Seabornia had to be registered in advance with the commodore of the marina, who had also received a discreet visit from the police. The following week, he told them that their suspect was planning to take out his boat on

Thursday, October 12. "We guessed that Lucie's body must be somewhere and that his plan was to dispose of the body," Udo said. "So we prepared to arrest him that morning." The Tokyo Public Prosecutors' Office hastily obtained an arrest warrant—not for Lucie's disappearance but for the rape of one of the other hostesses.

The suspect spent the night of October 11 in one of his Tokyo properties, a one-room apartment ten minutes' walk from Roppongi Crossing. The arrest was planned for early in the morning; everything was in place when Udo went to sleep that night.

At 3:00 a.m. he was woken by a telephone call from a Japanese journalist. *The Yomiuri Shimbun*, Japan's—and the world's—bestselling newspaper, was intending to run a front-page story in its earliest edition, reporting the imminent arrest of a man suspected of involvement in the disappearance of Lucie Blackman.

"I knew that this would be picked up and reported on television too," Udo said. "We had to act before he saw the morning news." It wasn't that the suspect might escape, for by now the surveillance of him was overwhelming. The fear was that, confronted with arrest, he would commit suicide.

At 6:00 a.m. the officers staking out the apartment building saw the man walk out and enter the convenience store on the corner. He emerged clutching a bundle of newspapers. They descended on him then and there, and arrested him on suspicion of the abduction and indecent assault of Clara Mendez on March 31, 1996. The newspapers that day named him as Joji Obara, a forty-eight-year-old businessman and company president. "When the arresting officers addressed him, he started trembling," Udo said, "and beads of sweat appeared."

PART FOUR OBARA

14. THE WEAK AND THE STRONG

Only a handful of photographs of Joji Obara ever reached the public domain and none was less than thirty years old.

All but one were from his school days. They showed a young man with a gentle, almost feminine face and a shyly diffident smile. He wore the black, high-collared Prussian-style uniform of the Japanese schoolboy. His hair, parted on the right, was short and well shaped. In one photograph, he looked away from the camera and bit down on his lower lip with an expression of nervous abstraction. He looked to be a soft, sensitive, slightly girlish boy. His lips were by far his most striking feature: full and sharply defined, forming a symmetrical Cupid's bow.

The most recent picture, very coarse and grainy, showed a man in his early twenties, his wide-collared shirt unbuttoned to reveal an isosceles of exposed chest. He was thinner than the schoolboy, with a longer, fuller head of hair. He smiled confidently into the camera through a pair of large sunglasses. The pose was self-consciously manly; one could read a confidence, even an arrogance, in the directness of his gaze. Most of these images had been cut out and enlarged from group photographs taken at formal school ceremonies. They were obtained by Japanese reporters in the feverish weeks following Obara's arrest, from old acquaintances at school or university.

But after that last one, which must have dated from the mid-1970s, there was nothing.

His elderly mother was said to possess a photograph or two. Otherwise, except for the purposes of unavoidable official documentation such as driver's license and passport, Joji Obara shunned photographers. Even in the Tokyo Metropolitan Police headquarters he twisted his head away from the camera and refused to display his face for the mug shot.

He was a hoarder and collector and recorder, a diarist and a memo maker, who seems to have found it impossible to throw anything away. He was incriminated by this habit; without the chaotic private archive they found in his properties, the police would never have been able to charge Joji Obara. But through the outer world, he moved, or labored to move, without a trace. It seemed to be a habit inherited from his family.

His past, even his most recent past, was dim and blurred. Stare long and hard enough (and I spent many months staring) and shapes and figures could be made out: flashes and flickers illuminating a face and an occasional snatch of speech. But it was difficult to name what was moving in the darkness.

Joji Obara had not always been Joji Obara. He was born in the city of Osaka on August 10, 1952. The following month, his father registered the child's name with three characters which, in isolation, meant Gold Star Bell. In Japanese, they were read as Seisho Kin, but the child's parents were Mr. and Mrs. Kim, and they would have called their baby Sung Jong. When it suited them, the family also identified itself by the Japanese surname Hoshiyama. It was entirely consistent with his later life that Kim Sung Jong/Seisho Kin/Seisho Hoshiyama entered the world with three names.

The Kim-Kin-Hoshiyamas were members of the population known as Zainichi Chosenjin or simply Zainichi—the ethnic Koreans of Japan. In 2000, when Lucie Blackman came to Tokyo, there were nine hundred thousand of them, but one could live in Japan for years and never be aware of their presence. They were an ethnic minority in a country that presented itself as racially homogeneous and undivided. Their origins were a tragedy, a by-product of the churning politics of early twentieth-century Asia.

Surrounded by powerful and aggressive neighbors, Korea had been a battlefield throughout its history. As far back as the sixteenth century, samurai armies had plundered the peninsula, returning across the narrow Strait of Tsushima with treasures, slaves, and the severed ears of slaughtered Korean warriors. Japan began to dominate Korea once again at the end of the nineteenth century; in 1910, the country was formally annexed into the emerging Japanese empire. The colonizers built roads, ports, railways, mines, and factories, introduced modern agricultural methods, and sent the children of the Korean elite to be educated in Tokyo. But whatever good Japanese power brought in the form of economic development was eclipsed by the racism, coercion, and violence of the imperial occupation.

The policies of the Japanese administration shifted over time. But by the late 1930s, its goal was not merely to control Koreans and exploit their resources but also to dissolve their culture and colonize their minds. The Japanese language was made compulsory in schools; students were required to worship at Shinto shrines, and Koreans were encouraged to take Japanese names. Infrequent uprisings were quelled with arrests, torture, and killings. And a vast and unequal human exchange took place, as Japanese bureaucrats and settlers were shipped over to govern and farm the new lands, and poor Koreans sailed in the opposite direction to find work in the industrial cities of Tokyo, Osaka, and Fukuoka.

At first, this migration was voluntary, but as the Pacific War turned against Japan, its colonial subjects were forcibly conscripted, both by the Imperial Army and civilian industry. By 1945, hundreds of thousands of Koreans were scattered across Asia with the Japanese forces, as soldiers, orderlies, camp guards, and military sex slaves (the "comfort women" whose existence was officially denied for almost fifty years). In Japan itself there were two million Zainichi, most of them concentrated in ghettos close to the mines and factories where they were set to work. As much as anything, it was the sudden presence of so many foreigners in the motherland that showed up the hypocrisy of Japanese colonialism.

Government policy was bent on the complete assimilation of Koreans, whose own culture and language would be swallowed up. But while Japan was content to obliterate their identity, it could not bring itself to allow Koreans the privileges and status enjoyed by its own people.

They were subjects of the emperor but never full citizens. Their voting rights were restricted, as was their representation in parliament. Koreans in the ghettos of Osaka and Kawasaki had lower standards of health and literacy than native Japanese. They were paid drastically less for the same work, earning them the hatred of many Japanese workers, whose own wages and labor were undercut. In everyday life, they encountered discrimination and contempt, which blocked opportunities in education, employment, and politics.

Many Japanese regarded them with dislike verging on disgust. They were held to be hot-tempered, stubborn, and quarrelsome, a dirty, smelly people who consumed obnoxious food. It is arguable whether one could ever tell Japanese and Koreans apart by their faces alone, but there was no doubt that they talked differently, moved differently, and distinguished themselves in a thousand small ways from the proudly homogeneous Japanese. Above all, they lacked that instinctive reserve and internalized respect for authority that is still so striking in Japanese today. The newspapers eagerly carried stories of crimes perpetrated by "rebellious" Koreans who, even when caught in the act, were notoriously reluctant to confess. At best, they were considered rowdy and unsavory; at worst, as violent, criminal, and subversive. Such prejudices and tensions were not always obvious, but they were close to the surface and, when they did express themselves, they could be explosive.

In 1923, an enormous earthquake destroyed Tokyo and neighboring Yokohama; 140,000 people died in the fires that consumed the wooden cities. In the stunned aftermath, rumors began to circulate—repeated by Japanese newspapers—that Koreans were starting fires, poisoning wells, rioting, raping women, and looting shops. There was no reason to believe any of the stories, but in the following few days thousands of Korean civilians were murdered by mobs of ordinary Japanese in a spontaneous eruption of hysterical violence.

"When they captured one, they shouted, 'Korean!'" according to a contemporary account.

> Many Japanese rushed to the scene, surrounding the victim. They tied him to a telephone pole, scooped out his eyes, cut off his nose, chopped open his stomach, and pulled out his internal organs. Sometimes they tied a Korean's neck to a car and dragged him around until he choked to death. They also captured women, grabbed their legs, pulled them in opposite directions, and tore their bodies. The Koreans resisted till the last moment, begging and insisting on their innocence. But the crowd never listened.

Two or three years after this, near the port city of Pusan, in what is now South Korea, Joji Obara's parents were born.

In Japan, a crime is regarded not merely as the act of a criminal; in some deep sense, it originates from within his family. Morally, if not legally, his closest relatives also bear a responsibility—hence the spectacle, surprisingly common in Japan, of a wrongdoer's parents (and sometimes siblings, school-teachers, even employers) bowing deeply before the cameras and offering tearful apologies for deeds over which they had no influence or control. So within hours of Obara's arrest, Japanese reporters were competing with one another to find out where he came from and who his people were.

The essential facts—name, age, and occupation—were quickly established. But there the flow of information stopped. A few years later, I spent several weeks inquiring into Obara's background. I spoke to a dozen Japanese journalists, veterans of solemn broadsheets and scandalous weekly magazines, who collectively had put in months of work. They were experienced investigative reporters; they had time, resources, and contacts. But between their efforts and mine, we assembled little more than scraps. "In most criminal cases," one magazine reporter told me, "even if you don't get anything from the family, then at least people around them will talk—friends, neighbors, business colleagues. But in Obara's case there was almost nothing."

His father's name was Kim Kyo Hak, his mother's Chun Ok Su. They came to Japan before the war, not as conscripts but as voluntary migrants. According to one of his sons, Kim Kyo Hak was imprisoned for two and a half years for his resistance to the Japanese, although where, when, and how this happened is not clear. But he was in Japan in 1945, and in little more than a decade he went from being a disenfranchised immigrant to one of the richest men in Japan's second-biggest city.

Japan immediately after the war was poor and chaotic, but for Koreans it was a moment of rare confidence and opportunity. One can imagine the powerful, even violent, exhilaration: after thirty-five years as despised underdogs, Zainichi stood suddenly alongside the victors, a liberated people in the heart of the defeated country. Osaka, like almost every other city, had been substantially destroyed by Allied bombing. Title deeds to property had been lost forever; in the confusion that followed, force was enough to make claims to land that might never be overturned. Black markets sprang up in the ruins, dominated by the Japanese yakuza on one side, and on the other by the people referred to as *sangokujin*, or "third-country people"—newly liberated citizens of the former colonies. There were murderous turf wars. The police looked on helplessly as armies of gangsters fought pitched battles with hundreds of Koreans, Taiwanese, and Chinese. Many Zainichi hurried back to Korea after liberation, but conditions there were as wretched and desperate as in Japan. And after the exultation of victory, those who stayed behind were soon faced with the reality of their situation. They were still poor, still disadvantaged, and still the victims of prejudice. And with the defeat of the empire and the liberation of Korea, they were unambiguously foreigners, stripped of even the basic rights of colonial subjects.

Zainichi formed themselves into two organizations: Mindan, affiliated with the right-wing American-backed dictatorship in the south of Korea; and Chōsen Sōren, which was loyal to the Communist north. In 1950, backed by the United States and China respectively, the two Koreas embarked on the three-year war that ruined and pauperized the peninsula all over again. The tragedy of the Korean War was Japan's good fortune, as the American military's demand for steel, uniforms, and supplies jerked its economy into recovery.

By the time the future Joji Obara was born in 1952 as Kim Sung Jong, his father, Kim Kyo Hak, was rich. Exactly how he made his fortune is difficult to tell, but for a man in his position the possibilities were limited. No large or respectable company would take on a Korean as anything but a manual laborer; no Japanese bank would lend him money. Apart from property, Kim Kyo Hak had at least three sources of income: parking lots, a taxi company, and pachinko—a uniquely Japanese arcade game, a kind of vertical electronic bagatelle, and one of the few forms of gambling tolerated by the law. The common feature of all these enterprises was that they demanded no large-scale capital investment. A shop or a restaurant required premises, staff, and stock. But having acquired a plot of vacant land, a car, or a pachinko machine, a man could start to make money from them immediately. Each day brought cash income, for the simple needs of survival or to reinvest (another car, a second machine). But even businesses as simple as this could not prosper in a vacuum.

Successful pachinko players were not rewarded directly with cash, but with prizes such as cigarettes or coupons that they could take to a discreet window nearby and exchange for money—by this means, the pachinko parlors bypassed the legal ban on gambling. The cash windows were operated by yakuza gangs, who creamed off a commission. The gangs also kept order in the markets, "resolved" ownership disputes over property, drove out unwanted tenants, made loans, and allocated the right of businesses to operate on a particular territory—all for the appropriate fee. The yakuza had always been a refuge for those with nowhere else to go, for the poor, outcast, and marginalized. Koreans were prominent in the great Japanese gang syndicates—the Yamaguchi-gumi in Osaka and Kobe, and the Sumiyoshi-kai in Tokyo—and there were Korean gangs too, such as the Yamagawa-gumi and the Meiyu-kai, notorious for their aggression, who defended Zainichi shops and ghettos.

There is no evidence that Kim Kyo Hak was a yakuza, or that he played any part in organized crime. He had no criminal record. But for many men of his background, in that place, at that time, and in those businesses, some kind of contact with the criminal syndicates was common. "It was inevitable," said Manabu Miyazaki, a journalist and the son of a yakuza boss. "For a Zainichi Korean, establishing relations with the yakuza was a condition of running a successful business."

■ ■ ■

"In the taxi business, he was the most successful," said an Osaka Korean who remembered Kim Kyo Hak. "In the pachinko business too. He was charming, sociable, talkative. He was rather fat, and none too tall. He always wore a jacket that was too big for him. He drove the most expensive cars. He began his career in the market." The man who told me this was a respected public servant in his fifties, distinguished in his field, with a foreign education and a fine collection of classical music recordings. His father, like Joji Obara's, had been a Korean immigrant, and he smiled as he recalled how he had supported his family by purchasing dead horses from the knacker's yards of the occupying American forces and selling their meat as beef.

Those who made a success of life in the Zainichi ghettos shared this spirit of opportunistic entrepreneurship. People who lived through the ten years after the war remember a period of acute hardship and food shortages, in which grown adults sometimes died of hunger, but they also talk of fellowship and camaraderie that are rarely present in times of prosperity and of a dark, gallows humor. The Kim family lived in the Abeno-ku area of Osaka, in a neighborhood of wooden homes thrown up hard by one another in narrow alleys off a street of shops and market stalls. It was a tough, cheerful, noisy place; one of the family's pachinko parlors was around the corner. But by the time the future Joji Obara was a toddler, the family had moved to an area little more than a mile south but a world apart in social status and glamour.

This was Kitabatake, an immaculate district of huge silent

houses surrounded by gardens in walled-off compounds, inhabited by the wealthiest and most respectable people in Osaka. They were people of restraint and breeding; however surprised they were at their new neighbors, they would have been unlikely to make any display of overt racism. But Korean immigrants in an area like this in the 1950s could not but have been conscious of their difference from those around them.

In secluding themselves in such an area, the Kims would also have detached themselves from the life of the Korean community at large. But perhaps this was happening anyway. Kim Kyo Hak was one of the wealthiest men in Osaka—yet now almost no one remembers him. Like his son after him, he strove to move through life without a trace.

Compelled, like all Zainichi, to make a choice of nationality after the war, he took that of South Korea. The rival residents' associations, Mindan and Chōsen Sōren, were central to the lives of many Koreans in Japan. They served as social clubs, schools, and cultural centers, where friends and contacts could be made. Associated with them were credit unions that lent money to businessmen who could raise nothing from the Japanese banks. But, most unusually, Mr. Kim was not affiliated to either of them.

The characters on the huge front gate in Kitabatake identified the family as Kim. But they also used the name Hoshiyama. Koreans often took new names because of the advantages to be had from fitting in, from being able to pass as Japanese. But the effort was self-defeating, because the names they chose still distinguished them as Koreans. Hoshiyama, for example, was the kind of name recognizable as typical of Zainichi. The Zainichi knew this, and it expressed their plight and their pride, and the pain of surrendering completely an identity as deep as that of race.

"That was the period when the gap began to open up between rich and poor Koreans," Manabu Miyazaki told me.

"The society was split between the extremes. People like Obara and his family were the winners, in that sense. They would have had faith in the future, in a life without discrimination. But in Japanese society, discrimination is not so easily overcome. The Japanese tribe wants always to keep itself separate from other people, to maintain the differences. For Koreans who believed in their equality, that sense of difference was a cause of fury."

"The first generation had great regard for their Korean identity," said the man whose father had sold horsemeat. "Among them were some who had success in business, charismatic figures who built their own empires. They couldn't find employment in the mainstream of Japanese society because of discrimination, and when they came across such discrimination, they asked themselves why. The answer they came up with was: education. They didn't have a decent education—my father only went through elementary school, for example. And so they wanted their children to have a better education than they had received themselves."

After his arrest, Joji Obara resisted all inquiries into his childhood and family. But a bizarre book, commissioned six years later by his lawyer, and that bears the signs of originating with Obara himself, dwells in detail on what he calls his "extreme special education for the gifted," which began in early childhood. In the absence of other information about the family, it is revealing about the intense pressure that Mr. and Mrs. Kim placed upon their children from an early age. "My father was in prison for two and a half years," Obara's younger brother told me in my one, strange encounter with him. "He was [in the] resistance, fighting the Japanese. But the only thing I can blame him [for] is [that] he has no time to take care of the family. But he always said the importance of education."

Two years before he went to elementary school, Kim Sung Jong was sent to a Roman Catholic nursery; every day when he got home from school, three private tutors were waiting for the little boy. Violin and piano lessons, according to the book, began "at the age of three years and ten months." On Saturdays, he studied with his music teachers from lunchtime until evening, and then played with an orchestra for an hour. On Sundays, there were more private tutorials in the morning and afternoon. "It was dreadful having no free time," the book, narrated in the third person, records. "[Obara] deliberately pretended to be not worthy of teaching in order to escape from the misery." He wrote his schoolwork with his left hand, instead of his right, to spoil his handwriting, and started on exam answers only when the time was nearly up. This later account summarizes the situation with an intriguing phrase: "He liberated himself by degrading himself."

At the age of six he entered the famous school attached to the Osaka University of Education, one of the best schools in the country. It was a self-consciously elitist institution, founded in emulation of a British public school. In the 1950s, many of the teachers were former officers of the disbanded Imperial Army and Navy, and the parents of the Osaka upper middle class—doctors, lawyers, and businessmen—competed to enrol their young sons.

At school, Kim Sung Jong was known as Seisho Kin. A man who was in his class at elementary school remembered wrestling and playing baseball with him. "He was a strong boy then, on the big side," he told me. "He had an older brother at the school, and I remember going to their house in Kitabatake, and his mother, who was very kind to me. He was a real Korean. He got angry quickly; he was very short-tempered. I thought his eyes were very strong. He had a strength in his eyes. But it would not be true to say that everyone liked him."

Another classmate from those days also played baseball with Seisho Kin. "He always wanted to be the pitcher," he remembered. "Not that he threw very fast or with great control. He always wanted to show off, but his technique didn't match his ambition. I don't remember seeing him laugh cheerfully as a child. And he wanted things his way, without paying attention to what other people might feel. I think he set up a wall between himself and others. His contacts with others were shallow or nonexistent. When you ask me now, I can't think who his close friends were."

These conversations were conducted half a century later, and several years after Joji Obara had been arrested and charged with a series of grave crimes. It was perhaps not surprising, although it was still striking, that of the ten people I tracked down who knew him as a child, not one described himself as a friend of Seisho Kin, or remembered anyone else who did.

Seisho was the second of four brothers. He was ten years older than Kosho, the youngest, and six years older than the third boy, Eisho. The oldest brother was Sosho, who had been born in 1948. In a traditional Korean family, it was he who should have carried the greatest burden of parental expectation and pride. But there were problems with Sosho Kin.

One of his schoolmates was Shingo Nishimura, who would go on to be elected to the House of Representatives of the Japanese diet. Nishimura was a member of the nationalist right wing, an ultrapatriot who believed that the Pacific War should be a source of pride rather than its opposite, and that Japan should arm itself against future war in Asia with nuclear weapons. Such people form a noisy but small minority in Japan; for one of them to be elected an MP is very unusual indeed. It was difficult to know to what degree Shingo Nishimura's chauvinism shaded his childhood recollection, but he spoke sadly and rather fondly of Sosho Kin.

His earliest memory was of a likable and well-adjusted boy who fitted in well enough in a class of high-spirited teenagers. "If people teased him, he took it in his stride and didn't let it bother him," Nishimura said. "I saw him at close quarters, and I always found him quite straightforward." He knew that Sosho's father was extremely rich, that he had made his money from pachinko, and that the family lived in the most expensive part of Osaka. "He was regarded as a bit different from others, but I wouldn't say that he was bullied. He was like a pet to us. In junior high school, he was a very loving character. But when we started in senior high school, all of a sudden he changed."

Between lessons, Sosho Kin would walk to the front of the class and chalk slogans on the blackboard, political slogans, full of resentment for Japan and the Japanese. "He would write, 'Down with Japanese imperialism!' and talk about how Japan was bad, and Japanese were bad, and Korea and Koreans were victims," Nishimura remembered. "And he said that he was being followed by the Korean CIA"—the notorious South Korean intelligence agency, which frequently abducted and tortured its political enemies.

This was the 1960s, a time of political tumult in Japan and Korea, with strikes and demonstrations against the Japan-U.S. Security Treaty and the Vietnam War. But the closest that the rich and pampered children of the school got to left-wing politics was listening to Joan Baez records; Sosho Kin's radical slogans were impossible for them to take seriously. "The other boys, we just watched him doing all this and laughed," Nishimura said. "People would say, 'Ah! He's at it again.' Some of them said, 'If you don't like it, why don't you go home?' When he talked that way, it was like watching a character in a comic. He took it so seriously, and the more seriously he took it, the less seriously everyone else did."

Towards the end of senior high school, Sosho Kin suddenly

stopped coming to classes. Shingo Nishimura never found out why. There were vague rumors that it was because of an inadequate academic performance; later, he heard that Sosho had gone to the United States. Nishimura went on to university in Kyoto and qualified as a lawyer, the most competitive and prestigious of the Japanese professions. Twenty-five years passed, and he forgot all about the strange Zainichi boy. And then late one night in 1989 he received a telephone call.

It was Sosho Kin, sounding terrified. He said that he needed to see Nishimura immediately. It was after midnight, but Nishimura found himself hurrying over, for the first time in his life, to the big house in Kitabatake. A maid admitted him; there seemed to be no one else at home. Sosho greeted him silently and produced a pad of paper on which he quickly began to write. "He wouldn't speak," Nishimura remembered. "He wrote everything down. He wrote, 'I'm being bugged so I can't talk. Even at home or on the train, someone is watching me and following me.'

"Well, I looked at my surroundings and thought that it could not be true. He was in this big, peaceful house with a maid looking after him. It was obvious that there was no one following him or bugging him, but he believed it passionately." Apart from expressing his paranoia about surveillance and pursuit, Sosho Kin wrote a little about his time in the United States. "I felt that his life there must have been very unhappy, that he must have suffered loneliness," Nishimura remembered. "He said a little about it. He told me that once he had been in a tent in the middle of the desert, and that he had shot a rattlesnake."

It wasn't clear from his scribbled sentences what Sosho Kin wanted his lawyer friend to do for him. Eventually, Nishimura took his leave. "What could I do?" he said. "I told him that he should have a good sleep and try to relax. Then I left."

Nishimura never heard from him again, although other contemporaries from the Osaka University of Education School did. Around the same time, a handful of ex-classmates had been contacted by Sosho Kin with a peculiar request. He wanted to borrow their copies of the school yearbook, and when the albums were returned, the faces of boys from Sosho's year had been cut out with a knife.

"At school, we knew that he was Korean," Nishimura said, "but we had no particular prejudice. We were friends, in the usual way. We got on well. But, thinking back, it seems that even leading that wealthy life, he was unhappy, and he believed that unhappiness was brought about by Japan and the Japanese."

■ ■ ■

The third of the boys, immediately junior to Joji Obara, was Eisho Kin. In different ways from his oldest brother, he too seems to have struggled with the face he presented to the world, and with his Korean identity.

Eisho went to the foreign-language university in nearby Kobe. He was a talented and creative young man. He spoke Chinese and English, as well as Japanese and Korean, and he had literary and intellectual ambitions. A group of like-minded young Zainichi used to meet at a library in Osaka to discuss literature and the politics of being a Korean in Japan; Eisho was one of them. They talked of Dostoyevsky, Sartre, and Camus, and of the prejudice they faced in their daily lives: invisible for most of the time but hard and high as a prison wall. These young men would never be offered jobs at a top Japanese bank or trading house. However outstanding their university careers, they would never be recruited into the fast track of the diplomatic service or the Ministry of Finance. "Most Zainichi Koreans aren't conscious of discrimination," an Osaka journalist told me. "That's just who they are—they get on with their lives. It's the people with ambition, who want to rise in society, they're the ones who hit the glass ceiling. Most of the time they don't realize they're captive. It's only the ones who try to escape who suddenly become aware of the cage. These are people who've grown up in Japan, speaking Japanese, eating Japanese food, never imagining that they are objects of discrimination. For people like this, in the second or third generation, the shock of discrimination is very great."

I met a man who had been a member of this group of young intellectuals and a friend of Eisho Kin. They had spent many hours together, talking of books and ideas. But he always found Eisho's company a strain. He was touchy and hesitant and defensive; the conversation never unfolded smoothly. "He was very stiff," the friend told me. "He couldn't be natural in the way he dealt with people. Whenever it got on to family matters, he always lost his composure. He was on guard all the time." Once, he visited Eisho Kin's home. The tone of their conversations, with their emphasis on radical philosophy and left-wing politics, had left him unprepared for its luxury and grandeur, and its garden filled with huge and expensive ornamental stones—immense, immovable manifestations of a family's wealth and power. "My impression is that he had difficulty in accepting that he had risen in social class," the man told me. "He couldn't deal with the distance between himself and other Koreans."

Eisho Kin had aspirations to be a writer. When he was twenty-two years old, a short story of his was published in a journal of Zainichi writing. It was an account of the sadness of a young man: hesitant, awkward, tormented by self-consciousness, disdainful of others, and humiliated by them.

The story is called "It Happened One Day," and its protagonist is a Zainichi named Bun'ichi Ri. He is sitting on the subway when three Japanese men of his own age board the train; he understands immediately that they are deaf. Unintelligible whooping sounds come from their mouths. They communicate with one another in sign language, with busily moving hands and exaggerated facial expressions. Bun'ichi wonders if subtle emotions and nuances of feeling can ever be expressed with fingers and eyebrows. But the deaf men are struggling so hard, with such physical effort, to communicate with one another. The sight of them moves him deeply.

Bun'ichi, we are told, had "problems at home." To escape them, he first put his energy into "social issues," also of an unspecified kind. But he became disillusioned with the "phoniness" of the Zainichi organizations in which he participated and preoccupied by painful questions about discrimination. He identifies this not only in the treatment of Koreans by Japanese but also in a sense of superiority over others that he recognizes in himself. If Bun'ichi is a victim of racism, he also has to own up to prejudices of his own. "What are we to do with this habit, this instinct to discriminate against others, to feel good in setting another below ourselves?" he asks. "In thinking about such things, he felt the weight of a stone on the top of his head." Bun'ichi feels himself to be divided within, to carry inside him a consciousness separate from his own—a cold, scrutinizing intelligence that passes judgment on him for saying one thing while intending another. It is the absence of this self-consciousness in the deaf men on the train that moves him so much. "They struggled without self-deception," he observes. "There was no dishonesty in their desperate struggle to communicate."

A drunk Japanese man walks down the subway train—in his shiny suit and white shoes, he looks like a yakuza. One of the deaf men unintentionally brushes against him. The drunk reacts furiously, grabbing his collar and demanding an apology; all the deaf man can do is whoop wordlessly. Bun'ichi stands up and shouts at the bully to leave his victim alone, and so the man turns upon him. In a fight between the stocky thug and the tenderhearted Bun'ichi, it is obvious who will come off best. But before any blows are exchanged, the three deaf passengers come between the two of them—and in the end, it is the handicapped men who save the Korean from a beating by the Japanese gangster.

Bun'ichi had intervened out of what he identified as a sense of fairness and justice. But in his humiliation, the voice in his head passes a harsher verdict. He acted because he had judged the deaf men to be weak and vulnerable. His anger against the drunken thug was actually based on a kind of prejudice and an assumption of superiority over the disabled—not so different from the prejudice he faces as a Zainichi. "Are we the strong if we name them the weak?" he asks himself. "Then what about Koreans in Japan who are discriminated against even in our jobs in this closed Japanese society? Which are we, the strong or the weak?"

He gets off the train and walks home from the station, filled with confusion and self-reproach. "Am I no different from those I despise?" he asks himself. "Why do human beings want to discriminate against human beings?"

He finds himself walking past a big house with an imposing front gate, a garden of "huge heavy stones, so huge that an ordinary house might be built with them." A Cadillac drives past with its headlights blazing. "Bun'ichi wondered if people who live in such a house would ever think about what troubled him."

This house, although few readers of the story could ever have known it, is recognizably the house of the Kin family in Kitabatake; the Cadillac is probably old Kim Kyo Hak's car. And so, in a story about self-reproach and isolation, Eisho Kin turns the final reproach against himself. He has created a sympathetic character, who articulates complicated feelings of alienation and self-disgust. But he has done so from a situation of unearned privilege, from behind the high walls in Kitabatake. Even the young man in his story, isolated as he is, is less isolated than the people in the big house. "Those parents and sons, so used to their wealthy life," Bun'ichi reflects, referring, although he doesn't know it, to his own creator. "What about me?"

"It Happened One Day" appeared in the Winter 1977 issue of *Sanzenri* magazine. It was singled out for commendation in a literary award. Eisho Kin was delighted and told his friends about his success—it seemed to impart to him the confidence he had lacked. But then he discovered that the competition had been judged by a famous Zainichi writer, a close friend of his mother since before he was born. He came to believe that his story had been commended for reasons of favoritism and family feeling, not for its literary qualities. And his confidence fled him once again.

■ ■ ■

At school, Seisho Kin, the future Joji Obara, "liberated himself by degrading himself." But when he chose, he could elevate himself ruthlessly. He demonstrated this when he passed the entrance examination for the senior high school attached to Keio, one of the most famous and prestigious private universities in the country. Boarding schools of the British kind were almost unknown, and for a teenager to leave home and move to another city was unusual, although not unheard of. But the arrangement his parents made for Seisho would be unusual in twenty-first-century Japan. In the 1960s, it was extraordinary.

At the age of fifteen, he left home and went to live in Tokyo, alone. With a female housekeeper to look after him, he was installed in Den-en Chofu, another neighborhood of the very rich, Tokyo's equivalent of Kitabatake. Today it is one of the few areas in the capital still dominated by traditional Japanese homes, set behind wooden fences in gardens of bamboo groves and moss. But the house where Seisho lived was aggressively modern, the epitome of late 1960s architectural chic. A six-foot brick wall and an inner cordon of fluffy pine trees closed it off from a narrow lane. Inside were an oval swimming pool and a wide two-story house with a façade of white plaster and brown tiles. The rooms were fronted by walls of sliding glass; those on the upper floor gave on to wide thrusting balconies, and a garage to one side had room for several cars. The traditional Japanese homes that surrounded it, like his parents' house in Osaka, were shadowy, cool, and somber, but this house was a fantasy of Hawaii or California, a place of light and brightness, made for sunbathing, barbecues, and dancing by the pool. And in the move here, the future Joji Obara underwent the next stage of his self-transformation. He left behind Seisho Kin and became Seisho Hoshiyama, and the weight of his family, his life in Osaka, and his Koreanness fell from his shoulders, like a man in springtime shrugging off a heavy winter coat.

Just as a criminal's family bears moral responsibility for his crimes, so—to an extent milder and more obscure—do his schoolmates. Those who knew him at Keio University School were reluctant to speak about Seisho Hoshiyama, and in the reluctance there was an element of shame. By the time I found them, the trial was under way; it was difficult for anyone to unimagine those charges, to reach back to memories untainted by hindsight. The man who came closest was Koji Akimoto, who shared a class with Seisho in their last year at the school.

"Every year the classes were changed around," he remembered, "and I had a friend who had been a classmate of Hoshiyama. He said to me, 'He's a strange guy.' But my first impression was of a rather amiable person. He was always neat. He had his hair carefully combed, in what we used to call the 'Kennedy cut,' like John F. Kennedy. He had smooth skin, a rather shiny face. He was a teenager, but he had good posture—he was well built but muscular, not at all plump. And he was always talking to people and trying to make friends. I thought that he seemed rather an interesting person, not strange at all. I said to my friend, 'What makes you say that he's strange?' And he said, 'Look at his eyes.'"

Akimoto looked, and immediately saw what his friend was talking about. Tiny scars were visible around Hoshiyama's eyelids, and, for his contemporaries at least, there was no doubt what they were—the marks of a surgery known as epicanthoplasty. The operation removed the epicanthic fold, a heavy lid of skin covering the inner angle of the eye, characteristic of many people from Central and East Asia. Surgery transformed the "single-fold" eyelid of the Asian to the "double-fold" of the Caucasian. It created eyes that were variously regarded as bigger, rounder, more "Western," and more attractive—and, to many Japanese, and without any basis in racial science, less Korean. Twenty years later, there would be a fashion for the expensive operation among Asian women. "But for a high school boy at that time to have that kind of plastic surgery—well, that was very unusual," said Akimoto. "But he seemed to have had the operation, and now he had the double fold. I thought that he must be a curious person."*

The two boys became close; two or three times Akimoto visited the house in Den-en Chofu. Plenty of the boys at Keio came from affluent families, but Hoshiyama's wealth was extraordinary. "It was a huge house," Akimoto said. "I thought

---

*In an account commissioned by Joji Obara's lawyer thirty-nine years later, it was reported that he had indeed undergone eye surgery at the age of sixteen, but that it was treatment for injuries when a pair of sunglasses broke against his face in a car accident.

that his family must have been rich for many generations. He had a big collection of records. And, even for Keio boys, those were expensive at that time. He told me that he had an annual income of ¥20 million a year—that was really an amazing amount. He said that he owned car parks. Somehow, maybe from him or maybe someone else, I heard that his parents came from Osaka. But he never talked about them really.

"There weren't any pictures or family photographs in the house. I think he said that he lived there with his grandfather, but the only person I ever saw there was the maid. I started to think that perhaps there was no grandfather. And he would often be late for lessons. I thought, 'It's because he lives alone, except for that maid. There's no one to wake him up in the morning and make sure he gets to school.' He was a clever guy, but his school results were bad. Because he wasn't living with his parents. Nobody looked after him. He created his own world; he lived in his own atmosphere."

It was difficult to describe. But something about him set Seisho Hoshiyama apart—a poise and an independence, which often seemed close to isolation and solitude. "Once he came back after the holidays with these wristwatches—Rolex, I think—which he was offering for sale. He said he'd bought them in Hong Kong, and, as boys, we were very impressed. Foreign watches, foreign travel—that was a world away from us then." Hoshiyama was a confident English-speaker, and a brilliant and charismatic musician—at least to the ears of the unworldly teenagers at Keio. "He was a very, very good singer," Akimoto remembered. "We had a school festival in the autumn, and we decided to put on a show with a band, sell bottles of Coca-Cola from a stall, and make a bit of money. Hoshiyama was the singer. He did Tom Jones—he was superb! He was exactly like Tom Jones, thrusting his hips, the whole act. I don't remember the song he did—it wasn't 'Delilah,' one of the other ones. He wore a long-sleeved shirt, a beautiful shirt in some kind of black satin or silk. That was an amazing shirt. By day, he didn't dress particularly sharply, but he had his own style and he looked good."

And yet, for Akimoto, it was impossible truly to befriend Seisho Hoshiyama. There was a fugitive quality in his personality and a hollowness, as if, below the promising exterior, the most important element, the substance of friendship, was being withheld—if, in fact, it was even present. "When I agreed to see you I thought hard about what he was like," Koji Akimoto told me. "It's very difficult to express. He built up a wall between himself and others. He never really understood his schoolmates. With friends you share a common feeling. You find things you agree on, and your conversation and understanding become deeper—even if it's just that you both like Honda motorbikes, or something like that.

"With Hoshiyama, I never had that experience. He would say, about someone in our class whom he wanted to become friends with, 'He's a cool guy.' But he never looked into people's characters. He was materialistic. He always lacked that subtle rapport which you enjoy when you're really communicating with someone's heart. He was interested in what he wanted to do, but he never made any compromise with others. He was the first person I ever knew who was like that and I've never known a person like that since. I kept my distance to some extent and observed him closely. But it was as if there was no room to step in and become a true friend. I still remember it."

Most impressive about Seisho was his assurance with girls. "He used to go out on his own to Jiyugaoka and Yokohama," Akimoto remembered. "In Yokohama, there was a famous disco, where he would go. Boys like me at that age, we might go out to play around in a group of two or three, but never on our own. But Hoshiyama had the confidence to do that. He behaved like an adult, he played around like an adult, and that was so unusual, so impressive.

"In our third year of high school he told me, 'I've got a date with a girl.' He said, 'Let me show you her picture.' I looked at it. They were sitting together in some expensive restaurant in the suburbs. It was a place schoolboys would never think of going. And there he was, in a white suit. Beside them there was a big bunch of flowers. The girl was half Japanese and half Western. Her name was Betty. I think that he was really serious about Betty, but she left him, and afterwards he rang up another friend of mine and he cried. She told him, 'If you can be a mature man, I'll come back to you.' He felt that he wasn't mature enough, but he was determined that he would become so. He was a human being, of course. Apart from everything else, he could be a true, loving person."

There were several ethnic Korean and Chinese students at Keio University School. But none of his schoolmates, at least among those I interviewed, ever knew that Seisho Hoshiyama was Zainichi. None of them ever met his parents or his brothers, or anyone from his early life in Osaka. And none heard anything of what must have been one of the defining moments of his teenage years: the sudden death in 1969 of his father, Kim Kyo Hak, in circumstances that have never been fully explained.

15. GEORGE O'HARA

Instead of Azabu Police Station, where they would have inter-
rogated the suspect in a more routine case, Superintendent
Udo's detectives took Joji Obara to the fortresslike headquarters of the Tokyo Metropolitan Police in the Kasumigaseki
district, the bureaucratic nerve center of Japan. The ministries
of Finance, Foreign Affairs, and Justice were strolling distance
away; in the space of this square mile was the greatest concentration of state power in the country. Within a few hours of
his arrest, hundreds of officers had descended with search
warrants on twenty of Obara's properties all over the country.
They included the apartment among the palm trees in Zushi
Marina, the room in Blue Sea Aburatsubo where the dead dog
had been laid, the building near Roppongi where he was arrested, and the big house in Den-en Chofu. Helicopters from
the Japanese television companies hovered close by, peeping
across the cordons. They captured images of search dogs
snorting over the grounds and policemen in overalls shoveling
mounds of earth. For days, police vans came and went carrying out articles of evidence. There were tools, clothes, notebooks, sheaves of documents, rolls of film, videotapes, audio
cassettes, photographic prints, bottles of fluid, and sachets of
powder. They were gathered in a storeroom in Kasumigaseki,
where Udo himself supervised their sifting. "There were fifteen
thousand items there," he told me. "It was the biggest room we

had available to us. There was so much dust, we were coughing and scratching, and there were dust mites biting our legs. But for us they were piles of treasure."

Obara was held in one of the cells inside the same building. In theory, criminal suspects in Japan are supposed to be kept in detention centers from which they travel in the morning for questioning and where they are dropped off after working hours. In fact, they are almost always held at a police station, where the organization investigating them also controls every aspect: visitors, the time and duration of their interrogations, their food, even the lighting in their cells.

Many of the rights regarded as fundamental in British and American justice are unavailable to the suspect in Japan— or, if available in theory, waived or ignored in practice. He has the right to see a lawyer, but the frequency and duration of the visits are decided by the police. He has the right to remain silent under questioning, but he is obliged to sit through the questions, which can go on for hour after hour through relays of fresh officers until the suspect is numb with boredom and fatigue. There is no obligation for detectives to record interrogations. Instead of a verbatim account, they produce at the end of the proceedings a summary (known within the justice system as the "prosecutor's essay") to which the exhausted suspect is simply asked to put his name.

An arrest warrant allows the police to hold a suspect for three days, but with the permission of a judge this can be extended, twice, by ten days at a time. The judge almost never refuses. For twenty-three days, then, a person can be incarcerated incommunicado by the police, without any access to lawyers, family, or friends, and without any charge being brought against him. "The formal legal system in Japan provides detectives with so many advantages that they rarely need to resort to obviously illegal tactics," writes the criminologist Setsuo Miyazawa. "The whole system is designed and implemented in such a way that the suspect will offer apparently voluntary confessions to his captors."

But the detectives and prosecutors work under one particular pressure of their own: the pressure to obtain a confession. Unlike a British or American court, where it is necessary only to prove the facts, Japanese courts attach great importance to motive. The reasoning and impulses that led to a crime must be proved in court; they are a crucial factor in determining a convicted criminal's sentence. The who, what, where, and when are not enough: a Japanese judge demands to know *why*. A detective, then, is obliged to get inside his suspect's skull. If he fails to do that, he is not considered to have done his job.

In reality, the only way to do this is by obtaining a confession. "Confession is king," one detective said. Everything else, including physical evidence, is secondary. In some cases, police prefer to carry out their physical investigation only *after* obtaining a confession. The hope is that a suspect will disclose incriminating information unknown to the detectives, which will then be confirmed by subsequent investigation, thus making the confession all the more convincing and allaying suspicions that it may have been obtained under duress. "We require proof beyond an unreasonable doubt," a Japanese prosecutor told the sociologist David Johnson, who writes that "confessions are the heart—the pump that keeps cases circulating in the system . . . Japanese prosecutors [are] characterized by an almost paralyzing fear to charge in the absence of confession."

And Japanese suspects do confess, whether they are guilty or not; over the years, they have confessed more and more. In 1984, eleven out of twelve people brought to criminal trial in Japanese courts admitted the charges against them. By 1998, the proportion was fifteen out of sixteen. From time to time, police and prosecutors break jaws, mash noses, and bruise genitals. ("To us Japanese, hitting in the head is not serious," one prosecutor said. "Kicking is serious.") But physical abuse is usually mild, intended to be humiliating rather than painful: slaps; light kicks; deprivation of sleep, food, and water; cigarette smoke blown in the face. More common is psychological intimidation; Johnson describes "suspects [who] were threatened, intimidated, worn down, led, induced, scolded, berated, manipulated, and deceived." But given the police's overwhelming power over those in their custody, such crude measures are rarely necessary. Japanese detectives, by and large, are calm, polite, detached, insistent, and relentless. They simply ask the same questions, over and over again, for the twenty-three days—or 552 hours, or 33,120 slow minutes—that they have suspects in their power. Most of the time, all they have to do is wait.

These, then, were the powers ranged against Joji Obara when he was arrested on October 12, 2000.

He didn't confess. He never bent at all. From the very beginning, when he refused to face the camera for the police mug shot, he offered no cooperation. It was clear that this was a suspect who knew, and would insist upon, his rights, and the Japanese police, in general, are wary of being caught overstepping the bounds of their considerable power. "When he was arrested he agreed to give fingerprints, but he wouldn't agree to the photograph," Superintendent Udo told me. "We couldn't make him face the camera. If you forced his chin up, for example, that might be taken to be torture. So the photograph we took has him looking down."

Udo was reluctant to go into detail about the police questioning of Joji Obara, probably because, from the police point of view, it went so badly. "At the beginning, he seemed very intimidated," Udo told me. "He sweated a lot, to the extent that his clothes got quite wet. He sweated, and sometimes he trembled. But he denied everything." The crimes for which he had been arrested were the abduction and indecent assault of

Clara Mendez. According to the rules, Udo emphasized, the detectives were supposed to confine their questions to that case alone. But everyone in the room knew that the true purpose of the interrogation was to find out what had happened to Lucie—and Udo conceded that the detectives "chatted" with their suspect about the Blackman case. But for a long time, Obara refused to talk to them. He confirmed his name; apart from that, he invoked his right to remain silent.

Two weeks passed; the police's twenty-three-day limit would soon expire. So the prosecutors employed another favorite technique. They charged Obara with the rape of Clara Mendez and immediately "rearrested" him for the indecent assault of Katie Vickers. With this, they gained another twenty-three days with their suspect, and they avoided losing him to the less pressured and intense environment of the detention center. They would use this questionable practice—not in itself illegal but verging on an abuse.

■ ■ ■

In 1969, at what was outwardly the peak of his success, Obara's father, Kim Kyo Hak, had gone on an overseas trip with a group of Osaka businessmen. He was forty-four at the time, and his sons ranged in age from seven to twenty-one years old. The details, like so much else about him, were sketchy. But the party certainly visited Hong Kong and there, on or before April 27, Kim Kyo Hak died.

Obara himself would insist later that the explanation was straightforward: his father's death was caused by a sudden stroke. But other people sensed something mysterious about the tragedy. The wake, which one would have expected to be large and lavish, was not held at the Kitabatake house, as would be customary, and the Kims displayed none of the conventional signs of mourning. The subject was hardly discussed within the family. Decades later, the youngest son, Kosho, who had been a boy at the time, did not know how exactly his father had died. Japanese magazines, and the Kim family's neighbors, speculated that it was an unnatural death, perhaps connected to a dispute over business. And afterwards, they reported that bulletproof glass was fitted in the windows of the big house in Den-en Chofu.

Whatever the truth, the death of their patriarch transformed the lives of the surviving Kims. His wealth was divided among his sons and widow. The taxi firm went to the troubled oldest boy, Sosho; the pachinko parlors went to Eisho, the aspiring writer. Seisho Hoshiyama, as Obara was still calling himself then, received the parking lots and property, including Den-en Chofu. It is not clear what Kosho inherited, but it seems to have been less than an equal share—alone among the brothers, he received a free state education rather than an expensive private one. The boys were fatherless now, but they were also rich.

It was about this time, when Seisho Hoshiyama was sixteen, that he was involved in the car crash that would be claimed later as the reason for his plastic surgery. "Glass pieces were taken out around his eyes," it was reported in the book about Obara privately commissioned by one of his lawyers. "Many slashes were stitched, some of which went up to his ear."* It was also around now, according to this same account, that he became an alcoholic. "[He] has been drinking since he was fifteen years old and has been addicted to alcohol ever since," the book says. "When he was hospitalised from the traffic accident, he couldn't drink alcohol through the mouth, so he tried inhaling it through the nose, which worked very

---

*Of the four acquaintances from Keio University School whom I interviewed, none remembered hearing anything about a car accident involving Seisho Hoshiyama, or his hospitalization.

well . . . He inhaled alcohol night after night and sank into a dreamy world."

Not surprisingly, his schoolwork was suffering. The whole point of Keio University School, for most of its students, was the all but guaranteed place it brought at Keio University— which, in its turn, was the ticket to a career in business, politics, law, or academia. For a student of Keio High School to be turned away from the university required more than average idleness, delinquency, or stupidity—and Hoshiyama was not stupid. In the book commissioned by his lawyer, it is claimed that he turned down the chance to go to the famous institution rather than being rejected. Either way, he graduated from high school in March 1971 at the age of nineteen without a place at Keio University.

After that, a fog descends over the life of Seisho Hoshiyama. At some point he studied at Komazawa University in Tokyo, a less glamorous institution than Keio. For three years, he traveled: according to the book, "he lived in Washington State, Stockholm, and moved around the world several times." He may have studied architecture, and at some point he claimed to have become acquainted with the famous American musician Carlos Santana—years later, he would show a photograph of himself with his celebrity friend to Christa Mackenzie. Around 1974, he returned to Japan and was accepted at Keio University on a correspondence course. Eventually, he was allowed to enroll as a regular undergraduate. He went on to take two degrees, in law and then in politics. On both occasions, he declined to be photographed for the graduation yearbook.

In 1971, around the time he left high school, he went through the next stage of his metamorphosis. He changed his nationality from South Korean to Japanese and took on a new name: Joji Obara. The first name, pronounced Jōji with a long *o* and written with the characters for "castle" and the number 2, was familiar enough, but Obara was a curiosity. Most Japanese ideographs can be read in two or more ways, depending on their context and the way they are combined with other characters. Common names have a standard reading, but more unusual ones have several possible pronunciations. Seisho Hoshiyama's newly adopted surname consisted of two characters (meaning "weave" and "field") and could be read as Obara, Ohara, or Orihara.

At the age of eighteen, he had already been through three names; in the thirty years before his arrest, he would employ dozens more. For a man who instinctively clouded his identity, who could not bear to be pinned down, captured, or summed up, even by a camera, it was appropriate that even his legal name should be evasive. But why this name in particular?

There was an actor called Joji Ohara (written with different kanji and pronounced with a long initial *o*) who starred in a series of soft-core porn films (*Seduction of Flesh, Lustful Companions*) of the kind that might have titillated a teenage boy in the late 1960s. A man of the same name was a Japanese cinematographer of the same period. But the Kim family, and others who knew him at this time, inferred another explanation.

The point about the new names was that each could be pronounced to sound as if it were English. Joji: Jorj: George. Obara: Ohara: O'Hara. Was this, then, the end point of his journey through identity: from Kim Sung Jong, the Korean baby; through Seisho Kin, the Japanese-born Korean child; Seisho Hoshiyama, the Japanese youth with round eyes; Joji Obara-Ohara-Orihara, the ambiguous, unphotographable Japanese citizen—to George O'Hara, cosmopolite, friend to the famous, man of the world?

■ ■ ■

Obara emerged from his twenties with two university degrees and a few years of desultory travel but with no obvious experience of having earned a living. Then, in his thirties, he put himself and his inheritance to work, in the occupation that epitomized the spirit of the age: property developing.

This was the time of Japan's notorious bubble economy, the period between the 1980s and early 1990s when Tokyo fleetingly became the wealthiest city in the history of the world. After forty years of steadily accelerating growth, the Japanese yen, the stock exchange, and, above all, the value of land began to rise with intoxicating speed. Anyone holding property became rich, whether they deserved it or not, and Japanese banks competed with one another to lend them money without asking very many questions.

These were giddy years in London and New York too, but nowhere was the consumption more conspicuous than in Tokyo. The grossness of bubble excess has become the stuff of urban legend: the nightclubs with mink covers on their lavatory seats, the cocktails sprinkled with gold leaf, and the banquets of sushi eaten off the naked bodies of young models. The Japanese who had lived through the war had seen Third World poverty and destitution; now their economy was close to overtaking that of the United States. Foreign tourists, who were accustomed to being the wealthiest people in the country, found themselves impoverished by the strong yen, which drew in a new working gaijin population of bankers, businessmen, English teachers, and laborers. And the Japanese took pride in this. Not only people of the poorer countries of Asia but now also Americans, Australians, and Europeans were coming to Tokyo, not as transient businessmen or idle backpackers but as worshippers at the shrine of Japanese economic might. The symbol of this was the gaijin hostess club, where the pretty foreign blond flirted submissively with the rich, newly potent salaryman.

In the glare of money, shades of difference—between Zainichi and Japanese, for example, or between old money and new—became less visible. Joji Obara was well placed to benefit from these shifts of wealth and power. With one of his Osaka parking lots as collateral, he took out loans and acquired some twenty buildings and apartments all over Japan, most of which he rented out. They ranged from warm Kyushu, the southernmost of the main Japanese islands, to chilly Hokkaido in the far north. They had typically bubble-era names, charged with received notions of foreign grandeur: Sasebo Lion Tower, Kushiro Passion Building, Ginza Brightness. Obara made at least one overseas purchase, another palpable token of affluence and prestige: an apartment on the thirty-third floor of the Waikiki Beach Tower in Hawaii. Some of these assets were held in Obara's name, but most were owned by nine companies that he established, including Atlantic Trading, Creation Inc., and the Plant Group. Each company had an address, a board of directors, and an auditor; on paper, they were perfectly legitimate. But later it would be reported that not all of those listed on these company documents even knew that they had been named as executives.

Obara bought the one-room apartment in Roppongi—the room where he would be arrested—in 1996; another of his residences, a huge flat overlooking the Togu Palace, where Japan's crown prince lived, was acquired in 1988. Nosy neighbors are an institution in Japan, but in each of these places it was remarkable how few people had distinct memories of Obara. He shunned casual contact; he turned himself away.

At the Roppongi apartment block, the staff had no idea who Joji Obara was until troops of police took him away. At Den-en Chofu, he would roar out of the high gate at full throttle in his white Rolls-Royce or silver Porsche, but otherwise his neighbors scarcely saw him. "We never talked to him, and I always assumed that he was just an ordinary man," said Mrs. Kurosaki, who lived three houses down from him. "But of course a young man on his own in a place that size stood out, and people talked about him. When he moved into that place with his own swimming pool, we were all envious."

Routine efforts to engage him in neighborly contact were ignored. Circulars delivered by the Den-en Chofu community association were never passed on, and Mitsuko Tanaka, the local housewife responsible for the national census forms, had great trouble extracting a completed form from the Obara house. Once, she chatted with the maid who was working there. "She was a nice friendly lady, said that he lived there on his own and that she cooked for him," Mrs. Tanaka told me. "I asked her how long she'd been working there, and she said it was just a few days. She came from a temporary-employment agency, and he asked them to send a different helper every week."

Even the identity of the occupant of the Den-en Chofu house was not clear. On the nameplate outside, written in the Roman alphabet, was OHARA, and below, in smaller letters, HOSHIYAMA. Whatever his name, the man who lived there was not without company. "There'd be young people going in and out, including foreigners," said Mrs. Kurosaki. "There was a high wall all around. I could hear women's voices, so I assumed most of them were women. You'd hear talking and chatting and playing from just inside the gate. You didn't see people, really. He didn't walk around the place. The gate would open and he'd zoom out in his open-topped car with a woman at his side, and when he returned he'd just zoom in again."

Mrs. Tanaka said, "I remember one particular woman. She had long, black hair like a Japanese, but she looked foreign in some way. She was around for quite a long time, but then I didn't see her anymore. After it happened, we wondered whatever became of that girl with the long hair."

What kind of man was Obara, and how, apart from running his businesses, did he spend his time? The absence of information was more striking than the few available facts; put aside speculation, rumor, and conjecture, and there was little left but fragments. He was proud of his charitable donations— he would later claim to have given more than ¥100 million to worthy causes, including the Japanese Society for Disabled Children and the Legal Aid Association. Despite (or perhaps because of) his Korean birth, he was a warm admirer of the Japanese imperial family—he spoke with pride of the occasion when he had been presented at a party to Emperor Akihito and Empress Michiko. As well as his rental businesses, he had a company, Ginza Foods, which operated a small ramen noodle restaurant in the most elegant part of Tokyo. He loved classic foreign cars, and at the time of his arrest owned nine of them, including a BMW, a Mercedes-Benz, a Ferrari, a 1962 Bentley Continental, and James Bond's favorite car, a silver 1964 Aston Martin DB5.

It is difficult to say much with certainty about Obara's adult life. In weeks of inquiry into his past, I found no one who could be described as his friend. In the period after his arrest, it would not be surprising if such people were reluctant to identify themselves. But perhaps they did not exist. I talked to Obara's neighbors, to the caretakers of his properties, to hostesses who entertained him, to shopkeepers and delivery men who served him. None ever described seeing him with anyone else or hearing him talk unambiguously of friend-ship—other than with Carlos Santana. After his arrest, he was visited during his long detention by one mysterious ac-quaintance, the owner of a pachinko company, but there seemed to have been no one else, apart from his elderly mother.

Other people who got to know him after his arrest formed a strong impression of his profound and elaborate isolation. "I've dealt with many different kinds of people," one of them told me, "but I don't think he ever had a true friend he could rely on, never in his life. Sometimes I see on his face a need to rely on me. Even when he's being very positive, I feel his lone-liness then too. I often felt sorry for him, very often. He's a man of great solitude. There's no one he can trust, or talk things over with. Sometimes I think it's because he has no one to rely on that he turned to women like that.

"He has no true friend. It's hard to say why I know this—it's just a feeling I have, from his eyes and the expression on his face. I try to look him in the eye, but he avoids direct eye contact. It's a complex feeling—not just simple sorrow, but pathos. He is so lonely, so lonely. There is something tragic about him."

The one creature for whom Obara had a straightforward love was his Shetland sheepdog, Irene, who would play such a bizarre posthumous role in the case of Lucie Blackman. In his few public statements, Obara mentioned her repeatedly, so we know that her favorite brand of dog food was Cesar boil-in-the-bag meat, and her favorite snack was dried filefish. By the side door of the entrance to the Den-en Chofu house was a life-size statue of the dog, with bared teeth and a glistening ceramic tongue. He referred to her as "my beloved dog" and "beloved dog Irene." After she died, on July 6, 1994, Obara preserved Irene's body for six years. "With the advancement of cloning technology," he wrote later, "in the hope of reviving the dog which I loved so much, I put her to rest in a large freezer. I also enclosed some roses and some of her favorite treats."

■ ■ ■

Obara's businesses flourished, for a while. The value of prop-erty, and the rents that a landlord could charge, were going up and up. At one point, it was later reported, the total value of his assets was ¥4 billion, about $38 million. But he also had debt, to which he kept on adding well after it was prudent to do so. Land prices in Japan had peaked in 1989, and by the early 1990s it had become obvious that the bubble was over forever. But in 1993, Obara established yet another company, for his most ambitious project so far—the construction of a skyscraper of offices and shops on the site of one of his Osaka parking lots. A prospectus was published with artists' impressions of the finished building, a soaring, gleaming, twelve-story structure of shiny blue glass, with a lofty, marbled atrium and an exterior busy with spikes and cylinders and sculptures of gleaming orbs within curving metallic crescents. "An outstandingly 'gorgeous' futuristic 'silhouette' in the Kita-Shinchi district, crowded with 'high society' shops," ran the promotional copy. "A wholly twenty-first-century 'landscape.'" The key words were English ones, clumsily Japanized: *gōjyasu, shiruetto, haisosaetii.* The Kita-Shinchi Tower was a monstrosity, a dog's dinner of bubble pretension and kitsch, dated even by 1993. And it would never be built. Three years later, Obara's creditors were suing him for recovery of unpaid loans, and in 1999 the house in Den-en Chofu was temporarily sequestered by the court.

The son of the Korean horsemeat trader said to me, "There were reasons why the second and third generations did not study hard. The best universities in Japan were supposed to offer the best jobs after graduation, but for people of my age at least, the opportunities were silently blocked off. So I can well imagine why he gave up studying in that social environment— that and the fact that he was so rich, he'd inherited such a huge fortune, that he didn't need to work. He was the most promising of the four brothers. But what was waiting for him at his expensive high school? Just booze and girls. Because he was rich. It's not surprising that he lost his motivation.

"My guess is that in the United States he felt accepted for himself—not as a Korean or a Japanese, just as himself. But when he came back to Japan he failed in business. He didn't have the talent. He wasted so much of his fortune. He managed to make money during the property bubble, but when the collapse came it was the familiar story of failure."

Manabu Miyazaki, the writer and son of a yakuza family, told me, "There's a typical type. You have a father who's a big success, a first-generation immigrant who got rich. But he's a simple man, maybe he can't even understand Japanese that well. So he wants to give his sons the best education possible. They're given all the opportunities but still they fail. They take over the father's business, but even with all their capital and education, it doesn't work out. Because they're not as aggressive as the father. They have the academic background but they're not interested in real business, and they always have to ask for help from the father's generation. And they still can't overcome their handicaps. They have money, but their life is not fulfilled. Seeking support, being scolded by the father's generation, their life is very twisted."

■ ■ ■

A month after Obara's arrest, his lawyer, Yoshinori Hamaguchi, issued a statement to the "reporters' club" of the Tokyo Metropolitan Police in the name of his client. Later, Obara would claim that Hamaguchi had written it and that he himself had not even seen it before it was released. But its style and content were in keeping with much of what was to come.

"I have in the past engaged in sexual activity with various gaijin hostesses and paid companions, all of whom were little more than glorified prostitutes," it began.

> I am presently being held for paying money to prostitutes for SEX PLAY, which I like to call "conquest play." Regarding the case for which I was arrested: I can't remember clearly because it took place a few years ago, but I had sexual rela-

tions with some of those so-called victims. They were all employed as gaijin bar hostesses or paid companions. Most of them took cocaine or other drugs right in front of my eyes. They were all willing to take money in return for SEX PLAY and I subsequently paid the appropriate sums. Therefore I do not believe that I am guilty of rape or sexual assault . . .

The police tell me that they are going to find every foreign hostess who has had SEX PLAY with me in the past, make them lodge complaints against me, and rearrest me repeatedly until they find the missing Miss Lucie Blackman. What is more, they are completely closing their eyes to illegal conduct, including illegal drugs, working illegally, prostitution, etc. committed by those gaijin hostess women. They intend to make me the scapegoat for everything.

Regarding Miss Lucie Blackman: I was served by Miss Lucie Blackman at a gaijin club once only, and introduced to a certain man. After that I found fragments of an address in my mail box, strange letters, and strange things happened one after another. There are many things I don't understand.

In late October, veteran detectives in charge of this case (Inspector Y, Assistant Inspector I) told me in a serious manner that a dangerous man had been observed in Britain, and that a suspicious British person arrived in Tokyo (I took it to be a sniper). I feel as if I've been sucked into something big, and that I've been framed, but I have nothing to do with the missing Miss Lucie Blackman . . . The media has portrayed me as if I were the criminal responsible for Miss Lucie's disappearance. This is not true . . .

The Tokyo Metropolitan Police keep telling me that Miss Lucie's disappearance is a very important case and that they have to solve it very soon. I think that they are hard pressed by Prime Minister Mori, and believe that unless they solve it quickly the national interest will be damaged . . . I now feel strongly that Japan is heading towards the revival of a police state . . . The authorities are putting the final touches to making me look all bad, all black. They set me up all right. The police say they will arrest someone for Lucie's disappearance and that until they do, they will continue arresting me on the charge of sexual assault and SEX PLAY with gaijin bar hostesses. I hope they catch the real criminal soon.

In different circumstances, this baffling document might have painted a sympathetic and persuasive picture of a scared and lonely eccentric, guilty of nothing more serious than consorting with prostitutes, now set up by the police in a desperate effort to dispose of the case that was giving them so much trouble. But this version of events could not withstand the emerging facts. For while Obara sat silent in his cell, Superintendent Udo and his men were on another floor engaged in what for Japanese detectives was an unfamiliar task: processing the thousands of objects removed from the properties and attempting to prove a case, by means of physical evidence, against a suspect who refused to confess.

16. CONQUEST PLAY

Joji Obara adored sushi; he had particular, and very expensive, tastes. Zushi Marina, where the palm trees grew and where he kept his apartment, was a community of second homes. Neighbors scarcely recognized neighbors, and there was no recollection of Obara among the people who shared the apartments next to number 4314. But one family remembered him distinctly: the proprietors of the local sushi shop.

He never went there in person, but he placed many orders for delivery by telephone. Weeks would pass when they heard nothing from him; then he would call the shop every day for three days. He always ordered the *tokujo*, or special set—nine pieces of the freshest and juiciest tuna belly, cod roe, and sea urchin on squeezed lumps of vinegared rice—and *awabi*, the abalone, or "Venus's-ear," a marine mollusk whose rubbery flesh was the most expensive item on the menu. His favorite was *kimo*, the liver of the abalone, a dish strange and exotic even to Japanese. To aficionados, the awabi was prized as an aphrodisiac; its innards were held to be especially potent in this regard. It was also a characteristic bubble delicacy, an advertisement for connoisseurship and extravagance: at the restaurant in Zushi, a single serving cost ¥6,000.

The young man who made the deliveries remembered Obara well, even before the police, and then the camera crews, had tracked him down, and he had repeated the story a dozen times. "There are some people you never notice, but there was something special about him," he said. "There was a funny atmosphere in that place—a bit creepy. I remember that whenever I pushed the bell, he always coughed twice just before he opened the door—*Khh-khh*. He'd often be in a white bathrobe and he wore dark glasses, even though he was inside. The light was so dim, it was difficult to make out his face. But there was a smell—like incense. Incense and cigars. Maybe eau de cologne.

"I never saw anyone else there. I never saw a woman's shoes in the entryway. But the food he ordered was too much for one. He always asked for a receipt, too—usually it came to ¥9,000 or more. He spoke softly, he was quite polite. Just one time, I forgot to bring the kimo and afterward he rang the shop and complained about that. He particularly loved that kimo."

■ ■ ■

Joji Obara kept meticulous records of his sexual encounters, beginning in April 1970, when he was seventeen years old. In court, he would dismiss these as fantasy, but if they were even partly true, then he was a prodigious womanizer. He would be criminally convicted of nine rapes, but they represented only a fragment of the activity recorded in the form of documents, photographs, and videotapes that were retrieved by the police from the house in Den-en Chofu and from the apartments in central Tokyo and Zushi Marina. The acts they recorded were not sudden explosions of violence and anger. From the descriptions of those who sifted through the evidence, they did not even seem to be principally about the discharge of lust. In documents discovered by the police, and in his own court testimony, Obara described in detail his sexual methods and tastes. He called it "conquest play."

He referred to the flat at Zushi Marina as his *kyoten*, a word meaning "foothold" or "hub," and suggesting something close to a strategic base. He kept video equipment, including professional lights, there, and he had attached hooks to the ceiling above the bed, the better to array his victims. Not every woman who visited it was raped; Obara, who was a small man, never pitted himself physically against his victims. The outcome of the play depended entirely on whether he could trick them into unconsciousness. If he failed in this, they walked away, aware of no more than fleeting social unease. But apart from the ladies' lavatory where he was caught peeping, there was no evidence that he perpetrated his crimes anywhere else.

It was weeks before Obara admitted it, but the detectives quickly dispelled any doubts that Lucie had been to Zushi Marina. Hundreds of strands of hair were removed from the apartment. Comparisons with the DNA from fingernail clippings provided by Jane and Tim Blackman confirmed that several of them belonged to their daughter. An undeveloped roll of film, one of many they recovered, was processed and found to contain two shots of her, the last images ever recorded of Lucie. She stood in front of a railing with the sea behind her and a town and hills visible across the bay. She wore her short black dress, the heart-shaped pendant glinted on her neck, and her sunglasses were pushed up over her hair. In her right hand she held a can of beer; if there was tension in her smile, it was barely perceptible. Only the position of her left arm, held away from her body at an awkward angle, suggested the artificiality and discomfort of her situation: simulating pleasure and ease for the sake of a stranger with a mobile phone to give away.

Experts analyzed the photographs in detail, and the police identified the precise spot by the marina where Lucie had been standing. The weather, the angle of the light, the appearance of the distant town, even the position of a buoy bobbing behind her right shoulder—all were consistent with it having been taken late on the afternoon of July 1, 2000.

The prepaid telephones, whose calls had been tracked so assiduously, were recovered too. And there was a handbag, a kind of male purse commonly carried by Japanese businessmen, containing two items of interest. The first was a gas bill, on which was scribbled the number of one of the prepaid mobiles from which Lucie had called Louise and Scott. The second was a sachet of powder. It was analyzed and identified as a powerful hypnotic drug called flunitrazepam. The name meant little in Japan, where it was occasionally administered as a treatment for the most severe insomnia. But under the brand name Rohypnol, it is the most notorious of the so-called date-rape drugs. The police found samples of another unusual pharmaceutical, commonly used for the same purpose—gamma-hydroxybutyric acid or GHB—and thirteen bottles of chloroform, two of them unopened.

The volume of documents taken away from the apartments—from thick notebooks and diaries to yellowing, decade-old receipts—was vast. The police and prosecutors would continue sifting through them, uncovering new and incriminating material. But early on, according to one Japanese newspaper, they came upon a list of about sixty women's names, Japanese and foreign. Beside each one were the aliases, almost all of them different, that Obara had used over the years: Yuji, Koji, Kazu, Kowa, Honda, Saito, Iwata, Iwasaki, Akira. The list went back years; some of the women were identified by just a single name, but for others there were telephone numbers or addresses.

The detectives also found receipts for several ambitious shopping expeditions that Obara had made in the early days of July. On Sunday the second, the day after Lucie's disappearance, he had bought twenty pounds of dry ice from a dealer near Blue Sea Aburatsubo, as well as a large packing box; the following day he had returned to the same place and bought twenty pounds more. "Is it for a big dog that's passed away?" the dealer asked, and Obara agreed that it was.

On Tuesday the fourth, he had gone to the Tokyo branch of L. L. Bean and purchased camping equipment, including three two-man tents, three groundsheets, a folding table, a seven-gallon cooler, flashlights, and a sleeping bag. The same day, at a hardware store, he bought a towel, three bags of cement, five cans of quick-setting agent for the cement, a stirrer, a plastic box, a paintbrush, a bucket, and a broom. At a third shop, he bought chisels, a hammer, wire, a knife, scissors, gloves, plastic bags, an axe, a handsaw, and a chain saw. The staff at several of the shops remembered that Obara had telephoned the day before, describing exactly what he needed and confirming that his requisites were in stock.

Then there were notebooks and diaries filled with Obara's handwriting and dating back to his high school days and audiocassettes recording telephone conversations and spoken memos to himself, manifestos of intention and resolve. One especially rich source of material was a binder containing loose leaves of paper, which was described at length in a document prepared by the prosecutors:

> The defendant lists the names of the women with whom he has had sexual relations since 1970 and the conduct of their sexual intercourse. In this notebook, starting with the entry "I administered sleeping drugs" in April 1970, he records sexual acts with numerous women after administering sleeping drugs and chloroform . . .
>
>   At the beginning of the book, there is a record of the number of people with whom he has had sexual relations in each year, such as "1990 nine people, 1991 nine people," and

there is a record of the number of people with whom he has had sexual relations by nationality . . . and there is also a record of the conduct of his sexual relations with 209 women between around 1970 when the defendant was 17 years old and 1995 when the defendant was 33 years old.

. . . There is a note (1970, 4th woman) to the effect that "I got a woman drunk and gave her a sleeping drug, but could not have intercourse because she was a virgin," regarding an experience in 1969. There is also a mention to the effect of using "Hyminal" [a sedative, also known as Quaalude] (1970, 3rd woman), "Chloroform, sleeping drug" (1973, woman no. 26), "SMYK (sleeping drug)" (1981, woman no. 63), "speciality SMY (sleeping drug)" (1983, woman no. 95), "CRO . . . HOL (chloroform)," "SMY" (1983, women no. 97, 98), and "sMY ice cream." It can be acknowledged that from his early days, he was repeatedly committing quasi-rape using sleeping drugs and chloroform.

Moreover, the defendant writes that having sex with women using sleeping drugs and chloroform is the defendant's modus operandi. For example

"I do it in the flat following the usual pattern. SY (sleeping drug) was good, but CRORO (chloroform) was unnecessary, and (she) ended up vomiting badly." (woman no. 150)

"Made her sleep in the flat with SMY ice cream + chocolate, and then PV (porn video)."

He writes that from around 1983, he has been taking photos of, and filming with a video camera, the rape scenes, such as "full-scale VTR (video) No. 1" (woman no. 139), "PV (porn video)," "PP (porn photo)" (woman no. 152), "foreigner video No. 1" (woman no. 160), "went to Zushi, like always, FC (fuck), PV" (woman no. 162).

The police pounced immediately upon the videos, of course. They littered the apartments, some unmarked, others with a woman's name and a date scribbled on a label. They dated back to the 1980s; some of them were in the long-obsolete Beta-max format. Once they had dug out and dusted off a machine capable of replaying them, the detectives worked in relays, loading and watching the flickering films, rewinding, carefully logging content and duration. It quickly became clear that the videos followed a pattern.

They were in color and of good quality. Some began with a brief preamble of one young woman or another laughing, raising a glass, and drinking. Then they cut abruptly to the central scene: the same young woman, naked, lying on a bed. Her eyes were closed, and she was motionless, but her slow breathing was visible. Sometimes she lay on her front and sometimes on her back; often, her legs were tied to hooks to keep them apart. Powerful lamps stood on either side of the bed to illuminate the activity on it.

The camera was steady and unwobbling, as if mounted on a tripod. In a moment, a man entered the picture. He too was naked. "His body was normal," someone who had seen the videos told me. "No sign that he exercised very much—the ordinary body of a middle-aged man." Only one thing about him was outstanding and sinister: in many of the films, he wore a mask.

I spoke to three people who had seen the videos or the detailed dossier of still photographs taken from them by the prosecutors, and each had a different recollection of the mask. One said that it was gray and concealed the entire face, like a bank robber; another remembered that it was black and covered only the eyes, like the mask of Zorro; the third thought that it had yellow and black stripes, like the skin of a tiger.

The penis of the man in the mask was erect. Before the steady gaze of the camera, he embarked on a long and rigorous violation of the unconscious woman.

"He does various things," one man who had seen the dossier told me. "Sex in a normal position. Sometimes anal sex. Sometimes he uses . . . tools, and objects. The kind of instruments that doctors use. He would look inside, if you understand what I mean. And a cucumber—insert it. His penis is . . . in a normal state. There were lights on both sides of the bed, and sometimes while . . . having sex enthusiastically, he failed to pay attention and the lights touched the woman's naked body."

Off camera there were two television monitors. According to Obara's own explanation, one of them played a foreign pornographic film, while another relayed the live image of him engaged in his "play." He would look up at these for further visual stimulation. "His libido was very strong," one witness to the videos told me. "He was always active, he never rested." After the completion of one sexual act, he would begin again. Sometimes, there were two, or even three, videotapes of the same woman filmed at a single session, which might go on for hours. "He treats women as things, not as people," I was told. "Those women show almost no reaction at all, they hardly made a noise." And whenever one of his costars did show signs of stirring from her stupor, Obara always did the same thing: he would reach for a piece of towel or gauze and hold it under the nose of his victim, close to, but not touching, the face. With that, her struggles would cease.

There were wildly different accounts of the quantity of videocassettes. One report said that the police had recovered a thousand of them, another that there were 4,800. Superintendent Udo told me that there were 170, and that they featured more than 150 different women. But the court noted that there were 40, and Obara claimed the number was as few as 9. By Udo's account, more than half of Obara's partners were foreigners, but many were Japanese. But there was something else about the two kinds of women that set them apart, other than their race.

Most of the foreign girls recognizably bore the hostess stamp: tall, slim, groomed, made up, and often, although not always, blond. But physically, the Japanese were of a different type. Many of them were stout and plump, or frankly fat, with none of the conventional prettiness of the gaijin girls. "With a Japanese girl, my preference is that she should be ugly and have no bodily curves," Obara would say later. "After I had talked to them often [on the telephone], I came to recognize their body type. Those who had a dry voice were skinny, while those with a moist voice were fat." He said, "I like an ugly girl. Selecting an ugly one is part of my play. I like ugly play with an ugly girl."

He chose his foreign partners, or so he claimed, according to the same criteria. "Foreign hostesses are all ugly," he said. "Not in the sense of appearance, but in their minds." Years later, an account would be published, in English, of "conquest play" from Obara's point of view. It is full of self-serving distortions and evasiveness, but it conveys the sacramental quality of the performance.

Before his "play" the accused pours into a small shot glass nasty liquid with [a] burning smell, commonly known as "Philippine liquor." Then he and his female "partner" drinks [*sic*] from the glass in turn. The accused drinks two glasses of the liquid.

As made clear at court, Obara loses the last bit of his sense of shame after drinking two glasses of the liquid. Then, the accused alone takes great quantity of a stimulant. His "partner," as she continues to drink the "Philippine liquor," loses her consciousness. Then the accused puts on a mask and begins the "play." This mask makes him turn into someone else, a person outside the ordinary. Then he gets into his nasty "play."

To "play" with, the accused preferred non-Japanese bar hostesses who were drug-addicted, punk women (with a mean personality), known as "bitches" . . . He also chose his "play partners" from those [Japanese] women searching for some male company over the phone. In such a case, the accused preferred waistless, plumpy women who were often compared to a pig or a hippopotamus. Under a mask, Obara had his nasty "play" with such ugly women.

After Obara's arrest, Clara Mendez was invited back to the investigation headquarters. There the police showed her images from the videos, of the night in 1996 when she had gone to Joji Obara's apartment in Zushi, and the missing hours after she had sipped her drink. "They spared me the worst of it," she said. "They were just pictures, still pictures they'd taken from the video so I could identify myself. It was just me, unconscious, lying on the bed, still in my clothes. It was . . . very creepy. I just looked like a doll, a girl-shaped doll."

■ ■ ■

Among the list of names and videos, the police found other women they knew: Katie Vickers and Christa Mackenzie. They followed the telephone numbers and addresses on the list and identified a dozen more. Much of the information was too vague to identify the victims, and many of the foreign girls had left Japan years before for untraceable destinations. Several of those whom they did find were unwilling to cooperate, out of shame, or timidity, or a wish to forget the whole story. Other cases would have been difficult to bring to trial for other reasons—such as Isobel Parker, who had taken her own action against Obara by successfully blackmailing him. But the detectives found several women for whom the combination of a video and the testimony of a credible victim made a strong case.

On November 17, the prosecutors formally charged Obara with drugging and raping Katie Vickers. They immediately "rearrested" him on suspicion of doing the same to a thirty-one-year-old Japanese woman named Fusako Yoshimoto. On December 8, they charged him with that rape and arrested him for another against twenty-year-old Itsuko Oshihara, followed in 2001 by twenty-five-year-old Megumi Mori. To the usual charge of rape and drugging was added one of causing a burn to Megumi Mori's leg—from the heat of the lights that had pressed against the skin of the unconscious woman.

The day after Lucie's disappearance, the police discovered, Obara had called the Zushi Fire Station, asking for Department Headquarters. According to one newspaper, he said, "Something serious has happened. Please tell me where the emergency hospital is." He called the number of the hospital that he was given. The conversation, in which he inquired about its opening hours, was recorded, but he never appeared. A few days later, he did turn up at a hospital in Tokyo, where he was treated for a rash caused by caterpillars.

The police were sure that they knew what had happened. They believed Obara had drugged and killed Lucie, and somehow disposed of her body. But how could they prove it? Lucie was not on the list of names, and there was no video of her. They could show that she and Obara had spent that afternoon together, and that after her disappearance he had behaved suspiciously. But what exactly had he done to her? And where was Lucie now?

The detectives searched the garden of the house at Den-en Chofu and open areas close to his other properties. They probed the ground with hollow rods of bamboo, and half a dozen policemen with sniffer dogs combed the beach and the cliffs close to Blue Sea Aburatsubo. It was anxious work, for the grass and weeds in the area were thick and littered with rubbish, and the detectives were afraid that they would disturb poisonous snakes.

17. CARITA

For Lucie's family and friends, there was little comfort in Joji Obara's arrest. In itself, the news did nothing to dent the mass of pain and uncertainty weighing down upon them. The Tokyo police never shared with the Blackmans their conviction that Lucie was dead; in fact, apart from the fact of Obara's arrest, they told them very little at all. The Blackmans gleaned a little of the leaked titbits that were published in the Japanese, and sometimes the British, newspapers, and the Lucie Hotline continued to generate sporadic, and useless, information. Louise Phillips, who had finally flown home after weeks of questioning, had been ordered by the police to tell the Blackmans nothing. Tim and Sophie flew out again to Tokyo in the middle of November but, in his meeting with them, Superintendent Mitsuzane maintained the official pretense—that, for the time being, Obara was being investigated for a series of rapes and, although the police were still pursuing Lucie's disappearance with vigor, there could not at present be said to be a connection between the two cases.

At his press conference after the meeting, Tim gave a skittish, unhappy performance, with flashes of his odd, out-of-kilter humor.

"How optimistic are you that you'll find Lucie?" a journalist asked.

"The optimism never dies," said Sophie, looking at her father.

Tim said, "There's realism in the fact that she's been missing for four months, and there's always the possibility that she's come to her end. But that's something you have to cross when you come to it. Whereas before it was a fifty-fifty chance, I suppose now it's an eighty-twenty chance that she is gone."

"My bid would be sixty-forty," said Sophie.

Tim gave an unnatural smile. "That's the realism of old age against the optimism of youth."

Christmas was approaching, a time of strain for any family divided by divorce. This year, each of the Blackmans dreaded the holiday for the way it would expose the absence in their lives. Jane, Sophie, and Rupert escaped to Barbados, and spent Christmas Day sunbathing on the beach, as far away as possible from any associations with Lucie. Tim was in the Isle of Wight with Josephine and her children. "I was trying to hold Lucie in one particular area of my head," he said. "I was trying not to let the trauma of what had happened overwhelm everything else. I was in my late forties. I had three children of my own and four children of Jo's to look after. Of course, Lucie was important, but I had to give time and priority to the other people I loved too.

"I used to drive from the Isle of Wight to work in Kent, an hour and a half's drive. There was a CD of music which Lucie used to like, and I'd listen to that in the car driving back and indulge my sorrow and my thoughts of Lucie. And that's what enabled me to be there for Jo, and for the other children, and to do my work."

Cautiously and steadily, Tim was loosening his grip on false hopes. He was abandoning the idea that Lucie might still be alive, the faith that had compelled him for six months and enabled him to find hope in con men, charlatans, and journalists. But he could not control his anger, which now directed itself not only against Lucie's abductor and the police but also against the system of collusion and institutional complacency that had made her disappearance possible. Two days before Christmas, he sent a furious e-mail to one of the detectives:

> It is six months since Lucie went missing, and incredibly I find that week after week goes by [and] I do not receive any communication from the Tokyo Metropolitan Police. I am very very upset and traumatised that the Police do not give a single consideration to how the family feels as victims, and it is disgraceful and inhumane that you do not provide any news or information to the family to help them cope with this terrible and tragic event . . .
>
> It is evident that many many girls have been abducted and raped from Roppongi in the last 5–6 years (some have disappeared). These are girls many of whom are working illegally on tourist visas. Because of this, some are not able to report the crime to the Police for fear of arrest and/or deportation. This puts all the girls in danger.
>
> However, some of these girls have reported the crime to the Police. Why has this man Obara, or others like him, been able to get away with these crimes for years, continuing to abduct and rape girls? Because the Police have not acted, and the Police have not arrested him. This makes the Police guilty of the disappearance of Lucie . . . and when the next girl is abducted and raped or murdered the Police and the Immigration Department will be guilty of that crime too.

■ ■ ■

So far, it was in Britain and Japan that Lucie's disappearance had drawn the most attention. But with the arrest of a suspect and the emergence of victims of other nationalities, the case was soon being reported all over the world. Stories about Joji

Obara popped up in Spain, Italy and Turkey, in Germany, Denmark and the Netherlands. One Friday in October, a thirty-five-year-old solicitor named Robert Finnigan was sitting at his desk in Sydney, Australia, when his eye fell upon an article on page 10 of the *Sydney Morning Herald*. "Fears of More Missing Women," ran the headline.

> Have Australian women fallen prey to the nightclub prowler believed responsible for the disappearance of Lucie Blackman, a British bar hostess? Newspapers have reported their fears that the main suspect in the case, Joji Obara, a Tokyo businessman, could have been involved in the disappearance of other foreign women . . . Australians are well represented among the foreigners working the Roppongi bar hostess trade, earning huge sums entertaining businessmen. It is believed that at least two Australians and one New Zealander contacted police through other channels to complain of being abused by Obara . . . The women all said Obara had lured them to his luxurious flat on the coast south of Tokyo and drugged them.

"It was lunchtime when I read it," Robert Finnigan told me later. "And straightaway, there was a moment of recognition. I knew instantly, even though I didn't have all the facts. It was just too similar. I wasn't surprised or shocked, because I'd had all those years to think about it. I didn't feel relieved. But I knew. There was an unanswered question, and this was the answer."

The question was: What had really happened to Carita Ridgway, the beautiful young Australian woman whom Robert had fallen in love with, and lost, almost nine years before?

Carita Ridgway grew up in Perth, on the far coast of Australia's immense Western Desert, one of the most isolated cities in the world. Her parents, Nigel and Annette, were creatures of the 1960s. They met when they were very young, married quickly, and soon found themselves deeply unhappy together. Annette, who was eighteen on their wedding day, was a seeker of enlightenment, a student of dreams and meditation and astrology. Nigel, who had emigrated from Britain in 1966, was a drummer in a rock-and-roll band called Purple Haze. "If I'm honest, I wasn't really a good boy," he told me years later, after he had remarried and become a respectable middle-aged primary-school teacher. "Not a model husband. I was easy prey for sex and booze. Not so much the booze, but the girls were always a temptation." Their marriage finally broke up in 1983, when their two daughters, Samantha and Carita, were fourteen and thirteen. "Again, that's something I look back on and cringe," Nigel said. "The girls were just getting into puberty, young womanhood, and their parents split up. Not a good time. I think it affected them a lot."

Carita had always been energetic and creative, a talented dancer who loved English literature and acting and the outdoors. After her parents' separation, she became quarrelsome, withdrawn, and depressed. At the same time, she emerged into her teens as a beauty, with long blond hair, curved red lips, and small, even features. Annette, who was struggling to support her two daughters, did not know how to help her. Carita's despair became deeper; she spoke of suicidal thoughts, and Annette was alarmed enough to have her committed to a psychiatric clinic. The enforced isolation from the outside world, and the attention of nurses and doctors, had a soothing effect on Carita, and for a while she seemed to be getting better. But then the hospital psychiatrist, who turned out to have a record of abusing his female patients, began taking her out for seductive lunches. He was sacked before any serious harm had been done. But by now Carita's education, and her self-confidence, had been thoroughly shredded. "If you don't have a strong family background, and you don't have self-esteem, it's almost a liability to be that good-looking," Annette said. "It's difficult to stand up for yourself. You get preyed on."

Carita left the psychiatric home and dropped out of school. She lingered in Perth for a year or two but soon became bored by its smallness and familiarity. When her best friend, Lynda Dark, suggested a move to Sydney, she seized the chance; together, the two of them hitchhiked east across the Western Desert. In Sydney, she met Robert Finnigan, newly arrived from Britain. The two of them fell in love and moved in together.

Annette, like any mother separated for the first time from her daughter, worried about Carita. Her anxieties took the form of intense nightmares and, being interested in such things, she recorded the details over the course of several years. There were scenes in which Carita was attacked and violated; mysterious robed strangers imparted warnings of danger and tragedy. Then there was a dream in which Carita came to her mother and comforted her, and placed a ring on her finger. Annette wrote down these visions meticulously, and subsequent events would impart a terrible resonance to her dream journal.

The worst of all the nightmares pictured Carita sitting at a table with a group of Asian men. She appeared happy and secure. Her companions, lightheartedly it seemed, were inviting Carita to choose one of them. Only Annette could understand the true meaning of the scene and the intense malevolence of the men. "She felt that she was quite safe," Annette said. "She had to choose one of the men. But they were so cold and calculating, and she didn't know, and couldn't see them for what they were. It was such a terrible, terrible nightmare. And I had these dreams but I didn't do anything about them. I thought they were symbolic, but they were precognitive. They were literal. I still have that dreadful feeling about it."

The attention she received from men disconcerted Carita. In an effort to deflect it, she dyed her blond hair auburn, but she remained outstandingly attractive. Robert Finnigan, who was serious, quietly spoken, and bespectacled, was overwhelmed by his feelings for her. He had arrived in Sydney after trailing around Southeast Asia; he and Carita had met in one of the city's many backpacker hostels. They would be together for the next five years. "I'd wake up in the morning and she would be there next to me," Robert said. "I just couldn't believe it. I remember walking on Bondi Beach, with beautiful women everywhere, women from the covers of magazines. And I'd look at Carita beside me—and she was more beautiful. We were young, so you can't be sure about these things. But I think we both expected we'd be together for the rest of our lives."

The two of them lived in a series of cheap rented houses in Sydney, shared with other young migrants to the city. They took casual jobs, Robert on a building site, Carita in a laun- derette and then at a restaurant. She designed and sold T-shirts, did a bit of modeling, and acted in a student film, but the two of them lived for traveling and for the long journeys that they would make together to the Philippines, Nepal, Mexico, and America, before returning to Sydney when their money ran out. Their first year together, 1987, was Australia's bicenten- nial, a round of barbecues, parties, and open-air celebrations. Then, in the summer of the following year, Carita's friend Lynda persuaded her to go with her to Japan to work as a bar hostess.

Robert was concerned, and not only because it meant an extended separation from his beautiful girlfriend. But Lynda had worked in Tokyo before, and she insisted that there was no danger in the work itself. "Like most people, I was led to believe that it was one of the safest societies in the world, that a woman can walk around the streets at two a.m. and nothing happen to her," Robert said. "This business of hostessing seemed a bit strange—paying someone to talk to you in a bar. But it was just one of the peculiarities of Japanese society, a bit pathetic to Westerners, but just a way for these businessmen to let off steam."

The months of separation were uneasy for Robert. It was difficult to imagine the kind of life that Carita was leading apart from him. There were postcards; she phoned once every week or two; he sent her cartoons of Sinbad, the ginger cat they had rescued as a stray. She and Lynda were in Utsunomiya, a colorless regional city an hour north of Tokyo. They worked at two clubs, Madam Adam and the Tiger's Lair, alongside Americans, Brazilians, Filipinas, and New Zealanders. Carita seemed cheerful enough. She quickly attracted regular customers, including one man who took her on a dōhan in his chauffeur-driven Ferrari. "And absolutely no monkey business either," she wrote to her mother. "The guys just love to take Western girls out to show them off . . . Japanese men have about three different women each. They leave their wives at home, take their girlfriends to the club, ignore their girlfriends and chat up the hostesses."

"I'd have been happier if she'd been teaching English or something more like that," Robert said. "But I didn't want to stifle Carita—sometimes you have to let people do what they want to do." And after a few months she left the Tiger's Lair, and Robert flew to Hong Kong to travel with Carita to Singapore and Thailand.

In 1990, she and Lynda went back for another three-month stint, this time at a club in Roppongi, where they had to "dance." Robert did not say as much, but this probably meant topless dancing. "I think Lynda was fine with it, but Carita was a bit embarrassed," he said. "She tried it a couple of times, but I don't think it worked out." By September, she was back with him in Sydney, waitressing and modeling again, and helping to support Robert as he applied to study law at the University of New South Wales.

The following year, Carita went back to Tokyo for a third time, accompanied by her sister, Samantha, who had a Japanese boyfriend. The two of them lived together in a gaijin house close to the language school where Sam was teaching. Carita was working at a Ginza club called Ayakoji, where the hostesses were expected to wear huge frilly, old-fashioned dresses with petticoats. The two sisters spent December and January of 1992 together in Japan. On Christmas Day, they ate spare ribs at the Lion restaurant in Ginza, and truffles sent from Perth by their father. On Boxing Day, snow fell over Tokyo, and at New Year they went to the countryside to stay with the family of Sam's boyfriend, Hideki.

Robert received exhilaratingly good news: he had won a university place to study law. Carita was delighted and told him how proud she was. Sometimes, people who knew them wondered whether they were well matched, and whether Robert's steadiness and calm were right for Carita, who had a taste for glamour and adventure, and was still only twenty-one. But if she had doubts, she did not speak of them. After five years together, it was difficult to imagine Robert and Carita apart.

Then one Monday in February, Samantha telephoned Robert in a state of confusion and distress. Carita had gone out for the weekend and not come back. And now she was in a Tokyo hospital, unconscious and dangerously ill.

■ ■ ■

Annette, Nigel, and Robert flew out to Tokyo together and went straight to Carita's bedside. It was impossible to digest what had happened. Carita, who was never sick, who didn't smoke or drink or take drugs, had been perfectly healthy on

Friday evening, when she had gone to work at the hostess club. Then on Monday, Sam had received a phone call announcing that she had been admitted to a nearby hospital. She hurried over, perplexed and annoyed, and prepared to give her sister a telling-off for not calling over the weekend. But Carita was barely conscious and was hardly able to acknowledge Sam's presence. She had been brought in that morning by a Japanese man named Akira Nishida, who had then abruptly left. Later that day, she fell unconscious. A few hours later, the doctors diagnosed acute liver failure and announced that Carita had less than a 50 percent chance of survival.

By Wednesday, when her parents and Robert got to the hospital, Carita was being kept alive with drips and breathing tubes, and her skin was yellow with jaundice. The following day, she fell into a deep coma. Robert and the Ridgway family took turns sitting by her hospital bed as the doctors carried out an expensive "blood-washing" procedure. There was no visible improvement, and Carita was moved to a bigger and better-equipped hospital. But by the weekend, unpurged by her liver, the toxins had built up in her body and she was experiencing convulsions. By the end of the following week, the doctors confirmed what was already unbearably obvious: Carita's brain was no longer functioning.

The doctors pressed needles into her skin, but there was no reaction. Beneath the lids, her eyes were blind and dull. Samantha and Robert found it impossible to accept. But Nigel and Annette agreed that there was no point in keeping her alive artificially. On Saturday, February 29—Leap Day—the four of them went to the hospital for the last time. "Carita was lying there, surrounded by tubes and machines and connected to the ventilator, and they removed all of those," said Nigel. "You could see the heartbeat get slower and slower and slower, until it was one long line. And when they'd taken the tubes out she looked like Carita again, and she looked beautiful and very peaceful. It wasn't a horrible experience, watching someone die. She was already dead; it was just letting her go. But Rob and Sam, and especially Rob, found it hard, so hard. And we were all crying, and hugging Carita, and then the nurses said could we go out for a moment. When we came back in, they'd dressed her in a beautiful pink kimono, with her hands folded neatly across her chest, and flowers, so many flowers, all around the bed."

Carita's body was placed in front of a Buddhist altar in the basement of the hospital. Annette and Nigel spent the night there, watching over her and lighting sticks of incense. The day after next, they made the long drive to the crematorium on the outer edges of suburban Tokyo. They said goodbye to Carita, who lay peacefully in a coffin full of rose petals, and watched her disappear behind the steel doors of the furnace. None of them was prepared for what came next.

After a pause, they were led into a room on the other side of the building, and each given a pair of white gloves and chopsticks. In the room, on a steel sheet, were Carita's remains as they had emerged from the heat of the furnace. The incineration was incomplete. Wood, cloth, hair, and flesh had burned away, but the biggest bones, of the legs and arms, as well as the skull, were cracked but recognizable. Rather than a neat box of ashes, the Ridgways were confronted with Carita's calcined skeleton. As the family, their task, a traditional part of every Japanese cremation, was to pick up her bones with the chopsticks and place them in the urn.

"Rob couldn't handle it at all," Nigel said. "He thought we were monsters even to think of it. But perhaps it's because we were the parents, and she was our daughter . . . It sounds macabre, as I tell you about it now, but it didn't feel that way at the time. It was something emotional. It almost made me feel calmer. I felt as if we were looking after Carita."

Nigel, Annette, and Sam picked up the bigger bones and placed them in the urn with the ashes. The bigger pieces of the skull went on the top.

■ ■ ■

Carita was dead three days before her twenty-second birthday because during the course of a single weekend her liver had suddenly stopped functioning. How was this possible? The doctors were unable to explain it. At first they had assumed that Carita was a drug user, but Sam and Robert, and everyone else who knew her well, insisted that she was not and had never been. Then the doctors proposed that her death was the result of viral hepatitis but failed to agree on which type or how she might have contracted it.

The only person in a position to explain was Mr. Nishida, the man who had dropped her off at the hospital on Monday morning. He had left no contact details. But he had Samantha's number, and during the week that her family was watching Carita die, he had called her several times.

He spoke fluent English. He was calm and solicitous, even when Sam became upset. He told her that he had met Carita at the hostess club and taken her to Kamakura, a seaside town south of Tokyo, where she had eaten a bad oyster and suffered food poisoning. He seemed pained to learn that she had become so terribly ill. Sam demanded his address and telephone number, but Mr. Nishida regretfully refused, but he always called again a day or two later. Robert Finnigan, in particular, was deeply suspicious. The unexplained nature of Carita's relationship with this man, and of the weekend they had spent together, were an additional torment to him. At his urging,

Sam's boyfriend, Hideki, contacted the police and urged them to investigate Mr. Nishida.

Two detectives came to the hospital to interview Sam and Hideki. It was a bizarre encounter. After perfunctory inquiries about Nishida, they accused Hideki of being a drug dealer, the implication being that it was he who was responsible for Carita's illness. "We didn't call the police again," Samantha said. "The truth is we felt more threatened and intimidated by the police than by the soft-spoken man who called himself Nishida and appeared to be concerned for us."

The day Carita died, Nishida telephoned again and talked at length to Hideki. He said that he wanted to make a contribution to the cost of the family's air fares and the funeral. He spoke of a sum of ¥1 million; he also wanted to talk to Nigel and Annette. The day after Carita's death, the family drove out to meet him in a hotel close to Tokyo's domestic airport.

They waited in the lobby for an hour until Mr. Nishida called them up to a room that he appeared to have taken for the occasion. It had been made clear that he wished to see only Carita's parents; Sam and Robert waited resentfully downstairs. In Annette's recollection, the hotel room was divided by a kind of screen, and she had the unnerving impression that there was someone else waiting and listening invisibly on the other side. Nishida himself made little impression: a man in early middle age, dressed in a dark suit, "not overly good-looking," as Annette remembered, "with an odd nose, a strange pinched nose." The most noticeable thing about him was perspiration; he mopped his sweating face constantly with a handkerchief or towel. "It was an uncomfortable situation," said Annette. "We had just seen Carita die. And here we were in this room, with the feeling that someone was going to jump out at any moment from the other side of the screen."

Mr. Nishida faced Nigel and Annette Ridgway across a low coffee table.

"I loved your daughter," he said to them. "And I wanted to spend more time with her."

"So did we," said Annette.

He described the weekend that they had spent together, beginning at the hostess club on Friday evening. "He said that on the Saturday evening, they were going to go out to dinner," Annette remembered. "But Carita wasn't feeling well so they'd stayed in. They went to bed—the way he told it, it didn't sound like the same bed—and in the middle of the night Carita got up. But when she came back, she wasn't the same as she'd been before. She was very unwell, and on the Sunday morning she was worse. So he called a doctor, and the doctor had given her an injection for the nausea and the pain. But then she got worse again, and by the time he took her to hospital on Monday she was nearly comatose. He was making out that he tried to care for her, to look after her, and that he didn't know what was wrong or why she was sick. He told us things in passing, comments which Carita had made to him, and they were the kind of thing which Carita really might have said—how she'd apologized for being sick and for not being good company, the sort of thing Carita would have said if she'd been ill."

Nigel remembered, "He kept saying how sorry he was about what had happened, what a dreadful thing it was. He seemed to know Carita well, as if she was his girlfriend. He was really upset. I said things like 'Dreadful accident,' 'Don't blame yourself.' I took him at face value."

After about three-quarters of an hour, Nishida produced two boxes and gave them to Nigel and Annette. One contained a gold necklace, the other a diamond ring. They were not wrapped, as a present would have been, and the ring was not clasped in velvet but rattled loose in its box. "He said again, 'I loved your daughter, and I wanted to spend much more time with her,'" Annette recalled. "He said, 'These would have been her birthday presents next week.'"

Later, Annette would turn over and over in her mind the significance of these objects and remember the dreams she had had about the predatory men and that other ring Carita had brought to her in her sleep. At the time, though, there was nothing to say and nothing more to do but to accept the gifts of gold and to leave. "We were very, very numb," Annette said. "And there is some information that you can only accept at face value. We couldn't accuse him of anything, because we didn't know what had been wrong with Carita. The police weren't interested, the Australian embassy was not interested. What he was saying sounded reasonable—that he'd done what he could."

The Ridgways made their awkward goodbyes, and stepped out into the corridor. As they were walking towards the elevators, Annette glanced back and saw Mr. Nishida looking out from the half-open door, peering after them as they disappeared out of sight, with an unreadable expression on his face.

■ ■ ■

They left Japan with Carita's ashes the day after the funeral. Samantha stayed on in Tokyo for a few months, the Ridgways flew to Perth, and Robert returned to Sydney and the apartment he had shared with Carita. For seven months, he wept every night as he went to sleep. He sleepwalked through his first year at the university. For much longer than that, he believed that he would never be able to lead a happy life. He stayed on alone in the apartment and looked after Sinbad. He finished his law degree, qualified as a solicitor, and got a job in

Sydney with Phillips Fox, one of the biggest law firms in Australia. And it was in their offices on Market Street that he was sitting that afternoon when he read the story in the *Sydney Morning Herald* and knew beyond any doubt that fishy Akira Nishida and Joji Obara were one and the same.

18. IN THE CAVE

The crumbling film and yellowing paper of Obara's seized possessions filled an entire room in the Tokyo Metropolitan Police headquarters. Superintendent Udo put in a lot of time there himself, supervising the younger detectives and looking over their finds. "I wanted to stay as close as possible to the evidence," he told me. "I checked as much as I could personally, because sometimes a less experienced investigator might fail to spot something which to me was a diamond." There, at the end of the year 2000, glittering among the dust and insects, he came upon such a jewel: a receipt from a hospital in western Tokyo for the treatment of Carita Ridgway.

Udo wanted to give the impression that the police would have nailed down this case anyway, by their own efforts. But there was no sign that they were aware of Carita Ridgway before November 2000, when, after prolonged pestering by Robert Finnigan in Sydney, they were contacted by the Australian embassy. Once the police had been alerted, however, the facts fell quickly together.

The receipt led to Hideshima Hospital, where Carita was first admitted, and to the Tokyo Women's Hospital, where she died. Equipped with a photograph of her, the police identified Carita among the unconscious foreign faces in Obara's video collection. During the rape, which extended over the course of several hours, he was seen shaking fluid from a bottle onto a cloth and holding it beneath her nose. At the Tokyo Women's Hospital was the most crucial evidence of all: a tiny sliver of Carita's liver, removed after her death and preserved for all these years through an administrative fluke. When the liver was analyzed, the police lab soon found what the doctors had inexplicably missed: traces of chloroform, which attacks and poisons the organ.

Robert had kept in touch only intermittently with the Ridgway family. But one day, when all doubts had been dispelled, he telephoned Annette in Perth to tell her that the man who had called himself Nishida was actually the accused serial rapist Joji Obara, and that rather than trying to save Carita, he had killed her. Robert and Annette traveled to Tokyo to talk to the police; Annette made a second trip alone and signed the documents necessary to file a criminal complaint.

Obara admitted that he had been Nishida, but he refused to own up to anything more. "I feel unspeakable indignation about the allegation that I raped and killed her," Obara said in a statement issued by his lawyers. "I had a romantic relationship with her and even took her to the hospital out of concern." Robert Finnigan had drafted a statement of his own, which was issued in the name of the Ridgways: "Not only has Obara drugged and raped women, he now insults his victims and humiliates their families. Obara is the worst type of human being. He shows no remorse whatsoever. It is hoped his true nature will be revealed in a Japanese court of law."

The police and prosecutors could prove now that Obara was a killer, and every few weeks, as they worked their way through the videos and notebooks, they were able to add a fresh charge of rape. But even the truth about Carita did not make up for their lack of progress in connecting Obara with the disappearance of Lucie—and after three months of solitary incarceration, he still refused to admit that he had done anything wrong at all. "The police underestimated Obara," I was told by someone close to the investigation. "They thought he was just another stupid criminal who would confess—'I'm sorry, I did it, I left the body here, I buried it like this.' But he was so stubborn. He always denied everything." The girls who alleged rape had been prostitutes, he insisted, when he bothered to speak at all; Carita had died of food poisoning, or because of misdiagnosis by the hospital; he had no idea what had happened to Lucie. "We go after him relentlessly until eleven, twelve at night," said one of the detectives. "We give him as little sleep as possible. We exhaust him physically and mentally. It's rough, but it's the only option remaining to us."

"The police are experienced in persuading people to confess," a senior detective told me. "We make efforts to let the criminal understand the consequences of their actions. We say things like, 'The sorrow of the victims is truly deep,' and 'Have you no sense of reflection on what you have done?' But he was not that kind of person. With him those tactics would never work." The detective had no difficulty explaining this quirk in Obara's character, although he hesitated a little in spelling it out to a foreigner. "It is hard for you to understand, perhaps. But it's because he is . . . not Japanese."

I got a sense, hearing people talk about the police, and hearing the police talk about themselves, that they felt hard done by. A fundamental rule—that criminals confess—was being willfully broken. Under such conditions, how could it be surprising that they struggled? The idea that cunning, stubbornness, and mendacity were to be expected from a criminal, that it was in order to deal with such people that the police existed, did not occur to many of the detectives, or not for much of the time. They were not incompetent or unimaginative or lazy or complacent—they were themselves victims of extremely bad and unusual luck: that one in a million in Japan, the dishonest criminal.

■ ■ ■

Winter in Japan is bright and bitter, but the cold keeps the vipers at bay. As he told it, this was when Superintendent Udo made a last attempt to find Lucie in the places known to have been frequented by Joji Obara. "It's a vast area," he said, "and there are many places where a body might be buried. I formed a team and told them to go out and not come back until they had found Lucie. In December and January, they dug in many places." One Monday early in February 2001, twenty-two plainclothes policemen checked into an inn on the beach in the village of Moroiso, a few hundred yards from the apartment at Blue Sea Aburatsubo. Their rooms were reserved for the whole month. Every morning, they went out with shovels and picks to different spots along the coast. The local people assumed that they were employed on some municipal project or other—except that, as one local woman said, "They didn't have the eyes of construction workers."

On Thursday, February 8, Udo sent his deputy down from Tokyo for consultations. It was concluded that the search area had been expanded too far and that the following morning they should begin again in the most obvious place of all—the 250 yards of beach that extended beneath a cliff next to Blue Sea Aburatsubo. It was there, five days after Lucie's disappearance, that Obara had arrived in a car with lumpy objects in the passenger seat. There, he had summoned a locksmith to break into his own apartment, from which banging noises had subsequently been heard. There, a sweating, shirtless Obara had first dismissed the police who had knocked at his door and later apologized to them, proffering the frozen corpse of his dead dog. Mr. Hirokawa, the caretaker's boyfriend, even claimed to have seen someone resembling him in the area of the beach in the middle of the night carrying a muddy shovel. Police dogs and police officers, of course, had sniffed and prodded the area after Obara's arrest in October. But now, in desperation, they were to go over it again.

The oblong block of Blue Sea Aburatsubo was the last structure before the road ended and the seashore began. It was a rocky coast; the cliff fell vertically to a beach strewn with large boulders and over which a cement path had been fashioned. It wasn't a charming or attractive beach. The sky was high and blue at this time of year, and the water was so clean and clear that you could see the forms of individual stones along the bottom. But the sand on the beach was gray and sticky, and the boulders were littered with dried and broken leaves. In the summer months—in early July, for example— they shimmered with thousands of vile brown beetles, which sucked on the seaweed rotting in the cracks of the rocks.

Around a curve of the beach, about two hundred yards from the apartment building and out of sight of human habitation, a portion of the cliff had tumbled away to form a tower of stone embedded in the beach. Just behind here, and concealed from view by it, was a cave. It was the kind of hideaway where rubbish is surreptitiously dumped and where teenagers go to smoke and canoodle. In a country less tidy and disciplined than Japan, it would have been littered with beer cans and discarded condoms. It scarcely qualified as a cave at all—more of a wide crevice in the dirty rock, eight feet wide at its mouth, ten feet high at its highest point, with walls and ceiling that narrowed and sloped to a dead end. Four crumbling plastic pipes protruded from its uneven ceiling and dripped onto the floor, an ancient attempt to channel rainwater from the cliffs above.

An old bathtub was partially submerged in the sand. At nine a.m., four of the policemen loosened it, hauled it out of the cave, and began to dig. Within a few moments, they encountered an obstacle that rustled against their spades. Tugged out of the sand, it emerged as a semitransparent plastic rubbish bag, containing three lumpy objects. They were immediately identifiable as a human arm, severed at the shoulder, and two human feet. The wrist was entangled with plants and seaweed. The flesh was white and waxy with decay, but the finger- and toenails were preserved, and the men with the spades observed how neat and well shaped they were, with traces of nail polish. The officer in charge called Udo at once on his mobile phone. "He was shedding tears as he spoke to me," Udo remembered. "He said, 'Boss, we found Lucie.'"

The four policemen stopped digging and awaited the arrival of the most senior and most specialized detectives from Tokyo. Udo went down, along with his own boss, the head of the First Investigation Section, Akira Hiromitsu. A judge quickly issued a warrant for a full and comprehensive search, and within two hours there were forty people at the cave: local police, Udo's Special Investigation Unit, and twenty officers from the Identification Division with cameras, sketch pads, rubber gloves, and plastic evidence bags. The news leaked quickly, and soon there were helicopters overhead, hired by the Japanese television companies, and photographers bobbing in boats a few yards offshore. An improvised marquee of blue tarpaulins was erected to conceal the mouth of the cave; all day, men in waist-length anoraks, rubber boots, and blue baseball caps came and went, with white cotton masks over their mouths and noses.

When the police had assembled, the digging resumed. The cave was scooped of its sand down to the bedrock, which was no more than two feet below the surface. The torso was the next part found, unwrapped and naked to the sand, thirteen inches down. Then two more rubbish bags, containing the second arm, two thighs, two lower legs, and what seemed to be the head, encrusted in a thick layer of concrete or cement.

Late in the afternoon, six of the searchers emerged carrying a heavy-looking blue vinyl zip-top bag, six feet long, which they manhandled awkwardly among them. It was driven first to Azabu Police Station and the next morning to a laboratory at Tokyo University Medical School. There the cement was prised away from the head, and the teeth were examined. They matched exactly dental records that had been sent from Sevenoaks. There was no doubt at all that the ten body parts on the examining table were the remains of Lucie Blackman.

Six times that weekend, senior detectives gave unattributable briefings to the reporters accredited to the Tokyo Metropolitan Police headquarters. The transcripts of these exchanges conveyed the excitement of the investigators, but also their defensiveness. "Now we have concrete evidence, his confession might not be necessary," one of the officers told the journalists on the evening of the discovery. "Don't you worry. The bottleneck was because we couldn't find the body. Once the identity [of the remains] is established, we'll have more than enough." Japanese reporters are rarely probing or aggressive with the representatives of the institutions to which they are assigned. But even they could not skirt the outstanding question: Why had it taken so long?

Rather ingeniously, the police attempted to present it not as a failure of basic detective work but as a triumph of tenacity. "Although we have looked at the search area previously, we weren't able to spot it at first glance," explained one officer. "Investigators went there repeatedly whenever they had some time. It was certainly a suspicious place, and our perseverance has paid off." Another officer of the Special Investigation Unit said, "Although we did search before, we couldn't find the body with just four or five people. There used to be a lot of weeds and we heard about vipers there, so we weren't able to find the body." The most memorable explanation of all came from an officer identified in the notes of one reporter as "Mr. S." "Detectives are like racehorses," Mr. S explained, "in that they can't use their instinct when they first visit a place. But as they run the course many times, they gradually start to shine. I thought it would be by Blue Sea Aburatsubo, without a doubt."

The body of a missing girl had been buried in a shallow grave two hundred yards from the apartment of the only suspect, an apartment in which he had been interviewed by the police for suspicious behavior five days after her disappearance. The detectives knew that shortly before he was arrested, Obara had moored a boat at a marina a few hundred yards away; it was their assumption that he was planning to dispose of a dead body. And then there was the most extravagantly clinching detail of all—the report of the suspect, late at night, close to the cave, carrying a spade.

Police sniffer dogs had been led over the area. But it had taken a specially formed team of forty elite detectives seven months to find the body. How could a modern police force have been so inept? The detectives looked more like plodding donkeys than sleek thoroughbreds. And among some of the journalists who followed their activities, an assumption became established: they must have known from very early on where Lucie had been buried, and the scene at the cave was an elaborately staged charade.

The reasoning went like this. The police were not stupid and must surely have found the body in such an obvious place. But they needed a confession, and a believable one. The most credible confession of all, which no subsequent recantation or legal sophistry could overturn, was the kind that told the police something that only the suspect knew. They were waiting patiently for Obara to talk, as virtually all suspects did eventually. When he did talk, he would tell them about the body in the cave, which they would promptly "discover," based on his information, thereby putting his guilt beyond any doubt. "The detectives had been to Blue Sea Aburatsubo, and they knew, they knew. I'm sure of it," someone close to the investigation told me. "But the police must not be the ones to find the body first. They need Obara to tell them where it is because then the case against him will go smoothly. Arresting someone is easy—the difficult thing is to prove that he is guilty."

But Obara didn't talk, and it gradually became obvious that he never would. Faced with this, and with time running out, the police were forced to take the second-best option and dig up the body themselves.

The problem was that seven months had passed. Because of the way it had been buried, sealed off from insects and bacteria in air-tight bags beneath wet sand, much of what remained of Lucie was partially mummified rather than skeletonized. But in the coolly euphemistic language of the autopsy, "the postmortem changes were extreme," and although the body was quickly identified, it was impossible to specify the cause of death.

Unsurprisingly, Superintendent Udo and all the detectives associated with the case insisted vehemently that they had no idea where the body had been until that day—to have admitted anything else would have laid them open to charges of perjury. But whatever the truth was, they emerged with shame. Either the police had conspired in a misguided cover-up that had resulted in the decay of precious forensic evidence; or they had achieved the same result through scarcely credible oversight and incompetence.

At home, Jane Blackman kept mementos of Lucie's life: a copy of *The Daily Express* from the day of her birth, the plastic hospital name bracelet she had worn as a newborn. There were childish drawings in crayon and felt tip, and school exercise books filled with Lucie's meticulous little girl's hand. Here she had written about playing in her paddling pool in the back garden, and making daisy chains with Louise, and practicing the recorder with her daddy accompanying her on the banjo, and going to the hospital with her toddler brother, Rupert, after he bit his tongue.

At the very end of January, Jane had flown back to Japan at the request of the police. In retrospect, this mysteriously secret visit would add to the suspicion that they knew more than they admitted about Lucie and the whereabouts of her body. The intrigue surrounding Jane's presence in Tokyo, a week before the scene in the cave, bordered on the sinister. Only a handful of people knew that she was in Japan. She had been checked into her hotel under a false name; even calls from her children were not connected to her room. Superintendent Mitsuzane told Jane nothing concrete about the progress of the investigation but bewildered her with bizarre and carefully prepared questions. One day she had spent more than an hour executing a detailed pencil drawing of the kind of hair clip Lucie used to wear. Another time she had been asked whether Lucie liked to eat eel. The questions about her daughter's diet were the ones that had given Jane the most intense sensation of chill and nausea. "Did she eat eel? Did she eat battered tempura? I had a horrible feeling about these questions," Jane said. "I couldn't bear it. I was staying in the Diamond Hotel, with that rabbit playing the piano. Once I saw a cockroach running across the floor. I just remember crying all the time. I didn't know why I was there."

"I love Mummy because she keeps the house tidy," Lucie had written in one of her exercise books from the Granville School, in an essay titled "Why I love Mummy."

Mummy is kind and she looks after me.

She cooks me lovely cakes and biscuits. Mummy makes a lovely pack lunch. I love Mummy she always keeps my bedroom tidy. Sometimes I don't like Mummy she shouts at me and sometimes I cry. But most of the time she is nice she cooks me a nice breakfast and a lovely tea. I love Mummy when she wears a pretty dress. I love Mummy very very much.

Jane had lost her own mother as a child and her sister as an adult. As a mother, her greatest fear had been the death of one of her children. It had been her life's mission to protect them. Now she was in Japan, speaking through an interpreter to policemen who seemed to be asking her to corroborate the contents of her dead daughter's stomach.

Two weeks after Lucie's body was found in the cave, her parents came to take her home. For the first time, Tim and Jane were in Japan at the same time, but they traveled there and back separately and never met or spoke to one another. Sophie and Rupert flew out with their father and then back with their mother, with Lucie in the hold of the airliner. Jane's friend Val Burman, who accompanied her, remembered the coffin as "macabre, like something out of a horror film, a huge, big, black wooden thing." When Tim visited the police, he was taken aback to be asked, more than once, if he wished to view Lucie's remains. "I was surprised," he said. "Is it a Japanese cultural thing? I didn't need those images. I can imagine them well enough without having them implanted in my head."

A heavy coffin, sealed and metal lined, was a necessity because of the condition of the remains.

Everyone gave a press conference. Jane, speaking at the Diamond Hotel, was as spare and searing as before. When the time came for questions, it was difficult to imagine what there was left to ask. But someone went ahead anyway and asked the default question for such situations, the question that is not a genuine inquiry so much as an invitation to dissolve into photogenic grief: Mrs. Blackman, how does it *feel* to be taking your daughter's body home?

Jane looked at the questioner witheringly and maintained her composure.

Tim, appearing with Sophie and Rupert at the Foreign Correspondents' Club of Japan, was as long-winded and informative as his ex-wife had been pithy and reticent. He thanked the media for their help over the months and spoke in detail about his feelings over Lucie's death, Obara's arrest, the Roppongi "system," and the role of the police. He also announced the foundation of the Lucie Blackman Trust, a fund that would be used to "ensure the safety of traveling children . . . so that Lucie's tragic death will not have been in vain." A flyer was handed out, bearing a photograph of Lucie and Tim embracing, and inviting donations to a Japanese bank account.

In my notes on the press conference, I wrote, "Grief takes people in different ways."

Tim confirmed that he and his children would be visiting the cave on the beach and asked that the media give them space and time to grieve in private. The message was clear enough: please leave us alone for a while. But in making this request, Tim had also announced exactly when and where they would be going.

It was Rupert Blackman's first visit to Japan. Throughout the whole agonizing, drawn-out period of Lucie's absence, he had been the member of the family least involved in the case. He was still a schoolboy, and he had done all he could to avoid contact with the reporters and photographers who intermittently rang the bell of their house in Sevenoaks. But he was conscious of a deep sense of loss and of being excluded from the intense activity that absorbed his mother, father, and sister. Journalists writing about Lucie's family got his name wrong, or left him out of their stories altogether. Many people, who knew only what they had read, were surprised on meeting him to discover that Lucie Blackman even had a brother. "The saddest thing of all is that I never really knew Lucie as a person," he told me. "She was always just my older sister, and I was the little brother. I didn't have the chance to build an adult relationship with Lucie, in the way that siblings do in their late teens or twenties. I was never mates with her, and I never will be." So Rupert needed no persuading to come to Japan when the time came to take Lucie's body home.

At Narita Airport, they were confronted by clicking photographers, trotting backwards and tripping over one another. It wasn't the only occasion when Rupert had to stifle the urge to laugh. "That was Lucie's spirit living through us, so we could still see the funny side of it and the absurdity of it all," he said. "It was just ridiculous, so ridiculous. Obviously we were devastated, but what the hell can you do about it? If you don't laugh, you cry. I remember at the press conference, just before it began, we were having a laugh about something, and Dad said, 'No, listen—you need to look somber and sad.'"

Rupert was fascinated by Japan: the vast, orderly throngs of people on the pavements and pedestrian crossings, the sight of thousands of umbrellas keeping off the early spring rain. "I'd never been anywhere like that," he said. "I love the respect that everyone has for one another. It's humbling to see that. But it made it even harder to accept that this thing had happened in this city." Towards the end of the week, the police drove them down to the beach at Moroiso, across the astonishing Rainbow Bridge, which curves in the sunlight across the breadth of Tokyo Bay.

They got out of the car above the cliff and descended to the beach down a set of rusty stairs. Rupert wanted to see the

place where Lucie had lain in the sand for seven months because he wanted to feel close to her. He wanted some of the
intimacy that they had never had, as a sensible big sister and
little scamp of a brother, and never would have now. Rupert
had flowers to leave for Lucie. They had stopped at a petrol
station so that he could buy paper and a pen to leave a farewell
note for his sister.

At the bottom of the steps, thirty or forty Japanese photographers and TV cameramen were waiting. Some of them
were standing or crouching in readiness, with their weighty
black cameras. Others had erected metal stepladders on the
sand to get a better view, no more than three or four yards in
front of the cave.

Rupert described it as "like a right hook," a punch to the
jaw, to descend onto the beach and find all these strangers
waiting.

The three of them walked forward with their flowers, and
the camera shutters hissed and whizzed. When Tim, Sophie,
and Rupert were facing the cave, the photographers crept even
closer behind them. Tim turned, and the cameramen paused,
and something caught light in both Tim and Sophie. Sophie
was swearing and screaming at the photographers, who scut-
tled back like crabs, and Tim was shouting too, and picking
up the abandoned ladders and hurling them awkwardly down
the beach. The cameramen kept shooting and filming, and
Rupert watched it all, and then turned away. "There was Dad
picking up these cameras and ladders, and shouting, and them
all shuffling back," he said. "And Sophie shouting too, telling
them all where to go." And there was Rupert, kneeling on the
slimy sand and weeping, staring into the dripping cave that
had been his sister's tomb.

PART FIVE JUSTICE

Lucie's funeral was at the end of April 2001. It would have been a grim occasion under any circumstances, and it was made doubly bleak by the palpable enmity between Jane and Tim.

It was organized by Jane and held in an Anglican church in the town of Chislehurst, twelve miles from Sevenoaks. It was a puzzling choice of venue. Sevenoaks has plenty of churches of its own, and Lucie, with Jane, had converted as a teenager from nominal membership of the Church of England to nominal Roman Catholicism. The church's principal significance in the lives of the Blackmans had been as the venue of Tim and Jane's wedding, twenty-five years earlier. Was this the point for Jane? I wondered. To reproach Tim, consciously or unconsciously, by tracing a link between his dead marriage and his dead daughter?

There were 260 people in the church; outside, a rabble of photographers and reporters were kept at bay behind aluminium barriers. There were flowers from Tony Blair and from the Japanese ambassador to London; the incense burned during the service was the gift of the Tokyo Metropolitan Police. Many of Lucie's contemporaries from Walthamstow Hall were there, as well as former colleagues from SocGen, a contingent from British Airways in their blue cabin uniforms, and even Helen Dove, who had worked with Lucie in Casablanca. Gayle

Blackman and Caroline Lawrence arrived together; at the last minute, Gayle decided that she could not face the church and had to be coaxed out of the car.

Several of those present would describe a sensation of lightness and depersonalization, almost of trance, as if they were watching the funeral at a remove from reality, as in a dream. The sensation was accentuated by the absence from the church of Lucie herself. The aura of decay about the coffin was too strong, so it was kept at the crematorium, and a large photograph of Lucie in a blue dress took its place. "That was the worst thing, that she wasn't there," Gayle said. "I'd written a card which I wanted to go with Lucie, and I took it to the undertaker before the service. It wasn't a question I'd ask now, but at the time it seemed necessary to know. I asked him, 'How bad is she?' And he said, 'It's bad.'"

There was no direct confrontation between Jane and Tim, who did not speak to one another at all. But black energies crackled between them. The friends who filled the church found themselves bent to their force, like iron filings arrayed around the field of a magnet. When the members of Tim's and Jane's families arrived, they seated themselves on opposite sides of the aisle, as if in parody of the wedding ceremony they had attended a quarter of a century before. Jane's seventy-four-year-old father, John Etheridge, was dying. He had heart disease and had recently had his second leg amputated. He was pushed into church in a wheelchair, a man who in his prime had been a strapping six three, now weighing little more than 125 pounds.

Even in their grief, her friends and family were struggling, mentally, for possession of Lucie. Gayle experienced a squirt of anger at the sight of a group from Walthamstow Hall, girls who had never known Lucie well or even liked her, who at various times had been her tormentors. "Jane had said no flowers, and Lucie's friends respected that," Gayle remembered. "But there were these girls from school, all dressed up and with their big bouquets. They were just there to be seen. You could hear them a couple of rows away, saying, 'Oh, look, so-and-so's here,' and 'Look who's with so-and-so!' It was disgusting. I didn't go to the crematorium after that. I couldn't face it."

No one had a more acute sense of detachment than Tim Blackman, and no one was under closer scrutiny. Many of the congregation were people whom Tim had never met and did not know, but they knew him, or versions of him, from his television appearances and newspaper interviews, and from the word of friends and acquaintances: Lucie's dad, who had worked so hard to find her, but whose demeanor and temperament remained, somehow, suspect. "I remember saying, 'I can't believe he's so composed,'" said Sarah Guest, one of the British Airways contingent. "He didn't give away his feelings at all, whereas the mum had a more normal reaction. I mean, I didn't know the guy at all, and I think people deal with grief in different ways. But people at the funeral were quite critical."

No one would have said so to their faces. But, among many of the mourners, a standard was being applied to those who had lost Lucie; a code of behavior was being invoked. Jane conformed to it; Tim, to the minds of people there, fell short.

■ ■ ■

A year and three days after she disappeared, on July 4, 2001, Joji Obara was brought to trial for the rape and killing of Lucie Blackman. The courtroom, in the towering judicial complex two hundred yards down the road from the Tokyo Metropolitan Police headquarters, was full to capacity. Obara had made seven previous court appearances and had been charged with five other counts of rape. Rather than being held day after day, Japanese trial hearings were held about once a month. So far,

most of those in the Obara trial had been held in closed court
so that the victims who were called on to testify—Clara Mendez, Katie Vickers, and the three Japanese women—could
give their evidence in private. But this morning nine hundred
people lined up for the sixty public seats, which were allocated
by computerized lottery. On the stroke of ten o'clock, Obara
entered the court, closely flanked by two uniformed guards.

He wore a charcoal gray suit and an open-necked shirt. He
was handcuffed, and a length of heavy-looking blue rope was
tied around his waist, its ends grasped by the guards who un-
cuffed and unknotted him after he had sat down. This was
routine in Japanese criminal cases, but I found myself registering a twinge of shock at a sight so out of keeping with the
gleam and modernity of Tokyo: a human being bound helplessly in ropes.

Obara was instructed to stand facing the panel of three
judges as the prosecutor read out the charges of *jungokan
chishi*—"rape resulting in death," a charge similar to manslaughter but short of murder—of Carita Simone Ridgway and
Lucie Jane Blackman. Defendants in Japanese criminal courts
do not respond with a simple plea of guilty or not guilty but,
after being reminded of their right to remain silent, are invited
to comment on the charges. Obara read aloud from a piece of
paper on the podium before him; his voice was clear but unexpectedly soft and lisping, almost soggy. He admitted to having been with Carita and Lucie on the nights in question, but
he denied any responsibility for their deaths. His sexual relationship with Carita had been one of mutual consent. He had
been entertained by Lucie in Casablanca (as "Mr. Kowa," the
lisping English-speaker whom Louise had vaguely remembered), but it was she who had asked to go out with him, not
vice versa; the question of a mobile phone had never come into
it. "We drank alcohol and watched videos at my apartment in
Zushi," he said. "We did not 'play'"—and he used the Japa-

nized English loan word *purei*—"even once that night. I did not make her consume drinks containing sleeping pills or any other drugs."

When he had left the apartment the next morning, he continued, Lucie had been fine. "I know that Lucie died," he said. "But I did not take any action which led to her death. Though I might have some responsibility for the incident, I didn't do anything listed in the criminal indictment."

A dozen reporters bustled out of the courtroom to file news of the plea for their television stations and wire services. Obara sat down again, and the chief prosecutor rose to read aloud the detailed indictment. He spoke in a breathless monotone, flipping over each page as he ended it, at a speed that was difficult for the reporters to follow. "By 1983 at the latest, using various names and without revealing his [real] identity," the indictment read, "the accused began taking women to Zushi Marina, giving them drugged drinks, causing them to lose consciousness, raping them while wearing a mask, and videoing it. He committed this crime quite regularly. He called it 'conquest play.'"

One thing stands out above all in considering the differences between the courts of Japan and those of Western Europe and North America: the conviction rate. Courts in the United States typically convict 73 percent of the criminal defendants who come before them, about the same as Britain. In Japan, the figure is 99.85 percent. Trial, in other words, brings almost guaranteed conviction: walk into a Japanese court, and you have the slimmest chance of leaving through the front door. And this is reflected in the way that the public, the media, and even lawyers regard defendants. In Japan, for all practical purposes, you are not innocent until proven guilty. "You're guilty from the moment of arrest," one of Obara's lawyers would tell me. "Look at the amount of space given to reports of criminal cases. In a newspaper, the arrest of the suspect is huge. When charges are brought, that's smaller. Conviction and sentencing is a minor story."

Even the Japanese language colludes in this assumption. From the moment of arrest, sometimes before charges have been laid, a suspect ceases to be referred to by the conventional honorifics, -*san* or -*shi*, and becomes -*yogisha*. Obara-yogisha: not Mister, but Criminal Suspect Obara.

Prosecutors insist that the conviction rate is high because they send to trial only cases in which the suspect's guilt is clear and certain. Guilt or innocence, in other words, is established during the investigation, behind closed doors, not publicly in the courtroom. "Prosecutors, like just about everyone in Japan, believe that only the guilty should be charged and that the charged are almost certainly guilty," writes the sociologist David Johnson. "The vast majority of Japan's criminal trials do not resemble fights, battles, or sporting events, as the adversarial logic of its laws seems to prescribe, but rather 'ceremonies' or 'empty shells,' devoid of even minor disagreements."

The converse of this is that acquittals, on the very few occasions they occur, are a humiliating blow for the authorities. In Western courts, defense lawyers win cases; in Japan, prosecutors lose them, and the loss can be devastating. When Joji Obara was led into court, bound and shackled, the odds were stacked overwhelmingly against him. But there was an enormous amount at stake for the other side too. The document being gabbled out in the courtroom that morning was the culmination of a year of joint effort by the detectives and prosecutors. Careers and reputations rested on it.

After setting out the facts of Carita's case—her swift and unstoppable decline, her chloroform-saturated liver, the masked man in the video—the indictment moved to Lucie and to Obara's movements during her last day of life.

At midnight on June 30, he had bought grapes, grapefruit, melon, and mandarin oranges from an all-night shop in the Akasaka district of Tokyo. Forty minutes later, he filled up his Mercedes-Benz at a nearby petrol station. At half past one the following afternoon, he phoned Lucie and postponed the time of their meeting. He went to the dry cleaner in the New Otani Hotel to drop off some laundry, then called Lucie again and picked her up in front of Sendagaya Station at three thirty. As they drove down to Zushi, at just after five o'clock, Lucie borrowed his phone to call Louise Phillips from the car. Obara took his photographs of her at five twenty judging from the quality of sun and shadow. By six o'clock, they had gone into apartment 4314 of Zushi Marina. Lucie, who had eaten little all day, must have been hungry by this point; Obara called a local restaurant and ordered fried chicken and deep-fried tempura of shrimp and eel. A notice had been delivered to the apartment reporting a fault with the gas supply, so he phoned Tokyo Gas and at seven fourteen a repairman appeared to carry out the routine job. It was while Obara was dealing with him that Lucie called Louise from the new phone that Obara had just given her. Then she left a message for Scott; and there she disappeared.

"Between that time and 2 July 2000, in the same apartment," the indictment explained, "the accused gave her a drink containing sleeping drugs and used chloroform to make her lose consciousness. He raped her, and around that time he caused her death through the effects of the aforementioned drugs, either through cardiac arrest or failure of respiration."

The prosecutors' narrative picked up again on Sunday afternoon, when Obara, traveling by train and taxi, visited one of his apartments in Tokyo, returning to Zushi Marina that evening. Early the following morning, he went back to Tokyo, where he activated another one of his large collection of prepaid mobile telephones. Just before half past five in the afternoon, he used it to call Louise Phillips.

"My name is Akira Takagi," he said. "Anyway, I'm ringing on behalf of Lucie Blackman."

Over the next two and a half hours, he made a series of further calls, to an electrical shop, a hardware shop, and L. L. Bean. The following afternoon, Tuesday, he visited them in turn and purchased tents, mats, a sleeping bag, flashlights, a hammer, cutters, a handsaw, a chain saw, a shovel, vessels and tools for mixing and stirring, three 35-pound sacks of cement, and a chemical agent to speed its setting.

On Wednesday, July 5, he drove to the apartment at Blue Sea Aburatsubo, in a Mercedes stuffed with objects covered by white sheets. The following day the caretaker became suspicious and called the police, who glimpsed the sweating Obara amid a mess of cement and bags, before he apologized to them, bearing the frozen body of his dog.

In the early hours of the following morning, the caretaker's boyfriend saw someone who looked like Obara walking near the beach with a shovel.

"Between 5 and 6 July 2000," the prosecutor droned, "with the use of an electric chain saw, either within Kanagawa prefecture or places nearby, or within apartment 401 of Blue Sea Aburatsubo, he cut off the head and arms and legs of Lucie. He put Lucie's head in cement and dried out the cement, and put it and the rest of the body into rubbish bags, and buried them in a cave under a cliff, and abandoned them."

On Sunday the ninth, Obara called a Japanese woman whom he had encountered on a telephone dating service. She had never met him in person and didn't know his real name. It was only by connecting the web of telephones and telephone calls that the police had tracked her down. But she remembered being told by Obara, "I've done something terrible, and I can't tell anyone about it."

Between late July and early October, he sent four letters to the police, two of them in English, signed in the name of

Lucie, listing her debts and enclosing money to pay them off. The police found the same list, along with drafts of the letters, in one of Obara's apartments.

In the cave where Lucie's body had been buried was a bag for a tent identical to the kind that Obara had purchased from L. L. Bean. The chain saw was never found, but the marks on Lucie's bones were consistent with the model he had bought on that same day. They found Lucie's notebook on Obara's property; they found chloroform and Rohypnol and GHB, and other powerful sleeping drugs.

The indictment was based upon evidence amassed over months by Superintendent Udo's men: telephone records, toll receipts, highway CCTV cameras, the testimony of the delivery boy, caretaker, and fruit vendor. Everything was documented; the twenty-eight files on the case filled three shelves in the corner of the courtroom. But between Saturday, July 1, and Sunday, July 2, and between the fifth and the seventh, there was a vacuum, a void in the narrative that the telephone calls, witnesses, and transactions failed to fill. A confession would have filled them; so would a sample of Obara's DNA—blood, hair, or semen—on Lucie's body. But—either because too much time had passed, or they had never been there—the forensic examiners never found a trace. Lucie had died, somehow. Someone, somewhere had cut her up with a chain saw and buried her in a cave. The circumstantial evidence posed the insistent question: If it hadn't been Joji Obara, who else could it have been? But literal, unimaginative, unforgiving Japanese justice demanded to know: How *exactly* did it happen?

■ ■ ■

The trial hearings were held in courtrooms of various sizes, but all of them were strip-lit, windowless inner chambers filled with dead, thermostatically regulated air. Japan passed from sweaty summer to cold, arid winter, but in court, the temperature never varied: neither cool nor warm, neither dry nor humid. The rooms were rectangular, with the public seats marked off by a wooden barrier. On the other side, the defense lawyers and prosecutors faced one another at parallel desks; between them was the upright podium for witnesses and the accused. A court clerk and a grimacing stenographer sat at the back facing the public; behind and above them were the three judges in high-backed chairs that reared over them like black halos.

The somnolence of the hearings, particularly after lunch, was often overwhelming. One of the judges, a plump, rather young man who sat on the chief judge's right, spent much of the trial with his eyes closed: whether he was concentrating profoundly, or simply asleep, it was difficult to tell. Obara's own lawyers had to poke awake one of their own number when he began snoring audibly one afternoon. In a British court, such an incident would be a cause for shame and reprimand. But here, the clerks snickered, the judges smiled indulgently, and it was immediately forgotten.

Japan had abandoned jury trials during the Second World War. Since then, exclusive power to determine guilt or innocence, and to impose sentence, lay with a panel of three judges.* Unlike Britain, where they are appointed from the ranks of senior barristers, Japanese judges form a dedicated legal class of their own. A young man, fresh from law school (and almost all are men), enters the judiciary and might do nothing else throughout his career. To Western eyes, junior judges, with their soft, plump faces and pimples, looked incongruously young. Their authority was emphasized by long black robes;

---

*"Lay judges"—members of the public who sit on the panel alongside the professional judges—were introduced in 2009, part of broader reforms intended to increase the pace and efficiency of Japanese criminal trials.

the occupants of the courtroom rose to their feet as they entered the chamber. Witnesses took a solemn oath before their testimony; lawyers and judges addressed one another politely and formally. But there was none of the dignified theatricality that one encounters in a British court, and little sense of the court as a place apart from the world around it.

Cross-examinations were pedestrian and anticlimactic. Statements were read gabblingly; legal motions were dry and unimpassioned. No one ever lost his temper or raised his voice, or displayed any personal care about the outcome of the proceedings. There was no oratory, no grandstanding, no conflict, no drama, and little display of emotion beyond occasional mild irritation. Rather than a majestic legal inquiry, the trial had about it the air of a teachers' staff meeting at a stuffy school.

Month after month, the voices of the lawyers droned, and the stenographer's fingers trembled over her keys. From time to time, I nodded off myself. But beneath the shroud of bureaucratic beige was a dreamlike suspense. It was as if a mosquito was buzzing somewhere, on the very threshold of human hearing; it was like the heightened reality before the breaking of a fever, or the chord of sensation—part sound, part vibration—that comes off an electrical pylon. It seemed to originate in Joji Obara himself.

Obara was transported to the monthly hearings from the Tokyo Detention Center, a twelve-story fortress in the suburb of Kosuge. His lawyers must have registered an objection, because after the first few hearings, he was never again seen shackled and bound by the heavy blue rope. He sat on the right-hand side of the court, with his defense team behind him and his two guards on either side.

He had the dignified, put-upon air of a man in regrettably reduced circumstances, who was struggling nonetheless to keep up appearances. In court, he always wore an open-necked shirt and a suit of navy blue or charcoal gray, smart and expensive-looking but wrinkled as though too recently removed from storage and inadequately sponged. His hair was soft, cut to medium length, and similarly unkempt, as if brushed and patted in a hurry: over eight years I watched grayness creep inwards from his temples, as thinness spread more slowly outwards from the crown. He wore spectacles with dark frames and always held a small blue towel with which he mopped the sweat from his face, his hands, and his neck. The court was a public space where it was unnecessary to remove outer footwear, and everyone else kept on their shoes. Only Obara had on his feet a pair of flappy plastic slippers, a further precaution, I assumed, intended to impede any attempt at escape.

The handful of snapshots of Obara were at least thirty years old, so for the Japanese media it was a matter of urgency to get an up-to-date picture out of the trial. Photography of any kind was banned in court, but professional artists, frowning and intent with their sketch pads and pastels, pushed their way busily to the seats in the front row.

But Obara foiled them, as he had foiled every other attempt to capture his image. From the moment he entered the courtroom, he turned his face at a three-quarter angle away from the public gallery and towards the judge. The drawings in the newspapers the next morning showed the last, and least interesting, quarter: hair, a neck, the collar of a jacket, and the rear left-hand side of Obara's jaw. Even under the scrutiny of the court, it was impossible to look at him full in the face.

Hearing by hearing, the prosecutors went through their case, filling out and corroborating the story they had told in the opening indictment.

In January 2003, a doctor gave evidence on the poisonous effects of chloroform. In April, an expert on anesthesia discussed the rape videos and explained that the pattern of breathing displayed by the victims was clearly the result of being drugged. The caretaker of Blue Sea Aburatsubo, and the police inspector who had responded to her call, described Obara's sudden appearance and strange behavior in the days after Lucie's disappearance. A police chemist testified that the cement encasing Lucie's head and the cement that Obara had purchased after her disappearance were of the same type. A woman named Yuka Takino, whose family owned a boat in the nearby marina, recounted a visit to the beach close to Blue Sea Aburatsubo two weeks after Lucie's disappearance. She had become aware of a man staring at her and her two children as they played on the sand. "He was watching my son with sharp, rather angry eyes," Mrs. Takino said. "I didn't get the impression that he was looking at them because he was the type who liked children."

Her young son was playing on the rocks: He called out to his mother and asked her if he could go into the cave. "He started running [towards the cave]," Mrs. Takino told the court. "Then the man looked startled, and he looked at my son, and he looked at me. He kept looking at us, and I thought it was very strange. So I called to my son, 'Come back here!' And when he was close, I told him, 'Don't go into the cave.'"

They packed up and left the beach, no more than mildly disconcerted. Seven months later, after the discovery of Lucie's body, she had remembered this strange incident and realized what a little boy with a bucket and spade might have turned up in the cave. Asked if the man at the beach was the man sitting in the court, Mrs. Takino turned to her right, where Obara was sitting with his head tilted towards her, five or six feet away. "He looks like the man I saw, but when I saw him he looked angry," she said. "Now he has a rather gentle smile on his face."

———

The prosecutors were keenly aware of the weaknesses in their case, and they confronted them head on. During weeks of searching, the police had stripped out carpets, tatami mats, and plumbing from Obara's properties, but they failed to find a speck of Lucie's blood. It was necessary to show the court that a man could have cut a body into ten pieces and disposed of them without leaving a trace of his victim's DNA. In May 2004, the police had attempted to do this by sawing up a dead pig inside a tent.

This experiment, a bizarre and gory operation that verged on black farce, was described by the officer in charge, Chief Inspector Nobuyoshi Akamine. He had begun by assembling the same kind of tents, mats, and chain saw that Obara had bought during his shopping expedition three days after Lucie's disappearance, and brought them to the courtyard of the forensic-medicine section of Tokyo University. Then he went to a butcher and procured a 150-pound pig, bisected along the spine. The carcass, of course, had been hung and bled, so the inspector and his men mixed red food dye in a bucket, and one of Tokyo University's professors of forensics painstakingly injected it into the corpse in simulation of fresh blood.

Of all the beasts in the butcher's shop, the chief inspector explained, the pig possessed bones and flesh closest to that of a human. The animal's right half was kept frozen, while its left half was thawed. On Chief Inspector Akamine's instructions, one of his officers lifted each half into the cramped tent and hacked it up with the chain saw. When the sawing was done, he splashed red food dye onto the tent's fabric to test its impermeability.

As it was described, the lawyers and judges consulted a little album of documents and images that recorded the procedure. I was sitting at the front of the courtroom; and by leaning forward, I could see photographs of the glistening cuts of wet pork. The prosecutors did not know with certainty whether

Obara had performed the dismemberment inside the apartment or somewhere in the countryside, and whether or not he had frozen Lucie's body. But when the pig experiment was done, Chief Inspector Akamine reported, not a trace of red fluid had escaped the tent.

Few journalists took any interest in the hearings once the pleas had been entered, but the public gallery was never less than half full, with an eccentric and marginal-looking crowd, distinct as members of a different tribe from the suited bureaucrats who strode the streets outside. One old man wore a brown trilby with a white flower in its band. Behind him, plump in their sailor suits, were two truanting schoolgirls. Once or twice, I identified someone with the gray, watery look of the Japanese homeless, the smartest and most presentable derelicts in the world. The most striking character was a man in his forties with a white-flecked beard, green-dyed hair, and a calf-length skirt, who continuously took notes in a school exercise book. At any one time, two or three people in the public gallery would be nodding off.

One of the most regular presences in the court was a small, pixielike young woman, who also took assiduous notes. Her name was Yuki Takahashi, and she was a founder and member of the Kasumikko Club, a group of friends who used their spare time to attend trials of defendants accused of atrocious crimes and published their observations on an Internet blog. There were a number of such blogger groupies—the green-haired man in the skirt, who called himself the Mighty Aso, turned out to be another. Yuki, along with her blogger friends Miki-san and Poison Carrot, was one of the most meticulous observers of Joji Obara.

"I like the Obara hearings very much," she wrote. "The schedule is fixed in my memory in the same place as the birthdays of my family."

I may be the person who knows more about the Obara case [than anyone else]. If there was an Obara quiz, I would win the Cup (rather than that, I'd like to be the one who set the questions). During the hearings, I even memorized the numbers of the mobile phones that Obara used. Sometimes, I wonder if I am a stalker! I like Obara a lot, but, to confess it honestly for the first time, I like the prosecutors very much, particularly the younger one. He's my type: cool. I do like the chief judge, of course. He's got a slight country accent—he sounds trustworthy. The day of the hearing is the day when all my favorite people get together in the same room, and I can't wait. The day before, the tension reaches a climax. Even the day after, the tension remains high.

One of the effects of Japan's astonishingly high conviction rate is that very, very few people want to be criminal defense lawyers. Why would they? Compared to commercial cases, such work is poorly paid and brings none of the compensations of glamour or social recognition. Japanese tend to regard criminal defenders suspiciously, as people who try to justify the actions of criminals—and, because almost everyone who comes to trial is convicted, there is a logic to this belief. Based on the prevailing rates, the average defense lawyer can expect to achieve an acquittal once every thirty-one years.

Lawyers are among the class of Japanese addressed as *sensei*, a word that means "teacher" but is also used as a form of address for doctors, academics, and politicians. Like a patient or student, a defendant is not expected to question the wisdom of his defending sensei. From the beginning, Obara rejected this assumption. He treated his defense as a war in which he was the general; he demanded that his lawyers accept his authority and their subordinate part in the struggle. His first legal team resigned en masse in October 2001 because they had "become unable to maintain good relations with the defendant," one of them was quoted as saying. The trial was put on hold for a year while the court cast around for lawyers willing to represent him. One of them remembered being told by Obara, "I don't want a reduced sentence, I want acquittal. As the defendant I'm denying all the charges. You are my lawyers, you must fight the prosecutors." In the West, this would have been no more than common sense, but to many Japanese lawyers, such determination was unprecedented. It was as difficult to accept as a patient who demanded to supervise his own surgery. It was another indication of Obara's singularity, and none of his lawyers had encountered anyone like him before.

They visited him in the Tokyo Detention Center. As a man technically innocent until proven guilty, he had greater liberty there than in prison. He could send and receive letters, and meet a visitor each weekday. Once a month at first, but with decreasing frequency, his old mother, Kimiko, made the journey by bullet train from Osaka. Otherwise, it was just the lawyers, at least one of whom saw him every day. He kept a distance from his guards, and few of the other inmates of the Tokyo Detention Center lingered for more than a few months. He would spend nine years in this small locked room with a bed and a washbasin; his only significant interactions were with his lawyers; his only occupation was his defense.

Obara's cell was his war room. The paperwork was stacked in columns from the floor to head height: letters, faxes, law books, sheaves of evidence. Apart from the eight rapes and the two rape-killings, Obara, like many former beneficiaries of the bubble economy, was being sued by his creditors. In the eighteen months before his arrest, the courts had sequestered several of his properties; in 2004, he was declared bankrupt, with liabilities of ¥23.8 billion. Separate teams of lawyers worked on the various cases; no one but Obara knew all their names, or even how many they were. At any one time, he had at least ten lawyers on retainer; over the course of his trial he probably went through dozens.

For a lawyer used to compliant and grateful clients, representing Obara could be a harrowing experience. It wasn't that he was rude or aggressive; the shock was that he expected to be in charge. "He's like a film director shooting a script written according to his own view of reality," one of them said. "He's clever and very suspicious. He doesn't trust anyone, including his lawyers. It's difficult to deal with him." In cross-examining witnesses, his lawyers literally followed a script of questions, and their discomfort was obvious. "It must be miserable for the lawyers," wrote Yuki Takahashi, the blogger groupie. "I watch them in court, working away with the eyes of dead fish because of all the orders he's giving them, all those questions completely irrelevant to the case. I can laugh at it, but it must be bad for them."

He had an immaculate recall of dates and details, and was intolerant of any lawyer who became muddled or confused. He was full of ideas, but they were often inconsistent or incoherent. "He's clever enough to devise many strategies, but he can't work out which is the best," one of the lawyers said. "So he tries to combine them all together, in a way, and I feel that it will be in vain."

The problem was simple: How to answer the library of evidence meticulously assembled against him? On the rape charges, the argument was obvious: the sexual acts that took place and were recorded on video may have been unusual, but they were consensual. As Yasuo Shionoya, probably Obara's most successful lawyer, told me, "Ladies who work as hostesses or the like—I believe that if they go to a man's apartment, they are giving their consent to sex. That's what Obara thought. He accepts that he caused injury by using drugs, he'll accept the charge of causing injury. But he cannot understand [the charge of] rape. That's his point. Logically, I think he may be right."

On the charge of raping, drugging, and killing Carita Ridgway, the defense was more complicated and depended on doubts about the cause of her death. Once again, Obara insisted that the sexual relationship had been consensual and that the video of him and the unconscious Carita had been made during an earlier encounter several weeks before her sudden illness. At the time, none of the doctors had concluded that the collapse of her liver had been caused by drugs. She might have been killed by inappropriate treatment after this misdiagnosis, or by a painkilling injection given to Carita by another doctor before Obara had taken her to the hospital.

But what about Lucie? To some of his legal team, this was the most straightforward case of all, because there was no direct proof. "The important thing was that Obara and Lucie were alone—no one else knew what happened," one of them said. "We don't need to prove that Obara *didn't* commit a crime. We just have to show that the prosecutors can't prove it and point out how weak the evidence is. No video. Cause of death unknown. How could he carry such a large dead body out of the Zushi apartment, on his own, in midsummer, without anyone seeing him? How could he carry it into his car and cut it up in his apartment and bury it all on his own? All we had to do was emphasise all these weak points."

The conventional strategy, in other words, was not to defend the accused but to undermine the story told by the prosecution. But this was not enough for Obara. He wanted to tell a story of his own; he needed to fill the man-shaped hole.

20. THE WHATEVERER

The early years of the twenty-first century were intense and eventful ones for a foreign correspondent. For weeks at a time, I found myself traveling far from home in Tokyo, to Pakistan, Afghanistan, and Iraq. Japan, for a while, became the peaceful, uneventful country where I restored myself between wars. But I was never able to forget entirely about Lucie Blackman and Joji Obara. The trial plodded along, at the rate of about one hearing a month, and whenever I could, I went to the Tokyo District Court myself, or sent a Japanese assistant who came back with pages of detailed and baffling notes. It was difficult to explain my continuing interest—two years after getting under way, the trial had lost its value as a news story. But somewhere deep within, it still itched and smarted and niggled; the mosquito whine continued to sound faintly in my ear.

Even allowing for their slow pace, Japanese criminal trials typically last for a year or so at the most. By 2005, when the prosecutors were still summoning pathologists and forensic experts, this one had already become exceptionally prolonged. Partly this was because of the number of separate charges and witnesses, and the disposition of Obara's defense team, whose frequent objections slowed the proceedings. But it also suggested a lack of confidence on the part of the prosecutors and a self-consciousness about the circumstantial character of some of their evidence. Finally, though, five years after Lucie's death, and fifty-six months after his first appearance in court, the last prosecution witness was called and Joji Obara began to set out his defense.

At this hearing, the public gallery was full. Sitting in the front row were Tim and Sophie Blackman, who had flown out for the hearing; a police interpreter scribbled notes for them as the proceedings unfolded. Obara sat between his guards, sharply angled, as usual, towards the judge and away from the gallery. He wore a light-gray suit; he looked very pale, like a man who has been long deprived of sunlight. As he stepped up to the witness stand, he carefully avoided directing his glance anywhere near Tim and Sophie.

In the weeks leading up to this hearing, an atmosphere of anticipatory tension had transmitted itself from within Obara's defense team. The fact that they were able to tolerate such a difficult client made his lawyers an unconventional and interesting group, and they were surprisingly chatty and frank about their client and his prospects. "His mood has swung throughout the hearings," one of them told me. "I think he's rather desperate in a way. Mixed feelings—irritable because he knows he can't be confident of winning. There's a risk he'll be found guilty and he's desperate to be acquitted. He swings back and forth between confidence and fear."

It was at this time that I established my own first, tentative contacts with Obara. One of his lawyers, who refused to talk to me himself, agreed to pass on my letter requesting an interview in the detention house, along with a list of questions. A reply, signed in the name of another lawyer but evidently dictated by Obara himself, was faxed back to me. "There are many fundamentals as well as important facts concerning the case of which the investigation side has not been able to know," it read. "We believe that facts concerning Question No. 5, for example, which was the most important question formerly asked by you, Mr. Parry, will also be brought to light . . . It is also possible for us to provide you with a scoop hereafter, because, as Mr. Obara says, your company comes from the same country as the native country of Lucie."

My fifth question was: "You have said you have no responsibility for the death of Ms. Blackman. Who do you believe is responsible for her death?"

The police and prosecutors had spent more than a year investigating and presenting their case on Lucie's death. But Obara had had five years. During that time he had employed lawyers and private detectives numbering in the dozens and sent them out from the confinement of his cell. The version of events presented by the prosecutors was overwhelming in its detail and in the logic of its central question: If Obara hadn't killed and sawed up Lucie, who had? Now Obara was to confront it with his own version of reality. It would have to be a masterpiece.

He stood at the podium and began to read aloud his opening statement, a sheaf of closely handwritten pages. "To tell the truth about Lucie's character will shame her family and make them depressed," he lisped softly. "Parents always want to see their daughter as a pure creature, and every sister wants to respect her sister. I don't want to ruin their image of her; I haven't changed in my wish to avoid revealing her character. But it was because of it that I became embroiled in this terrible incident."

Obara's defense had two elements. The first was to question and undermine every line of the prosecution case, to poke at its weak spots and expose its gaps, and to stifle its details with baffling details of his own. The second was to paint an alternative portrait of Lucie herself. This was the "scoop" that Obara had vouchsafed to me in a second fax sent shortly before the hearing: that far from being the blithe young woman described by her family and friends, she was tormented and self-destructive, and had died after consuming an overdose of illegal drugs.

Under cross-examination by his own lawyers, Obara began to quote from Lucie's diary, translating it into Japanese as he went. The passages he selected were those describing her most miserable moments—her mood swings, her loneliness and homesickness, her failures as a hostess and her envy of Louise's success. "We have drunk more alcohol in the last 20 days than I have ever consumed in my whole drinking lifetime," Obara read. "I am so fucking up to my neck in debt . . . I feel such a sense of disorientation and being lost . . . I can not stop crying . . . I feel so ugly & fat & invisible."

> I hate the way I look, I hate my hair, I hate my face, I hate my nose, I hate my slanty eyes, I hate the mole on my face, I hate my teeth, I hate my chin, I hate my profile, I hate my neck, I hate my boobs, I hate my fat hips, I hate my fat stomach, I hate my flabby bum, I HATE my birthmark, I hate my bashed up legs, I feel so disgusting & ugly & average.

On May 4, Lucie had written, "We have been on a never ending quest for . . . music (anything but Craig David), postcards & drugs!" Rather ingeniously, the police interpreter had taken the most incriminating word in this sentence to be "dugs" and declared that it made no sense. "But I consulted five professional translators," Obara told the court, "and they all agreed it should be read as 'drugs.'"

"What's the significance of buying postcards and drugs?" asked the defense lawyer, who once again gave the impression of reading from a prepared script of questions.

"When young people travel overseas, it's common for them to buy postcards," Obara explained with worldly confidence. "And among drug users, it's a common pattern that they buy postcards and drugs."

There was another unlikely discussion about a passage from the diary, which Obara read as follows: "As usual no matter where I am—I feel alone. It's not toaks, it's me." Obara explained that a "toak," more commonly spelled "toke," was youthful slang for a marijuana cigarette. This admission of illegal drug use was an embarrassment to the prosecutors, who offered no response or rebuttal. But if they had consulted a native speaker, they would have learned that what Lucie had actually written was not "toaks" but "7oaks," an abbreviated reference to her hometown.

The chief judge was a man named Tsutomu Tochigi, who had very white and very even teeth that flashed in a smile even at moments of irritation and tension. Often, in fact, Justice Tochigi's grin seemed to be a sign of his displeasure, rather than the opposite. It grew wider and wider, as Obara plowed on through the most lachrymose and self-pitying sections of Lucie's diary.

"It's torture listening to these translations," the judge said finally. "What does this have to do with the trial?" But now, Obara's narrative shifted to the events of June and July 2000 and became stranger than ever.

The summer of that year had evidently been a complicated time for Obara. He was deep in negotiation with his creditors about the rescheduling of his debts. In June he had been hospitalized after a van drove into the back of his car, painfully wrenching his neck and damaging his eardrum. He was trying to sell off several of his properties, including the apartment in Blue Sea Aburatsubo. Weighing most heavily on his mind was beloved Irene, the Shetland sheepdog whose body he had preserved in the freezer of the house at Den-en Chofu. Having abandoned hope of resurrection through cloning, Obara decided to bury her in a plot of forest land that he owned on the Izu Peninsula. This was not a straightforward task, for there were large trees that would have to be cleared. But Obara, as he explained to the court, knew just the man for the job. He identified him as A-san—"Mr. A." He was described as a *nandemo-ya*, literally a "purveyor of anything" or a "whateverer": a jack-of-all-trades, or a fixer.

Mr. A's unexplained code name turned out to be one of the less unlikely things about him. Obara's defense was so thick with bizarre detail that it became impossible to keep a mental account of it all. No sooner had one outré claim lurched into view than three or four more chased it in close succession. In 1997, he told the court, his car had exploded in an underground garage. (There was no further explanation of this alarming happening; evidently, this was just the kind of misfortune that befell Obara.) To investigate it, he had hired Mr. A, whom he had originally met by chance near Tokyo's Shinjuku Station, when the nandemo-ya had offered him drugs. For ¥500,000, Mr. A agreed to clear the burial plot for beloved Irene. The task was scheduled for July 5 and 6, the second day being the sixth anniversary of the pet's demise. And this explained one of the most persuasive pieces of circumstantial evidence against Obara: the tent, saws, and shovel he bought after Lucie's disappearance. These, he was now able to explain, were not for dismembering and disposing of a dead woman but for camping out overnight, felling trees, and burying a dog.

The plan was canceled because of unforeseen events the weekend before.

Obara had met Lucie in Casablanca in the second half of June and agreed, at her request, to take her to the seaside. In its factual outlines, his account of that day matched the story told by the prosecutors—the drive to Zushi Marina, the photograph by the sea, the visit by the gas repairman, and the telephone calls to Louise and Scott. But Obara was in a position to describe what no one else could: Lucie's conduct in the hours before her death.

"Lucie was very excited," Obara said. "This was not be-cause of alcohol, but because of the influence of the 'things' which she had brought with her." The "things" were pills of crystal meth, Ecstasy, and "toaks." "Lucie had a high toler-ance for alcohol and she continued to talk while drinking wine, champagne, then spirits such as gin and tequila," Obara told the court. "Lucie told me she was a manic-depressive. In fact, she was in a manic state at the beginning, but as the time went on, she seemed to go into a depressive state . . . Of course, this was the influence of drugs too."

Lucie and Obara talked "about many things." She com-plained to him about her debts and said that she was consider-ing taking work at a "special club" in Roppongi to repay them more quickly (the implication was that this was a place of prostitution). He talked about his car accident and the pain he had in his neck. Lucie offered to give him a massage. "Al-though her massage was good, the pain didn't go," the book commissioned by his lawyer recorded, "so Lucie recommended the drugs she had. She told him any pain and discomfort would disappear, so Obara took them. That night, Obara took three different kinds of pills . . . Lucie showed her pierced navel to Obara, and told him she would pierce her left nipple . . . Obara was walking in the clouds from the pills Lucie gave him, and their powerful effect continued for more than an hour."

Tim and Sophie Blackman sat in silence in the front row of the gallery, as the police interpreter scrawled summaries of Obara's words on the pages of a notebook. It was upsetting, of course, and a little humiliating, to hear Lucie's sad little diary exposed like this—and disturbing in what it revealed of Obara's ruthlessness and cunning. "As a parent it would be foolish for me to say definitively that Lucie had never taken drugs," Tim said afterwards. "She may have had small amounts recreationally, as many people do. But I don't believe that she was endangering her own life, and she certainly didn't take Rohypnol herself." To anyone who knew Lucie, the picture Obara painted of a drunken, psychologically disturbed coke slut was absurd to the point of being laughable. But would this be obvious to the judges?

Obara's defense was a concoction of opportunistic manipulations, distortions, and, in some cases, outright lies. The lies were not surprising: what was most sickening was the core of truth visible through the glaze of elaboration. Obara knew a painful amount about Lucie, intimate things, which he could have heard only from her in person. Whatever had really happened in the hours they spent alone, it was clear that they had talked at length and that Lucie had shared with him secrets that she would have entrusted to very few people.

Obara's account continued on to the following day, Sunday, July 2. By this time, the prosecutors asserted, Lucie was already dead or dying. According to him, she was vigorously alive and continuing her drug-fueled binge. Obara traveled by train to Tokyo, but Lucie chose to remain behind in the apartment, working her way through her supply of pills. In the evening, he phoned from his apartment in the city, and "she started talking about strange things—I thought she was overdosing." He rang a few hospital emergency departments in case Lucie needed medical treatment and got back to the room in Zushi shortly before midnight. "I told Lucie that she had taken too many drugs, and that she should go to hospital in Tokyo," he said. "But Lucie was reluctant to go for fear that if the drugs were detected, she might be deported."

What Obara told the court next was the most chilling thing of all, not because it was a lie but again because of what was true. "My neck was aching from the car accident and I was not feeling well, so I became irritated with Lucie ignoring my advice," he said. "Lucie then kept repeating some very bad jokes. She said, 'Jane's side of the family is cursed. They have a defect of the brain. Jane's mother died at the age of forty-one. Jane's sister died at the age of thirty-one.'"

The family history was accurate. Had Obara gleaned this by remote control, from British detectives at work in Sevenoaks? Or was it a measure of how he had worked upon Lucie, and how far he had drawn her out, to have learned such secrets during the course of that evening?

"She kept saying, 'There is a curse,'" Obara continued. "She said, 'Jane's mother died at the age of forty-one. Jane's sister died at the age of thirty-one. Jane's daughter will die at the age of twenty-one. And Jane's granddaughter will die at the age of eleven.' She kept repeating these bad jokes, and I became irritated. So I contacted a certain person and said that there was a foreign hostess who had overdosed on drugs, and asked him to take her home. This person was Mr. A."

According to Obara, he went back to Tokyo on Monday morning. Before leaving Zushi Marina, he had left some food out for the stoned Lucie and told her that someone would be coming over to take her home. He hid the money for Mr. A in a lambskin slipper by the entrance to the apartment.

As if Mr. A were not mysterious enough, at this point another character entered the narrative: an ethnic Chinese known as Sato, a still more shadowy figure whose identity would never be fully explained. Mr. Sato telephoned Obara later that morning to say that he, rather than A, was driving Lucie to hospital. He passed the phone to a foreign woman, who sounded like Lucie, and Obara talked briefly to her. Later, when Obara asked Sato about Lucie, he was told, "Ask Mr. A." "When Obara asked A," it would later be explained, "he said that Lucie had not objected to going to hospital. And he said that he had introduced her to his acquaintance, a rich man, because she asked for drugs. They got along well and did what they pleased."

In other words, Obara did not know what had happened to Lucie. He had last seen her in the Zushi apartment—drugged to the point of incoherence but alive. He had entrusted her to the custody of a vague acquaintance, who reported having passed her on to still shadier people. And after that he had set about his principal task for that week—the interment of his frozen dog.

He spent the rest of Monday and Tuesday equipping himself with tools, camping equipment, and cement, picked up the corpse of Irene from the freezer of his Den-en Chofu house, and swaddled her in dry ice. He was driving towards the burial place on the morning of Wednesday, July 5, when Mr. A abruptly called to postpone the appointment, blaming "urgent business." Disappointed, Obara diverted to Blue Sea Aburatsubo and checked into a nearby inn. Lacking a key, he had to summon a locksmith to let him into his apartment, where he began work on what was to be Irene's gravestone: an "art piece" that he would make with his own hands. The following evening, Thursday, he answered a ring at the door to find several policemen outside, including Inspector Harada, who would go on to describe Obara's strange behavior in court. But the policemen got it all wrong. The cement they saw was for the construction of the "art piece," not the entombment of a severed head. It was true that Obara had behaved angrily and uncooperatively towards the officers, but he had an explanation for this—after he had stepped through the front door of the apartment, the inspector had inadvertently kicked the blanket-wrapped corpse of Irene. What animal lover would not have become a little upset at seeing a uniformed policeman trip over his frozen pet?

For that night, Thursday the seventh, Obara offered no alibi. He said that he had gone for a walk and had walked until morning. He was bitten by poisonous caterpillars, and the bite swelled and made him feverish. So he telephoned Mr. A and put off the ill-fated plan to bury beloved Irene in the forest at Izu. He returned to Tokyo and went to the hospital to have his rash treated. Over the next few days, he held various meetings with his bankers and accountant.

The following week, Lucie's disappearance was all over the Japanese news. There were missing-person posters in railway stations and on public billboards. Television crews were broadcasting live from Roppongi and running long interviews with Lucie's family, who begged for information from anyone who had seen her.

How did Obara react to all this? He was "surprised," according to the book commissioned by his lawyer. He contacted Mr. A, who told him that Lucie was "traveling with a man."

A and Obara were supposed to meet again on July 15 to make Irene's grave. But again A called to cancel. When Obara asked him once more about Lucie, he was told, "She's having fun taking drugs at the home of my acquaintance." When Obara mentioned all the fuss about her disappearance, A said, "It's ridiculous—she's just doing what she wants to do."

It was an extraordinary story. It was difficult enough to believe that Lucie was a drug addict; it was harder still to accept Obara's failure to go straight to the police. Who was Sato, the errand boy of the errand boy? And who was the "rich man" with whom Lucie had allegedly been enjoying her debauch? One man was in a position to answer these questions. So who—and where—was Mr. A?

His name was Satoru Katsuta, known to his acquaintance by the diminutive "Kacchan." In 2001, he had been living in the Tokyo suburb of Mitaka. He was about five six, with long hair and a mustache. He had been born in the southern island of Kyushu in 1953, a year after Joji Obara. In his twenties, for reasons unspecified, he had once attempted to disembowel himself in the ritual suicide known as seppuku or hara-kiri.

He had survived but had contracted hepatitis C from the transfusions of blood used to save his life.

The Tokyo District Court learned all of this in December 2005 from an old man named Issei Mizuta, who was called as a witness for the defense. Mizuta knew Katsuta and employed him regularly as a driver and odd-job man. One of Katsuta's various occupations, Mizuta confirmed, had been as a dealer in crystal methamphetamine, or shabu, which he sold around Shinjuku Station. One day, early in December 2001, the two men were sitting in the car together when Kacchan said, "I'm very anxious. I need to ask your advice." He said that it was to do with Lucie Blackman and the man on trial for killing her, Joji Obara.

Kacchan said that one day the previous summer he had been called by Obara and asked to pick up a foreign hostess and drive her to Tokyo. The woman had been Lucie. She was already high on drugs, and when Kacchan arrived to take her home she begged him for more. He gave her shabu, not just once, but repeatedly. Under oath, Mizuta stated, "Katsuta told me, 'Lucie took too many drugs and died.' He said that she died in front of him . . . He said that he took her body somewhere, but he didn't say where . . . He didn't tell Obara about Lucie's death."

Mizuta continued, "I was the only one he told about Lucie's death and the abandonment of the corpse—no one else knew." After Katsuta told him the story, Mizuta remembered something else: the previous summer, at the time when Lucie's disappearance was being most intensely reported by the newspapers and television, Katsuta had appeared "restless and unsettled," and all his hair had fallen out. "I told him that I wanted to hear about it in more detail," Mizuta told the court. "I was planning to ask him about it at our New Year party. I was thinking about whether or not I should take him to the police, after he told me the story in detail." But he lost the chance.

A few days later, Katsuta went into the hospital, suffering from advanced liver cancer. Two weeks later, in a state of terminal illness, he called Mizuta, crying and shouting deliriously, "I have set Lucie on fire! Lucie is burning!"

The story told by Mizuta exactly corroborated what Obara had previously said in court. But there were two difficulties. The first was that Katsuta, who had been so tormented by guilt for causing Lucie's death, was not around to attest to the truth of the story. He had died a few days after Mizuta's last, anguished conversation with him.

The second problem was Mizuta himself. As he readily stated when he identified himself after taking the oath, he was an *oyabun*, the boss of a gang that formed part of the notorious Sumiyoshi-kai yakuza syndicate. Obara's star witness, in other words, the man on whose testimony his hopes of acquittal rested, was a self-confessed leader of the Japanese mafia.

■ ■ ■

"It doesn't fill us with dread," Tim Blackman said, when I asked what it felt like to be back in Japan. "I don't know why it doesn't, but it doesn't. It's the same process that takes people back to a grave even though they know it will make them unhappy. But it's part of the process, it's part of keeping in touch. Would we just not want to have anything to do with it? The answer is no. We do it because we have to do it and we want to do it."

Tim operated his business out of a two-story wooden office in the garden of his home in the Isle of Wight, where I visited him repeatedly over the years. Since 2000, his work as a property developer had been pushed to one side. "I've spent months on matters relating to Lucie's death," he said. "Something crops up almost on a daily basis. An entire section of the office is given over to it—filing cabinets, files, the Lucie Blackman Trust. It's like a little industry. It occupies fifty percent of my life." Tim had hoped that with the trial under way, it would become simpler and easier to keep abreast of events in Tokyo. But the opposite was true. The proceedings were so slow and dense that they were difficult enough to follow inside the courtroom in Tokyo. From Tim's garden shed, they were hopelessly remote and opaque.

A few days after each hearing, the Tokyo Metropolitan Police would forward a brief, baffling summary of the proceedings, which went into Tim's extensive filing system. "The amount of information we get is minute," Tim said. "We read very carefully the few words we get. Obara making a statement— those are huge words for us. Whatever mind-set he's developed, we very much believe that our presence there—Sophie's presence, my presence—ups the stakes for him. It's one thing sitting in a cell, it's quite another to stand up in front of the sister and father. If he's not being straight, he'll be under pressure."

It was impossible to tell whether this was true and whether Joji Obara did indeed feel the weight of Tim and Sophie's presence in court. But as he stood to take the witness stand at the next trial hearing, he did something that he had never done before. He turned towards the public gallery, and to Tim and Sophie, and gave an expressionless bob of the head— more than a nod, less than a bow, not an expression of courtesy but an acknowledgment. Sophie passed the long hours in the hearing by executing a sketch of him in ink, which captured this unexpected moment of noncommittal intensity.

Later, in one of many long conversations with Tim, I asked him about Obara and what it was like to see him face-to-face. Tim paused, which he rarely did in conversation. He said, "It's been quite a revelation to me, and whether or not I'm a bit odd—well, I could easily be a bit odd, I'm prepared to admit that." There was another pause, and Tim sighed. "The emotion

I get is . . . I see somebody who is the same age as me, and who has by their actions produced the most terrible, terrible trouble for themselves, and done something so appalling to someone else's life. And in a very strange way, there's a degree of . . . pathos that tends to neutralize what might be more natural anger."

I asked, with more surprise in my voice than I intended, "Do you feel sorry for him?" and Tim said, "I do feel sorry for him. I do. I do feel sorry for him."

Tim and Obara had been born just eleven months apart. They both owned boats; both of them made their money in property. Nothing better caught the complexity of Tim's own character, his stubborn unorthodoxy, which to me was so likable and admirable but which to many people was repellent. Almost on principle, he refused the obvious point of view and the temptations of conventional morality. The high ground was his for the taking, but instead of marching ahead to claim it, he dawdled and skirted around it, finding shades of pathos and ambiguity where others could see only black and white. Onlookers were not merely puzzled by this—they were appalled.

If Lucie Blackman's killing was not a straightforward example of good against evil, then what was? To be told by none other than her father that there was complexity here, to see Tim striving to be fair and sympathetic to his own daughter's killer, undermined people's certainty in their own sense of right. They took Tim's lack of orthodoxy as an affront to their own. They identified him as a transgressor, almost a blasphemer, against acceptable ways of feeling.

21. SMYK

In its evasive cunning and squirming, acrobatic dexterity, Obara's defense would have been extraordinary in any courtroom. In Japan, where it was rare for the defense to challenge the prosecution seriously, it was unprecedented. At times, it was bafflingly foggy and vague; at others, it was baroque in its detail and ornamentation. It was also an obvious farrago of distortions, omissions, and libels on the dead. Plenty of Obara's own lawyers did not believe that it would do him any good. "The story told by Mizuta about Kacchan has no significance as evidence," one of them told me. "It's hearsay, apart from the fact that both of them are gangsters. The judge kept asking, 'Why didn't you mention this earlier?' which shows he didn't trust what he heard. Why didn't Obara say from the beginning that Lucie was on drugs? In the first four years of his defense he made no mention of it at all. When he started talking about her like that, I found it a little offensive. Why start shaming the dead?"

Like men plugging the leaks in a dissolving dam, Obara's lawyers attempted to shore up his defense by putting to him some of the obvious questions hanging over his story.

Why didn't Obara go to the police immediately after it was announced that Lucie had gone missing?

Because he had accepted three Ecstasy pills from Lucie and was afraid of being prosecuted for using illegal drugs.

What about the woman who had heard Obara say over the telephone that he had "done something terrible, but I can't tell anyone about it"?

He was simply referring to the traffic accident that he had been involved in.

What was Obara doing with all those bottles of chloroform?

They did not, in fact, contain any chloroform. Obara had emptied out the original contents and replaced them with vodka, and it was this which he held below the noses of the girls in the videos.

Several of the exchanges were comic in their self-serving artificiality.

LAWYER: You donated a lot of money to charity. Will you tell us about it?

OBARA: I have donated money since I was a high-school student. I did not use my real name, though. In total, I must have spent several tens of millions of yen on donations. I had a special sympathy for children. UNICEF was one of the organisations I sent money to.

LAWYER: On 16 April 1991, you met the emperor and the empress at the Hotel Okura. Is this true?

OBARA: Indeed, yes. We met at a charity event there. They invited me to become involved in several charity events.

LAWYER: Will you tell us about your childhood? Is it true that you had an IQ of 200?

OBARA: Yes . . . etc., etc.

Then, in March 2006, it was the prosecution's turn to cross-examine Obara. Face-to-face with the prosecutor, his self-assurance deserted him.

The prosecutor, whose name was Mizoguchi, began by

asking about the various letters that had been received by the police, including two signed in Lucie's name, the drafts of which had been found in Obara's properties.

"Some letters were written by me, after messages from Katsuta," Obara admitted.

"What kind of messages?" Prosecutor Mizoguchi asked.

"The messages were messages," Obara answered. "I can't say more than that."

"Did Katsuta explain why you had to write a letter to Azabu Police Station?" the prosecutor asked.

Obara said, "There was a message about it."

"What was the purpose of the letter?"

"May I refrain from commenting?"

"You mean you don't want to answer the question?"

"I did it because there was a message."

"You can't explain in any more detail?"

"At the moment I can't."

As always, Obara held in his hands the small blue hand towel that he used to dab at his perspiring face and neck. Even viewed from behind, his unease had become obvious in his physical stance. His shoulders were slumping, and his head was angled towards the floor. Prosecutor Mizoguchi continued. "On July third, after leaving Zushi Marina at midnight and coming back to Moto-Akasaka Towers, what did you do that morning?"

Obara gave no answer.

"Do you remember doing a search on the Internet using your home computer?"

"No," Obara said. "I don't remember."

"You have a computer at home, don't you?"

"Yes, I have one at Moto-Akasaka Towers."

"In the report on the use of that computer on July third, there is mention of an Internet search done on that day from around eight fifty. Do you remember that?"

Mizoguchi was holding up a sheaf of papers, densely printed. It was impossible to see Obara's reaction, but evidently he registered surprise. "Let me show this to the defendant," the prosecutor said, "as he seems not to have seen it before."

Obara took the document.

"This is a list of searches performed using that personal computer from the middle of June," Mizoguchi explained. "On July third, two thousand, between eight forty-four and eight fifty-seven, six searches were performed. Looking at those searches now, do you remember anything?"

Obara paused. The sentences that followed were fragmentary and difficult to follow, even in Japanese. "From around late midnight of the first, taken drugs," he began falteringly (it was unclear who was supposed to have taken what drugs). "On July second with Lucie, we were talking about a Japanese woman who'd gone missing in Britain. She had been kidnapped and was still missing. Lucie said it was a well-known story, and I suggested that she might already have been killed then, although I didn't know the story. That story was in my mind. I mean that kidnap case in Britain."

The prosecutor listed the Internet searches that Obara had made that morning. The first was for *Datura metel*, the herb known as devil's trumpet, which causes hallucinations and even death if eaten. The second was for Nachi Harbor, a place from which elderly Buddhist monks approaching the end of their lives would set sail on a final, fatal journey. The third was "how to get chloroform." The fourth was "synthesis of GHB," the date-rape drug. "Why were you looking at such sites?" asked Mizoguchi.

"You ask why—it's like asking why someone watches crime films," Obara said. "You don't watch a crime film to commit a crime. You watch it just to reduce your stress. Actually, you'll see that I looked at various sites of this kind."

Mizoguchi pointed out the final searches that Obara had made that morning. "You accessed other websites about the process of producing sulphuric acid, and how to buy sulphuric acid. You were searching with a view to making a purchase, weren't you?"

Obara made no response.

The prosecutor flicked through the document and pointed to another page. "This one here says 'a possible method is to use a high-temperature furnace to burn even the bones to ashes, but this is too difficult.' And also, 'one way to melt down even bones is by immersing the bones in concentrated sulphuric acid.' This is about disposing of a dead body, isn't it?"

"I [also] looked up pages like that in June," Obara said. "It wasn't from the motive that Prosecutor Mizoguchi suggests."

"Then why did you look at such sites again on that day?"

"It's just because, as I told you, I chatted with Lucie about the kidnap case in London."*

"Do you remember those two methods [incineration and dissolution in acid] being described as 'too difficult'?"

"I don't remember."

This was a rare thing in a Japanese court: a psychological contest, a struggle of wits between accuser and accused. Obara dabbed at his perspiration. How his heart must have turned over in his chest when Mizoguchi presented the next piece of evidence, a heavy folder containing yellowing pages.

This was where Obara had recorded his sexual adventures, the logbook of his "play." Having quoted from Lucie's diary, Obara was now being confronted with his own.

"Here is a book in which you made notes, from around 1970," the prosecutor said.

---

*I have been unable to find any record of the missing-person case to which Obara referred.

Obara had no difficulty remembering this document. He said, "I wrote about my relationships with girls five years after they actually happened. Waiting five years made the stories more interesting. So I wrote it after five years had passed, and made the stories more pornographic."

"So the stories written here are fiction?"

"Not all of them are. The girls mentioned exist, but the stories are fables."

The log of sexual encounters was numbered and in some cases dated, from 1970 to 1995, from 1 to 209. "Take a look at number sixty-three, line three," Mizoguchi asked Obara. "What do you mean by SMYK?"

"This is just something I wrote to make it more interesting, five years later."

"What does it mean?"

A pause, then: "I won't answer that."

"Number four—'I gave her sleeping drugs.' Number twenty-one—'Today, I gave her sleeping drugs.'"

The Japanese word for sleeping drug is *suiminyaku*.

"That is what you wrote," the prosecutor said. "Does SMYK mean *sui min ya ku*?"

"I don't want to answer that."

"Number one hundred forty—'Gave too much SMY and CHM. I was very shaken up.' What is the meaning of this CHM?"

"I forget."

"In number one hundred fifty, you write about 'CRORO.' What does this mean?"

"I don't want to answer that."

"It means chloroform [in Japanese: *kurorohorumu*, pronounced "crororo-hormu"], doesn't it?"

"I don't know."

Mizoguchi turned over the pages of the notebook. "Number one hundred ninety. You wrote, 'She realized in the middle of it, and I made an excuse, but she knows.' What does this mean?"

"This too is 'play,' so I'm not answering."

"Judging from what's written in the notebook, it seems you were very shaken up when [the girls] realized that you had performed 'conquest play' without consent."

"No. It's not true. It was 'play.'"

"So, what kind of 'play' was it?"

"I'm not answering."

"Number one hundred seventy-nine, February 1992. 'Met Nanae, and later Carita.' Is this Carita the same Carita in this criminal case?"

Obara said nothing. It was maddening to be unable to see his face.

"You insisted that you didn't use chloroform on Carita," said Mizoguchi.

"I didn't [use it]."

"Number one hundred ninety-eight. 'Used SMY and CROCRO. Used too much CROCRO. [Although I] used CROCRO in the case of CARITA, the drug from the hospital was the cause, I think.' This is what you wrote. You did use chloroform, didn't you?"

Obara said, "It's fiction."

A few hearings later, he had a go at repairing some of the damage done in this cross-examination by having his own lawyers question him about the Internet searches and the sex diary. Over the months, he had browsed many websites, he pointed out; it was unreasonable to take in isolation those which he visited on that morning. As for the diary, CRORO and CROCRO and CRO and the other code words referred not to chloroform but to various alcoholic spirits that Obara and his female companions used to sniff and snort from plastic bags. But having taken the stand on his own behalf, he had to submit himself to another grilling from the prosecutor. Mizoguchi's first question was a simple one: "Does SMY mean *sui min yaku*?"

"SM means 'Super Magic,'" said Obara. "And, in foreign countries, Y is a general term for hallucination. The letter Y expresses something unknown. Yellow sunshine . . . er, *yesca* . . . y . . ." He trailed off into incoherence.

Justice Tochigi flashed his beautiful teeth. "What are you talking about?" he asked.

■ ■ ■

Amid all of this, in April 2006, Jane Blackman, Tim Blackman, and Carita Ridgway's mother, Annette, flew out to Tokyo to give evidence of their own. Sensitive to the state of relations between Lucie's parents, the prosecutors scheduled the two women to appear first, and Tim five days later.

The prospect of a face-to-face confrontation between the accused killer and the bereaved parents packed the public gallery. But the ushers were late in admitting the press and public to the courtroom; when the doors were opened, Jane and Annette were sitting at the front of the public gallery, but Obara's usual space was empty.

Chief Justice Tochigi was beaming warmly. "The court has received word," he said, "that the defendant has refused to appear before the court today."

By law, he explained, a criminal trial could not proceed without the presence of the accused. But this rule could be waived if the defendant had received a summons and had no good reason for not being present. Obara had indeed been informed in the usual way, and the officers of the Tokyo Detention Center had gone to his cell that morning and requested him to come to court. "But he has been taking off his clothes and clinging to the sink, and he refuses to appear," Justice Tochigi explained. "The defendant hasn't given any justifiable reason for not appearing. Given that the bereaved families have come from abroad, the court has decided that despite the absence of the defendant, we won't wait for him."

Jane took the witness stand first. She spoke of her memories of Lucie as a baby, and as a child and a young woman, and of their closeness, like that of sisters. "I used to believe that the sorrow of any parent losing a child is the greatest sorrow anyone can know," she said. "I was wrong. To lose a child and know her body was desecrated in such an inhuman way is the greatest and most unrelenting pain I have ever had to endure." She went on: "The fact that Obara has refused to attend court today is very dishonorable and a clear sign of his guilt. He is a coward."

Annette was next. She talked about the effect of Carita's death on her older daughter, Samantha, and on Carita's boyfriend, Robert Finnigan. "Even though fourteen years have passed, I still think of her every day and feel the pain of her loss," Annette said. "She was a wonderful daughter and nothing can replace her. My preference for Obara's sentence is that he should be executed. However, in the circumstances that is impossible. Therefore, he should be in prison until he dies."*

---

*Japan retains the death penalty for murder, and a handful of death-row inmates are hanged every year. But capital punishment is imposed only in the most extreme cases—child murders, multiple murders, and premeditated killings carried out for cynical motives such as life-insurance fraud. No one ever accused Joji Obara of deliberately attempting to kill his victims— although the prosecutors might have chosen to argue that, having unintentionally killed Carita Ridgway with an excess of illegally administered drugs, his recklessness in repeating the mistake with Lucie Blackman amounted to murder. But given their reliance upon circumstantial evidence in proving Obara's guilt, they concluded that a lesser charge of "rape resulting in death" was more likely to secure a conviction.

Annette's final comments speak to what, in a Western jurisdiction, are two crucially distinct duties of the court: the adjudication of guilt or

Five days later, Tim appeared in court. Obara was absent again. This time, the judge reported, he had squeezed himself into a narrow niche in the walls of his cell and refused to come out.

Tim spoke for nearly half an hour. "The death of my daughter, Lucie Blackman, has been the most terrible, terrible event of my life," Tim's statement began. "The shock and trauma . . . has changed me."

> Lucie lived for eight thousand days and I carry many images of her in my mind, and there are many things in everyday life which I see which make me cry in public, which make me cry in business meetings, which make me cry when with friends and which make me cry in the night.
> Sometimes when I see a child in a pushchair I can see Lucie and tears come to my eyes. Sometimes I see children playing with their daddy in a park and their fun and joy makes

---

innocence, and the sentencing of a convicted defendant. If Obara had pleaded, or been found, guilty, then the views of his victims' families would reasonably have been taken into account in deciding his sentence. But at this stage, he was a defendant who vigorously denied all the charges against him.

To invite the views of the bereaved at this stage, when the accused should still have been under the presumption of innocence, reinforced the impression given by so many other aspects of the Japanese justice system that the defendant's guilt had been unofficially established before he stepped into court and that the trial was a hollow ritual.

"I have never accepted any count of the criminal prosecution on this trial," Obara wrote in a statement prepared for these hearings. "On the other hand, the statements by the relatives of Carita Ridgway and Lucie Blackman are supposed to be directed towards the offender. Therefore, if I appear in court, I am afraid that I would be regarded as the offender and I would be supposed to accept it . . . I am afraid that this must reduce the criminal court to a venue for retaliation and criticism, resulting in hatred and regret." Justice Tochigi refused to allow this document to be read out in court.

me so sad for Lucie. I may be standing next to a lovely twenty-five-year-old young woman on a train and Lucie fills my eyes with tears. Seeing a young woman with her young children makes me think of how Lucie will never be . . .

I will never feel her loving arms around my neck and feel warm breath as she tells me she loves me. I cannot stop myself thinking of the moment when her life stopped; the moment when her brain stem ceased to function; her last deep and tragic breath. Was she in pain, was she terrified, did she call for me?

Now I have images in my head of her cut-up body, the chain saw marks on her bones, her rotting, decomposing flesh . . . her parts in plastic bags buried beneath the sand, the grief on Sophie and Rupert's faces. These images will stay with me for the rest of my life and when I am reminded of Lucie, when I see a little child, I see these terrible images too.

I hear her voice in my sleep and, for a moment, I forget she is dead. For a moment I feel the joy of hearing her voice and then the pain hits me because I know she is not there, and I know that I can only dream of her now.

I have been changed by all these things . . . I have been left distraught and traumatized with a depth of indescribable sadness. I do not sleep properly. I cry very often uncontrollably. I am frightened to meet with friends and family because I know how upset it will make me as I see the grief in their eyes . . . Some days I find it impossible to concentrate on my work and am too upset to make important decisions at work, as it seems so pointless and unimportant.

I feel guilt for all the times when I could have seen Lucie but was maybe too busy; guilt for the times I was cross with her as a girl; guilt for not giving her the money she needed and guilt for not being with her at the times when she needed me most. This guilt may not be logical, but it will always be with me and makes me feel terrible and deepens the terrible wound left by Lucie's death.

But the worst guilt of all is the feeling of guilt I have when I do not think of her, the guilt I feel when I am happy for a moment about something. This guilt feeling makes it impossible to ever be really free during my life from the devastating effect of her [death]—and part of me knows that I will never be free from this tragedy until I am able to be with her in my future life. Only death will release me from this pain. Only knowing that when I die I will feel her arms around my neck again helps me live my life.

It was the most powerful statement that Tim had ever made. The Tokyo District Court was a colorless and unemotional place, but the impact of these words was unquestionable. The prosecutor's case was tight and consistent; Obara's defense was a thicket of contradictions: And now, here was the father of dead Lucie, setting out in searing terms the anguish brought about by their deaths and pleading for the heaviest penalty. So it was all the more jolting to learn, later that year, that Tim Blackman had accepted half a million pounds from Obara and signed a document questioning the evidence against him.

22. CONDOLENCE

"Lucie's funeral meant that she was no longer missing," Sophie Blackman said. "That period of limbo was done with; we didn't have to keep looking for her anymore. But it was the burial of her ashes—that, to me, was when I understood that her life was over. More so than her funeral. The burial was her death to me." It came close to being the death of Sophie too.

Four years separated the cremation and the interment of the remains. They were marked by a destructive, stubborn argument among the surviving Blackmans about what should be done with Lucie's ashes. At first, Tim had suggested scattering them from his boat into the waters of the Solent, where the family used to go sailing when Lucie was a child. Rupert preferred a burial place somewhere close to Sevenoaks, where it would be accessible to all the members of the family. But the heat and bitterness in this debate were between mother and daughter. Sophie desperately, achingly, wanted the ashes to be divided among the four members of the family. She wanted to be able to recapture her visit to the cave in Moroiso, when, for the first time since Lucie's death, she had felt close to her sister in spirit. "I would like to have some of Lucie's ashes placed in a beautiful, delicate silver trinket box which I can keep in my life," she wrote in a passionate letter addressed jointly to her mother, father, and brother. "I am not ready to sacrifice Lucie to the earth. I want to have her with me a little while longer.

Somewhere I can talk to her every day. And perhaps in my future, when I have my own family, or my own house, I can bury her at the perfect place where I can be with her forever."

But Jane was immovable. In 2002, she had been named by the court as administrator of Lucie's estate, which gave her the final say in all such matters, an authority that she was determined to wield. At one point, she placed the ashes in a household safe bought specially for the purpose. Her fear, although she stopped short of spelling it out, appeared to be that Tim or Sophie might steal Lucie's remains. The strength of these feelings had much to do with the aspect of Lucie's death that haunted and horrified Jane the most—the dismemberment and destruction of her body. "Lucie had been cut up," she said. "There was no way that her ashes were going to be divided too. I felt very strongly about that. I didn't want half of my daughter." The interment of the ashes was arranged for March 23, 2005, at St. Peter and St. Paul Church in the village of Seal, a mile from where Jane lived.

Since she was a teenager, Sophie had always had ferocious quarrels with her mother. It was as the mediator of these squabbles that Lucie had become so precious to both of them. At the age of fourteen, Sophie had left home and moved in with the family of a friend for several months; she had dropped out of school halfway through the sixth form. When Lucie went missing, Sophie was studying to be a cardiac technician, the specialist who monitors pacemakers and tests people's hearts. She flew to Tokyo expecting to spend a few days there at the most. In the end, she lived in the Diamond Hotel for weeks. In between visits to Japan, she returned to London and resumed the life of a medical trainee. But with Lucie's sudden, violent absence, the elements of Sophie's life shifted and resettled in patterns that cut her off from the consolation of human contact. Some friends, she found, avoided her, at a loss for what to do or say; these, she despised. Others displayed an exaggerated, stifling wish to comfort and support; them, she rejected. Sophie's pride and defensiveness, manifested so often as aggression and contempt, drove away many of those who might naturally have helped her.

She got along far better with Tim, but he had long been an absent father, living hours away in the Isle of Wight with his large new stepfamily. "I isolated myself, quite happily," she said. "And really, truly, the only person in my life who has ever been consistent or reliable was Lucie. I got myself in a situation where the more depressed I became, the fewer and fewer people I could turn to. I ended up on the day of Lucie's burial with no one."

It was agreed from the beginning that it would be a private ceremony for the four members of the immediate family. But journalists somehow got wind of it, and so to avoid the inevitable scrum of reporters and photographers, the burial was brought forward at the last minute from four o'clock to one. Jane's seething conviction that Tim had tipped off the press added to the awkwardness of the whole day.

It was a short and very simple service. Almost five years after her death, Lucie's urn was buried in a plot in Seal churchyard, overlooking the fields and low hills of west Kent. Rupert placed in the grave a CD of songs that he had written and recorded for Lucie. Sophie had had two silver plaques made, engraved with the opening lines of Lucie's favorite poem, "An Irish Airman Foresees His Death" by W. B. Yeats. The first line she placed in the grave with Lucie:

I know that I shall meet my fate

The second Sophie kept with her and resolved to carry with her wherever she went, for the rest of her life:

Somewhere among the clouds above

After the service, the four Blackmans went for a late lunch. They drove to the Rendezvous, a restaurant where, as a younger and happier family, they had celebrated Lucie's birthday. It was the first time that Tim and Jane had been in such close proximity since soon after their divorce. Tim ordered champagne and was surprised to find the occasion "reasonably okay—it was really quite convivial. The children could never resist quips and laughs." Jane even found her ex-husband's presence less unbearable than usual. "Everyone was civil to one another," she said. "Tim told me I looked nice. I wouldn't have chosen to spend the day like that, but we did it for the sake of Rupert and Sophie." But for Sophie, it was a moment of horror and hypocrisy. Beneath a cheerful exterior, her emotions were writhing within her heart.

"It was fucked up. It was weird," Sophie said, and four years later, her voice broke as she spoke of it. "Because everyone was trying to be nice to each other, playing the game of let's pretend that we're a happy family, sitting in a restaurant—and we'd just buried Lucie. It was weird, this pretense of everyone being united, when actually there was nothing between us anymore, there was nothing that related us. Even now, I find it very upsetting. It made no sense. What was most glaringly obvious was how Lucie's death had changed the relationships between all of us, and how as a brother and a sister, and a mum and a dad, we were just four strangers sitting round a table."

It was Sophie's pride that caused her to conceal her feelings and to set her unhappiness as a challenge to her friends and family. "The only small sign I put out that I was not really okay," she said, "was that I invited everyone to come back to my flat. After wanting to run away from that awful lunch, I then extended my time with them. And that was me saying, 'Don't leave me quite yet. I'm not ready.'" The Blackmans had a few more drinks and cups of tea at Sophie's, then said their goodbyes. Sophie's flatmate, Emma, who worked as a flight attendant, was going out—so, on the night of Lucie's burial, she was to be alone. "I didn't say, 'Please stay, I really need you to be here,'" Sophie recalled. "It's true that I should ask people to help me when I need it. But the test I laid down for people was whether or not they could see that for themselves. Surely, if they knew me, they wouldn't even have to ask—they would just be there.

"So I was very alone. The burying of Lucie's ashes was the most significant day of all for me. For me, that was the end of her life—I would never see her again, and I didn't feel in a position to get through it."

Over the past year, Sophie had been prescribed a series of antidepressants. She had tried several different drugs; none had helped very much. But now, in between shots of neat vodka, and after carefully and neatly disposing of the empty packets, she laid out her collection of pills.

"I was sitting there on my own, getting obliterated. I don't clearly know what I was thinking. I don't remember making a decision about what I wanted to do. But at some point I took every tablet I could find. I can remember doing it in handfuls. I was popping them out of the packets and taking them in handfuls and handfuls. People say, 'Wasn't it just a cry for help?' But it wasn't. I just wanted to die. I didn't want to be alive. I didn't see the point."

Emma and her boyfriend returned home to find Sophie asleep on the sofa in what they took to be no more than a vodka stupor and lifted her into bed. The next day, Emma left at dawn for two days of flying. Recollections differ about what happened next. Tim had the idea that it was Emma's mother who raised the alarm, but Sophie remembered coming to groggy consciousness and phoning for an ambulance herself. Either way, it was early on Friday morning, more than twenty-four hours after she took her overdose, that the ambulance took her to the hospital, where her life was saved.

Rupert was the first to get the news of what had happened. He rushed to the psychiatric clinic to which Sophie had been transferred and was appalled to see her shuffling and mumbling and rubbing her hands together compulsively, more like a zombie than the scathing, energetic sister with whom he had had a boozy meal just two days earlier. Tim drove over from the Isle of Wight and had Sophie transferred to a private clinic, where she was briefly committed under the Mental Health Act. He was struck by the pallor of her skin and by the way that, even after the drugs had been flushed from her system, she still seemed to be hallucinating. Jane was the last to be tracked down. When she visited the hospital she saw for the first time the scars on Sophie's arms where for several months she had been cutting herself.

After a few days, Sophie was discharged into her father's care and went to the Isle of Wight to live in the old vicarage with Tim, Jo, and her children. She spent ten weeks there, calmly and happily, and finished the dissertation required to complete her degree in clinical physiology at the City of Westminster College. When the results were published that summer, she was awarded a first-class degree.

The following year, she was admitted as a residential patient at Cassel Hospital in Richmond-upon-Thames, which specialized in treating people with severe psychiatric problems related to their families. She spent nine months there. She didn't see Jane again.

"You might think that a disaster like Lucie's death would draw everyone back together," Tim said. "In fact, even in a happy family, people often unravel after something like that. They blame one another, they withdraw from one another. When things have already broken up, as in our case, the pain makes you less able to cope. So it becomes even more difficult to deal with the strain and stresses which were already there." One summer day in 2006, Tim visited Sophie in the hospital with news that would add to the pressure on the Blackmans: Joji Obara had offered him half a million pounds and he had decided to accept it.

This approach had first been made in March 2006, in the form of an e-mail from one of Obara's lawyers. The offer was for a one-off cash payment of £200,000; in return, Tim would promise not to make a statement to the Tokyo District Court. Jane received a similar proposal and responded with contemptuous rejection. But Tim entered into a brief e-mail correspondence on the subject—although not, he insisted to me at the time, with the intention of accepting any money. "Here I was, almost in direct contact with Obara," he said. "I wanted the opportunity to engage with him. I wrote back, pretending to negotiate—first, to see how far it would go, and second, to raise his hopes and then dash them in a pathetic effort at having a stab at him . . . I was just playing . . . There is no agreement, there is no money [that has been paid], and there is no forgiveness."

But Obara's lawyers were keeping copies of the e-mails, and they were taping and transcribing their telephone conversations with Tim. When these were published the following year, they suggested that he was more eager to accept the money than he admitted. "I have received the offer from the accused," Tim wrote. "I am prepared to consider it and prepared to consider the condition." He asked for £500,000; Obara made a counteroffer of £300,000; and for this Tim agreed to a series of statements to be delivered to the court. "The accused has shown contrition and expressed sorrow at Lucie's death," he promised to say. "As Lucie's father and as a Christian, I am able to forgive the accused, and . . . our relationship is resolved. I hope that he will rehabilitate himself into the community." A few days later, however, Tim abruptly withdrew from the negotiation.

He explained in a telephone call to one of Obara's middlemen, which was duly recorded, transcribed, and published, "I am informed by the British police, who talked to the [Japanese] prosecutors," Tim said, "that they are not happy for me to receive money and then go to court."

Carita's mother, Annette Ridgway, had been approached with a similar offer, which she too had rejected. All three parents went to Tokyo the following month and described the effect on their lives of the loss of their daughters. "The terrible, terrible acts played out on my beautiful girl are acts of a disgusting creature, a filthy animal preying on beauty and vulnerability," Tim told the court. "These are acts of depravity by a monster which has grown unchecked for decades in a hothouse atmosphere without law or control."

> This monster has shown not a single tear of contrition, shame, or guilt for the perversion or crime against humanity. Instead there are only lies and denial; from denial at the start, of even knowing Lucie, to denial in her death. Quite simply, my beautiful daughter would be alive today if she had not been preyed upon by this creature . . .
>
> These despicable crimes against us must receive the absolute maximum penalty, and longest possible sentence. The eyes of the world believe the charge should be murder—the sentence death. I concur. Any sentence less than the maximum permissible will not deliver the deserved justice and would be a dishonorable insult to Lucie's life and Lucie's death.

But over the next six months, Tim resumed his exchanges with Obara's team. At the end of September, he traveled to Tokyo and met them in the New Otani Hotel. The timing was no coincidence: in October, Obara's lawyers would begin their closing arguments in his defense. Just five days before, ¥100 million, which at the time was worth $850,000, was wired to Tim's bank account in the Isle of Wight.

The payment of cash from perpetrator to victim is a well-established procedure in Japanese criminal cases, frequently encouraged by prosecutors. A dangerous driver who has injured a pedestrian, a shoplifter, even a rapist, can reduce his sentence, and occasionally avoid prosecution altogether, by making a financial settlement, often accompanied by statements of forgiveness or appeals for leniency from his victim. To a Western mind, such agreements are a dangerous interference with the impersonal workings of justice. But to many Japanese it is common sense that an offender should do what he can to compensate someone whom he has hurt. In one gang-rape case, for example, defendants who paid ¥1.5 million to the victim received a three-year jail sentence, compared to four years for those who did not, or could not, find the money. "In cases of this kind, ¥1.5 million is about the 'exchange rate' for a one-year reduction of sentence," writes David Johnson. "In murder cases, where terms of imprisonment range from three years to life (and capital punishment is a possibility), the desires of the victim's survivors have an effect that must be measured in years, if not in life itself."

But there was a difference between this practice and the settlement being proposed by Obara. In a conventional case, the accused offers money as an expression of atonement, a concrete token of his desire to put right a wrong for which he has admitted responsibility. But Obara admitted nothing. The hundreds of thousands of pounds that his lawyers flourished were not accompanied by apology or confession. In fact, they were careful to point out that this was not compensation, but rather *mimaikin*—a "solatium" or "consolation money"—which implied no criminal liability whatsoever. Obara had done nothing wrong but, like many decent people, he was terribly sad about what had happened to Lucie and Carita and wanted simply to help the families in their grief.

If he had pleaded guilty, then reparation to his victims might have persuaded the judges to reduce his sentence. But to pay money to someone to whom he had done no harm made little sense. Several of his lawyers deplored the strategy. But Obara pursued the goal of distributing this charity with aggressive determination.

Lawyers and private detectives tracked down each of the eight surviving women he was accused of raping, offering them ¥2 million each. Several of the women refused, but the offer was repeated with a persistence that verged on harassment. A lawyer named Mikiko Asao acted for three of the rape victims. She advised them that they were entitled to compensation from Obara but that if they accepted money, they should give in return nothing more than a receipt—no statement, no request for leniency, nothing that might influence the deliberations of the court. Most of the victims signed anyway. The documents drafted by Obara's lawyers acknowledged receipt of "nuisance compensation," agreed that the case was now "settled completely," and asked the court "to withdraw the prosecution and the complaint on my case . . . because I do not have [the] intention of seeking his criminal punishment."

"These detectives contacted them repeatedly," Mikiko Asao told me. "At their jobs, at home, on their mobiles. Even when they changed their mobile phone numbers, they found them out. They even found out their private e-mail addresses. This is how they get what they want—by telling lies, by making threats, by upsetting them psychologically. As soon as I heard about this, I protested to the defense lawyers. But it didn't stop, and they forced them to sign these documents."

No one made threats to Tim Blackman. But on the same day as the bank transfer of ¥100 million, he signed and fingerprinted the following document, which would be presented to the judges by Obara's lawyers the following week.

Written Statement

I did not know that the cause of death of my daughter Lucie Blackman was unknown, the DNA or so on of defendant Obara were not detected from the body of my daughter at all and the defendant Obara lodged at the Japanese style hotel on that day and at the time supposed when my daughter would have been dismembered and deserted.

I would like to state and ask to the Japanese Court the following matters:

1. What was the real black material flooded from mouth at all, and what was the real black material veiled the head of my daughter Lucie Blackman at all?*

2. Constituent Analysis of the concrete veiled the head of my daughter Lucie Blackman.

3. When and how transferred my daughter Lucie Blackman from Zushi Marina to Aburatsubo?

Hereinbefore, and as father of Lucie Blackman, I would like to wish you please inspect the most important these three points supposed to be able to clarify the cause of death and this case.

---

*The existence of a "black substance" on Lucie's head was raised repeatedly by the defense. Postmortem photographs showed a tarry liquid on her head and in her mouth. The lawyers never spelled out what they thought it was, but the implication seemed to be that it was formed when the head was burned, and that this further exculpated Obara because none of the witnesses to his behavior in the days after Lucie's disappearance had reported signs of a fire.

If the black material filled in the mouth and veiled over the face that could be clarified the cause of death would be discarded by the Police or the Prosecution, such act is illegal, and as a father who loves his daughter, I can not forgive even if that person will be a policeman or a prosecutor.

The clotted grammar and preoccupation with baffling detail made it obvious that none of these were Tim's words, that he had signed it without caring, and perhaps not really understanding, what it said. But for many people it was all the more shocking that he would casually undermine the prosecution case for nothing more complicated than half a million pounds.

"In public, I was very supportive of Dad's decision," Sophie said. "In fact, I didn't support it at all. It's not that I disapproved of him taking the money in itself. I just knew that he was going to commit public suicide by doing it, that he'd be torn to shreds by Mum and by the media. Everyone would have an opinion, and no matter how he justified it, people would judge him, and it would affect his life, his livelihood, everything. And it has."

It was Obara's lawyers who announced the payment, the day after Tim's return to England. The weekend papers in Britain all carried the story; their headline was supplied by Jane's description of the transaction: "blood money." "I have rejected all and any payments from the accused, as have my daughter, Sophie, and my son, Rupert," she said in a statement. "He is conducting these negotiations against my wishes and the pleas of his children. Lucie's loyal family and friends are sickened by Tim Blackman's utter betrayal."

Many people in his situation would have discreetly gone to earth until the brouhaha had abated. But Tim had never sought to avoid journalists, and he did not begin now. Dutifully, he submitted to a round of television and newspaper interviews, all with the same question: Why? He talked about the losses he had suffered during the months that Lucie had been missing, and of the Lucie Blackman Trust and his hopes of putting it on a secure financial footing. He pointed out that because of the expense and duration of Japanese litigation, and Obara's status as a bankrupt, there was no chance of winning compensation through a civil case. He didn't help himself with certain of his claims: that the payment had been made not by Obara himself but by a university "friend" of Obara, a Mr. Tsuji, and that far from helping Obara, the payment "could actually make him look more guilty." He came across as tepid and defensive. The television interviewers, who had formerly addressed him with simpering compassion, were hectoring and self-righteous. Rather than the bereaved father of a slain daughter, it was as if Tim Blackman had become an offender himself.

It got worse the following week, when the *Daily Mail*, beneath the headline "A Father's Betrayal," ran a two-thousand-word character assassination of Tim. "It is an astonishing U-turn, and one that has caused immense anguish to Lucie's mother, Jane," the paper reported. "Intriguingly, however, while his conduct may have caused grievous upset, it has not, it seems, come as a huge surprise to many who know Tim Blackman well." Nowhere in the article was Jane quoted directly; instead "friends" described her "quiet dignity" in the face of betrayal by Tim. "They paint a picture of a shallow and vain man who callously abandoned his family ten years ago to live with another woman, refusing to support them financially in any way . . . an arrogant and selfish man who quickly eroded the well of goodwill among the [Tokyo] community."

Of the "many," only one was quoted by name: Huw Shakeshaft, or "Sir Huw of Roppongi," the financial adviser who had turned so violently against Tim in Tokyo.* "I have long felt shocked and disappointed by the way he behaved," Huw "revealed" to the *Mail*. "I have kept quiet until now but after hearing what he has done, I felt I could no longer keep silent." Huw rehearsed his complaints: the liberties that Tim had taken with his office, the use of Huw's restaurant tab to entertain journalists, Tim's decision to leave Sophie on her own in Tokyo for two days. Another "friend" of Jane had further revelations about how little maintenance Tim had paid her, his relationship with Lucie ("To say they were close is laughable"), and his failure to consult with Jane about the founding of the Lucie Blackman Trust. The *Mail* had further "learned" that Jane was planning to write to the charity's trustees "to question her former husband's suitability" in running the organization.

Tim sent a stricken letter to the court in Tokyo. "The condolence from [Obara's] friend is accepted just as we have received condolences from around the world," he wrote. "It is accepted because it makes the defendant more guilty of the crime against Lucie. Because he is bankrupt and this adds to his punishment. The defendant is guilty and continues to pretend he is innocent. He is a mad and wicked criminal, preying on our daughters." It was too late: no one was listening. A month after receiving the money from Obara, it would later come out, Tim spent £64,500 on a yacht—his second. He tried to explain that the boat was an investment purchased on behalf of a yacht charter company that he ran, but no one was interested in this either.

Jane Blackman's shyness about speaking of Tim in her own words was conquered a few months later, when she gave

---

*Huw had by now moved to Kuala Lumpur. He had embarked on a short-lived engagement to a Malaysian princess, and had a new business, as the partner of the psychic Ron Bard.

an on-the-record interview to the *Mail*. The headline to this
piece was "HE IS IMMORAL." "It is like fighting two battles, one against her killer and one against my former husband," she said. "Whose side is he on? How is this helping
justice for our daughter? . . . As far as I am concerned, Tim
accepted a hundred million pieces of silver. Judas was content
with just thirty."

■ ■ ■

The first time I met Roger Steare, Jane's second husband, he
gave me some advice. "You need to understand at the outset
that there are two versions of this story," he said. "There's Tim's
version, and then there is the truth, which Jane will tell you."

Jane had met Roger two and half years after Lucie's death.
There was no doubt that his love and practical support enabled
her to emerge from a period of the most extreme desolation.
She had been alone since 1995. "I thought that I would never
meet anyone," she said. "I thought that that side of my life was
over." One evening some friends offered to introduce her to a
single man they knew and, rather tipsily, she agreed. The date
had an auspicious beginning. In the years after Lucie's death,
Jane had become aware of small signs, rarely noticed by other
people, that had to her a profound significance. Butterflies,
white feathers, stars, the image of angels in pictures and de-
signs, the singing of a bird, the unusual behavior of objects
and machines—all of them, Jane became convinced, were
manifestations of Lucie. "She's been here recently," she told me
on my second visit to her home. "Things have been going missing, the fire alarm went off for no reason."

Rather self-conscious about going out on a blind date at
the age of forty-nine, Jane arrived at the agreed pub and parked
next to a silver car with its interior lights on. This, it turned
out, was the car of the man she was meeting.

"I said to him, 'Is that silver Mercedes in the car park yours? Because your inside lights are on.' He said, 'That's impossible,' but he went out to have a look. When he came back in, he said, 'You were right. But if that's your car next to mine, then your inside lights are on too.' And now it was my turn to say, 'No, that's impossible.' But when I went out, he was right too."

The name Lucie, of course, comes from the Latin word for light. And light, Jane had discovered, was as important to Lucie in death as it had been in life; its unexpected flickering was a reliable sign of her presence. "It was Lucie," Jane said. "She was giving her approval, telling me it was okay." Roger proposed to Jane five weeks later. Eight months after that, in August 2003, they were married.

Roger was five years younger than Jane. Like her, he had been married and divorced. He was the son of a Methodist minister; he had worked as a banker, a social worker, a City of London headhunter, and a self-employed career adviser. At the time he married Jane, he was establishing himself as a "corporate philosopher," advising companies on moral and ethical issues. He published a book titled *ethicability®: how to decide what's right and find the courage to do it*. "Moral values such as humility, courage and self-discipline are the keys to success, well-being and sustainability," his website explained. "ethicability®"—the lowercase *e*, one gathered, was as important as the ®—"is a decision-making and cultural framework that helps people stop, think, talk, unite—and then do the right thing." Roger would go on to be appointed a professor of "organisational ethics" at Cass Business School in London. He was also the unofficial secretary of a concerted campaign devoted to the prosecution and criminal conviction of Tim Blackman.

Roger was a bearded, gentle-faced man in his fifties. The first time I met him, he seemed to find the insecurity of being a self-employed, self-published philosopher a mild, but constant, strain. In the photograph on the ethicability® website, he leans forward into the camera, smiling confidingly through heavy black-rimmed spectacles. Beneath his pin-striped jacket, he wears a flowery open-necked shirt. But Roger always struck me as more at home in Marks & Spencer than Paul Smith. His love and respect for Jane, and his desire to protect her from the harsher aspects of her situation, were obvious and unaffected, and it was natural that he should help her with the practical aspects of being the mother of Lucie Blackman.

When Jane saw Lucie in a butterfly that crossed their path on a country walk, Roger saw her too. When she faltered, as she often did during my conversations with her, over a painful—or an unbearably happy—memory, Roger was always there with an outstretched hand or a cup of tea. But I was taken aback by the zeal he brought to the struggle against Tim and the extent to which he had taken on his wife's fight for moral supremacy as his own. At times, he seemed to vie with Jane to outdo her in his contempt for Tim, a man whom he had never met.

I spent hours talking to Jane in the house they shared in Kemsing, outside Sevenoaks, usually with Roger on hand. Sometimes, it was difficult to get an answer from her, so avid was he to answer every question I asked. "I think I am quite a perceptive person because I've been a social worker and I do understand behaviors and I do understand personality types," Roger told me. "And Tim has all the signs of a serious personality disorder. He's a Walter Mitty character . . . He switched from being a genuinely caring father, and great with the kids—and brought Lucie back when she was having her fit, and saved her life—to becoming someone who lashed out and ended up hurting not only [Jane], but the children. He's an ideal psychologist's case study in that respect."

"It's called a sociopath," said Jane at this point.

"Yes, I believe he's a sociopath, basically."

The legal campaign against Tim began in the months following his acceptance of the "blood money." Another of the former volunteers in Tokyo, a British banker who like Huw had acquired a powerful loathing for Tim, paid for Jane to engage Mark Stephens, a flamboyant media lawyer. With Stephens's help, the Steares persuaded the Hampshire police, Tim's local constabulary, to investigate him on suspicion of fraud.

It was an ingenious accusation, which on the face of it had little to support it. Whom had Tim defrauded, after all? Not Obara, who had pleaded with him to accept the money. Not Jane, who had repeatedly refused a similar payout. "Lucie's estate was the victim," Roger explained to me. One of the statements drafted by Obara's lawyers and signed by Tim affirmed that he accepted the ¥100 million "representing on [sic] the family of Lucie." But it was Jane who administered the estate; by misrepresenting himself, the argument went, Tim had defrauded not a living person but dead Lucie. This argument was considered strong enough for the Hampshire police to dispatch a detective sergeant to take a statement from Jane and for the Crown Prosecution Service to write to the Japanese authorities requesting more information.

Jane had a particular resentment for the Lucie Blackman Trust. It had become one of the battlefields on which Lucie's parents struggled for possession of her spirit. Over five years, the trust had evolved into a small charity with a handful of paid and volunteer staff. It sold safety equipment aimed at young people, such as rape alarms and kits for testing whether a drink had been spiked. Tim would visit schools to tell Lucie's story and talk about the importance of personal safety at home and abroad. Jane wrote to the Charity Commission, lobbying for the trust's charitable status to be revoked, and to the trustees, urging them to disassociate themselves from Tim. Roger e-mailed one journalist, "off the record and strictly unattributable," urging her to investigate the trust's finances. Another line of attack was opened up in April 2007, when Roger received an e-mail from a woman named Heidi Black, formerly Tim's assistant and "deputy chief executive" of the trust. Ms. Black had been sacked the month before; she was contesting her dismissal at an industrial tribunal. She had also made a complaint to the police about money donated to the trust that she claimed had gone missing. The same week that she wrote to Roger, the information found its way to the *Daily Mail*. "Lucie's Father in Trust Fraud Probe" ran its headline. The following day, Matt Searle, the trust's only full-time employee, was arrested and questioned.

After five weeks of investigation, he was cleared. Having been through the trust's accounts, the police had found nothing to suggest that money had gone missing, or that any other crime had been committed. There was nothing in the complaints made to the Charity Commission, nor in the claim of fraud against Lucie's estate, either. By the middle of 2007, all Roger and Jane's efforts had come to nothing.

"This is why I don't have contact with my mum," Sophie said. "This need that Mum has to seek out and destroy Dad and what he's doing, irrespective of the consequences and the impact that it would have on me and Rupert. She puts herself before us and our emotional needs, or any needs at all. I think that's an unforgivable trait in a parent.

"If you're over him, and have moved on and remarried, then let him be. How happy and secure is she in her life and in her new marriage if the focus of her interest is her ex-husband? And Roger—he needs to man up a bit. What's that about? Spending so much time investigating the workings of your wife's ex-husband when you're the current husband—isn't that just a bit weird?"

23. THE VERDICT

Over the years, I kept on trying to bring about a meeting with Joji Obara. I sent repeated letters through his lawyers asking to be allowed to interview him in the Tokyo Detention Center. I wrote of the unresolved mysteries about the case (of which there were several) and of my wish (which was sincere) to balance my reporting of the victims and police with his own point of view. I sent lists of the kinds of questions that I knew he liked to answer, about the evidence against him, the "condolence money," and the work of the police. But what I really wanted to ask him about was growing up in rich Osaka as a Korean pachinko magnate's son, and living with a disturbed older brother, and how he had heard the news that his father was dead in Hong Kong, and what he used to see when he looked in the mirror in the years before he changed his face.

Once, he replied, asking me to get hold of Lucie's health records, the same information his lawyers had tried to obtain through British private detectives. The implication was that my cooperation would be rewarded with his. I declined. After another of my letters, one of Obara's lawyers, a brooding, unsmiling man named Kiyohisa Arai, called me to his office in central Tokyo.

He began by reading to me a personal message from Joji Obara. "I'm quite grateful to receive such a letter from you," it began. "Sooner or later I'll have a chance to meet you, but before that please have a look at the materials which I can provide." Across the table, Mr. Arai pushed a sheaf of documents—court transcripts, Lucie's diaries, photographs of Christa Mackenzie in Obara's apartment. Most were reprinted in the strange book that would later be commissioned, but several were not and could never be. These were police photographs of Lucie's remains as they had been recovered from the cave—her head, her arms, her torso, her thighs, her calves, her feet and ankles—coldly arrayed on the pathologist's table. The images were appalling, of course, and after the visceral shock of beholding a dismembered body came a sense of shame, the shame that pornography imparts. "Of course, these are terrible and unbearable to see," Mr. Arai said as he passed them over. "We all feel great pity." He seemed to be observing my reaction as I looked over them.

Ostensibly, the point of the photographs was to draw attention to the "black substance" on Lucie's head and in her mouth, which the prosecutors, in Obara's view, had never satisfactorily explained. But later, I wondered if there was more to it than this, and if it wasn't, in fact, a kind of warning, or even a threat aimed at me personally—a tipping ajar of the trapdoor above the pit, a glimpse into the hellishness of what had befallen Lucie, and the mind of the person who had done it.*

I received two other letters from Obara's lawyers, alleging inaccuracies in stories I had published—dates, the nationality

---

*Mr. Arai encouraged me to take away the photographs; I sent them back to him, as he had asked, the following week. Four months later, in an indignant letter, he accused me of "delivering copies to Scotland Yard which then showed the copies to the family of the deceased Ms Lucie Blackman." He went on: "This act of yours not only violated the promise you owed to your source and damaged a relationship of mutual trust, but also hurt the family and increased their grief. Such an act should never be forgiven as a journalist and as a human being." There was no truth whatever to any of these assertions.

of one of Obara's victims, the sequence of events. "What is more," Obara's lawyer Shinya Sakane wrote indignantly, "the dog kept in the . . . freezer was reported as being a German shepherd, although it was in fact a Shetland sheepdog. So this is also contrary to the facts." I expressed my thanks for this correction and asked again for an interview. Again, there was no response. But in May 2006, after years of rebuffs, Obara reached out to me in his own way, in the intimate embrace of a legal action.

Obara, represented by the grave Mr. Arai, was suing me for defamation. It would have been more conventional to have gone after my newspaper, as the publisher of the alleged libel, but he had chosen to pursue me personally. He was demanding damages of ¥30 million, and I was summoned to appear three weeks later at the Tokyo District Court. The legal language of the written complaint was dense and intimidating, but on examination, the complaints that it contained were characteristically and comically bizarre. The most unexpected of them concerned the hearing at which Jane had given her evidence, for which Obara had failed to appear in court. At the time, as I and every other journalist present had reported, the judge announced that Obara had taken off his clothes and clung to the basin in his cell. But according to Mr. Arai, this was an absurd and damaging libel. "There are no facts whatsoever which indicate that the Plaintiff . . . stripped himself naked to avoid appearing in court on that date," the complaint insisted. "The Plaintiff's reputation has been severely marred by this act of tort."

The Times engaged a firm of Tokyo lawyers on my behalf. There were meetings and conference calls, notes and documents were mustered, and lengthy drafts of my rebuttal were passed back and forth. Alarm at my new status as a defendant gave way to excitement and curiosity. Would I face Obara in court? What would it feel like on the far side of the courtroom that I knew so well? So it was disappointing to learn that Obara was not required to appear for any of the hearings—and that I didn't need to either. Even more than a criminal trial, civil litigation was a bureaucratic procedure, conducted between lawyers, in which the presence or absence of plaintiff and defendant made no difference whatever. I went to one of the hearings anyway and sat on the defendant's bench. The proceedings lasted less than ten minutes. My lawyer presented items of evidence, statements from other reporters attesting that they too had heard Justice Tochigi describe Obara's *déshabillé*.* These were scrutinized and accepted by Mr. Arai and the judge and then the three of them set a date for the next hearing. My case had attracted no public attention whatsoever; the three people in the public gallery were not spectators but lawyers waiting for the next case to come up. Yet for all the banality of the proceedings, I could identify the thrill, and the terror, of being a defendant, of being under the eye of the law. It was the opposite sensation of sitting on the other side, taking notes; it was like being on a stage, but as director as well as actor.

■ ■ ■

The last two hearings in Joji Obara's trial—the sixtieth and sixty-first—were set aside for the closing arguments of prosecution and defense. There was nothing new to say, but both sides spoke at length anyway. Obara was on his feet for two hours, gnawing away at the holes in the prosecution story. How could he—a small man—have maneuvered the body of

---

*The principal article of evidence, of course, was the stenographer's transcript of the hearing. But although the trial was conducted in public, this was not a public document and it required the permission of the judge for it to be made available to my lawyers.

such a large woman into a car without being spotted? How could anyone be sure about the truth of a charge that contained so many unanswered questions? "There is no decisive evidence, nor is the cause of the victim's death clear," the defense statement read. "Nothing has been found that can be traced back to the defendant's [involvement] in her death, including his DNA. No chloroform has been detected in the corpse, even though prosecutors say she was killed by such drugs."

The prosecution laid out the now familiar evidence—Obara's long and self-documented history of "conquest play," the accounts of the surviving women, the videos and drugs, the whole sequence of suspicious phone calls, purchases, and Internet searches in the days after Lucie's disappearance. It attempted to turn Obara's own defense against him, or the most far-fetched part of it, the unbelievable story about Katsuta, the "whateverer," whose involvement was revealed so late in the case. "The irrational quality of his excuses," the statement observed, "is itself evidence of his guilt."

Bureaucratic understatement, rather than emotionalism, is the characteristic mode of the Japanese courtroom. The young prosecutor's delivery was as droning and uninflected as ever, but in its language the statement summoned an indignation seldom heard in an official setting. "This is an unprecedentedly bizarre and vicious case," it read. "The chances of Obara committing the same crime are extremely high. He is nothing but a cunning beast, who has shown not a trace of human remorse, nor paid heed to the voices of the bereaved families. We see in him not a trace of humanity; he has displayed no feeling of contrition. This case is extraordinary in the annals of sexual crime. Therefore we insist on lifetime imprisonment for the defendant."

Before the reading of this statement, Obara's lawyers made repeated requests that Tim Blackman should be called to give evidence in person.

"What do you want to examine him about?" asked Justice Tochigi, with his customary beam of irritation.

"About the fact that he received one hundred million yen. Although he had been rejecting the money, now he has accepted it. We wish to understand that thought process . . . He is an important witness in considering mitigation. So I want an examination."

"We have already questioned him fully enough," Tochigi said.

The lawyer muttered something inaudible, and Tochigi spoke forcefully. "I will not permit anything of the kind. Rejected."

"I object," said the lawyer.

"Rejected!"

Justice Tochigi invited the prosecutors to begin their closing argument. "I object," said Obara's lawyer again. "I object to the decision of the court. This goes against the court's obligation to fully examine the case."

"Rejected," said Justice Tochigi. "Raising meaningless objections can be regarded as contempt. Watch your step."

It seemed hopelessly misguided, an obvious tactical misjudgment deliberately to provoke, in the fading moments of the trial, the man who would decide Obara's guilt or innocence. On December 11, 2006, the trial came to an end. The court would deliver its verdict in five months' time. There was little doubt what that verdict would be.

■ ■ ■

The sixty-one sessions had extended over the course of six years. Even at the pace of a British court, with hearings five days a week, morning and afternoon, it would have lasted for more than a month and a half. Obara had brought to bear every resource at his disposal—legal, financial, investigative, technological. In 2004, according to the account of a British newspaper, one of his lawyers had hired British private detectives to investigate the backgrounds of Tim, Jane, and Lucie, as well as Louise Phillips and her sister, Emma. Two years later, a website materialized in cyberspace. In English and Japanese, it presented at rambling length Obara's version of events, as well as parts of Lucie's diary, the documents signed by Tim, and selected transcripts of the court hearings.* And in 2007, a few days before the verdict was due to be delivered, a book appeared on the shelves of a few shops in central Tokyo with a cover photograph of a dead dog.

This was *The Truth About the Lucie Case*, a distillation of the tedium, creativity, and grotesquerie of the defense—the Bible of Joji Obara studies. The cover carried a lengthy subtitle: *Elite Prosecutors vs Defendant Joji Obara Who Has an IQ of 180—In No Other Case in Recent Years Have the Reporting and the Reality Been So Different.* "Why did the prosecutors in this case run amok?" ran the blurb. "Revealed: Destruction of Evidence and Forgery of Official Documents by Prosecutors." It was two inches thick, 798 pages long, and weighed two pounds.

The book was "written and edited" by the "Team Seeking the Truth of Lucie's Case," who were also credited on the website. Who were these independent crusaders for veracity, and why were they so shy of identifying themselves? In fact, the book was a vanity publication commissioned by Obara's lawyer; its publishers, for one, believed that he did so at the instigation,

---

*It was forbidden to make public official documents such as this without the court's permission; police muttered angrily of a prosecution for publishing evidence in an ongoing criminal case. But somebody had thought of this: the website—with its suffix ".cx"—was hosted in the obscure Australian territory of Christmas Island. No criminal investigation was ever pursued.

and under the supervision, of Obara himself.* It included page after page of court transcripts, articles of evidence, and long narratives describing in the third person Obara's early life, alcoholic adolescence, and the events before and after his fateful evening with Lucie. There were photographs of the interior of Blue Sea Aburatsubo and of Obara's Mercedes-Benz sports car. There was a series of pictures of Christa Mackenzie apparently smoking heroin on Obara's sofa. Tim's e-mails negotiating the payment of condolence money were reproduced in full, together with transcripts of his telephone conversations with Obara's agent, and a receipt for ¥3.2 million paid to Tanya Nebogatov, the Ukrainian woman whom Obara had raped. There was Lucie's diary again, reproduced and annotated in English and Japanese. There were drawings of the cave, indicating exactly where Lucie's body parts had been found, and a photograph of the beach being battered by a typhoon.

Most of these materials could be seen to make some point or other, or raise a question that might be seen to work to Obara's advantage. Questions such as "Isn't that car rather small for transporting a dead body?" And "How could the body have remained undisturbed in the cave through the winter, inundated by high seas?" Points such as "Foreign hostesses—drug-crazed sluts" and "so he actually *did* freeze his dog after all."

But the body of material was so vast, so promiscuously inclusive and unfocused, that any value it had was overwhelmed in a slurping swamp of weirdness and tedium. Did Obara genuinely believe that anyone would digest all this raw documentary matter? Whom did he expect to influence by its publication? The judges had heard it all in court. Even if they were assumed to be susceptible to public opinion, there was

*For a fuller account of the publication of *The Truth About the Lucie Case*, see pp. 448–49.

nothing here, if any member of the public bothered to read it, to sway it in his favor. Obara did it because he could do it, because he had to do something, and because by this stage there was nothing else left to do.

And yet there was one obvious ploy to which he had never resorted. Japanese courts attach much credit to evidence of previous good behavior and to the testimony of character witnesses. The upstanding fraud, the philanthropic arsonist, and the well-liked flasher who offer evidence of their worthiness can all expect to be treated more leniently. Obara understood this, which was why he had boasted of his ongoing charitable donations—in May 2006 alone, he gave ¥5 million each to Save the Children, Amnesty International, and the Japan Red Cross.

Much more valuable would have been the personal testimony of those who knew, and liked, Obara: the childhood classmate, the old schoolmaster, the university chum, the business partner—anyone with anything at all good to say about him.* Obara had tried everything else; he would surely have produced such people if they existed. But, on the face of it at least, this was one of the most extraordinary of the many extraordinary things about him—he had advanced through childhood, youth, and well into middle age without possessing a single friend.

■ ■ ■

The verdict was to be delivered at 10:00 a.m. on Tuesday, April 24, 2007. This was 1:00 a.m. in Britain; if all went to schedule,

---

* *The Truth About the Lucie Case* (pp. 751–52) refers to various former teachers who "doted" on Obara, but none was ever called in his defense. In particular, "Professor Emeritus Sekiguchi" of Keio University is described as having been "shocked" at the news of Obara's arrest. Unfortunately, the professor died shortly before his former student was charged.

it would just be possible for me to get the news in the last edition of that morning's newspaper. But the timing would be uncomfortably tight, particularly if there was a delay. That morning I woke early and wrote the draft of a news story to which I could add details over the telephone after the verdict was announced.

It began:

> The Japanese property owner Joji Obara was convicted of the killing of the British bar hostess Lucie Blackman this morning and sentenced to life in jail [to be confirmed] after a sensational six and a half year trial.
>
> [Insert family reaction in court, judge's words]
>
> The verdict is a vindication for Ms Blackman's family, especially her father, Tim, who spent months in Japan pressing the police to search for his daughter after her disappearance in July 2000 . . .

I e-mailed this draft to London, drank a cup of coffee, and gathered up my laptop and notebooks. There would be a crowd at the court this morning; I needed to leave home early to get a place. My stomach was light with excitement, almost with trepidation.

Next week, it would be seven years since the day of Lucie's arrival in Japan. It was fifteen years since Carita Ridgway's life support had been switched off, and twenty-seven years since Tim had saved the baby Lucie from febrile convulsion. Thirty-eight years ago this week, Joji Obara's father had died, or been murdered, in Hong Kong, and around that time his second son, the repository of his hopes, had had his heart broken by the half-American girl named Betty. It was seventy years since Obara's parents had come to Osaka as poor colonial immigrants and eighty-four years since the pogrom after the Great Kanto Earthquake, when Japanese had killed Koreans like animals. Something connected all those moments, if only I could see it. I pictured the image of a tree, with sap circulating from roots deep in the earth. Its branches spread immeasurably high and broad; from them bristled an infinity of lesser limbs, each one quickened with moisture from deep below. Obara's distorted life was a twig of one of these; Lucie's death, her family's grief, and Sophie's near death were its fruit. No one of us had eyes capable of encompassing more than a tiny part of this twisted black tree; it was impossible to describe it in words. But this morning, Justice Tochigi would make official pronouncement on a tiny part of it. His terms—of guilt and innocence, harshness and leniency—were crudely narrow, but perhaps they were the best that anyone would manage. Out of the human mess of Lucie's and Carita's deaths and Obara's strange life, some kind of meaning was to be unpacked.

After all these years, it was momentous. I wrote in my notebook, "Can there be any chance that he will be acquitted? Surely not. The mass of circumstantial evidence. The absurdity of the defence. The overwhelming weighting of the scales of justice in favour of the prosecution. And yet . . ."

On the verge of leaving the house, anxiously aware of how late it had become, I switched on my laptop again and hastily wrote a second draft of the news story that began as follows:

The Japanese property owner Joji Obara was acquitted of the killing of the British bar hostess Lucie Blackman this morning after a sensational six and a half year trial.

[Insert family reaction in court, judge's words]

The verdict is a devastating blow for Ms Blackman's family, especially her father, Tim Blackman, who spent months in Japan pressing the police to search for his daughter after her disappearance in July 2000 . . .

In the end, 232 people lined up for the public seats, barely a quarter of the number at the opening hearing. It confirmed the view of the Japanese trial as a hollow ceremony: people were not interested in verdicts because they were so predictable. But every seat in the court was occupied. I could see the blond heads of Tim and Sophie in the front row, and beside them Annette, Nigel, and Samantha Ridgway. Obara was already seated, looking away from everyone and everything. I took my own seat. I had not expected this sensation of fluttering nervousness. But my deadline was so close. I found myself looking every fifteen seconds at my watch and then up again at the faces of the people in the courtroom around me, several of whom had become familiar. There was Yuki, the blogger groupie. There were the frowning court artists, and a detective whom I recognized, and behind him the old man with the flower in his trilby. A young and rather gaunt blond man in a mackintosh was seated in the very back row, taking notes.

The judges swept in abruptly from the back of the court, and everyone rose to their feet.

Eight minutes later I was in the open air outside the courthouse, stabbing at my mobile phone, with other reporters milling all about me. "It's the second version," I said when the voice in London answered.

"Go with the second version. He's been acquitted. But he's got a life sentence. Well, I'm sorry, that's what the judge said. I know, I know. I don't understand it myself."

From: Lloyd Parry, Richard
Sent: Tue 4/24/2007 14:36
To: Times Online; Times Foreign Desk
Subject: Lucie Blackman verdict copy—refile

[Resending this, having talked again to the lawyers. I think I've finally got it straight now.]

Richard Lloyd Parry
Tokyo

The Japanese property owner Joji Obara was acquitted of raping and killing the British bar hostess Lucie Blackman this morning in a devastating blow for her family and a grave embarrassment for Tokyo police and prosecutors.

Obara received a life sentence in prison, nonetheless, after guilty verdicts on eight other charges of rape and one of raping and killing an Australian hostess, Carita Ridgway. His legal team immediately said that he would appeal.

The chief judge in the Tokyo District Court, Tsutomu Tochigi, acquitted Obara of the abduction, rape, killing and dismemberment of Lucie Blackman, whose body was found buried in a seaside cave close to his home seven months after she went out for the day with him.

Justice Tochigi said that, despite circumstantial evidence, there was no direct proof—such as DNA evidence—linking Mr Obara to Ms Blackman's death.

But the text of the judgement reveals the court's revulsion for Mr Obara and the crimes of which he is convicted. "You treated these women as sexual objects to satisfy your lust," the judge told Mr Obara as he faced him in the dock.

"Your behaviour is not healthy sexual behaviour, but a filthy crime. Furthermore, you used lethal drugs such as chloroform that can cause death due to disordering of the liver function. One opinion might be that these women were careless, but I believe that they could not anticipate your deviant behaviour . . . You repeated the same routine, treating their lives and their bodies carelessly.

"It is rooted in your self-centred attitude based on your perverted sexual taste and deserves the most severe reproach."

Ms Blackman's family expressed outrage at Obara's acquittal on the charges relating to Lucie's death, and disgust at the Tokyo prosecutors for failing to construct a watertight case against him.

"I'm afraid to say the lack of justice for us today has been the failure of the prosecution team to develop the case adequately," said her father, Tim, who attended the hearing with Lucie's younger sister, Sophie. "Lucie has been robbed of her justice."

Ms Blackman's mother, Jane Steare, said in a statement from her home in Sevenoaks, Kent: "My worst fears have come true. As for my darling Lucie, I miss you so much. This aching void in my heart feels like it will never go away, but I truly believe that one day we will hug each other again. Your mummy will never give up hope of finding justice and the truth."

Mrs Steare, who divorced Mr Blackman before their daughter's disappearance, has denounced him for accepting ¥100 million from "a friend" of Obara in return for signing a statement questioning some of the evidence against him. But yesterday's ruling made it clear that the judge was moved to acquit Obara, not because of

the payment, but because of the lack of a
"smoking gun" linking him directly to Ms
Blackman's death.

"The defendant is recognised as being
involved in the damage and abandonment of Lucie's
dead body in some form," Justice Tochigi said.
"There is a suspicion that he was involved in the
death of Lucie in one way or another. [The fact]
that the defendant . . . gave false information
as if Lucie was alive and tried to cover up the
death supports such recognition. Then the problem
is how the defendant was involved in the death
of Lucie."

In Japan, both prosecutors and the defence
are allowed to appeal against an acquittal, so
it is likely that the case will continue for
several more years.

ends

PART SIX LIFE AFTER DEATH

24. HOW JAPANESE

"When the police were done, I flew back home to England and I was in a trance," said Louise Phillips. "I didn't sleep. I cried all the time. I thought that there were people coming to get me. I drank my way through it. I took a lot of drugs. I hated myself; I just didn't care about anything. I was staying at home, at my mum's house in Kent, and I was terrible to live with. It was terrible for my family too. I suppose that I didn't want to be alive. I had nightmares too, about being chased by someone, or trying to save Lucie from a house, and the house was burning down. Or about Lucie coming back, and saying, 'Here I am, I've been looking for you.' And about that phone call—the phone ringing and a voice saying, 'You'll never see her again.'"

The experience of bereavement is often compared to the loss of a limb, but rarely is it a neatly sutured surgical amputation. In the case of a young person who dies violently and unexpectedly, it is like the tearing of an arm from its socket. Muscles and arteries are ripped open; the shock and loss of blood threaten the functioning of organs far from the wound. After Lucie died, the private world through which she had moved was tipped permanently off its axis. The pain of the event surged outwards, afflicting not only her immediate family and close friends but people she had never known.

Sophie narrowly failed to kill herself and spent nine months in psychiatric care. During his first term at university, Rupert

Blackman became severely depressed. He came home and lived with Jane and spent much of his time alone in his room, weeping. Lucie's friend Gayle Blackman spent a year in counseling, and Jamie Gascoigne, the ex-boyfriend of Lucie who had gone out with Sophie to look for her in Tokyo, went through months of anger management. "After I found out what had happened, I just wanted to kill someone," he said. "I was a really horrible person. After a few months I started seeing a girl I worked with. I was an arsehole. I was brought up to treat women with one hundred percent respect, but the way I treated her was disgusting."

But the most stricken of all was Louise, who spent years in the clutch of suicidal thoughts. Booze and cocaine did less and less to keep them at bay. The ordeal was made all the harder by the promise, solemnly extracted by the police, that she say nothing about the case to the Blackman family. As a result, Lucie's closest friends, and Jane Blackman herself, shunned Louise, convinced that she was concealing some crucial article of evidence. She lived at home; apart from intermittent stints as a waitress, she never worked. Eventually, she fell in love and married a man she had first known as a teenager in Bromley, but always the dark shape of Lucie's death loomed on the edge of her vision, ready at any moment to roll in and black out her happiness. "Nobody was talking to me," Louise said. "Everybody blamed me. The guilt was crushing. I felt guilty at Christmas, guilty on my birthday. I felt guilty on my wedding day—so guilty that I was getting married, and she wasn't. I felt guilty for being happy, guilty for getting older. It seemed like it was my fault that I was here and she wasn't."

Lucie had gone away, and it had been understood that she would be invisible for a while. But, invisibly, she died; for the seven months that her limbs lay in the cave, she was nowhere. It would have been easier to assimilate if she had been struck down in public, in full view of family and friends. None of them was surprised when she was found to have been killed. Privately, although they would never have owned up to it, all had admitted to themselves that she was never coming back.

But when she was found, it was in a state that might have been calculated to inflict the greatest sense of violation on those who knew her. "I remember thinking about it while Lucie was missing," said Sophie. "I thought, 'She's probably not going to come back now—she's gone, and I can begin to accept that, but please don't let her have been chopped up.'" As the photographs that had been thrust before me confirmed, there could be no question of saying goodbye to Lucie's remains in person. Even her hair—Lucie's great pride, reflective of the light, the emblem of her loveliness—had been hacked or burned off. And then there was the baffling, protracted trial: grim and comic, lurid and tedious at the same time, with dead pigs in tents, frozen dogs, politely obliging gangsters, and the dark, evasive villain at the center of it.

A crew-cutted thug, a svelte psychopath, or a twitching inadequate—any of them would have been more satisfactory than Joji Obara, with his lisp and his loneliness and his fastidious, outlandish determination. Finally there was the verdict, which pronounced him guilty of everything except harming Lucie, and not because the judge thought he hadn't done it but because of the inadequacy of the evidence. And now the appeals, by prosecution as well as defense, with a further appeal available after that, and the possibility of all ten verdicts, convictions as well as acquittals, being reversed. There was nothing that could be taken for granted in this case; none of the comforting clichés applied, about just deserts and patience rewarded. Everything seemed designed to deny its victims the consolation of a familiar storyline.

The stresses generated by the case were centrifugal: they forced people apart rather than bringing them together. This was true not only within the Blackman family; many of those who knew Lucie well found themselves becoming alienated from friends, family, and one another. To those who cared about her, almost any reaction to Lucie's death was unsatisfactory. People were either coldly indifferent or intrusively curious. Everyone had a confidently held opinion, based on superficial exposure to newspaper and television reports, and often implying a judgment about the shadiness of Lucie's hostessing work and her stupidity in climbing into a stranger's car. Equally enraging were those acquaintances who exaggerated their closeness to Lucie, because of the glamour of association with such a celebrated victim and the status bestowed by an affected grief.

Even true friends found it difficult to broach the subject with one another. Jane described how her circles of acquaintances shrank, as people she had formerly known well confronted an uncommon challenge of social etiquette: What do you say to the woman whose daughter has recently been chopped up and buried in a cave?

Lucie's friend Caroline Lawrence came back to Sevenoaks for the Christmas after her disappearance and avoided all her old friends. "I didn't want to see, hear, think about it," she said. "I didn't go out at all. Once, I saw Sophie passing in the street and I hid. So selfish, but I couldn't bring myself to talk to her." It wasn't only the struggle to find appropriate words for Sophie. Her jolting physical resemblance to her sister, which became more pronounced as the years went by, gave more than one person the sensation of standing in the presence of the dead.

Sophie detected this, and her anger at the arbitrariness of such treatment (was she to be punished for resembling her sister?) increased her loneliness. She felt like a ghost for so much of the time anyway; she didn't need to see it in the eyes of others. Two years after Lucie's death, Sophie became conscious of having crossed an appalling threshold. It dawned on her that in the passing of time she had become older than her own older sister. It was impossible to explain to anyone how strange and desolating that felt.

■■■

Obara's libel case against me was dismissed by the Tokyo District Court in September 2007. He made an appeal to the High Court, and that too was thrown out eight months later. Perhaps he never expected to win; the point may not have been to prove himself right but simply to harry and intimidate me with a burden of time, paperwork, and expense. Japanese courts, in defamation actions, do not award costs against an unsuccessful plaintiff, and the legal bill for defending the action was £60,000, or about $90,000. *The Times* covered this without a flicker of hesitation or hint of reproach. A threshold had been crossed now, although this became obvious to me only later. For years, I had regarded the story from the detached and privileged distance of a reporter; now it had stepped up and tapped me on the shoulder. Japanese friends, in particular, wondered aloud if I should not ease off on my reporting of the case. But it was impossible to contemplate going back now.

I was not the only object of Obara's complaints. He sued, and won damages from, several Japanese weekly magazines, and from *Time* magazine, which in 2002 had made the mistake of reporting that he had associations with the yakuza. How could a bankrupt afford these expensive actions, on top of his retinue of criminal lawyers, private detectives, webmasters, and publishers, and the large disbursements of "condolence money"? The answer was his family. Control of Obara's assets had been passed to relatives, including his mother, Kimiko, now in her eighties; it was them, or their agents, who settled his lavish legal bills. I had heard that Kimiko was alive and still lived in the house where Obara had grown up. The youngest of her sons, Kosho Hoshiyama, also lived in Osaka, where he worked as a dentist and avoided journalists. Then there was the third brother, the aspirant writer, who called himself Eisho Kin. None of the family had ever attended the trial or given an on-the-record interview. Apart from submitting their bills, even Obara's lawyers had only fleeting and infrequent contact with them. From Tokyo I took the bullet train to Osaka in search of the Kim-Kin-Hoshiyama family.

The cab I caught from the station was owned by Kokusai Takushii—International Taxis, the firm, still owned by Kimiko, on which the family fortune had been built. I went to the plot of land where Obara had planned to build his bubble tower and found it occupied by an empty multistory car park. I found the home where the family had first lived, a shabby house on an alley off a cheap shopping street. It too was deserted; around the corner, one of the family pachinko parlors was shuttered and dark. From there I went to the rich residential district of Kitabatake, where houses were still built in the traditional style, with high walls of clay-covered brick and heavy front gateways roofed in tiles. In front of one of these was a plate bearing the name of Obara's mother. I pressed the button on the intercom, and after a long wait, the voice of an elderly lady answered.

"Is that Mrs. Kim?"

"She's not here," the voice said faintly.

"You're not Mrs. Kim?"

"I'm the housekeeper."

"When will Mrs. Kim be back?"

"I don't know."

I was fairly sure that this was Mrs. Kim.

As I walked away, a man came out of the next-door gate. He was about fifty years old, wore a crumpled white shirt untucked over black trousers, and carried two plastic bags stuffed with rubbish or dirty laundry. He walked at frantic speed, his head tilted forward. I knew that this must be Eisho Kin.

"Mr. Kin!" I called out as I trotted to catch him up. "Mr. Kin, may I speak to you?" He paused and turned as I introduced myself, and with the introduction he became immediately enraged. I was used to situations where my presence as a reporter was not welcomed, but Eisho Kin was one of the angriest people I had ever met. There were no preliminaries to his outburst, no buildup of irritation. As soon as I had handed him my business card and identified myself, he simply exploded with fury.

"I am a publisher!" he snarled, apropos of nothing in particular. "You should read my books!"

"Well, Mr. Kin, I read your story, about the Korean man and the deaf boys," I said. "I was interested by it. Could I talk to you sometime?"

"I haven't seen my brother for thirty years," he said. "If you ever come back here, I will take certain measures. I don't want you to come any closer to me." Mr. Kin stopped, and I stopped too. But he kept talking, placing his bags on the pavement and jabbing his finger at me with rolling eyes.

"If these girls come to a foreign country and follow a guy, a guy who isn't good-looking, to his apartment—what do you really think about that? Why would she do that?"

"Well, I don't know, Mr. Kin. If you mean Lucie Blackman, she thought that Mr. Obara was going to give her a present."

"You are *stupid*!" he said, and he was pacing ahead again with his bags, looking back over his shoulder at me as I tried to keep up. "It's absurd. You must have bigger issues to pick up than this minor thing. *What about global warming?*"

"Well, I write about various issues—"

"How many times have you seen in Thailand a beautiful girl with some ugly guy?"

"Quite often, I sup—"

"It's a waste of time."

"I'm sorry if—"

"Are you doing this for money?"

"It's my job, if that's what you mean. I—"

"My father was in prison for two and a half years," he said in English. He had stopped walking again and put down his bags. "He was resistance, fighting the Japanese. But the only thing I can blame him is, he has no time to take care of the family. But he always said the importance of education."

I nodded in a way that I hoped would communicate empathy and understanding.

"I don't go abroad, but I speak Japanese, Korean, Chinese, and English."

I kept nodding.

"I'm not rich," he said. "The Japanese media say that my brother is the property tycoon of eastern Japan. Such stupid . . ." He waved his hand in disgust.

"Don't come here again," he said. "Never come back. Never come close to me. If you come back, I'll take certain measures."

"Mr. Kin, I don't wish to bother you, I just have a few . . ."

He was stamping away down the street with his rubbish or laundry, still muttering and shaking his head as he went.

■ ■ ■

In March 2007, a month before the verdict in the Tokyo District Court, a twenty-two-year-old British woman named Lindsay Hawker was murdered in Tokyo's eastern suburbs. She was a teacher of English. One Sunday, she went to the apartment of a twenty-eight-year-old man named Tatsuya Ichihashi after giving him a conversation lesson and never returned home. When the police called there the following day, Ichihashi fled from them in his stockinged feet. The officers found Lindsay buried in a soil-filled bathtub. She had been beaten, raped, and throttled.

Her father, Bill Hawker, a driving instructor from the Midlands, flew out to Japan to identify her body and bring it home. Like Tim Blackman before him, he gave a press conference, at a hotel close to Narita Airport. The circumstances were different, of course: unlike Lucie, Lindsay's fate was immediately known, and the only mystery was the whereabouts of her killer. But in Bill Hawker I recognized the model of the grieving parent, the role in which circumstances had cast Tim Blackman, and that he had always refused to play.

Bill Hawker was a man possessed by pain, quite incapable of calculation or control. Grief for his daughter overwhelmed anger at her killer. It was hard to look at him. It seemed shameful that he should be required to weep and choke before strangers, and heartless to ask questions. We asked them anyway, and the camera flashes illuminated the twisted mask of his face. Bill Hawker was everything that Tim had not been, and everything the world expected of a man in his situation: broken, helpless, turned inside out by loss.

Tatsuya Ichihashi, meanwhile, had vanished in his socks: it would be thirty-two months before the police caught up with him. It turned out that he had a history of approaching foreign women and had followed Lindsay home one evening after encountering her on a station platform. The nationality of the victim and the method of disposing of the body made it an extraordinary and freakish crime, and yet, for many people, there was something naggingly appropriate about the fact that this murder had taken place in Tokyo.

How many times foreigners—in Japan and in Britain—commented on "how Japanese" Lindsay Hawker's death was, without ever being able to say exactly why. The case spoke to unarticulated but deep-seated stereotypes. A jumble of images and ideas were called to mind, involving stalkers, repressed and perverted sexuality, pornographic comic books, and notions about the way Japanese men regarded Western women. It was as if, far from being an appalling aberration, the death of Lindsay Hawker was an accident waiting to happen. Japanese too had an anxious sense of this, especially since Bill Hawker's pronouncement at the press conference that the murder of his daughter had "brought shame on your country." That weekend, Japanese television nervously sent a film crew onto the streets of London to ask passersby whether Lindsay's death had sullied their image of Japan.

The sense of déjà vu, of course, was a result of Lucie's case, and as the years passed, people became so confused between the British girl buried in the cave and the British girl in the bathtub that they came to seem like a single incident. But apart from the country where they occurred, the nationality and youth of the victims were all that the crimes had in common. Two women had been killed, seven years apart—that was all. And yet for many people the compulsion to draw conclusions from their deaths, about Japan and Japanese people as a whole, was irresistible.

In the media, much of this generalization was concerned with Japanese sexuality and particularly the imagined tastes of Japanese men. The *chikan*, gropers who operated on crowded trains, were cited, as were Japan's "infamously" pornographic manga comics, with their representations of wide-eyed foreign-looking beauties vigorously violated by frowning salarymen. Former gaijin English teachers and hostesses were wheeled out by the newspapers to tell "horrifying" stories of Japanese stalkers. "What is the fascination that Western women seem to hold for Japanese men?" asked one tabloid reporter, who found his answers on a pub crawl through Roppongi.

> "They look down upon us, yet at the same time they look up to us, if that makes sense," one 24-year-old language teacher from Liverpool told me as she drank with friends in a bar at the start of the weekend.

"It makes it difficult for us to really understand them. I've been trying to translate their behaviour for the entire year that I've been here and I still don't know how to read them." While some British women described the attitude of the men they encounter here as strange, uncomfortable and unpredictable, others talked of the awe and mystique Western women hold for the Japanese male.

Taller, more independent and liberated than their female Japanese counterparts, they are regarded with a curious combination of attraction, fear and disapproval . . . "They view the more beautiful Western women, particularly the taller ones, as goddesses," says a British woman working for a Tokyo stockbroking firm who was with friends in Roppongi's Hub Bar last night . . . "The Japanese are so very different to us that I wonder sometimes if we will ever really understand them."

The implication of all this was spelled out in the story's headline: "Japanese Men, Smoky Bars and the Obsession with Beautiful Western Girls That Cost Lindsay Her Life."

Japan has a population more than double that of Britain, but in 2005 it recorded 2.56 million crimes, fewer than half the 5.6 million reported in England and Wales. Most remarkably, only 3.5 percent of these were crimes of violence, compared to 21 percent in Britain. How many young British women had been murdered in New York, Johannesburg, or Moscow in the years separating the deaths of Lucie Blackman and Lindsay Hawker? Nobody was interested in finding out. By the standards of any comparably developed Western nation, Tokyo is a fantastically safe place to live: break-ins are rare, car theft is virtually unknown, and women can walk the streets alone, without anxiety, at all times of the day and night. One of the reasons why Japan's police frequently appeared so bumbling was that they had so little practice fighting real crime.

The notion that Japanese men are "obsessed" with Western women is a racist cliché: cocky, skirt-chasing foreign men with an appetite for Japanese girls are far more in evidence than the famous gropers. Japanese pornography and manga are unique in their style, but the idea that the Japanese masturbators are greater consumers of porn than their counterparts in the West is contradicted by all the facts. And anyone who believes that this is a sexually repressed country has only to spend a Friday night among the Roppongi girls, who feed on foreign men with equal enthusiasm and appetite.

What makes Japan "so very different"? Not merely the characters on the signs and the faces of the people. There is something far deeper, a fugitive quality, difficult to put into words, the source of so much of the pleasure, as well as the frustration, of the life of the gaijin: a drastic unfamiliarity about the atmosphere of the streets, gesture of individuals, and the emotion of the crowd. An intense and thrilling energy drives Tokyo, but it is narrowly channeled by constraints of convention and conformity. The closest most people come to identifying this is to talk of Japanese "restraint" and "politeness," and it greatly complicates the business of reading people and understanding situations.

Japanese men rarely make the overt displays of aggressive masculinity that Westerners deploy to impress or intimidate. They seldom preen or strut; almost all of the time, they are the opposite of menacing and sinister. To newcomers like Lindsay or Lucie, with no command of Japanese, they appeared "sweet," "shy," often "boring." In fifteen years, I have seen only two fistfights in Japan. Each one exploded out of nowhere, with no preliminary shouting or goading or facing off, and came to an end with equal abruptness.

The effect of this, for many foreigners, is to disable instincts of caution and suspicion that guide and protect them at home. This is what united Lindsay Hawker with Lucie Blackman, conventional, "respectable" Englishwomen who would not have contemplated going to the apartment of a strange British man or working as a hostess in a London nightclub. Japan felt safe; Japan was safe; and under its enchantment they made decisions that they would never have made anywhere else.

Why did Lucie go to the apartment in Zushi with Joji Obara? Even those closest to her wondered whether she had not been foolish. "To go off with a man like that is just silly," her brother, Rupert, said. "I've always thought it was a very avoidable situation. If I try to imagine myself in her shoes, there's always a point along that journey where I would have said, 'Enough's enough. I'm not coming inside.'" But to Lucie herself, the events of that day would have flowed quite naturally. It was part of her assailant's cunning, perhaps, to avoid ever confronting her with a decision that aroused doubt or caution.

Meeting men in her own time was a hostess's job, and Lucie, struggling to meet her dōhan quota, close to being sacked, needed regular customers more than most. Then there was the promise of the mobile phone, which would have brought ease and convenience to her work, her friendships, and, especially, to her new love affair. About Obara himself, there was nothing obviously threatening. With his good English and his visible wealth, he was distinctly more desirable than many of Casablanca's clientele. And the original arrangement had been for nothing more than lunch, after all. It was Obara who had arrived so late and who proposed, out of nowhere, a journey to that homely, unmenacing, and comfortingly British-sounding place—"the seaside."

Lucie would have had little sense of how far, or in which direction, the seaside lay. By the time they reached it, after an uneventful drive, it was too late to worry about. Obara made no attempt to rush her into the apartment—first came the photographs by the sea and then, perhaps, the reasonable suggestion that, since it was so late, they might order in food rather than going to a restaurant. Once inside the apartment, the promised mobile phone was quickly handed over and activated. No one knew what happened next. The court made no detailed finding, and Joji Obara was acquitted of causing Lucie's death. But, after such a day with such a man, would it have seemed incautious or unusual to have accepted a glass of champagne, to have raised a toast, and to have drunk?

Many young women would have done the same thing in similar circumstances. Many more will in the future, and only the smallest fraction of them will ever come to harm. This, I began to think, was the sad and mundane truth about the death of Lucie Blackman: not that she was rash or idiotic, but that—in a safe, yet complex, society—she was very, very unlucky.

I put this once to Tim Blackman, and he immediately disagreed. "I don't think Lucie was unlucky," he said. "She was preyed upon by someone, someone who should not have been at large. Not unlucky. It was the failure of society to control someone who should not have been free. She was the victim of a failure of law and order."

Superintendent Udo, and the handful of other officers of the Tokyo Metropolitan Police who agreed to talk to me, were sincere, committed men who worked night and day in the hunt for Lucie's killer. Unfortunately, they served an institution that was, and is, arrogant, complacent, and frequently incompetent. The inadequacy of its police force is one of the mysterious taboos of Japanese society, a subject that the media and politicians strain to avoid confronting, or even acknowledging.*

At the local level, as directors of traffic, helpers of confused old ladies, and chastisers of the drunk and disorderly, they are outstanding. In cases of more serious crime, they are

---

*Other taboos include the power of organized crime and the ultranationalist far right, and the Imperial Family and its role.

competent at wringing confessions out of conventional Japanese criminals. But against almost any out-of-the-ordinary crime, they are lamentably ill equipped—sclerotic, unimaginative, prejudiced, and procedure-bound, a liability to a modern nation. Their performance, in the Lucie Blackman case and many others, suggests that the true reason for Japan's lack of crime lies not with its guardians but with its people, who are law-abiding, mutually respectful, and nonviolent not because of but despite the performance of the Japanese police.

Allowances must be made, of course, for the complications brought to the case by the victim's foreign nationality. The Japanese family of a daughter missing in Britain would have surely faced many of the same frustrations the Blackmans endured. But the true scandal was not the investigation itself, which was no more than routinely shoddy, with its slow start, the patchy tailing of Obara, the failure to spot the body in the cave. The most serious failure of the police was in not identifying and bringing Obara to justice years before. Katie Vickers, for one, had reported him in 1997; she was ignored. How many others, who have never told their stories publicly, experienced similar treatment? The greatest disgrace had been another five years before that, when the police dismissed the suspicions of Carita Ridgway's family about "Nishida," the man who brought their dying daughter to hospital. The failure was one of imagination, an institutional inability to think other than in clichés. People were types, and types were to be relied upon. The young hostess who went to a customer's place and then claimed rape must be trying it on; the respectable chap who talked of a bad oyster and food poisoning was to be believed. Against Obara, the Japanese police offered no protection whatsoever; he slipped freely in and out of the coarse mesh of their net. Lucie Blackman had been thirteen years old when Carita died: it might have ended there and then. "If the police had located Obara at that time, all they would have had to do was search his home, and they would have uncovered his decades-long crime spree," the Ridgways wrote in a statement on the eve of the verdict. "Obara spent thirty years as a serial rapist, drugging his victims. If the police had acted in 1992, as we had asked, Lucie Blackman would still be alive and many other girls, both Japanese and Western, would not have been drugged and raped."

■ ■ ■

Early in 2009, a year after the unsuccessful efforts to sue me for libel, a sequence of curious events occurred in my own life. It is important to begin by saying this: I have no evidence that they had any connection with Joji Obara.

A large, stiff envelope was delivered one morning to my home in Tokyo. It had taken several days to reach me; official marks indicated that it had bounced among several sub–post offices. It was addressed to someone called Kengo Namai at the Save the Nation Bulletin Co., but the address on the front of the envelope, an apartment on the far side of Tokyo, was unknown to the post office. The sender identified himself as "a Comrade" but provided no further contact information. Lacking a return address, the post office had opened it and, finding my name inside, had redirected it to me.

My home address was to be found on a sheet of paper inside the envelope, below a photocopy of my business card. The envelope also contained a stapled sheaf of printed documents, a couple sheets of photographs, and a hardback book in Japanese with the cover image of a woman in a tiara.

I looked at the photographs first. There were ten of them photocopied in color on two sheets of paper. They were photographs of me, sometimes alone, sometimes alongside friends. It was obvious that they had been taken covertly, by someone who had been following me for the purposes of surveillance.

Five of them were from three months earlier. I remembered the events of the day clearly: a bright Saturday afternoon in autumn, a late lunch with visitors from London. In the photographs, I was talking and smiling with my guests as we strolled home along a busy street of shops. Other images were harder to place. One might have been taken in an elevator, by a security camera; two others seemed to show me speaking in public, at some kind of lecture or gathering. I strained to remember these occasions and for the image of a furtive figure with a camera, but nothing came to mind. He—or she—had been there anyway, following me as I went about my unremarkable daily business, in streets close to my home.

Now I examined the other contents of the envelope. The book was one I recognized. It was the Japanese translation of *Princess Masako: Prisoner of the Chrysanthemum Throne* by an Australian journalist named Ben Hills, which had been published in a brief blaze of notoriety three years earlier. It told the unhappy story of Japan's crown princess, a bright and internationally educated former diplomat, who had been driven to chronic depression by the stifling demands of the imperial court, a state of affairs that was covered up for months by the palace bureaucracy. On publication, the book had been angrily denounced by the Japanese government; the offices of its Tokyo publisher had been picketed by angry ultranationalists. I had met Ben Hills once, when he interviewed me during his research, and his book quoted one or two of my articles about Princess Masako. In the copy of the translation that I held in my hands, each of the references to my name had been highlighted in yellow and the pages carefully marked with adhesive notes.

The last object in the envelope was the stapled document, six laser-printed sheets. It began abruptly, without salutation or introductory phrases: "The goal of Richard Lloyd Parry is to bring down the Japanese imperial family and after that to bring Japan itself under the control of Britain."

Princess Masako, a calumnious book about the imperial family, uses material provided by Richard Parry, who manipulated the Australian journalist, Ben Hills, and had him publish it. Although he has the title Tokyo Bureau Chief, Richard Parry has just one employee, and gets away with whatever he likes . . . He persists in insulting the imperial family overseas and if he is allowed, the situation will be beyond repair. We hope for a hero who will deal with Richard Parry.

At the moment, the items which calumniate the imperial family cannot be found on the Internet (they are not allowed to be found). What follows is the gist of articles, photographs, and other materials which used to be on the Internet.

Richard Parry, a man who plots against Japan, should not be tolerated anymore. The Parry clan slaughtered 186 Japanese soldiers during the Second World War. He insulted the imperial family and threw Japan into confusion . . . He provided materials to Ben Hills, who claims to be an Australian journalist, for the purpose of plotting against the Japanese imperial family by writing and publishing a book . . . We should not allow Richard Parry to insult the imperial family and throw Japan into confusion anymore.

This was a great deal of strangeness contained within a single envelope.

It was not the first time that I had been called an enemy of the imperial family, and other journalists who had reported on the depression of the crown princess had been accused of the same thing. To be named as the puppet master behind an Australian author, and of serving as an agent of British imperial ambitions, was a first. But the outstanding item among all this was the nugget of wartime history (completely new to me) and the image of wartime Lloyd Parry "clansmen" standing atop a heap of Japanese corpses. It was almost too far-fetched to be made up. I found myself smiling as I read. It reminded me of somebody . . .

But it was clear what had happened. Somebody, most likely a private detective, had carefully compiled this dossier. Judging from its impersonal tone, he had probably made multiple copies of it and sent out a wave of mail shots to numerous addresses, among them the Save the Nation Bulletin Co. But either the organization had moved or gone out of business and so, by chance, this envelope had ended up in my hands—the last person it was intended for.

Its name suggested that the Save the Nation Bulletin Co. was a right-wing ultranationalist group—one of many, large and small, that exist across Japan and that mount noisy demonstrations against people and organizations deemed insufficiently patriotic. Academics or public officials who disparage Japan's wartime conduct, the embassies of Russia, South Korea, and China, journalists held to have embarrassed the imperial family—all of these, from time to time, incur the displeasure of the *uyoku*, or rightists, which inevitably expresses itself in the same form—a visit by one or more black vans blaring denunciations through high-powered loudspeakers, with rippling Rising Sun flags mounted on their roofs. Sometimes these groups have links to yakuza gangs; very rarely, acts of violence are associated with them. Whoever had sent this package hoped to inflame the anger of such people against me personally, in the hope that one of them would take it upon himself to visit my home or office and "deal with" me.

The word used for this expression is *seibai*. The Japanese friend to whom I showed the document puzzled over how to translate it. "'Deal with' is probably okay," she told me. "You could also say 'judge' or 'punish.' 'Subjugate,' 'vanquish' even. It isn't a good word. Not a good word at all. I think that you should take this to the police."

I didn't expect the police to take it seriously, but I was wrong. Within a few minutes of my arrival, four detectives were sitting in the small interview room examining the envelope and its contents with gloved hands. I was asked if I had ever been conscious of being followed, whether I'd received any strange telephone calls recently or seen any suspicious people or vehicles loitering near my home or office. The answer to all of these questions was no.

"Have you made any enemies?" asked the chief detective, a small, weathered-looking man with a heavily lined smoker's face.

Occasionally, of course, people had been upset by articles I had written. Like every reporter who writes about the imperial family, particularly about the sad story of Princess Masako, I had received an angry letter and a barking phone call or two, and been denounced anonymously in the more obscure reaches of the Internet. But only one person had taken any serious action against me.

"You were right to bring this to us," said the chief detective. "It's this word *seibai*—it's an unusual word to use in a letter like this. But it implies violence. Do you watch TV samurai dramas? It's the word that samurai use about attacking their enemies. And when the samurai deal with someone, they do it with a samurai sword."

The detectives kept the package to check it for fingerprints. I asked whether I needed to take any precautions. The chief frowned and nodded his head. "When you take the subway, don't stand close to the edge of the platform," he said. "Stand back. That makes it difficult for someone to push you in front of the train. Same when you're crossing the road—stay back from the curb. Otherwise just keep an eye open for anything suspicious and call us straightaway if you spot anything. We'll inform the local police station, so the officers on patrol will be aware of this and keep an eye on your place."

One of the police detectives specialized in following the

activities of the far right. He knew of the Save the Nation Bulletin Co. and Kengo Namai, and he telephoned him there and then. The group's address had indeed changed, Mr. Namai confirmed—and he had never received a copy of this, or any similar, package. The detective described its contents and asked him what he made of it. Mr. Namai was unimpressed. Ultranationalists receive plentiful crank mail, he said. No right-ist with any gumption would act on the promptings of an un-signed, unsourced screed such as this.

■ ■ ■

There is nothing like the suspicion that you are being followed to open your senses to the world around you. Over the next few weeks, Tokyo took on a dreamlike sheen and burnish, as if shot through exquisite filters by a visionary cinematographer. Details to which I had never before paid attention suddenly glowed with powerful and sinister significance—cameras, sunglasses, the color and make of parked vehicles, the clothes and features of people I passed in the street. I found myself living every mo-ment as if I might have to give a detailed account of it, under oath. The most mundane part of the day, the fifteen-minute subway journey to my office, became a heroic struggle to avoid assassination. It was laughably ridiculous and queasily alarming.

The months passed. There were no attempts to pitch me into the path of a commuter train, no blows from glinting samurai swords, no more strange letters, phone calls, or anom-alies of any kind. A detective called one day to say that none of the fingerprints on the envelope had come up on the police database. I was starting to become almost blasé about the act of crossing the road, when, in June 2009, a telephone call came from the police station close to my office. A group of ultranationalists, calling themselves the School of the Refined Heart, intended to carry out a demonstration against me, and—

in the orderly and law-abiding way of the Japanese extremist—had filed a formal notification of their plans. The police could not stop them from invoking their right to free speech, but they were giving me due warning.

The School of the Refined Heart appeared as arranged a few days later—four middle-aged men in an elderly flag-draped black van. It was the classic uyoku protest: a few turns around the office building, and an amplified broadcast of their demand—that Richard Parry of *The Times* apologize for insulting the imperial family. The men tried to enter the building, but the security guards politely blocked them. They presented a letter addressed to me; it was refused. They posted it in the mailbox in front of the building—but because they had failed to attach a stamp, it never arrived.

After half an hour they drove away in their black van. They came back a month and a half later, and performed the same drill, with van, slogans, and letter. And after that I didn't hear from them, or anyone like them, again.

The whole affair remained a mystery. I still cannot say who it was who went to such extravagant lengths to encourage fascists to "deal with" me, or what was his—or her—motive. But the incident was impossible to forget, and it had an intriguing coda. Months afterwards, I met Yasuo Shionoya, one of Joji Obara's lawyers, whom I had contacted in a final, and unsuccessful, attempt to gain an audience with his client. I told him the story of the strange package, and the photographs, and the men in the black vans—and a complicated expression crossed Mr. Shionoya's face, part amusement, part surprise. He said, "I was talking to Mr. Obara once, and your name came up in conversation. He talked about articles you had written, about the Japanese royal family. He said, 'Parry's articles made the right-wingers angry. I think that he may get some trouble from them, one of these days.' I asked, 'What kind of trouble?' and he said, 'Oh, I don't know.'"

25. WHAT I REALLY AM

What was Joji Obara, and what made him what he was? I spent years thinking about him, talking about him, and watching him in court—but how much did I truly know? Stretches of his life were a blank: his years of traveling after school, much of the period between his return to Japan and his arrest. I had exhausted the obvious sources of information. His family was hostile and uncooperative; from Obara himself, I had had only evasiveness and writs. The police, who made a fuller reckoning of his life than anyone else, were incurious about anything that could not be used in court. Even Carlos Santana, his most celebrated and unexpected "friend," refused to talk about him. And long before he had committed any crime, Obara himself had begun the task of erasing himself from his life as he moved through it, of frustrating anyone who might draw out patterns and make connections between the past and present. He changed his eyelids, he changed his name, he changed his nationality. He wore dark glasses and built up his shoes. He avoided the fixing gaze of the camera with the fervor of those isolated peoples who believe that a photograph snatches away a man's soul. Even his sexual assaults were furtive, the opposite of rape as an assertion of male power: most of his victims, until they were shown the videos recovered by the police, did not know with certainty what had been done to them.

Was that why he formed so few close relationships? Because friendship, among other things, represented a personal trace, a clue to identity as unique as a fingerprint, left upon the wider world? These days we are all amateur psychiatrists, and the connections between early experience and adult patterns of behavior are readily and sometimes glibly made. In Obara's case there were obvious pressures on him even as a young boy—the expectations of his mother, the presence of a disturbed older brother, the loss of a father, the covert, instinctive prejudice experienced by all Koreans in Japan, and the dizzying, devastating liberation from duty and discipline brought by his sudden inheritance. But there were countless anxious children in Japan, and millions of disturbed families, spoiled rich kids, and victims of racism, and none but a tiny fraction of them went on to become serial rapists and killers.

During the trial, the question of Obara's sanity, or the lack of it, never came up; no psychiatric evaluation was carried out. Superficially, the characteristics attributed to Obara in Justice Tochigi's judgment matched some descriptions of the psychopath—"a self-centered, callous, and remorseless person profoundly lacking in empathy . . . a person who functions without the restraints of conscience," according to one definition. But I have my doubts about such diagnoses, which represent a convenient moral, as well as clinical, judgment, designed to offer spurious and unearned comfort to society at large. By attaching a label to extreme behavior—monstrous, psychopathic, "evil"—and placing its perpetrators in a category reassuringly apart from "good" people, we could all worry a bit less about the complexities of human nature and the extent to which we might all, at one time or other, behave callously or without remorse. There was a similar impulse at work in the Japanese commentary—much in evidence on the Internet but rarely intruding into the mainstream media—that empha-

sized Obara's status as a Korean, as if the fact of foreign an-
cestry exculpated Japanese society of responsibility for him.

Whatever Joji Obara was, he came out of Japan—but it
was so difficult to say exactly where. At first, I suppose, I
had hoped to achieve the conventional feat of "getting inside"
Obara's mind. If I could imagine the kinds of thoughts he entertained, alone in his cell, or kneeling in front of the breathing, unconscious body of one of his victims, then I could
congratulate myself on having "understood" my subject. But
such knowledge was an illusion. Unlike their words or actions, the thoughts and emotions of other people are unavailable to us. Even those we know best are strangers, whom we
understand, if we ever do, intermittently. Perhaps Obara had a
rich interior life, denied to the world at large. Perhaps I could
unlock it, but I would never know whether I had truly succeeded, or if I was just the victim of my own vanity, or Obara's
play.

Or perhaps there was nothing to understand. What if
there was no inside but only what was visible? Perhaps the
truth would have been boring, perhaps there was actually little
to say, and perhaps this was the great secret that Obara was at
pains to conceal. From what I could see, his life was most
strongly characterized by the absence of close personal relationships, almost to the extent of complete isolation. There
must have been reasons, painful and fascinating, why he had
closed himself off from the world, but they were locked fath-
oms deep. It made more sense to think of him as an absence
too, in the way that sudden and intense cold is nothing more
than the absence of heat, and blackness is the lack of light.
Obara came like a blizzard of darkness and withered the lives
he came into contact with. This was his true measure—not a
"self" that was available for scrutiny and evaluation but the
effect he had on others.

In court, he had presented receipts for his charitable work and asked to be judged by the good this brought about. Why not, in the same way, judge the damage he did, and let that be the measure of his character? Shape-shifter, he was the pain of his victims; whatever mysteries he kept close, he was the damage he had done.

He was Jane's crusading fury over the "blood money" and Tim's stubbornness and humiliation in accepting it. He was the pills and vodka in Sophie's blood, and Rupert's lost year of mental breakdown. He was the rage kindled in Jamie Gascoigne. He was the effect of all of this pain at two or three removes—the suffering and confusion it brought to Jamie's girlfriend, the family memory of dead Lucie—aunt, great-aunt—in children yet unborn.

Humans are conditioned to look for truth that is singular and focused, hanging for all to see, like a clear, full moon in a cloudless sky. Books about crime are expected to deliver such a photographic image, to serve up a story as dry as a shelled and salted nut. But as a subject, Joji Obara sucked away brightness; all that was visible was smoke or haze, and the twinkling upon it of external light. The shell, in other words, was all that was to be had of the nut. But the surface of the shell turned out to be fascinating in itself.

■ ■ ■

Everyone who came into contact with the Blackmans, and many of those who knew them only through newspapers, formed powerful and entrenched opinions about their story. Everyone insisted on being in the right. Not only about the question of Joji Obara's guilt but also about Lucie herself, her family, and Japan as a nation. This drive to pass judgment was one of the extraordinary effects of the case.

It was focused most intensely upon Tim and his decision

to accept the ¥100 million. In the weeks that followed, it often felt as if he had been convicted of a crime equivalent to that of Obara. "His pain will be twofold," a columnist in the *Daily Mail* prophesied. "He will agonise over what he could have done differently to save his beautiful daughter from the tawdry hostess career that led to her death; and he'll be racked by guilt over the part he played in denying her the justice she deserved." Or as Jane said to me, "I feel I've been fighting two men. I've been struggling to bring them both to justice— Obara and Lucie's father."

What precisely had Tim done wrong? There was a single question to be answered about the condolence money, and an undeniably important one: Did it influence in any way the outcome of the case? In their written decision, the judges had stated explicitly that the payments received by the rape victims had made no difference to the life sentence that they had imposed, the maximum that the law allowed. In Japanese justice, this was the only effect that a payment of this kind was capable of making. Japanese courts can be reproached for various shortcomings, but acquitting killers because they have money is not one of them. Obara was found not guilty of harming Lucie because the court, rightly or wrongly, found the evidence to be lacking.

Of course, the popular verdict passed upon Tim was not legal but moral. "How could any father take cash [from] his daughter's [accused killer]?" asked one reader of *The Sun* newspaper, in a page of similar letters. "Tim Blackman should now hang his head in shame." It was one of those pronouncements that serve as a statement of one's own superiority of character. In between the lines of each of these letters flickered the unspoken brag: *I would never do such a thing.* To which my instinctive response was: *How do you know?* and *Why do you care anyway?*

It is exciting to imagine ourselves in extreme circumstances in which we are tested, morally and physically; in our own minds, we always pass such a test. Everyone who has children has dreamed of their deaths and understood it to be the worst of all losses. But beyond that, we can do no more than fantasize. We may hope that we would behave with dignity, restraint, and determination. But none of us can know with certainty, any more than we can predict the course of a rare and life-threatening disease.

This is all the more true when the element of money is introduced. The letters pages of the newspapers were full of sneers about the "price" that Tim was accused of having set on Lucie's life. But there are few people for whom money, at some level or other, is not a crucial element in many of the choices they make. Justice was unaffected by ¥100 million paid to Tim Blackman; he harmed no one else by his decision. And the leisure it purchased for him brought ease to a life that had been twisted out of shape by anxiety and pain. He put some of it into the Lucie Blackman Trust, he promised to set some of it aside for Sophie and Rupert, and he spent part of it on the purchase of a classic yacht, the sixty-year-old *Infanta*, in which he would spend a happy year sailing around the world in 2008.

There was much public tutting about such indulgence. But if the money had come from a court victory, or from an officially administrated compensation fund, it would not be considered anyone's business how it was spent. Most people, in Tim's circumstances, would also discover their "price." If the money proffered was enough to wipe out a burdensome debt, or bring comfort to a sick relative, or see a surviving child through her education, or provide security for retirement, how many of us, given a certain level of reward, would not eventually say, "I have suffered: I deserve this"?

I hope that I never have to confront a loss like that of the Blackmans, and that I never discover my own set of those particular moral bearings. Perhaps I would grieve like Jane, or like poor Bill Hawker. Perhaps I would be all energy and action like Tim. I might reject any financial compensation, or I might regard it as the very least to which I was entitled. I don't know, and nor does anyone else—and none of us has the right to judge those who have been unlucky enough to suffer such a torment.

Jane Steare was in a position to pass that judgment, and so were Annette, Nigel, and Samantha Ridgway. The Ridgways shared Tim's loss exactly, and despite repeated blandishments from Obara's lawyer, they consistently rejected the same offer of money. Jane took comfort in this solidarity with the Australian family. She and Annette used to speak to one another over the phone, and they became friends of a kind, united by the loss of their daughters. Until July 2008—when Nigel Ridgway, with the agreement of his ex-wife and daughter, signed a document stating that he believed Obara was capable of "rehabilitation" and questioning some of the evidence used to convict him of killing Carita. In return, the Ridgway family received ¥100 million of their own. They had suffered; there were no other sources of compensation; they felt they deserved it. Jane received the news with deep distress. Carita's father, mother, and sister, she told me, had "all sold out to evil."

■ ■ ■

People are afraid of stories like Lucie's, stories about meaningless, brutal, premature death, but most of them cannot own up to their fear. So they take comfort in the certainty of moral judgments, which they brandish like burning branches waved in the night to keep off the wolves.

Jane, too, needed to be right about Lucie, and she needed those who felt differently, including her daughter, and above all her ex-husband, to be in the wrong. Her own conviction was not enough; she wanted Tim's wrongness to be proclaimed upon him in court. But there is no right and wrong to loss, to grief. The pain is circular; it is its own fulfilment. Summoning the strength to break out of it was the task each of the Blackmans faced.

Part of the struggle was to find some good in Lucie's death, a silver lining to the black fog. Tim looked for it in the Lucie Blackman Trust. It had begun as a bank account number handed out in Tokyo at one of his press conferences. Eventually, and despite Jane and Roger Steare's efforts, it was legally registered as a charity. Apart from the rape alarms and antispiking kits, its website carried commonsense information about safety for young people traveling and nightclubbing. There were fund-raising events, patronized by a comic actor and a famous model; in 2007, a teenage Liverpudlian named Nathalie was "crowned" Miss Lucie Blackman Trust. Not all its schemes worked out—the manufacturer of a gadget called the BuddySafe, promoted by the trust, went bust within a few months; and several of the links on the website were broken and nonfunctional.

But Tim was proud of the trust's Missing Abroad program, which offered help to British families in the same situation in which he had found himself after Lucie's disappearance. Once, he would have thought of his experience as unique in its exotic awfulness. But every few months, there was a new case very like it.

There was Wendy Singh, a thirty-nine-year-old mother, murdered by her husband in Fiji. There was Amy Fitzpatrick, a shy Irish girl of fifteen, who disappeared close to her mother's home in Spain on New Year's Day. There was Michael Dixon, a thirty-three-year-old journalist, who vanished during a holiday in Costa Rica. And there was Alex Humphrey, a twenty-nine-year-old health-care worker, who walked out of a hotel in Panama on his way to visit a famous waterfall and never returned.

None of these missing people conjured the intensity of coverage given to Lucie's case: because the victims were older or less photogenic, because there was no international summit meeting in Fiji or Costa Rica that season and no Tony Blair to take an interest in the case—chance, in other words. Tim's trust did the kinds of things for the families of the missing or killed that the Foreign and Commonwealth Office could not do—provide twenty-four-hour hotlines for tip-offs and sightings, upload posters and case histories onto its website, and pay for visits by relatives and the repatriation of bodies. The FCO lent its support as a partner to the scheme; and, also as a result of Lucie's disappearance, the Metropolitan Police instituted a system of family-liaison officers for the relatives of those who had gone missing abroad.

All of this brought a kind of satisfaction, but Tim smiled wryly and shook his head when well-meaning people spoke tentatively to him of the possibility of "closure." No success imaginable—in his charity, in his professional or personal life—was ever going to equal or exceed or cancel out the loss of Lucie. The most he could hope for was to contain the loss and prevent it from overwhelming everything else in his life. The image came to his mind of a bulging black rubbish bag, stuffed with all the grief and frustration and regret associated with Lucie and her fate. The thought of opening the bag and sifting through its slimy contents made him feel that he was unraveling. He never acted upon suicidal thoughts, but they occurred frequently. It was not only the urge to escape from the heaviness of life but also the hope that, in dying, he would be reunited with Lucie.

"Lucie was dead," Tim said. "Sophie was an inpatient in a sanatorium. Rupert had flunked out of university and had a nervous breakdown. It had been such a burden for such a long, long time, and instead of getting better it was actually all getting worse. I was feeling in great danger. It was hard to see that I'd ever, ever come out on the other side." Certain days were especially bad—the anniversaries of Lucie's life and death, which were spaced out regularly throughout the year, so that there was never more than a few months without a reminder of what had happened. "She was lost on 1 July," Tim said, "her birthday was 1 September, she was found in February, and Christmas is difficult in any household, but worse when people are missing. The day she died is the worst, and I like to spend it sailing out in the Solent. She loved that stretch of water, and when I'm there I have a huge sense that she's not there with me."

■ ■ ■

Tim was at sea on December 16, 2008, when the satellite telephone on the *Infanta* rang. It was the deepest hour of the night. When he picked up it was my voice on the other end.

For the second time in two years, I was standing in front of the Tokyo courts complex, surrounded by reporters stammering into mobile phones. The judges in the High Court had just given their ruling on the appeals by Obara and the prosecutors. They had upheld Obara's convictions for the eight rapes and the rape and killing of Carita Ridgway. And they had partly overturned the acquittals on the Lucie Blackman charges. Obara had been found guilty of the abduction, drugging, attempted rape, and dismemberment of Lucie, and of illegally disposing of her body. The life sentence against him was confirmed.

"To violate the dignity of so many victims, using drugs, in order to satisfy his lust, is unprecedented and extremely evil," the chief appeal judge, Hiroshi Kadono, said. "There are no extenuating circumstances whatsoever for acts based on determined and twisted motives."

The verdict was complicated because on a single charge—of causing Lucie's death—Obara had once again been acquitted. It was true that the postmortem had not identified what killed Lucie, and it was impossible to know with certainty what had happened in the hours after her last telephone call. But Japanese courts could, and did, convict on circumstantial evidence.* It was very difficult to understand how, in the absence of any other suspect, a man could be found guilty of drugging, raping, and carving up a woman who had spent her last evening in his company—but not of killing her. Still, these new convictions were as surprising as the original acquittals; everyone I knew had expected the judges to rubber-stamp the earlier verdicts. Jane Steare, who was in court with Roger beside her, wept tears of relief. "This has been a harrowing ordeal, not just for today, but for over eight years," she said afterwards. "But at last we have two guilty verdicts and a life sentence . . . Today, truth and honor have prevailed, not only for Lucie, but for all victims of violent sexual crime."

I told Tim all of this over the satellite telephone line, and there was a silence filled with the hiss of the atmosphere. I had never known Tim to be speechless; I thought at first that the connection had been broken. I had to coax out of him the phrases that I needed for my newspaper story. "It is fantastic, and completely unexpected, and no less than Lucie deserves,"

---

*The most notorious such case was the "Wakayama curry killings." In 1998, two adults and two children died after consuming curry served at a village festival in Wakayama prefecture. A forty-seven-year-old woman, Masumi Hayashi, was eventually sentenced to death for the murders, after traces of arsenic were found in her home. Hayashi insisted that the poison was the residue of a pest-control business once operated by her husband. No one saw her lacing the curry, and the prosecutors failed to adduce a convincing motive for the indiscriminate killings.

he said eventually. "It's been such a long haul, such a merciless torture. But for the police and prosecutors to get him like this is a great achievement."

Tim thanked me for calling him and hung up. The *Infanta* was between Morocco and the West Indies, halfway through a transatlantic yacht race. There was almost no wind; sea and air were stilled by a dense tropical heat. On board his yacht, eight thousand five hundred miles from Tokyo, Tim was becalmed.

■ ■ ■

Obara appealed again, to the Supreme Court. This time his lawyers directed their attention to the story told in the prosecution indictment. They wanted to demonstrate the physical impossibility of maneuvering a dead body out of the apartment in Zushi Marina, back to Tokyo, down to Blue Sea Aburatsubo, and into the cave. This argument had been made before, and rejected, in the lower courts; this time, Obara attempted to make his point by means of a bizarre experiment. He had his lawyers purchase the same model of refrigerator in which he was accused of having stored the corpse in the house at Den-en Chofu, and he spent ¥1 million on a precisely molded mannequin of Lucie. "The mannequin is very delicate, and its skin is like human skin," his lawyer Yasuo Shionoya told me. "It weighs the same [as Lucie] and the size is the same. One of the lawyers who is about the same size as Obara tried to carry it and to put it into the freezer—it was completely impossible." A video of the fellow's exertions formed a central part of the appeal dossier.

From his cell in the Tokyo Detention Center, Obara continued to direct his legal battles, suing the *Yomiuri* newspaper for libel and fighting a claim for unpaid fees from the publisher of the strange book with the dead dog on the cover.

Shionoya talked about the appeal with modest confidence; there would be no verdict, he predicted, until the middle of 2011 at the earliest. But then, early in December 2010, Tim, Jane, and the Ridgways in Australia each received a telephone call from the Tokyo police with unexpected news. The appeal had been rejected by the Supreme Court. The guilty verdicts and the life sentence were now confirmed irrevocably; there was nowhere left for Joji Obara to run.* A life sentence in a Japanese court rarely means life, but on average the term served before parole is more than thirty years. Even counting the decade he served in detention, Joji Obara is unlikely to walk free before 2030, when he will be seventy-eight years old. As a convicted criminal, he was transferred to a prison with a regime drastically different from the detention center where he had lived since 2001. He shares a cell with other convicts; he is allowed none of the books and documents that furnished his life for the past decade. Visits are allowed just once a month, and even then only from members of his immediate family. Prisoners are not barred from seeing their lawyers, but permission must be obtained for each visit and is typically granted only once every few weeks.

"Until now, Obara has been his own chief lawyer, but that is impossible for him in prison," Shionoya told me. His legal team spent the last days before his incarceration huddled with their client, making hasty arrangements so that they could continue to manage his affairs without the daily contact to which they had grown accustomed.

The prosecutors had not appealed to the Supreme Court,

---

*In fact, a single legal avenue remained open: a retrial. Obara's lawyers argued that there was new evidence that had not been heard in the lower courts. But all of this had already been submitted to, and rejected by, the supreme court. As a means of winning Obara's freedom, retrial appeared to be a theoretical possibility only.

and so the single acquittal, on the charge of killing Lucie Blackman, stood. Jane held fast to her view that even the partial conviction of Obara was a victory, if not for Lucie then for Obara's victims in general. It was true, of course, and yet emotionally it hardly mattered at all. Well before the conclusion of Obara's trial, it had become impossible for those most closely connected with the case to hold it and all its details in mind.

It was not that justice was unimportant. But it altered nothing, or nothing that really mattered. It was as if, after a frantic contest of strength between two equally determined and unyielding opponents, one had simply relaxed its grip and walked away. Lucie was still gone—and what could ever make a difference to that? Such a loss was unquenchable. What might have been consolations—arrest of suspect, trial, a guilty verdict, ¥100 million—evaporated into it like spoonfuls of water tossed into a desert. What if Obara had admitted guilt, begged forgiveness, wept out his black heart? What if he had been charged with murder, rather than manslaughter, and sentenced to hang? Imagine the most extreme vindication and retribution—nothing that mattered would be alleviated or improved by it. There was no satisfaction that could be imagined, only greater and lesser degrees of humiliation and pain. Lucie had been a unique being, a precious, beloved human creature. She was dead, and nothing would ever bring her back.

All about me

I would like a magic ring that
would make me and my sister
fairies. We could have a castle and
flying ponys and powers.

WHAT I REALLY AM. I am kind and quite sensible says mummy and daddy. I can get very cross with my sister and brother. I am very thoughtful to other people and helpful to other people. I do not like racing my work even though someone is racing me. I am not keen on playing in the playground. I hate to eat omelets and swede [rutabaga] and peas. They are all my worst. I will tell you the thing I do not like but not my worst.

It is mushy peas.

"I used to think all the time about what he did to her," Jane said. "That was the worst thing of all—imagining Obara cutting up Lucie. My skull would want to burst with it; I thought I'd never get it out of my head. I'd hear a chain saw in a field, where someone was chopping down a tree, and I'd physically shake." Jane had been to see a psychotherapist, and she had talked to the mothers of other murdered children in Japan as well as Britain. All were kind and sympathetic, but none of it helped. Then she was introduced to a treatment called eye movement desensitization and reprocessing, or EMDR, widely used to treat post-traumatic stress disorder in soldiers returning from Iraq and Afghanistan. It was a mysterious therapy that often worked dramatically for reasons that even its practitioners could not fully explain.

"What would make you feel better?" the therapist asked during his first meeting with Jane.

"Just to know that she's safe," she answered.

"So then he told me to think of the horrible things that Obara did to Lucie," Jane recalled. "And then I had to follow his fingers, and he moves his fingers from side to side. And I'm thinking about it, and he's saying, 'She is safe, she is safe . . .'" Jane attended four sessions, and they were the only treatment that did any good. "Now, when I'm sitting in court, and the interpreter's going over these terrible things that Obara did, I repeat to myself, 'She is safe, she is safe . . .' and it helps. I think that was the turning point in saving me from going mad."

Jane said, "I don't believe in this thing called 'closure' or 'moving on.' What do you close, and where do you move on to? You learn to live with it. But I'll never be the same again. I can be in a supermarket and be feeling perfectly okay. And then I'll see a little girl who reminds me of Lucie when she was tiny, and my eyes will well up with tears, and I have no control." As the years passed, friends of Lucie had children of their own. Louise Phillips's baby was christened Lucia, and Samantha Burman's daughter was Grace Lucie. Jane was glad, and moved by the love of these young friends, but it was searing to be reminded of the kind of life Lucie would have enjoyed, if she had lived.

■ ■ ■

Jane hated everything about the Lucie Blackman Trust; in the war for possession of Lucie, it represented a devastating defeat. She hated the hypocrisy she saw in it—the good works of a father who had walked out, as Jane insisted, on his wife and children. Despite the conclusions of the British police and prosecutors, she still suspected it of concealing embezzlement and fraud. She wanted nothing to do with the trust and its work, but she still resented its existence and the way it had co-opted Lucie's name without any reference to Jane.

She found her own consolation in Lucie's death, in a dark fatalism that viewed her daughter as the tool of an impersonal destiny—a death, as well as a life, preordained. "I've told you this before," she said, "and I'm not making it up—but I knew that I would never see her again. I arranged for her to see a medium before she went to Japan, but she wouldn't go. When she was little, she was always so grown up—in a way, she was like my mother. And I feel that this was her destiny, Lucie's destiny. She was born for it. She was put on this earth to stop Obara. She wasn't meant to make old bones."

Lucie had to die, in other words; her death had been ines-capable, and Jane had foreseen it. She had been right again, and right to tell Lucie not to go to Japan. In all her sad story, from the death of her mother to her falling out with Sophie, Jane had not been wrong. Even in her choice of Tim, she had made no mistake, because the man she had married was not the husband who left her. "He was a different person," Jane said. "The man I lived with for nineteen years didn't exist." It was the only way that the facts could be compelled to make any bearable sense.

She was comforted at all times by an unwavering faith in Lucie's continued presence. Jane attended sessions with a me-dium, a woman named Tracy who lived in the London suburb of Penge. "I went to see her, and Lucie came through," Jane told me. "It was like I was speaking to Lucie for an hour. She was telling me things that she did—she said, 'Lucie's doing this with her hair, and you used to like stroking her hair.' And I did, I did like stroking it. Cynics would think that she's just saying that, but there were lots of things that she said, names that people just wouldn't know . . . I don't want to talk about them, but I know it was Lucie."

Jane said: "I do talk to her, in my mind. We went for a walk a few months ago and we saw a lovely house for sale and made an appointment to have a look. I said to Lucie, 'If you think this is right for us, give me some signs.' The signs are always butterflies and stars. On the front door was a little printed sign that said, 'Gone to the Beach.' Well, that's un-usual, isn't it, in the middle of the countryside? But the beach is where her body was found. Then we went inside and there were butterfly stickers all over the wall. Then upstairs there was a lampshade in the shape of a star, and in the garden there were butterflies dancing round, and a big topiary of a butter-fly. So I said, 'Okay, Lucie—thanks. We got the message.'"

Once Jane saw a healer, who told her that a robin would

come to her garden. As she had predicted, it appeared a few weeks later, lolloping across the lawn. Jane and Roger fed the robin; it quickly shed its fear and became almost a pet. "That's Lucie," the healer said, and Jane knew that it was true.

It happened again on the day of the funeral, as Jane stepped out of the dark church into the light. Perched in a tree opposite the door was a blackbird, and as the service came to an end it fetched up a loud singing that filled the air above the graves. Lucie's friends and family milled outside in small groups and gradually broke off and left the churchyard, while above them the blackbird trilled and fluted in the branches of the tree. "It started up as we were all walking out," Jane remembered, "and I said to myself at once, 'That's Lucie.' Everyone noticed, it was so loud. Tim even looked up at it and commented on it—'Listen to that bird! Isn't that bird making a lot of noise?' I just smiled to myself." And how sweet death would be, if it could all have ended there, with the image of a bird in a tree, pouring out its song.

NOTES

This book is a factual account, and the events recounted in it were observed by me, attested to by other witnesses, or documented by reliable written or broadcast sources. Inevitably, in a story like this, versions of some events differ. I have tried to distinguish between what is credible and what is not, and in cases where this is difficult, to say as much. Unless stated in the following notes, factual information and quotations are from personal correspondence, face-to-face interviews conducted by me, press conferences I attended, and documents in the personal archives of Tim Blackman, Annette Ridgway, Nigel Ridgway, and Jane Steare.

Most of the hearings in Joji Obara's trial and appeal were attended by Japanese researchers employed by me who took detailed notes on the proceedings. The official transcripts of Japanese criminal trials are not routinely available to journalists, but in many cases I have been able to obtain copies of these through other channels. I also consulted copies of the English-language reports on the trial hearings prepared for the victims and their families by the Tokyo Metropolitan Police.

In a few cases, noted below, I have changed names and identifying details of people in this story. I have done so for three reasons: because anonymity was requested by the interviewee; because, for various reasons, I have been unable to contact the person concerned; and, as a matter of principle, for all living victims of sexual crime. For those in the last category, I have gone to some lengths to make it impossible for the person to be identified, even by close friends and relatives. In some cases, this has required me to alter biographical details, as well as names, although I have preserved chronology. None of these changes have any bearing on the principal subjects of this story.

The ordering of personal names is a complicated matter in a narrative that includes Japanese, Korean, and Korean-Japanese names, sometimes for the same person. I have followed the style commonly used in English-language newspapers. All Japanese and Korean-Japanese names are in the Western order: given name first, family name second. Korean names are in the traditional order: family name first, personal name (or names) second. So in the names Joji Obara,

Seisho Kin, and Kim Sung Jong, the family name is Obara, Kin, and Kim, respectively.

The phrase "people who eat darkness" is inspired by Toru Matsugaki, *Yami o Kuu Hitobito* (Tokyo, 2006). I am very grateful to Mr. Matsugaki for his warm support.

PROLOGUE: LIFE BEFORE DEATH

9   *"Something has happened to Lucie"*: *Mail on Sunday,* July 16, 2000.
10 *"I asked what was known of the client"*: "Lucie Jane Blackman—Report as of Close of Play 4 July 2000," British embassy memo by Iain Ferguson, vice-consul.

RULES

39 *a twenty-one-day training course*: Details of the British Airways training course are from my interview with Lucie's BA colleagues Ben and Sarah Guest.
41 Jim, Robert, and Greg are pseudonyms.

HIGH TOUCH TOWN

59 *"Life here means never taking life for granted"*: Donald Richie, *The Japan Journals, 1947–2004* (Berkeley: Stone Bridge Press, 2004), p. 280.

GEISHA GIRL! (JOKE)

68 Hajime Imura is a pseudonym.
69 Ichiro Watanabe is a pseudonym.
70 *The novelist Mo Hayder worked as a hostess*: Janice Turner, "My Life as a Tokyo Bar Hostess," *The Times*, May 7, 2004.
70 Helen Dove is a pseudonym.
75 For the history of paid female companionship in Japan, see Liza Dalby, *Geisha* (Berkeley: University of California Press, 1983), and Edward Seidensticker, *Tokyo Rising: The City Since the Great Earthquake* (Cambridge, MA: Harvard University Press, 1990). Seidensticker's observation about the decline of the geisha is on pp. 54–55.
75 *Roppongi began to emerge as a place of recreation*: For the history of Roppongi, see Seidensticker, *Tokyo Rising*, and Robert Whiting, *Tokyo Underworld: The Fast Times and Hard Life of an American Gangster in Japan* (New York: Vintage, 1999).
76 *the slogan on the walls of the Roppongi expressway*: To the regret of many habitués of Roppongi, the "High Touch Town" sign was removed in 2008.
77 *Anne Allison was*: Anne Allison, *Nightwork: Sexuality, Pleasure and Corporate Masculinity in a Tokyo Hostess Club* (Chicago: University of Chicago Press, 1994). The quotations in this chapter are from pp. 160 and 48.

78 *"We were taught three things when we started"*: Anne Allison, "Personal Services," *The Times,* July 14, 2000.

86 Kenji Suzuki is a pseudonym.

TOKYO IS THE EXTREME LAND

95 Kai Miyazawa is a pseudonym; Club Kai is not the real name.

100 *"Some hostesses don't consider themselves part of the mizu shōbai"*: Quoted in Evan Alan Wright, "Death of a Hostess," *Time,* May 14, 2001.

100 *"There is something dirty about [the hostess]"*: Allison, *Nightwork,* pp. 173–74.

108 *"She was deliriously happy"*: Quoted in Paul Henderson, "I Told Lucie I Loved Her—They Were the Last Words We Ever Spoke Together," *Mail on Sunday,* July 30, 2000.

SOMETHING TERRIBLE HAS HAPPENED

115 *There are two versions of the conversation*: They are based on interviews with Rupert Blackman, Sophie Blackman, Tim Blackman, Valerie Burman, Josephine Burr, and Jane Steare.

118 *the confusion of the reporters was evident*: John Coles, "BA Girl Lucie 'Held as Cult Sex Slave,'" *Sun,* July 11, 2000; Mark Dowdney and Lucy Rock, "Snatched by a Cult," *Mirror,* July 11, 2000; Richard Lloyd Parry, "Missing Hostess Vanished after Meeting at Club," *Independent,* July 11, 2000; "Japanese Journalists Fear the Mob May Be Involved," *Sevenoaks Chronicle,* July 20, 2000.

121 *The embassy press secretary had earlier advised*: Letter to Tim Blackman from Sue Kinoshita, press and public affairs officer, British Embassy, July 12, 2000.

122 *At school, Tim played the four-string banjo*: Stephen Pritchard, "Why I Took '100 Million Pieces of Silver' for My Daughter's Death," *Observer,* April 29, 2007.

126 *There was much lurid reporting*: Frank Thorne, "Peril of Jap Vice Trap," *People,* July 16, 2000; Gary Ralston, "21st Century Geisha Girls," *Daily Record,* July 14, 2000; John Coles, "From High Life to Hostess," *Sun,* July 13, 2000.

127 *the headlines told a much more compelling human tale*: "I Will Never Leave Japan Without My Lucie, I Just Pray That She's Safe," *Daily Express,* July 13, 2000; John Coles, "I'm Not Leaving Without My Sis," *Sun,* July 13, 2000; "Family Pleas for 'Cult' Woman," *Daily Telegraph,* July 13, 2000; John Coles, "Why Us?," *Sun,* July 14, 2000.

133 *the effigy of a giant white rabbit*: Sadly, the Diamond Hotel has since been demolished and rebuilt, and its animatronic bunny is nowhere to be seen.

UNINTELLIGIBLE SPEECH

134 *Tony Blair met Tim and Sophie*: Contemporary newspaper reports; British embassy, Tokyo, "Consular Case: Missing British Citizen: Miss Lucie

Blackman—Notes of Main Points in Case and Actions Taken by Embassy," August 2, 2000.

139 Tania is a pseudonym.

142 *Dozens of calls began to come in to the Lucie Hotline*: These and other calls to the Lucie Hotline are from a memo in the possession of Tim Blackman, dated July 31, 2000, and a document sent to Tim Blackman from the British vice-consul, Iain Ferguson, October 13, 2000.

144 *claimed to have supernatural gifts*: Details about Jane's state of mind at this time, and the information supplied by the psychics, are from interviews with Jane Steare; e-mails to Sophie Blackman from Jane Steare on July 26, 27, and 29, and August 2, 2000; and a fax from N. T. Crowther to Josephine Burr, July 26, 2000.

146 *Tim asked the Tokyo Metropolitan Police*: From British embassy, Tokyo, "Consular Case: Missing British Citizen."

146 *He wrote to Tony Blair*: Letter from Tim Blackman to Tony Blair, July 28, 2000.

THE FLICKERING LIGHT

148 *The next day, a Saturday, Tim received a telephone call*: The section on Mike Hills is based on letters and documents supplied by Tim Blackman, including e-mail and fax correspondence from Hills, and Tim's statement to the Essex police, October 31, 2000; on interviews with Tim Blackman, Adam Whittington, and Sophie Blackman; and on British newspaper coverage of the kidnapping of Paul Winder in 2000, and of the arrest, trial, and conviction of Mike Hills in 2003.

150 *"We did not have a clue where Lucie was"*: David Sapsted, "Lucie Blackman's Family Gave Cruel Conman £15,000," *Daily Telegraph*, April 24, 2003.

152 *"I'm sorry if this is not to your liking"*: Fax from Mike Hills to Tim Blackman, August 6, 2000.

S & M

165 *Canadian hostess named Tiffany Fordham*: The story of Tiffany Fordham's disappearance is told in Miroi Cernetig, "Red-light Alert in Tokyo—Police Hunt for Missing Briton and Canadian Turns up Chilling Evidence of Risks Women Run in Hostess-Bar Scene," *Globe and Mail,* October 28, 2000; and Tim Cook, "Family of Woman Missing in Japan Fears for Her Life—Police Seek Possible Link to Rape Suspect," *Toronto Star,* October 30, 2000.

By the time Lucie disappeared in 2000, Tiffany's disappearance in 1997 had faded completely from the minds of the Roppongi police. When I mentioned it to Superintendent Udo, the detective in charge of the Lucie investigation, the name Tiffany Fordham meant nothing to him; he appeared never to have heard of the case.

165 Isobel Parker and Clara Mendez are pseudonyms.

166 *One day in August, a Japanese man called*: The account of the S & M circle

and the death of "Akio Takamoto" are based on notes of interviews with "Makoto Ono" by Ken Katayama; on interviews with Tim Blackman, Dai Davies, Ken Katayama, "Yoshi Kuroda," and Adam Whittington; and on articles in the magazines *Shukan Hoseki*, August 23, 2000, and *Shukan Gendai*, October 11, 2000. All names of sadomasochists have been altered, as well as some biographical details.

172 Yoshi Kuroda is a pseudonym.

THE MAN-SHAPED HOLE

178 *One day, Tim was out in Roppongi*: This incident is recounted in Wm. Penn, "Fuji TV Mounts the Podium for Fair Play," *Daily Yomiuri*, October 5, 2000.

179 *Tim went to the police station with Alan Sutton*: Based on notes of the meeting by Josephine Burr.

182 "*I think most of all is the fear that in ten, twenty years' time*": Interview with Sophie Blackman by Kentaro Katayama of Tokyo Broadcasting System, September 1, 2000.

182 *Jane was accompanied by the latest addition*: The account of Dai Davies and his work is based on interviews with Sophie Blackman, Tim Blackman, Dai Davies, Jane Steare, and Adam Whittington; and on Dai Davies, "Preliminary Report and Executive Summary," September 17, 2000.

184 *Dai Davies got on well with journalists*: For example, "Family's Fears for Missing Brit in 'Murder Riddle,'" *Express on Sunday*, July 7, 2002.

184 "*super-sleuth*": David Powell, "Private Eye Goes on Trail of Missing Girl Louise," *Daily Post* (Liverpool), January 11, 2002.

184 *the disappearance of another Kent girl*: By a remarkable coincidence, Louise Kerton was a classmate of Lucie at Walthamstow Hall. On July 31, 2001, at the age of twenty-four, she vanished while returning home from a trip to Germany to visit the family of her fiancé. The mystery of her disappearance has never been solved.

184 Mandy Wallace is a pseudonym.

184 *There he produced a photofit*: Metropolitan Police Facial Imaging Team, FIT Ref: NW058/00.

185 *a growing hostility towards Tim*: This section is based on interviews with Sophie Blackman, Tim Blackman, Dai Davies, Huw Shakeshaft, Jane Steare, and Adam Whittington; on Huw Shakeshaft, "Lucie Blackman," privately circulated document, 2006; and "A Father's Betrayal," *Daily Mail*, October 1, 2006.

188 *Tim gave an interview to a British Sunday tabloid*: Katy Weitz, "Why I Must Find Lucie," *Sunday People*, September 17, 2000.

DIGNITY OF THE POLICE

On the Japanese police and prosecutors, I have consulted Walter L. Ames, *Police and Community in Japan* (Berkeley: University of California Press, 1981); David H. Bayley, *Forces of Order: Policing Modern Japan* (Berkeley: University of California Press, 1991); David T. Johnson, *The Japanese Way of Justice: Prosecuting Crime in Japan* (New York: Oxford University Press, 2002); Setsuo Miyazawa, *Policing in Japan: A Study on Making Crime* (Albany: SUNY Press, 1992); and L. Craig Parker Jr., *The Japanese Police System Today: An American Perspective* (New York: Kodansha, 1984).

192 *Christabel Mackenzie had come to Tokyo*: As well as her name, biographical details about Christabel Mackenzie have been altered to conceal her identity.

200 *On the face of it, they are astonishingly and uniquely successful*: On Japanese crime rates, see Johnson, *Japanese Way of Justice*, pp. 22–23.

200 *the Japanese police were facing their most vociferous criticism*: Quotations from Naoki Inose, "Japanese Police Must Lift Shroud of Secrecy," *Daily Yomiuri*, September 20, 1999; and Doug Struck, "Japan's Police Wear Tarnished Badge of Honor: Reputation of Once-Admired Constables Plummets with the Rise of Scandals and Corruption," *Washington Post*, March 3, 2000.

205 *"There are so many, though"*: Jonathan Watts, *Guardian*, July 11, 2000.

205 *Almost two weeks after Lucie's disappearance*: Interview with Superintendent Toshihiko Mii, Azabu Police Station; and Richard Lloyd Parry, "Free Her Now, Father Urges Tokyo Captor," *Independent on Sunday*, July 16, 2000.

THE PALM TREES BY THE SEA

210 Clara, Isobel, Charmaine, Ronia, Katie, Lana, and Tanya are all references to actual women, based on interviews and court documents. All names, and in some cases nationalities, have been changed.

211 *a young American woman named Katie Vickers*: The account of "Katie Vickers" is based on an interview with "Kai Miyazawa"; opening statement by Tokyo Public Prosecutors, December 2000; and correspondence with "Katie Vickers."

218 *there was only a single sex offender*: Interview with Toshiaki Udo; "Alleged Rapist of Foreigners Fined for Obscenity in 1998," Kyodo News, October 30, 2000; Rushii jiken shinritsu kyumeihan, *Rushii jiken shinritsu* [Team seeking the truth about the Lucie case, *The Truth About the Lucie Case*] (Tokyo: Asaka Shinsha, 2007), p. 757.

218 *he had been arrested for peeping*: Opening statement of supplementary indictment submitted to the Tokyo District Court by the Tokyo District Prosecutor's Office, April 27, 2001. The relevant section reads, "In addition to having a previous record of violating the Minor Offenses Act for peeping into a ladies' toilet, the defendant also has a previous record of violating the Minor Offenses Act and being subject to a 9,000-yen fine for peeping at a woman going to the toilet in a public lavatory, using a handy camera on October 12, 1998."

220 *"He was half naked"*: Testimony by Naoki Harada in the Tokyo District Court, December 25, 2003; Richard Lloyd Parry, "Blackman Suspect Had Her Severed Head, Say Police," *The Times*, December 26, 2003.

THE WEAK AND THE STRONG

228 *His elderly mother was said to possess*: Information from a source close to the Kim/Hoshiyama family, Osaka, July 2006.

228 *Obara shunned photographers*: "Cops: Obara Hid Identity with Dozens of Aliases," *Daily Yomiuri*, November 20, 2000.

229 *As far back as the sixteenth century*: My account of Japan's colonization of Korea, the lives of Koreans in Japan, and the postwar period draws on Changsoo Lee and George De Vos, eds., *Koreans in Japan: Ethnic Conflict and Accommodation* (Berkeley: University of California Press, 1981); Yasunori Fukuoka, *Lives of Young Koreans in Japan* (Melbourne: Trans Pacific Press, 2000); John W. Dower, *Embracing Defeat: Japan in the Wake of World War II* (New York: Norton, 1999); Peter B. E. Hill, *The Japanese Mafia: Yakuza, Law, and the State* (New York: Oxford University Press, 2003), and David Kaplan and Alec Dubro, *Yakuza: The Explosive Account of Japan's Criminal Underworld* (Reading, MA: Addison-Wesley, 1986).

231 *"they shouted, 'Korean!'"*: Quoted in Lee and de Vos, *Koreans in Japan*, p. 22.

231 *near the port city of Pusan*: Information from a source close to the Kim/Hoshiyama family, Osaka, July 2006.

232 *They came to Japan before the war*: Ibid.

232 *According to one of his sons*: Conversation with Eisho Kin, Osaka, July 4, 2007.

234 *He had no criminal record*: According to a Japanese newspaper reporter in Osaka, who received the information from contacts in the Osaka police.

237 *a bizarre book*: *The Truth About the Lucie Case*. See p. 385 and pp. 448–49 for a fuller account of this book and its origins.

238 *founded in emulation of a British public school*: Interview with Shingo Nishimura.

243 *a short story of his was published*: Eisho Kin, "Aru Hi no Koto" (It Happened One Day), *Sanzenri*, Tokyo/Osaka, Winter 1977.

247 Koji Akimoto is a pseudonym.

248 *an account commissioned by Joji Obara's lawyer*: From *The Truth About the Lucie Case*, p. 753.

GEORGE O'HARA

254 *"Confession is king"*: Johnson, *Japanese Way of Justice*, p. 158. The chapter (pp. 243–75) on the role of confessions in Japanese justice, and the ways they are obtained, is fascinating and chilling.

254 *"We require proof beyond an unreasonable doubt"*: Ibid., p. 237.

254 *"confessions are the heart—the pump"*: Ibid., p. 243.

254 *"To us Japanese, hitting in the head is not serious"*: Ibid., p. 255.

255 *Udo was reluctant to go into detail*: Superintendent Udo was not personally present during Obara's interrogation, which was supervised by Detective Yamashiro.

256 *Obara himself would insist:* Letter to the author from Shinya Sakane, lawyer representing Joji Obara, September 14, 2005.

256 *But other people sensed something mysterious*: Information about the death, funeral, and disposal of the estate of Kim Kyo Hak is drawn from public documents on the Kim/Hoshiyama family companies; interviews with neighbors of the Kim/Hoshiyama family in Kitabatake, July 2007; interviews with a source close to the Kim/Hoshiyama family, Osaka, May 2006; articles in the magazines *Shukan Bunshun*, February 22, 2001, and *Shukan Josei*, November 21, 2001; and Tokyo Public Prosecutors' indictment of Joji Obara, December 14, 2000.

257 *Japanese magazines*: The suggestion that Obara's father's death was connected in any way with the underworld was denied by Shinya Sakane in his letter on behalf of Joji Obara.

257 *"Glass pieces were taken out around his eyes,"*: From *The Truth About the Lucie Case*, p. 753.

258 *He may have studied architecture*: Interview with a person close to the Kim family.

259 *another explanation*: Interview with a person close to the Kim family.

261 *With one of his Osaka car parks as collateral*: Information on Obara's business activities comes from a list of companies provided to the media by the Tokyo Metropolitan Police; from public documents on those companies; from interviews with people close to the case; and from "Obara Hid Identity with Dozens of Aliases," *Daily Yomiuri*, November 20, 2000, and "Blackman Suspect Obara Threw Nothing Away, Even Evidence," Kyodo News, February 16, 2001.

261 *not all of those listed on these company documents*: "Obara Hid Identity with Dozens of Aliases," *Daily Yomiuri*, November 20, 2000.

266 *Later, Obara would claim that Hamaguchi*: From *The Truth About the Lucie Case*, p. 758. He is referred to there as "Lawyer H."

CONQUEST PLAY

270 *Joji Obara kept meticulous records of his sexual encounters*: "Statement of Reasons for Appeal," Number 1294, 2007, Tokyo Public Prosecutors, pp. 68–69.

271 *He referred to the flat at Zushi Marina as his* kyoten: Ibid., p. 71.

272 *a list of about sixty women's names*: "Obara Hid Identity with Dozens of Aliases," *Daily Yomiuri*, November 20, 2000.

273 *"Is it for a big dog that's passed away?"*: Interview with Wataru Fujisaki.

273 *"The defendant lists the names of the women"*: "Statement of Reasons for Appeal," Number 1294, pp. 69–70.

276 *"He does various things"*: Based on interviews with Toshiaki Udo and two other people who had seen the dossier of still images.

276 *Off camera there were two television monitors*: Testimony of Joji Obara in the Tokyo District Court, March 8, 2006.

276 *One report said that the police had recovered a thousand of them*: "Obara In-

dicted over 1992 Death of Australian Woman," Kyodo News, February 16, 2001, and "Police View 4,800 Videos from Obara's Condominium," *Daily Yomiuri*, April 10, 2001.

277 *"With a Japanese girl, my preference"*: Testimony of Joji Obara in the Tokyo District Court, March 8, 2006.

277 *"Foreign hostesses are all ugly"*: Ibid.

277 *"Before his 'play' the accused pours into a small shot glass"*: From the website The Truth of Lucie's Case, http://lucies-case.to.cx/case1_e.html, accessed June 2010.

279 Fusako Yoshimoto, Itsuko Oshihara, and Megumi Mori are pseudonyms.

279 *"Something serious has happened"*: "Photograph Links Obara to Blackman," *Daily Yomiuri*, February 17, 2001.

CARITA

284 *"Fears of More Missing Women"*: *Sydney Morning Herald*, October 27, 2000.

IN THE CAVE

299 *"We go after him relentlessly"*: *Mainichi Daily News*, February 20, 2001.

301 *Mr. Hirokawa, the caretaker's boyfriend"*: The judge in the first trial discounted his testimony as unreliable.

302 *They were immediately identifiable as a human arm*: The details of the exhumation are from personal observation, contemporary press reports, and notes provided to me of a briefing to members of the Tokyo Metropolitan Police Agency reporters' club on February 9, 2001.

303 *Six times that weekend*: These details come from notes provided to me from Tokyo Metropolitan Police briefings on February 9, 10, and 11, 2001, and an interview with a former member of the Tokyo Metropolitan Police Agency reporters' club.

304 *The most memorable explanation of all*: Notes on a briefing to members of the Tokyo Metropolitan Police reporters' club by a detective of the First Investigation Division, April 9, 2001.

305 *"The detectives had been to Blue Sea Aburatsubo"*: Interview, 2007.

305 *"the postmortem changes were extreme"*: Assessment by Dr. Masahiko Ueno, February 7, 2006, on the postmortem conducted on February 10, 2001, by Dr. Masahiko Kobayashi.

CEREMONIES

313 *Lucie's funeral was at the end of April 2001*: Accounts of Lucie's funeral are from interviews with her family and friends, and from contemporary press reports, including William Hollingworth, "Family, Friends Say Goodbye to Murdered British Hostess Lucie," Kyodo News, March 29, 2001.

317 *One thing stands out above all*: Data on Japanese conviction rates are from Johnson, *Japanese Way of Justice*, pp. 62, 216. Johnson writes, "Even in an

unusually 'good' year for defendants, only one in 265 cases ended in acquittal. Typically the proportion is closer to one in 800 . . . It would take Japanese
judges 175 years to acquit as many defendants as American courts acquit in
one year."

318 *"Prosecutors, like just about everyone in Japan"*: Ibid., p. 165.

318 *"The vast majority of Japan's criminal trials"*: Ibid., p. 47.

320 *"I've done something terrible"*: "Photograph Links Obara to Blackman," *Daily
Yomiuri*, February 17, 2001; "50th Hearing of Joji OBARA," English
summary of court proceedings prepared by Tokyo Metropolitan Police,
December 24, 2006.

324 *a doctor gave evidence on the poisonous effects of chloroform*: Trial of Joji Obara,
13th hearing, Tokyo District Court, January 22, 2003.

324 *In April, an expert on anesthesia*: 17th hearing, April 16, 2003.

325 *The caretaker of Blue Sea Aburatsubo*: 25th hearing, November 27, 2003.

325 *the police inspector who had responded to her call*: 26th hearing, December 25,
2003.

325 *A police chemist testified*: 28th and 29th hearings, January 30 and February
17, 2004.

325 *A woman named Yuka Takino*: 31st hearing, March 26, 2004.

326 *This experiment, a bizarre and gory operation*: 32nd hearing, May 25, 2004.

327 *"I like the Obara hearings very much"*: Yuki Takahashi, Miki Takigawa,
Rei Hasegawa, and Haruko Kagami, *Kasumikko Kurabu: Musume-tachi no
Saiban Bōchōki* (*Kasumi Kids' Club: Girls' Diary of Court Watching*) (Tokyo,
2006).

328 *He treated his defense as a war*: Information on Joji Obara in the Tokyo Detention Center, on his relations with his lawyers, and on his legal affairs are
from interviews with members of his defense team and people close to the
case. See also Richard Lloyd Parry, "How the Bubble Burst for Lucie's Alleged Killer," *The Times*, August 17, 2005.

328 *His first legal team resigned en masse*: "All Defense Lawyers for Obara in
Blackman Case Resign," Kyodo News, October 12, 2001.

THE WHATEVERER

333 *"There are many fundamentals"*: Letter to the author from Tomonori Sugo,
lawyer representing Joji Obara, received July 8, 2005.

334 *My fifth question*: Letter from the author to Joji Obara, June 23, 2005.

334 *"To tell the truth about Lucie's character"*: 42nd hearing, July 27, 2005.

335 *"What's the significance of buying postcards and drugs?"*: Ibid.

340 *"When Obara asked A," it would later be explained*: From *The Truth About the
Lucie Case*, p. 293.

341 *the inspector had inadvertently kicked the blanket-wrapped corpse*: Ibid.,
p. 300.

342 *He was "surprised," according to the book*: Ibid., p. 301.

342 *"She's having fun taking drugs"*: Ibid., p. 303.

342 *His name was Satoru Katsuta*: Information on Katsuta is from the trial of Joji Obara, 47th hearing, Tokyo District Court, December 22, 2005.

SMYK

347 *Obara's lawyers attempted to shore up his defense*: The examples that follow are from the 49th, 50th, and 51st trial hearings, February 8 and 24, and March 8, 2006. The exchange about Obara's charitable activities occurred in the 51st hearing.

348 *Then, in March 2006*: 52nd hearing, March 2, 2006.

354 *Jane Blackman, Tim Blackman, and Carita Ridgway's mother, Annette, flew out*: They appeared at the 53rd and 54th hearings on April 20 and 25, 2006.

CONDOLENCE

365 *"I have received the offer from the accused"*: E-mail reprinted in *The Truth About the Lucie Case*, p. 73.

365 *"The accused has shown contrition"*: E-mail reprinted in ibid., p. 75.

366 *He explained in a telephone call*: Transcript of telephone conversation, ibid., pp. 78–79.

366 *"The terrible, terrible acts played out on my beautiful girl"*: 54th hearing, April 25, 2006.

367 *"In cases of this kind, ¥1.5 million"*: Johnson, *Japanese Way of Justice*, p. 202.

369 *"I did not know that the cause of death of my daughter"*: In *The Truth About the Lucie Case*, p. 97.

370 *"blood money"*: Glen Owen, "Now Father of Murdered Lucie Accepts £450,000 'Blood Money,'" *Mail on Sunday*, October 1, 2006.

370 *"I have rejected all and any payments"*: Natalie Clarke and Neil Sears, "An Utter Betrayal of My Dear Lucie," *Daily Mail*, October 2, 2006.

371 *a two-thousand-word character assassination*: "A Father's Betrayal," *Daily Mail*, October 7, 2006.

373 *an on-the-record interview to the* Mail: Kathryn Knight, "He Is Immoral," *Daily Mail*, April 23, 2007.

377 *e-mailed one journalist*: Roger Steare to Indira Das-Gupta, May 17, 2007.

377 *the information found its way to the* Daily Mail: Daniel Boffey, "Lucie's Father in Trust Fraud Probe," *Mail on Sunday*, April 29, 2007.

THE VERDICT

378 *I sent repeated letters through his lawyers*: Author to Joji Obara, January 25 and June 23, 2005, February 23, 2006, and October 27, 2008; to Tomonori Sugo, lawyer to Joji Obara, July 8 and 20, 2005; to Shinya Sakane, lawyer to Joji Obara, November 17, 2005; and to Akira Tsujishima, lawyer to Joji Obara, December 5, 2008.

378 *asking me to get hold of Lucie's health records*: Letter to the author from Tomonori Sugo, lawyer to Joji Obara, July 19, 2005.

379 *he accused me of "delivering copies to Scotland Yard"*: Letter from Kiyohisa
Arai, lawyer to Joji Obara, May 17, 2006.

380 *Obara's lawyer Shinya Sakane wrote indignantly*: Shinya Sakane to the author, November 14, 2005.

382 *"There is no decisive evidence"*: 61st hearing, December 11, 2006.

384 *one of his lawyers had hired British private detectives*: Jason Lewis, "Lucie
Murder Suspect and a Sinister Plot to Smear Her," *Mail on Sunday,* May
13, 2007.

384 *a website materialized in cyberspace*: http://lucies-case.to.cx. The English
version of the website is at http://lucies-case.to.cx/index_e.html.

385 *publication of* The Truth About the Lucie Case: In February 2010, the publisher of *The Truth About the Lucie Case*, Asuka Shinsha, sued Joji Obara and
his lawyer Akira Tsujishima for ¥13,146,481 (at that time about $148,000)
in unpaid fees. According to the complaint filed with that court, the book
was a vanity publication, "part of a campaign to give an advantage to Obara."
It was commissioned in December 2006, soon after the judges in the Tokyo
District Court withdrew to consider their judgment. As well as the Japanese
edition, there was to have been an English translation published in Britain.
The agreement signed with the publisher was in the name of the "Team
Seeking the Truth About the Lucie Case," and their agent, Obara's lawyer,
Kiyohisa Arai.

On the face of it, then, the book was the work of independent third
parties campaigning on Obara's behalf. "The truth seekers," the book ex-
plains, "are composed of persons such as journalists, law school staff and
members of the legal community, including former prosecutors" (p. 31).
But there seems to have been no one working on the project who was not
paid to do so. Asuka Shinsha and Yorishige Fujita, the freelance editor responsible for the book, received their instructions from lawyers employed
by Joji Obara.

"In order to pretend that the campaign is a neutral activity, the defendants pretend that those in charge of the campaign are a specific organisation composed of third parties," the publisher's complaint reads. "But
needless to say, the truth seekers are neither a corporate body with a judicial personality, nor . . . an unincorporated association. In reality, they are
no more than individuals, such as the defendants."

Hidetoshi Okuhara, an editor at Asuka Shinsha, described to me the
confusion that followed when different, and sometimes contradictory, instructions were given by Mr. Arai, Akira Tsujishima, Yasuo Shionoya, and
another of Obara's lawyers, Katsura Maki.

"The instructions varied from lawyer to lawyer, and the plantiff [Asuka
Shinsha] was often left baffled," the company's complaint says. "It is pre-
sumed that the reason behind such a situation was that these lawyers were

seeing Obara in regards to the content of the manuscript for a point-by-point confirmation, and on these occasions, Obara's story often changed."

The result, according to Asuka Shinsha's complaint, was delay as well as confusion. After what should have been the final version of the book went into production, Katsura Maki complained that it contained errors. The publishers proposed inserting an errata slip, to which Mr. Arai agreed—but then Mr. Shionoya ordered that the print run be stopped. Thus the book did not appear on the shelves until just before the verdict of the Tokyo District Court in April 2007. The English-language edition was canceled, and the costs of the translation, which had been largely completed, were never paid by the "truth seekers."

385 Tanya Nebogatov is a pseudonym.

HOW JAPANESE

399 *He sued, and won damages from*: Information on Japanese magazines and *Time* magazine from two separate sources close to those cases.

399 *The answer was his family*: Interviews with lawyers representing Joji Obara and source close to the Obara family.

402 *a twenty-two-year-old British woman named Lindsay Hawker*: For an overview of the Lindsay Hawker case, see Richard Lloyd Parry, "Police Catch Fugitive Suspected of Killing British Woman," *The Times*, November 11, 2009. In July 2011, Tatsuya Ichihashi received a life sentence for the rape and murder of Lindsay Hawker.

405 *"Japanese Men, Smoky Bars and the Obsession with Beautiful Western Girls"*: Richard Shears, *Daily Mail*, March 31, 2007.

406 *Japanese masturbators are greater consumers of porn*: The greatest consumer and producer of pornography is the United States. Duncan Campbell, "With pot and porn outstripping corn, America's black economy is flying high," *Guardian*, May 2, 2003.

411 *The book was one I recognized*: Ben Hills, *Princess Masako: Prisoner of the Chrysanthemum Throne* (New York: Tarcher, 2006). Translated as *Purinsesu Masako* (Tokyo: Daisan Shokan, 2007).

WHAT I REALLY AM

417 *Even Carlos Santana*: I put Obara's claim about his friendship with Carlos Santana to the musician's representative, Susan Stewart. She responded, "Carlos Santana will not be able to assist in this." E-mail to author, August 18, 2007.

418 *"a self-centered, callous, and remorseless person"*: Robert D. Hare, *Without Conscience: The Disturbing World of the Psychopaths Among Us* (New York: Guilford Press, 1999), p. 2.

418 *I have my doubts about such diagnoses*: This point is made by Janet Malcolm in *The Journalist and the Murderer* (New York: Knopf, 1990), p. 75. "The concept of the psychopath is, in fact, an admission of failure to solve the

mystery of evil—it is merely a restatement of the mystery—and only offers an escape valve for the frustration felt by psychiatrists, social workers, and police officers, who daily encounter its force."

421 *"His pain will be twofold"*: Amanda Platell, "A Betrayal That Will Haunt Lucie's Dad for Ever," *Daily Mail*, April 28, 2007.

421 *one reader of* The Sun: "Lucie's Dad Has Sold Out," *Sun*, April 27, 2007.

424 *Missing Abroad*: www.missingabroad.org.

425 *The image came to his mind of a bulging black rubbish bag*: Dee O'Connell, "What Happened Next?," *Observer*, January 12, 2003.

426 *"To violate the dignity of so many victims"*: 7th appeal hearing, Tokyo High Court, December 16, 2008.

428 *There was almost no wind*: Blog entry on *Infanta* website, http://infanta .square-space.com/log/2008/12/15/winch-handle-sniffer-outed.html.

428 *Obara appealed again*: On his Supreme Court appeal, see Richard Lloyd Parry, "Lawyers Will Use Lucie Mannequin in Attempt to Win Killer's Freedom," *The Times*, December 15, 2009.

429 *on average the term served before parole*: "Mukikei, kari shakuhou made 30-nen . . . gembatsuka de nagabiku" (30 Years Before Parole for Life Imprisonment . . . Increased by the Trend for Stricter Punishment), *Yomiuri Shimbun*, November 22, 2010.

ACKNOWLEDGMENTS

Many people helped me in researching this story, but none gave more than the Blackman/Steare and Ridgway families. In repeated meetings, telephone calls, and e-mail exchanges, they submitted uncomplainingly to interviews that must at times have been unbearably painful. This book could easily have been subtitled *The Fate of Carita Ridgway*, and I'm sorry that I didn't have the space to devote more of it to Carita and the endurance and tenacity of her family. I thank Rupert Blackman, Sophie Blackman, Tim Blackman and Josephine Burr, Annette Ridgway, Nigel and Aileen Ridgway, Jane and Roger Steare, and Samantha Termini (née Ridgway). I also thank Louise Phillips and Robert Finnigan, who did so much for Lucie and Carita, in life and death; and Lucie's friends Valerie Burman, Gayle Cotton (née Blackman), Jamie Gascoigne, Samantha Goddard (née Burman), Caroline Lawrence, and Caroline Ryan.

Some of those to whom I owe the most have chosen not to be identified, but I am grateful to all of them, particularly to the surviving victims of Joji Obara. Among those I can name, I thank the following for recollections, documents, contacts, support, ideas, research, proofreading, translation, interpretation, and hospitality: Kozo Abe, Jake Adelstein, Peter Alford, Kiyohisa Arai, Nahoko Araki, Mikiko Asao, Ian Ash, Charles Boundy, Alex Bowler, Everett Brown, Josephine Burr, Chris Cleave, Jamie Coleman, Rob Cox, David Seaborn "Dai" Davies, Tomomi Deguchi, Michael Denby, Toby Eady and all at Toby Eady Associates, the Foreign Correspondents' Club of Japan, the Foreign Press in Japan, Dan Franklin and all at Jonathan Cape, Wataru Fujisaki, Benjamin Fulford, Ben Goodyear, Ben and Sarah Guest, Samar Hammam, Thomas Hardy, Atsushi Hosoya, Hideo Igarashi, Noriyuki Imanishi, Stuart Isett, Shoshin Iwamoto, Lea Jacobson, Jenn Joel, Eric Johnston, Colin Joyce, Kentaro Katayama, Velisarios Kattoulas, Hideo Kawaguchi, Taeko Kawamura, Lee Hyon Suk, Leo Lewis, the Lloyd Parry family, Hamish Macaskill and the English Agency, Justin McCurry, Sean McDonald and all at Farrar, Straus and Giroux, Toshio Maeda, the late William Miller, Vanessa Milton, Manabu Miyawaki, Giles Murray, Chika Nakayama, Shingo Nishimura, Katsuro Nitto, Hidetoshi Okuhara, Akihiro Otani, Tsuyoshi Otani, David Parrish, David Peace, Dave

Russell, Julian Ryall, Issei Sagawa, Hiro Saso, Masato Sato, Junzo Sawa, Matt Searle, Huw Shakeshaft, Alex Spillius, Mark Stephens, Jeremy Sutton-Hibbert, Hiroko Tabuchi, Yuki Takahashi, Gillian Tett, Chika Tonooka, Michiko Toyama, Adam Whittington, Fiona Wilson, Shigeru Yamamoto, and Yuji Yoshitomi.

My former employer, *The Independent*, sponsored much of the early research for this book; my present one, *The Times*, generously gave me time off to research and write, and unhesitatingly defended me against accusations of libel. At the former, I thank especially Leonard Doyle, and at the latter, Richard Beeston, Pat Burge, Martin Fletcher, Anne Spackman, and Roland Watson, as well as Keiji Isaji and Matthew Whittle of Clifford Chance in Tokyo. Friends and colleagues at *The Yomiuri Shimbun* have also been a reliable source of information and support.

Although this book is critical of the Japanese police, the officers whom I met in the course of writing it were, with rare exceptions, kind, honorable, and hardworking men, justifiably proud of their service. My criticisms are not of their work as individuals but of a system which many people believe to be in need of reform. I thank Fusanori Matsumoto, Toshihiko Mii, the late Toshiaki Udo, and all those others who have chosen not to be named here.

The website of the Lucie Blackman Trust is at www.lucieblackmantrust.org.

Jane Steare supports the Hospice in the Weald: www.hospiceintheweald.org.uk.